Marivaux
Plays

The Double Inconstancy, The False Servant, The Game of Love and Chance, Careless Vows, The Feigned Inconstancy *with* Harlequin's Lesson in Love, Slave Island, The Will, A Matter of Dispute, The Constant Players

For too long hidden behind the towering stature of Molière, Marivaux's light-hearted comedies of love and intrigue are at last enjoying a vigorous revival. Fresh new translations have enabled a new generation to re-discover the depth and range of his characterisation quite distinct from the heroic splendour of French classical tradition or Molière's precisely-carved caricature.

As Claude Schumacher, who has selected the ten plays in this volume, explains in his introduction, Marivaux's theatre illustrates that 'eloquence is action', there is no 'infernal machine', which relentlessly carries the characters to their inescapable doom. Marivaux is the first French drama-tist to dissect the soul, to sow doubt about the immutability of human nature.

Pierre Carlet (later to adopt the name of **Marivaux**) was born in Paris in February 1688. He was the son of a provincial official of comfortable means. He studied law in Paris but became more interested in the world of literary salons. In 1721, he was ruined by the collapse of the banker Law's financial schemes and obliged to earn his living by writing. Over the next twenty years he worked closely with the Italian *commedia dell'arte* troupe in Paris and the Comédie-Française, producing some thirty plays, most of them comedies. He also wrote a major novel *The Life of Marianne* (1731) and was elected to the Académie Française in 1742. Of his many plays, the best known in English are: *Harlequin's Lesson in Love* (1719), *Surprised by Love* (1722), *The Double Inconstancy* (1723), *The False Servant* (1724), *The Game of Love and Chance* (1730), *The Triumph of Love* (1732), *Careless Vows* (1732), *The Feigned Inconstancy* (1733), *The Constant Players* (1757). Marivaux died in 1763.

MARIVAUX

Plays

The Double Inconstancy
translated by Nicholas Wright

The False Servant
translated by Michael Sadler

The Game of Love and Chance
translated by John Walters

Careless Vows
translated by John Walters

The Feigned Inconstancy
translated by John Bowen
with

Harlequin's Lesson in Love
translated by Donald Watson

Slave Island
translated by Nicholas Wright

The Will
translated by Michael Sadler

A Matter of Dispute
translated by John Walters

The Constant Players
translated by Donald Watson

introduced by Claude Schumacher

METHUEN DRAMA

METHUEN WORLD CLASSICS

3 5 7 9 10 8 6 4 2

These translations first published in Great Britain
by Methuen in 1988
Reissued with a new cover in 1997 by Methuen Drama
Random House, 20 Vauxhall Bridge Road, London SW1V 2SA
and Australia, New Zealand and South Africa
and distributed in the United States of America
by Heinemann, a division of Reed Elsevier Inc.
361 Hanover Street, Portsmouth, New Hampshire
NH 03801 3959

Harlequin's Lesson in Love & *The Constant Players*
translation copyright © Donald Watson 1988
Slave Island & *The Double Inconstancy*
translation copyright © Nicholas Wright 1988
The Will & *The False Servant*
translation copyright © Michael Sadler 1988
A Matter of Dispute, The Game of Love and Chance & *Careless Vows*
translation copyright © John Walters 1988
The Feigned Inconstancy
translation copyright © John Bowen 1988
Introduction and selection copyright © Methuen 1988
The authors and translators have asserted their moral rights

ISBN 0–413–18560–5

Random House UK Limited Reg. No. 954009

A CIP catalogue record for this book
is available from the British Library

Printed and bound in Great Britain by
Cox & Wyman Ltd, Reading

Contents

Marivaux: a Chronology   *page* vi

Introduction   x

The Double Inconstancy   39

The False Servant   107

The Game of Love and Chance   185

Careless Vows   245

The Feigned Inconstancy   317

Harlequin's Lesson in Love   393

Slave Island   423

The Will   455

A Matter of Dispute   501

The Constant Players   533

Marivaux
A Chronology

[We mention only the significant events of Marivaux's theatrical career, to the almost total exclusion of his other literary activities. Titles preceded by an asterisk are included in this anthology. The other titles are given in French only in order to avoid confusion.]

1673	Death of Molière in Paris.
1677	First performance of Racine's *Phèdre* at the Hôtel de Bourgogne.
1680	Creation of the Comédie-Française by Louis XIV.
1684	Death of Corneille in Paris.
1688	4 February. Pierre Carlet (later to adopt the name of Marivaux), son of Nicolas Carlet and Marie Bulet, was born in Paris.
	8 February. Pierre Carlet is baptised, parish of Saint-Gervais.
1694	Birth of Voltaire.
1697	The Italian *Commedia dell'arte* players are exiled from France by Louis XIV. They were accused of lampooning Mme de Maintenon.
1699	Death of Racine in Paris.
1700	Birth of Gianetta Rosa Benozzi, stage name Silvia, who will become the most famous interpreter of Marivaux's theatre.
1710–13	Pierre Carlet (Petrus Decarlet parisiensis) studies law at the University of Paris. He will graduate only in 1721.
1712	Anonymous publication of *Le Père prudent et équitable* in Limoges, which marks the entry of Marivaux into literature. The dedicatory notice is signed 'M'. This early comedy in alexandrines probably had a private performance in Limoges.
1712	Birth of Rousseau.
1713–20	Marivaux makes a name for himself in Parisian literary and social circles. He publishes regularly burlesque, satirical, journalistic and moral writings.
1715	1 September. Death of Louis XIV.
1716	The Regent, the Duke of Orléans, calls back the Italian Comedians, under the direction of Luigi Riccoboni (Lelio). They return to the theatre they occupied before 1697, the Hôtel de Bourgogne.

1716	Pierre Carlet signs for the first time: 'Carlet de MARIVAUX'.
1717	Marivaux marries Colombe Bollogne, a well-to-do heiress. Writes for the literary journal, *Le Mercure*.
	Dominique Biancolelli, stage name Trivelin, joins Riccoboni's company.
1719	Death of Marivaux's father; birth of his only daughter, Colombe Prosper, who will become a nun in 1745.
1720	3 March. *L'Amour et la vérité*, one-act comedy written in collaboration, now lost, unsuccessfully staged by the Italian Comedians.
	17 October. *Arlequin poli par l'amour* (Harlequin's Lesson in Love) is successfully staged by the Italian Comedians. Initial run of 12 performances.
	16 December. *Annibal*, tragedy in alexandrines. Only three performances at the Comédie-Française.
	The English banker Law becomes Finance Minister, but his system fails and brings about financial chaos.
1721	Marivaux is ruined. He must now write to earn a living.
	Death of the painter Watteau. Personal reign of Louis XV.
1722	3 May. *La Surprise de l'amour*, three acts, Italian Comedians, run of 13 performances. Great success.
	Marivaux and Silvia start a very fruitful artistic partnership.
1723	6 April. *La Double Inconstance* (The Double Inconstancy), three acts, Italian Comedians, run of 15 performances. Great success.
	Death of Marivaux's wife.
	The Italian Comedians given title of 'Les Comédiens du Roi' (The King's Actors).
1724	5 February. *Le Prince travesti*, three acts, Italian Comedians, run of 16 performances. Great success.
	8 July. *La Fausse Suivante* (The False Servant), three acts, Italian Comedians, run of 13 performances. Great success.
	2 December. *Le Dénouement imprévu*, one act, Comédie-Française, run of 6 performances. Small success.
1725	5 March. *L'Ile des esclaves* (Slave Island), one act, Italian Comedians, run of 21 performances. Enormous success.
	19 August. *L'Héritier du village*, one act, Italian Comedians, run of 9 performances.
1727	11 September. *Les Petits Hommes ou l'île de la raison*, three acts, Comédie-Française, run of 4 performances. Booed.
	31 December. *La Seconde Surprise de l'amour*, three acts,

	Comédie-Française, run of 14 performances without being an overwhelming success.
1728	22 April. *Le Triomphe de Plutus*, one act, Italian Comedians, run of 12 performances. Very successful.
1729	18 June. *La Nouvelle Colonie ou la ligue des femmes*, three acts, Italian Comedians, failure.
1730	23 January. *Le Jeu de l'amour et du hasard* (The Game of Love and Chance), three acts, Italian Comedians, run of 14 performances. Great success.
1731	Marivaux starts the publication of his most successful novel, *La Vie de Marianne* (The Life of Marianne) which he will pursue in 11 instalments until 1741 and leave unfinished.
	5 November. *La Réunion des amours*, heroic comedy in one act, Comédie-Française, run of 9 well received performances.
1732	12 March. *Le Triomphe de l'amour*, three acts, Italian Comedians, only 5 performances in town, but the play is successful at Court.
	8 June.* *Les Serments indiscrets* (Careless Vows), Marivaux's only five-act play, Comédie-Française, run of 9 unsuccessful and even rowdy performances.
	25 July. *L'École des mères*, one act, Italian Comedians, run of 18 very successful performances.
1732	Birth of Beaumarchais and Fragonard.
1733	6 June. *L'Heureux Stratagème* (The Feigned Inconstancy), three acts, Italian Comedians, run of 18 very successful performances.
1734	Death of Dominique-Trivelin.
	Publication of the first instalments of *Le Paysan parvenu*, another successful novel but never finished.
	16 August. *La Méprise*, one act, Italian Comedians, unsuccessful.
	6 November. *Le Petit-Maître corrigé*, three acts, Comédie-Française, single, interrupted performance.
1735	9 May. *La Mère confidente*, three acts, Italian Comedians, run of 18 most successful performances.
1736	11 June.* *Le Legs* (The Will), one act, Comédie-Française, run of 7 performances.
	Début of Mlle Clairon in *Slave Island*.
1737	16 March. *La Fausse Confidence*, three acts, Italian Comedians, run of 5 performances.

CHRONOLOGY

1738	7 July. *La Joie imprévue*, one act, Italian Comedians, written to accompany a revival of the previous play under the new title of *Les Fausses Confidences*.
1739	13 January. *Les Sincères*: one-act comedy, was performed with great success, but anonymously, by the Italian Comedians. The following day the author's name was revealed and a 'cabal' ensured production's failure. 19 August. Death of Thomassin Vicentini-Harlequin.
1740	19 November. *L'Épreuve*, one act, Italian Comedians, run of 17 very successful performances. Marivaux's last play written for the Italian Comedians.
1741	Marivaux writes a comedy in one act, *La Commère*, inspired by an episode of his novel *La Paysan parvenu*. Text lost until 1965. The Comédie-Française staged it in 1967.
1742	Marivaux is unanimously elected to the Académie Française, in preference to Voltaire.
1744	19 October. *La Dispute* (A Matter of Dispute), one act, Comédie-Française, single unsuccessful performance.
1746	6 August. *Le Préjugé vaincu*, one act, Comédie-Française, run of 7 successful performances.
1753	Michel van Loo paints Marivaux's portrait.
1755	24 August. *La Femme fidèle*, a comedy in one act is performed by amateurs of the Théâtre de Société de Berny.
1757	The Comédie-Française contemplates the production of *Félicie*, a comedy in one act, and of *L'Amante frivole*. These two plays were never staged and the latter text is lost. Anonymous publication of *Les Acteurs de bonne foi* (The Constant Players). No contemporary record of production.
1758	First publication of Marivaux's *Oeuvres de Théâtre* (Complete Plays).
1760	Silvia's daughter, Manon Balletti, makes her début with the Italian Comedians, in *L'Épreuve*. The Italian Comedians, in dire financial trouble, turn to Goldoni.
1761	Anonymous publication of *La Provinciale*, one-act play.
1762	Merger of the Italian Comedians and the Opéra-Comique. Actors who cannot sing are sacked. Disbanded by the King in 1779.
1763	12 February. Death of Marivaux.
1775	Beaumarchais's *Le Barbier de Séville* (The Barber of Seville), followed in 1784 by *Le Mariage de Figaro* (The Marriage of Figaro).

Introduction

At the beginning of the eighteenth century, the French theatre was dominated by two companies: the Comédie-Française and the Comédie-Italienne. Marivaux wrote exclusively for these two companies, but while the 'Italian' productions of his plays were very successful, those staged by the Comédie-Française were almost virtually all failures.

Created by a royal decree of Louis XIV in 1680, the Comédie-Française brought together Molière's former company – adrift since his death in 1673 – and the tragic actors ('les Grands Comédiens') of the Hôtel de Bourgogne. This company, which still exists today, was given a new theatre in 1689 in the rue des Fossés-Saint-Germain-des Prés (now known as the rue de l'Ancienne-Comédie), where it remained until 1770. Regarded as the most prestigious company in Paris (and so hence in France also), the Comédie-Francaise specialized in the 'grand style', favoured tragedy to the detriment of comedy, followed a traditional and overblown style of acting and was suspicious of newcomers with unorthodox ideas.

Italian *commedia dell'arte* actors had been performing in France since the second half of the sixteenth century. Throughout the seventeenth century they were deeply appreciated by their French audiences, both at court and in Paris. Originally they performed in Italian, first because they did not speak French and, second, because the actors of the Hôtel de Bourgogne had a monopoly on French acting and did not allow competition from foreign colleagues. This obligation to perform in a language which only a minority of their spectators could understand made the Italians develop a very physical style of acting and kept alive the acrobatic tradition of *commedia dell'arte*.

'Unfortunately' for the diversity of dramatic art, in 1684 the

Italians obtained from Louis XIV a concession which they had been seeking for many years, to be allowed to perform in French. This act of kindness resulted only in disastrous consequences for the Italians themselves and for theatre as a whole. Given the freedom to speak French and in view of the satirical vein in the *commedia*, the Italians soon got into trouble with the authorities: in 1697, after a performance of *La Fausse Prude*, a play in which Madame de Maintenon was lampooned, they were expelled from Paris. Even if it had not been for that play, another pretext would have been found: the end of Louis's reign was sad and sombre, the court was sinking into gloom and devotion, and the fun of the *commedia* masks was in any case out of place in a court pervaded by religion.

Their exile lasted for almost twenty years and, during their absence, two new theatres opened in Paris, the so-called 'théâtres de la foire', which performed at the two main fairs of Paris: the fair of Saint-Germain, from 3 February to Easter, held on the same spot as the present-day Saint-Germain market, and the fair of Saint-Laurent, from 25 July to 29 September, on the ground where the Gare de l'Est was subsequently built. These 'théâtres de la foire' presented circus performers, and puppet as well as live plays. They too had to face the hostility of the 'Comédiens Français', the successors of the 'Grands Comédiens', and were subjected to many petty limitations. When not banned from performing altogther, they were obliged to perform only monologues or to play 'à la muette', i.e. to perform silently. They were perhaps the first to use 'subtitles' or 'captions' to keep their audience informed about the plot by unrolling banners. In 1714, the fairground theatres were given permission to sing and so, by accident, they started a new tradition which later in the century was to blossom into the very successful genre of the 'opéra-comique'. That particular right was denied them in 1718, then granted again in 1724. Despite further setbacks, they went from strength to strength and, by 1783, the 'Opéra-Comique' had become the second theatre of Paris, having amalgamated with the Comédie-Italienne in 1762.

Louis XIV died in 1715, and the following year the Regent, Philippe d'Orléans, welcomed back a new company of Italian actors who returned to their 'own' theatre, the Hôtel de Bourgogne, which had remained empty during their absence and was refurbished for their use. The company consisted of experienced Italian actors, who did not speak French fluently, if at all, and of younger artists at the beginning of their career, such as the future 'Silvia', who were slightly more proficient in French.

The main actors of the new company were:

Luigi Riccoboni, the director who adopted the stage name of	*Lélio*
Elena Balletti, his wife	*Flaminia*
Antoine Balletti, her brother	*Mario*
Zanetta Benozzi, his wife	*Silvia*
Thomasso Vicentini, known as Thomassin	*Arlequin*
Margarita Rusca, his wife	*Violette*
Dominique Biancolelli junior, who joined them in 1717	*Trivelin*

This company gave its first performances in Italian, but the eighteenth-century audiences, unlike their seventeenth-century predecessors, refused to sit through plays if they could not understand the text, and they soon forced a change. First the Italians had recourse to résumés in French which they distributed before the performance; and then they tried including a few French scenes in their Italian repertoire, but to no avail. In 1718 they had to bow to the inevitable, and performed plays entirely in French. They started with a translation of an Italian scenario already in their repertoire, *Colombine, avocat pour et contre*, followed with an original French play with an ominous title, *Le Naufrage au Port-à-l'Anglais*, which scored a fair success. But the question of language would, in time, be the cause of their downfall.

In a prologue to the play, Autreau, the author, allowed them to voice their apprehension at having to perform in an unfamiliar language:

SILVIA. We're going to speak French; that makes me tremble with fear.

FLAMMINA. Why be afraid? What we're going to play isn't difficult. It's only a light little play, with no strongly defined characters; we shall only be playing more or less what we really are – Italian women newly arrived in Paris. Our faulty pronunciation will be to our credit. People will think we're doing it deliberately.

SILVIA. All this doesn't really reassure me.

Silvia was right to be wary. Her own success was immediate and lasted all her life, but ultimately the adoption of French was to destroy the Italians' distinctive theatrical genius.

From 1718 to 1750, the Italian Comedians performed regularly in French and in Italian and, during that period, they premièred over 200 Italian plays and almost 350 French plays. Some French authors, now forgotten, wrote exclusively for them while others, like Marivaux, wrote for the Comédie-Française as well as for the Comédie-Italienne.

The repertory of the Italians, in either language, was richer, more varied, livelier – in a word, more theatrical – than the repertory of the Comédie-Française. The Italians had not forgotten their *commedia* inheritance; they still used improvisation within a scripted play, included songs and dance in their productions and added excitement to their theatrical entertainment by using fireworks. But despite their unstinting inventiveness, they were not able to woo and command the loyalty of a large enough public. The first half of the eighteenth century was notoriously bad for Parisian theatre companies. While the drop in attendance during the last years of Louis XIV's reign can be explained, a reversal of the situation might reasonably have been expected during the Regency and the early years of Louis XV's reign. Yet this did not come about. Average attendance during the first half of the century fell to about 30% at the Comédie-Française, in a theatre seating 1300 spectators, and the situation was worse at the Hôtel de Bourgogne, which was even larger (1700 seats). There was a slight, short-lived improvement around the middle of the century, but – in 1762 – the Italians were obliged to seek an alliance with the 'théâtres de la foire' to give themselves a wider repertoire and a larger potential audience. They also called the Italian playwright Goldoni to the rescue. These two desperate measures, far from saving the company from ruin, sealed their fate: the more popular Opéra-Comique incorporated them into the troupe, only to get rid of them when they sacked all the actors who were not also singers. The disappearance of the Italian Comedians from the French stage was, indeed, an inestimable loss, for they were the last representatives of a tradition which stretches back to the beginning of the sixteenth century, and even beyond to the dim and distant traditions of the middle ages.

But the real claim to fame of the Comédie-Italienne in the eighteenth century lies in their brilliant collaboration with Marivaux. The first plays performed by the Italians after their return from exile already seemed to have a Marivaudian ring: in 1716 they put on *L'Heureuse Surprise*, *Les Équivoques de l'amour* and *Les Stratégies de l'amour*, all plays written and performed in Italian. As with all *commedia dell'arte* companies, the actors who had joined Riccoboni had either specialized in a particular role or were to make their mark in a type of part which would be theirs throughout their career. These types, in the traditional *commedia* companies, were Harlequin, Pantalone, the Doctor, the braggart soldier . . . who wore masks, and the unmasked lovers or maid-servants. The French theatre also had its stock characters such as the noble fathers, the juvenile leads, the maid-servants or soubrettes . . . and such a nomenclature is still in use at the Comédie-Française today.

Luigi Riccoboni, the director of the company (and, incidentally, a fine scholar and historian of the theatre), performed, under the name of Lélio, the 'premiers amoureux' or leading lovers' roles, while Antoine Balletti (as Mario) played the 'seconds amoureux jaloux' or the rival and jealous lovers; the two comic masked men-servants were the speciality of Vicentini (Harlequin) and Biancolelli (Trivelin). Flaminia, played by Elena Balletti, was usually the first female lead ('première amoureuse') and Silvia, Giovanna-Rosa Benozzi, was known as the second female lead and ingénue; the role of the female servant or soubrette was taken by Margerita Rusca under the name of Violette. The company also comprised actors who filled the roles of the fathers (Pantalone, Il Dottore) – although these characters do not appear as such in Marivaux – and at least one singer, the 'cantarina'. Riccoboni's troupe never grew larger than the average *commedia* company of about ten regular players. This fixed number, together with the necessity to write parts for practically all the leading players, explains why Marivaux's plays have an average of six main roles, with a minimum of five and a maximum of ten; so, although Marivaux's plays written for the Italians became more and more 'French' as time went on, the characters, however faintly, retained some vestige of their Italian origins.

The meeting of Marivaux and the Italians was one of those rare occurrences in the history of the theatre when author and actors not only benefit from one another's expertise, but also when the genius of the author brings out the best in a company, and vice versa. In France it happened with Molière and the actors who gathered around him between 1658 and 1673 and, more recently, when Jean Giraudoux and Louis Jouvet combined their talents in the 20s and 30s of this century.

The first play which Marivaux presented to the Italians had been written in collaboration with another writer, and it flopped lamentably: *L'Amour et la vérité* had its only performance on 3 March 1720. But Marivaux's dramatic career was really launched with a play that is still successfully performed nowadays: *Arlequin poli par l'amour* (Harlequin's Lesson in Love). This was written specifically for the Italians with each role tailored not only to suit the histrionic talents of the performer but also designed to accommodate each one's proficiency in French, and was rapturously received on 17 October 1720. Even the sternest critics of the Comédie-Italienne had to concede that it was full of charm and grace. This success was immediately followed by failure: Marivaux's only tragedy, *La Mort d'Annibal*, had just three performances in November 1720 at the Comédie-Française and the contrast between the 'Italian hit' and the 'French flop' was to become a permanent feature of Marivaux's career.

If *Harlequin* was a kind of Italianate 'pantomime', relying as it does on spectacular effects, on physical acting and the *commedia* tradition, Marivaux's next play, *La Surprise de l'amour* (3 May 1722) started the process of 'de-italianization' which was to be completed in 1736 when the Italians performed *L'Heureux Stratagème* (The Feigned Inconstancy), a play containing not a single *commedia* character, although Arlequin made a brief reappearance in *Les Fausses Confidences* the following year. In *La Surprise de l'amour*, then, although Harlequin, Columbine and Lélio retain their original stage names and characteristics, they are already accorded a far greater amount of text. Both the actors playing Lélio and Harlequin were required to learn and deliver long, intricate and stylistically complex speeches; the same was true of the actor playing the Baron (performed by the specialist of Pantalone) and, above all, by Silvia herself, who played the part of the Countess. Flaminia and Mario were 'frenchified' into Jacqueline and Pierre and they spoke that particular form of lively theatrical speech of Marivaux's invention which convincingly, and humorously, represents the colloquial dialect of country folks on the stage.

Although Marivaux's plays increasingly reflected French society rather than duplicating any Italian mode, the playwright remained faithful to his most successful interpreters, until his fateful election to the Académie française which, in many ways, marked the end of his creative career.

Marivaux at the Comédie-Française

During Marivaux's lifetime, twelve of his plays were accepted for performance by the Comédie-Française, but only ten were staged. Of the two remaining plays, one (*L'Amante frivole*) is now lost and the other (*Félicie*) has yet to be performed.

Today, twenty-six of Marivaux's forty plays belong to the repertoire of the Comédie-Française, but some titles are rarely performed. Although Marivaux's plays were often cooly received when presented by the Comédie-Française, it cannot be claimed, as is too often the case, that he failed to achieve popular success, and that he owes his 'newly-found fame' to the better taste of modern critics. Between 1720 and 1750, he occupied the tenth place in the league of authors staged at the Comédie-Française. Admittedly his score of 292 performances playing to some 30,000 spectators compares unfavourably with Voltaire's impressive 400,000 spectators during the same period.

But, of course, Voltaire did not write for the Italian Comedians, who were as popular in Paris as their French rivals and the

'Italian league' (by no means a second division) was headed by Marivaux with a total of some 240,000 spectators officially recorded from 1720 to 1750. Furthermore, attendance figures are missing for eight of these thirty seasons and they do not take into account the spectators who applauded Marivaux's one act plays when they were part of a double or triple bill with longer plays by other playwrights. According to Lagrave, it is no exaggeration to claim that Marivaux's popular success, for the thirty most prolific years of his life, was equal to that of Voltaire, whose plays were exclusively performed at the Comédie-Française. Nowadays Voltaire is not even considered a playwright at all, whereas Marivaux's plays are regularly revived by the best French companies and interest in his work is growing abroad as well.

Since 1970 the following plays by Marivaux have been performed in the main house of the Comédie-Française in Paris. Some of these productions have toured in the provinces and abroad. These additional performances do not figure in our totals.

	Performances in Paris since 1970
Les Acteurs de bonne foi	57
Annibal	8
Arlequin poli par l'amour	nil (but 115 performances from 1892 to 1960)
La Colonie	68
La Commère, premièred in 1967	107 (163 since 1967)
La Dispute	1 (1 in 1744; 24 in all)
La Double Inconstance	60
L'Éducation d'un prince, premièred in 1981	60
L'Épreuve	77
Les Fausses Confidences	93
L'Ile de la raison, premièred anew in 1975	38 (had only 4 in 1730)
L'Ile des esclaves, premièred in 1939	49
Le Jeu de l'amour et du hasard	137 (total to date: 1547)*

La Joie imprévue, premièred in 1962	25
Le Legs	nil (total to date: 696)*
La Méprise, premièred in 1959	nil
La Mère confidente, premièred in 1810	nil
Le Petit-Maître corrigé, premièred in 1734	nil (total to date: 2)
Le Préjugé vaincu	nil (91 before 1870)
Le Prince travesti, premièred in 1949	60
La Réunion des amours	nil
La Seconde Surprise de l'amour	68
Les Serments Indiscrets	nil (35 in 1956-7)
Les Sincères, premièred anew in 1950	37**
La Surprise de l'amour	nil (40 from 1911 to 1950)
Le Triomphe de l'amour, premièred in 1978	97

* For Marivaux's tercentenary the Comédie-Française staged a double bill of *Le Jeu de l'amour et du hasard* and *Le legs*, which opened in Paris in May 1988, after an extended world tour.

** *Les Sincères* had a most successful opening night in 1739, but a conspiracy of Marivaux's literary enemies ensured its subsequent failure.

Marivaux's Originality

Not only was Marivaux deliberately 'modern' in his rejection of Greek classical models (his enemies, the 'Ancients', blamed his ignorance), but he also turned his back on Molière's approach to comedy at a time when the latter was hailed above Plautus and Terence. 'Molière became the one model to imitate, the symbol of perfection. Contemporary comedies are strictly judged with reference to Molière, yet Molière is also said to be inimitable.' (Lagrave) The highest ideal, then, was the five-act comedy of characters, written in alexandrines (rhyming couplets of twelve syllables each) and adhering to neo-classical rules.

Marivaux wrote only one play in five acts *and* in alexandrines: the ill-fated tragedy *Annibal*. His first attempt at comedy, *Le Père prudent et équitable*, published in 1712 and never produced professionally was also written in ungainly rhyming couplets. Of his mature comedies, only *Les Serments Indiscreets* (Careless Vows) is in five acts, but in prose. All his other plays (in one or three acts) were written in prose.

Molière's comedy of character relies on the depiction of stereotypes (the miser, the misanthropist, the religious bigot, the womanizer, the cheat . . .) and on a solidly-constructed plot. Marivaux rejected this kind of narrative and created plays in which the action takes place in the mind of the character and in which dialogue is of primordial importance. Deloffre admires in Marivaux 'the finely-observed psychological approach in which the pain felt by the character, just as much as that which the character inflicts, becomes the touchstone for true love'. According to Marivaux himself, the dramatic expression of these feelings requires that 'the actors do not seem aware of the value of what they are saying', and Deloffre adds: 'In Marivaux's plays the stress is above all on the word itself, not on what the word represents. But in each repeated word we are aware of different nuances of interpretation, quibbling over meaning, arguing, sudden unexpected twists – in a word, dramatic progression. Language is no longer the sign of the action, it becomes instead its very substance.'

Even more than with the tragic theatre of Racine (though that too is dependent on the precise usage of word), Marivaux's theatre illustrates that 'eloquence is action', for in the universe of the eighteenth-century playwright there is no 'infernal machine' which relentlessly carries the characters to their inescapable doom. Marivaux is the first dramatist to dissect the soul, to sow doubt about the immutability of human nature – the first in fact to open up for the theatre what Nathalie Sarraute has, in the twentieth century, termed 'l'ère du soupçon' (the era of doubt).

Marivaux maintained, then, that actors must not feel the value of what they are saying – i.e., the actor must not put himself above his character and pass judgement on him as he interprets the role. Louis Jouvet, in his classes at the Conservatoire, stated that to play Marivaux 'you have to play at playing'. This is anything but a contradiction, for it is Marivaux's character himself (a modern concept if ever there was one) who is caught up, partly by his own choosing and partly willy-nilly, in a network of conflicting strategems. To take an obvious example (although there are very many others scattered throughout the plays), let us consider the position at the start of *Le Jeu de l'amour et du hasard*. Dorante and Silvia choose to disguise themselves as servants to size each other up before agreeing to the marriage arranged by their fathers and, in order to do this, they need to confide in their servants who have to assume the identity of the masters. The four 'characters' are aware of the role they are playing but when they unexpectedly fall in love, they are forced to play a role they had not bargained for and for which they are not prepared. What this means is that throughout the play the actor, without shedding the identity of the character he played at the outset, has to superimpose a second character on the first; and this second character has to convey the impression that he is improvising without knowing where all this will lead him. The situation is further complicated by the fact that Silvia's father, Orgon, who has agreed to go along with the trick, forbids his daughter and her servant Lisette to reveal their identity before the experiment is over.

With each twist of the basic situation, which evolves with every revelation or discovery of secret feelings, the 'playing actor' must reassess his position and readjust his response. Silvia, for example, is convinced that she is in control, that she 'knows' who the master (her future husband, Dorante) is, and that she 'knows' the identity of his man-servant. But when the men arrive, she takes an instant dislike to the master and is 'attracted' to his lackey. As if this were not bad enough, the valet woos her, and she responds all too readily! Eventually she is inextricably ensnared in an impossible situation of her own making and, literally, no longer knows who she is:

Oh, how my poor heart aches! What is it that mingles with my present confusion to make this whole business so distressing? I distrust every face, I am content with nobody, I am not content with myself. (p. 222)

Fortunately for her, this is the moment when Dorante reveals his true identity. 'Ah, exclaims Silvia, now I see clear into my heart.' (p. 224) But instead of putting an end to the game, she sparks off a further series of disguises, casting her brother into a new role. But, interestingly, even when Silvia *knows* the *true* identity of all the other characters, and even though she has instructed her brother on the way he should behave, she is again the victim of her own stratagem and is made to suffer one last time before she can rejoice in Dorante's love.

Marivaux, (and the spectator of his play) is the only one to understand his character's inner motives. Obviously the actor knows as well (and it is all the more imperative that he knows the more complicated the play becomes) but he must never *show* that he knows since the character he is playing is ignorant of the true facts of the situation.

The appreciation of the complexity of this psychological interplay, which should have relegated the one-dimensional character to oblivion a long time ago, even if he were not always fully recognized by Marivaux's contemporaries, did not have to await the twentieth century to be acknowledged. As early as 1809, Barante wrote:

Marivaux, that fine observer of the minutiae of the behaviour of the human species, made a special study of recognizing the slightest nuances behind our feelings and resolutions. Therein lay his talent, and it is impossible to disagree with the truth of his observations; but we must not be misled by this kind of attitude and we should be aware that by putting undue stress on it, you lessen its effect. Marivaux does not present us with the result of his observation, but shows us observation in action. The words of each character are always geared to show us that what lay in his heart was well known to the dramatist. A scene from Molière is a representation of human nature, a scene from Marivaux is a commentary on that selfsame human nature. (Lagrave, p. 175)

The irony of this perceptive analysis is that it was made, not to stress Marivaux's modernity or his original achievement, but to condemn him for the lack of theatrical qualities in his plays. Théophile Gautier, some 40 years later, was the first to draw attention to the affinity between Shakespeare and Marivaux; he did not make a claim for any direct influence, but underlined the rich complexity of the masterpieces of both playwrights. His further comparison between Molière and Marivaux again highlighted the eighteenth-century writer's profound psychologism, his 'serious analysis of love', opposed to Molière's mechanistic painting of human emotions. As Gautier put it: Molière 'depicts lovers, if you like, but never people who are in love.'

The novelist Nathalie Sarraute, author of *L'Ère du soupçon*, who late in her career was prevailed upon to write for the theatre, helps us understand Marivaux's thought process when writing his dialogue as she refers to her own approach to the construction of dialogue in her plays:

> What would, in my novels, have constituted the dramatic action of the sub-conversation and the pre-dialogue, in which sensations, impressions and feeling are conveyed to the reader through images and rhythms, was here displayed within the dialogue itself. The sub-conversation became conversation. Thus the inside became the outside, so that a critic was able later on, and quite rightly, to describe this shift from the novel to the play, as a sort of 'glove turned inside out'.

It might be excessive to make the same claim for Marivaux's dialogue, but Sarraute's analysis, applied to Marivaux's plays, leads to a better understanding of his art. In a further passage, perhaps even more pertinent to the study of Marivaux, she writes:

> In all my plays action is absent; it is replaced by the ebb and flow of language. The emphasis on the role of language in literature is so great these days, it is to such a degree considered the sole substance of every literary work, its point of departure and its 'generator', it has become to such a degree the theme-song of literary criticism, that I hesitate to mention

its importance in my plays. It is, however, a fact that these plays contain no external action. It is a fact that language plays in them the role of detonator.

Of Marivaux, d'Alembert had already said that his plays were 'without any real action, because everything takes place in discourse rather than by developments in the plot'.

Such concentration on internal action (so disconcerting to eighteenth-century critics) is precisely what, today, stimulates the creative activity of those directors who choose to stage Marivaux's work.

Marivaux on the post-war stage

Early in Marivaux's career as a dramatist, his enemies coined the word 'marivaudage' to qualify, disparagingly, what they saw as his hair-splitting, precious and mannered dialogue. They also spoke with derision of his 'metaphysics of the heart' and Voltaire, who crudely lampooned Marivaux in a satirical poem, summed up 'marivaudage' as the art 'of weighing flies' eggs on scales made from a spider's web'.

In more recent times, and in theatrical parlance, 'marivaudage' has also come to mean a light-weight love intrigue without much substance and a precious style of behaviour, almost synonymous with 'minaudage' (affected simpering). Theatre practitioners in France must take part of the blame for spreading this acceptation of the word and thus fostering a distorted image of Marivaux, since too many productions of his plays have simply striven towards elegance, glamour and 'good taste'. So much so that André Gide, who had listed *La Vie de Marianne* among the ten best French novels, once damned a play by declaring it 'as boring as Marivaux'.

Since the end of World War II, however, the situation has been radically altered. Not that Marivaux has yet again been 'rediscovered', but directors have decided to clear away all the cobwebs (not just Voltaire's), which surrounded Marivaux's theatre and to look at his plays without preconceptions and reject a three-century old, but nonetheless spurious, 'tradition'.

The new era was opened by Jean-Louis Barrault with his two important *mises en scène* of *Les Fausses Confidences* (1946) and *La Seconde Surprise de l'amour* (1949), followed by Jean Vilar's *Le Triomphe de l'amour* (1956), *L'Heureux Stratagème* (1960) et *La Fausse Suivante* (1962). The truly modern departure, however, came with Roger Planchon's *La Seconde Surprise de l'amour* (1959) which prompted a fundamental reappraisal not only of Marivaux himself, but of classics in general, and a reassessment of the role of the director in the theatre and the status of *mise en scène*. Since the late 50s, Marivaux has become the French classical dramatist whose plays are most often revived, and the best and most adventurous directors have been seduced by his plays. In addition to the three directors already mentioned Marcel Bluwal (French TV), Jean-Paul Roussillon (Comédie-Française), Patrice Chéreau (TNP and Nanterre), Alfredo Arias (Groupe TSE), Jacques Lassalle, Claude Stratz, Antoine Vitez . . . have all put on Marivaux in a spirit of artistic and intellectual experimentation.

Needless to say, there is no question of their 'revivals' being staged as historical reconstructions, quite the contrary. Nowadays a director deciding to produce a classic is well aware that, apart from the written word, all the other conditions contributing to the presentation of a play from the past have changed. The social context of, say, the 1720s has not much in common with that pertaining today; the theatrical organization has altered radically (new audiences, new buildings, different actors, changed financial structures and so on . . .) and the acting traditions, whether those of the improvised Italian *commedia* or of French academicism, are now nothing more than theoretical concepts for theatre historians to muse on and are of no immediate value to the practitioner faced with the task of directing or performing a text and confronted with the obligation of creating a theatrical language of his own, adapted – as *he* sees it – to the particular demands of each play.

Some thirty years ago, Jan Kott disturbed the critical fraternity with his provoking *Shakespeare Our Contemporary* and the publication of the book inspired, directly or indirectly, Shakespearian productions world-wide. Something not dissimilar happened in

France in the case of Marivaux in the wake of Planchon's *La Seconde Surprise de l'amour*. His *mise en scène* threw overboard all respect for the sacrosanct unities and the revered notion of decorum ('la bienséance'). The unique, unspecified location in which the action is 'supposed' to take place was 'blown up' into a series of contrasting locations, from the Marquise's bedroom to the skivvy's washroom; so much for the unity of place. The unity of time disappeared with the help of lighting changes which clearly marked the passing of time and a strategically-placed interval. The unity of tone, which would require the play to be performed and perceived as a straightforward comedy, was flouted by the many shifts in atmosphere and the seesawing between serious, comic and even 'naturalistic' scenes. Planchon also augmented the basic cast of six actors by an array of extras, maids and servants of the Marquise's household: their constant presence and their unceasing, but silent activity, contributed a striking commentary on their betters, engaged in the idle pursuit of love.

What caused the greatest scandal, though, was the obtrusive presence on the set of the Marquise's bed. Obviously it does not appear in Marivaux's text and, even if the play is all about sex, the reality of it was always safely tucked away in the wings. But not content with forcing the spectator to stare at a bed, Planchon had the Marquise lying on it in a suggestive négligé, first on her own, and – after the interval – with the Comte, inferring unequivocally that they had put the luxury of silk sheets to good use. Planchon was obviously not offering a perverse reading of Marivaux's play rather he had foregrounded what the eighteenth-century playwright knew was the more secret kernel of his comedies. New audiences expect new *mises en scène*, but fresh approaches do not mean, as traditional critics would like us to think, a betrayal of the 'intentions' of the playwright. It was, after all, Marivaux himself who wrote: 'Every woman understands that she is desired when she is told, "I love you"; and she is only grateful for the compliment because it really means, "I want you".' In 1949, after Barrault's revival of the same play, a critic was moved to concede that 'the torments of the flesh' were indeed part of Marivaux's discourse, but he also stated that they should remain in the background. Planchon restored the body, in its physical presence, where it belongs, i.e., centre stage, and presented human beings as moral and physical individuals *and* as members of the society to which they belong: 'Our main aim,' wrote Planchon, 'is to bring to the fore the mainsprings of human action: love, self-interest, perversity, feminist demands, class warfare.'

Such a Brechtian programme was even taken on board by the Comédie-Française in Roussillon's production of *The Game of Love and Chance* in 1976. Roussillon set the play inside the plush, eighteenth-century drawing-room of Orgon's family whose members belonged to solid, not to say stolid, bourgeois stock. His was a 'naturalist' *mise en scène* in which two wealthy, spoilt but decent, responsible children played a safe game under the benevolent gaze of an all-controlling father. The clear-cut class distinction between masters and servants, underlined by the strict differentiation in acting, serious and parodic, and the omission of the creative ambiguity which one would expect in our 'democratic' age, robbed the play of any tension; the game was thus turned into a 'slice of life' sentimentalized by the appeal made to the kind heart of the spectator by the valet Pasquin (the French counterpart of Arlequin, a change which eliminated any Italian influence from the production) and Lisette, after their discovery that they would not, after all, marry into the bourgeoisie. In this instance, the play was applauded by the press and it received the prize for the best production of 1976; watered down and made safe, Planchon's revolutionary insights had gained acceptance (and a bed has since been seen on the set for *La Surprise* at the Comédie-Française!).

More recently (1986-7), the Théâtre TSE, under the direction of Alfredo Arias, has presented another award-winning production of *The Game of Love and Chance*, but the contrast could not have been greater. Set in an eighteenth-century folly, a minimal cast of six great apes, dressed in colourful costumes *à la Watteau*, jumped, danced, squealed, laughed and, on rare occasions, cried their way through the game. The ape-like characteristics of every character made it unnecesaary for them to behave like ladies or gentlemen and allowed the actors to express the instincts or the desires of the characters ('the torments of their flesh'!) without the need to don the mask of hypocritical decency. Indeed, the mask of the ape stood paradoxically for the absence of mask and helped to reveal the innermost urges of the characters. The tone was set very firmly in the opening scene between Lisette and Silvia: the maid, unable to understand her mistress's bizarre aversion to a good-looking husband and inflamed by talk of an imminent marriage, not only collapsed on the ground in hysterics but showed her excitement without inhibition: she flung her legs high into the air – showing off immaculate nineteenth-century drawers (given the absence of an equivalent eighteenth-century garment) – and furiously scratched where it itched. A large party of pubescent school-girls who attended the performance I saw were stunned into silence, then giggled uncomfortably, but they soon got into the spirit of things and left the theatre exhilarated, having received a most subtle lesson in human amorous behaviour delivered with exuberant playfulness.

Playfulness was conspicuously absent in Chéreau's *A Matter of Dispute* (TNP, 1976) whose radical production highlighted what he saw as Marivaux's violence and cruelty, not to say his Sadian or sadistic qualities. This play, long regarded as a minor work, had had a number of unsuccessful productions at the Comédie-Française, but was nonetheless considered as the epitome of 'marivaudage' since its theme is the question of whether man or woman was guilty of the first infidelity. Put this way, the question would indeed appear to be the worst kind of 'metaphysics of the heart'.

Chéreau and his dramaturge, François Regnault, wrote a framing prologue to the play for their *mise en scène*, using extracts of scenes, dialogue and speeches taken from Marivaux's works (journalistic writings, novels as well as plays). The prologue was set in the 1930s in some mid-European decadent court whose Prince, at a party given in honour of his fiancée, Hermiane (who is shown to be his prisoner and victim at least as much as his partner), reveals the cruel experiment put in motion by his father almost twenty years earlier: four children, two girls and two boys, had been brought up 'in solitary confinement' until adulthood, with two black servants as their sole human contacts. Marivaux's first scene reads as a simple and uncomplicated theatrical device to introduce a playful and harmless demonstration, which, predictably, concludes that fickleness is not the privilege of either sex. Chéreau, however, sees in the play far more sinister forces at work and refuses to believe in the innocence of the experiment. His Prince is an all-powerful figure who tyrannically controls the members of his court and who watches gleefully as the youngsters discover that they are not the only 'person' on earth and that coming to terms with the existence of the 'other', of one's sexual impulses and the freedom of newly-encountered 'persons' can be a very traumatic experience. In Chéreau's *mise en scène*, Hermiane is made to watch by force, although she finds the spectacle distasteful and distressing, all the more so as it ends in tragedy when one of the youngsters, unable to accept in himself and in others the deceitfulness he has just discovered in human nature, chooses to take his own life. In *A Matter of Dispute*, Chéreau gave us a Marivaux contemporary with the Marquis de Sade, a Marivaux who has read Freud, who is aware of Nazi experiments, a Marivaux who, since Planchon's epoch-making production, has lost faith in humanism.

Our anthology

The ten plays contained in this volume span the entire career of Marivaux as an accomplished playwright. *Harlequin* (1720) was his first success staged by the Italians and *The Constant Players* (1757) was the last play he wrote. Our selection reflects the division between plays written for and performed by the Italian company and those presented by the Comédie-Française and reflects also the proportion of successes and failures of the first productions.

Harlequin's Lesson in Love (Italians, 1720), although specifically written to show the Italians' skills at their best (pantomimic acting by traditional *commedia* masks, interludes with songs and dance, clever scene changes), introduces one of the central themes of Marivaux's theatre: the distinction between nature (represented by Harlequin and Silvia), and artifice (the Fairy and her world of fantasy). The action revolves around a sophisticated fairy who wishes to cast a spell on the uncouth Harlequin, while –

at the same time – she is trying to hide from 'the great Magician Merlin' (p. 395) whom she has jilted. Unfortunately for her, Harlequin is not only unresponsive, but resists all her attempts to refine him. His grossness and stupidity seem incurable. His first entrance, which is his first appearance in Marivaux's theatre, is typical of the character: he enters 'hanging his head or in any other silly posture he likes'. (p. 397) His speech is just as clumsy. To the Fairy's engaging: 'How now, sweet youth! You look sad. Is there something that displeased you?', he replies grumpily: 'I dunno!' But, in the following scene, on meeting Silvia, he requires no prompting and is instantly endowed with a smooth tongue:

HARLEQUIN (*approaching* SILVIA *and revealing his happiness in little laughs*). How pretty you are.

SILVIA. You're very kind.

HARLEQUIN. Oh, no, I'm telling the truth.

SILVIA (*laughing a little in her turn*). You're pretty too. (p. 402)

The sun shines throughout the action. Harlequin and Silvia outwit the fairy who is generously forgiven for her scheming ways, Harlequin declares himself king and the play ends in songs and dances.

The same pair of lovers is central to *The Double Inconstancy* (Italians, 1723) as well. They are still in love, but the threat to their happiness is this time very real: Silvia has been kidnapped by the Prince who wants to marry her and he is ready to buy off Harlequin. In the early stages, the contrast between court and country is absolute: the Prince and his sycophantic courtiers do their utmost to seduce the two villagers, but the country folk cling to their simple honour and seem immune to temptation. The Prince, priding himself on not being as tyrannical as he could be, marvels at Silvia's 'phenomenal' constancy, but Flaminia laughs at him: 'My Lord, don't listen to [these] strange phenomena; they are all very well in fairy-tales; I know my sex; the only phenomenal thing about us is our vanity.' (p. 44) Indeed, she knows her subject well. In the second act, Silvia explains that she loves Harlequin, *faute de mieux*, and finds that she is no longer able to resist Flaminia's flattery:

FLAMINIA. . . . You have taste and wit . . . he's portentous and crude, he isn't your style . . .

SILVIA. Put yourself in my place; he was the most suitable
man in my part of the world . . . (p. 83)

From here on Harlequin's fate is sealed. But it would be wrong to
cast him in the role of victim; he, more basically, succumbs to the
temptation of good food and the temptation of the flesh. Flaminia
having decided to sacrifice herself to the happiness of her Prince
has no difficulty in inflaming the yokel. As the title implies, the
action does not chart the burgeoning of adult love after an initial
youthful but chaste infatuation, but shows rather the power of
seduction, the triumph of falsehood and the defeat of honour and
decency. The court corrupts and no one is immune from the
disease it spreads.

In *The False Servant* (Italians, 1724) Silvia scored an immense
success in a breeches part and the play was often revived during
her lifetime. Superficially it is a play of intrigue and of mistaken
identity; the 'Chevalier', who is in fact a rich young heiress, has
by chance met Lélio one evening at a masked ball; he is the
husband-to-be her family has chosen for her, and, as she is in
disguise, she decides to continue to play her masculine role to
discover what Lélio is really like. What she sees appals her. Lélio
is not only expecting to marry '*her*' and pocket her dowry, he is
also carrying on an affair with a rich countess whom he is double-
crossing and cheating out of thousands of pounds. Money and
greed motivate him and love, as far as the word has any meaning
at all, is obviously devoid of any romantic connotations and
merely a snare to trap fools. Lélios's eventual exposure is not a
cathartic experience and leaves a very bitter taste in the mouth.
Recent productions have highlighted the harshness of the
situation and stressed the tragic potential of the play. No wonder
that this is the text that introduces the cynical, self-seeking and
unscrupulous servant, Trivelin, who epitomizes this society in
which notions of honour and decency are nothing but sham.
Listening to him, one hears already the ringing tones of
Beaumarchais's Figaro:

TRIVELIN. Over the fifteen odd years that I've been making
my way in this world of ours, you know the lengths to which
I've gone in my attempt to settle down. It had come to my

notice that scrupulous men rarely make money. So to give myself an even chance, I laid scruples aside. If it was profitable to be honourable, then I was a man of honour. If I deemed it pertinent to be devious, then, once my conscience had heaved a deep sigh of regret, I was devious. On occastions I have indeed been rich. But how is one to lend performance to such a situation, when our path is littered with rocks? The odd flutter, the odd fling, the odd beverage. How is one to avoid such temptation?

FRONTIN. True.

TRIVELIN. What else can I say? One day upstairs. The next day downstairs. Ever prudent. Ever industrious. Befriending crooks by design and gentlemen by inclination. Respected in one disguise, horse whipped in another . . . (p. 112)

The spectators of the 1720s were fond of 'philosophical comedies' and *Slave Island* (Italians, 1725) belongs to a repertoire of plays which depict a social Utopia. On Slave Island, the descendants of Greek slaves have established an egalitarian republic and if ever 'masters' land there, the islanders either kill or enslave them, unless they mend their ways. After a shipwreck they capture Iphicrate, a young Athenian nobleman who is accompanied by his slave Harlequin and Euphrosine, a flighty Athenian lady of fashion with her slave Cleanthis. Trivelin, the democratic ruler of the island, puts them to the test of swapping roles with their slave; furthermore, the masters have to listen, without protest, to their slaves' complaints and to the unflattering portraits made of them, in order to make them 'rational, empathetic and humane for the rest of [their] life'. (p. 431) Harlequin, as Trivelin did in the previous play, foreshadows Figaro, when he lays into his master: 'All he has contributed to the world, to date, is a lot of wasted money and a certain amount of bother to other people. Born without too much in the way of surplus brain, he devoted his life to the art of mindlessness, on the principle that women preferred him that way. Spent money like water. Was mean when he should have been generous, generous when he should be mean. Good at borrowing, bad at paying it back. Strangely terrified of seeming clever . . .' (p. 441) Cleanthis is no less forthright with Euphrosine. But, basically, we are dealing here with noble hearts who have erred: the masters recognize the error of their ways and the servants resume their 'natural' place. The play ends in kisses and tears of joy, and it is the 'republican' Trivelin who concludes: 'Degree between man and man is given us by the gods, not as a set of rules to follow blindly, but to test our humanity.' (p. 454) No wonder that such statements did not endear Marivaux to revolutionary spirits; but it should not be read as an authorial pronouncement (especially not today) but as a lucid recognition of the world-view held by society at that time.

Class distinction and nobility of the heart are the twin themes of *The Game of Love and Chance* (Italians, 1730): despite their disguise as servants, Dorante and Silvia recognize one another at first sight (even if they do not *know* who they are) as in their hearts they instinctively see each other's true worth. Their genuine quality shines through the servants' livery just as much as the vulgarity of the real servants cheapens the elegance of their borrowed finery. In *The Game* the gulf between the upper and the lower classes appears unbridgeable: Dorante is always a gentleman but nothing could lift Harlequin above his 'innate' vulgarity. But although class is an important factor, the problems it gives rise to are not brought into sharp focus. In fact, Marivaux evades the issue by carefully avoiding writing scenes between Silvia and the real Harlequin (the one who is supposed to be her husband-to-be) and between Dorante and the real Lisette: decorum (la bienséance), so dear to the French theatre-going public, would have been flouted. The important feature of *The Game* is that it is the only play, among the ten presented in this volume, which presents a pair of ideal lovers, the only one in which love is genuine and not complicated by overweening pride or sordid financial considerations.

With *Careless Vows* (Comédie-Française, 1732) we come at last to a play presented by the French actors. According to Marivaux himself it was booed on the first night, it 'pleased on the second night, was applauded on the third and then it was praised'. But it had only a total of nine performances. In recent years it has scarcely been more successful. It was, however, one of Marivaux's favourite plays and, after its failure, he wrote a preface to accompany its publication. 'This play,' he writes, 'is about two people between whom a marriage has been arranged, who do not know each other at all and who, in their heart of hearts have the same aversion to marriage . . .' Lucile and Damis have agreed to meet, as did Silvia and Dorante, to please their fathers, but they have both resolved to be frank and to declare openly to one another their dislike of marriage. Given such a premise, the play could not even get past the first scene were it not for Lucile's curiosity. Instead of facing Damis on his entrance, she hides in a little room to spy on him and on learning of his resolve not to marry, she is piqued and comes out fighting. There can be little doubt that Damis is won over by the beauty and the vivacity of the girl. But her motives for falling in love are more complex and more questionable. As she explains to Lisette, whose love for the valet Frontin is healthy and uncomplicated, it is clear that she does not understand her own feelings:

> LUCILE. I don't know about that, Lisette, because when I think about it, our love doesn't always reflect credit on the loved one. More often, it implies criticism of the one who is in love. I am only too well aware of this. What are the great sources of our passions? Our vanity, and our flirtatiousness. That's where men, most often, derive all their worth. They aren't left with many admirable qualities, once you've taken away the weakness of our hearts. That little room where I hid while Damis was talking to you – take that away from my little story, and perhaps I wouldn't have been in love . . . (p. 310)

And she goes on to ask, 'After all, why am I in love?' and her reply is blunt and unromantic, 'I wanted vengeance for my face'. Lucile plays a game of love and pique whose conclusion is an unwanted marriage – not to mention a broken friendship with her sister who was cruelly abused by Lucile's self-seeking caprices.

The Feigned Inconstancy (Italians, 1733) brought Marivaux his next success and on that occasion he was praised for having 'a perfect knowledge of the human heart' and for offering an 'in-depth analysis of what is going on in the heart of women'. The plot revolves around a quartet of lovers: the Countess has jilted Dorante, who loves her, in favour of the Chevalier who, for his part, has betrayed the Marquise. To revenge herself, the Marquise has the bright idea of proposing to Dorante that they, the injured parties, should pretend that they had fallen deeply in love. Her aim is to arouse the jealousy of their former partners. Just like Marivaux, the Marquise knows the difference between 'amour' (love) and 'amour-propre' (self-esteem) and she, rightly, suspects that the bruised pride of the Countess will restore her love for Dorante. The trick works despite the fact that the Countess does indeed see through her rival's stratagem. The play appears to reach a happy conclusion as the initial couples are reunited, yet it belongs to the 'unpleasant' category, to use Anouilh's definition, and its characters are quite unlovable. At her first entrance, for instance, the Countess lectures Lisette on the joys of infidelity and on the absolute duty of women to follow their every whim:

> COUNTESS. It is in the nature of a woman's heart to give one's word a thousand times, and break it a thousand times, for the heart must be led by feelings, and I'm sure our feelings are not to be confined. If we do else, we break our heart's natural laws, and by being untrue to our own natures we deceive the world, which we should never do. (p. 329)

This is not idle talk; the Countess is actively trying to corrupt Lisette's more simple heart, and her maid will, as a consequence, experience a few anguished moments. The Countess has also the unpleasant habit of splitting hairs and of making a distinction between 'singling out' a man and 'loving' him. Dorante, she asserts, was singled out by her, not loved; and, in any case, the Chevalier who, in her eyes, has the charm of novelty is infinitely preferable. Dorante, the least objectionable character of the quartet, lacks strength and, above all, emotional and intellectual perspicacity and he therefore fails to enlist our sympathy. As for the Marquise, her motives are ambiguous. Locked into a contest of seduction with the Countess, her attitude *vis-à-vis* Dorante is not as open as would at first appear and we get the impression that she would happily forget her Chevalier, a stupid, insensitive, boastful, macho, ineffectual bore, if Dorante entered the game in earnest. Approached psychologically *The Feigned Inconstancy* is one of Marivaux's darker comedies, but obviously the 'unpleasant-ness' could easily be ironed out if the play were staged as a *commedia* variation on the theme of light-hearted sexual toings and froings.

The Will (Comédie-Française, 1736) got a good reception, perhaps because Marivaux took the precaution of presenting it anonymously on the first night. Not only was the play judged to be 'extremely witty and stylishly written' but the acting was also highly praised. To date, with *Le Jeu de l'amour et du hasard*, *Le Legs* is Marivaux's most frequently revived comedy (together, these two plays make up the double bill with which the Comédie-Française celebrated Marivaux's tercentenary in 1988). Superficially it seems that once again we are dealing with a 'triumph of love', as the Marquis and the Countess find a way of admitting to one another that they are in love, thus enabling their friends Hortense and the Chevalier, who are entangled in their love and money dealings, to conclude a long desired match. Indeed love is seen to be triumphant as the curtain falls with two marriages about to take place. But does it? To the Chevalier's joyful exclamation: 'This, Countess, is the happy end we have all been waiting for', she tartly retorts: 'Then there's no point in waiting any longer, is there?' and storms out, without giving the photographer a chance to take a few smiling snapshots of the engagements. The Countess, a youthful and rich widow, despising love and romantic inclinations, is worried about some pending court cases and could do with a man about the house. The Marquis is such a man, as he himself is obsessed with money and finds matters of the heart quite troublesome. 'In love' with the Countess, this rich man is prepared to marry his cousin Hortense for the sake of an additional inheritance of 200,000 francs. He declares to the Countess:

> MARQUIS. You can say what you like. She's going to be my wife. But, and here's the clever bit, I'm going to be her husband. Aha. That's going to give her something to think about. Today the contract, tomorrow the wedding, tonight locked up in her room. That's the way it is. She's put me in one of my moods. (p. 489)

Richer, and more sensible than the petulant Marquis, the Countess buys him off to make an end of it and to assert her superiority. This is how she explains her position in a 'romantic' aside before concluding the bargain:

> COUNTESS. I am, I must admit, more and more sorely
> tempted, prompted by no more than impatience, to tell him
> outright, yes, I do love him. There. Only to show him . . .
> what a stupid idiot he is. (p. 492)

And to Lisette she confesses: 'I wouldn't go as far as to say that my
feelings could be characterized as passion. But on the other hand
I have nothing with which to reproach him.' (p. 496)

When Lépine, the Marquis's servant, tries to explain Lisette's
self-seeking action to the Countess, he delivers a strong, tongue-
in-cheek critique of the upper class so-called nobility of mind and
generosity of heart:

> LEPINE. . . . that kind of mentality, you doubtless find
> repugnant. Your sensitivity is sorely offended. That's what
> makes you a Countess. But, everyone is not a Countess, are
> they? What I've just told you, that's how a servant's mind
> works. And servants . . . you just have to accept them for
> what they are. I mean. Do we get angry with ants for
> crawling? You get my point. Lowly status, lowly ideas.
> (p. 493)

All Lisette and Lépine can hope for is to pick up a few crumbs and
they need their wits about them in order to survive. Yet their
masters who are very comfortably off are prepared to turn their
lives into living hell for the sake of ever more money in the bank.
These marriages will pay handsome financial dividends, but they
spell the bankruptcy of human decency.

Until its revelation by Patrice Chéreau [see above, p. xxvii]
A Matter of Dispute (Comédie-Française, 1744) was just about
tolerated within Marivaux's œuvre. It had a disastrous first night
and was immediately dropped from the repertoire. Modern
revivals at the Comédie-Française have hardly been more
successful. If in *Harlequin's Lesson in Love* we witnessed the
enchanted discovery of love by 'children' who suddenly and
generously experience a warmth of feeling hitherto unknown to
them, the four 'innocents' of *La Dispute* do not so much discover
love as discover themselves as objects of admiration for themselves and for others. When Eglea, for the first time in her life,
catches a glimpse of herself in the stream, she is overwhelmed:

EGLEA. What! Is that me, is that my face?

CARISA. It certainly is.

EGLEA. But do you realize it's beautiful, it's delightful to look at? What a shame I didn't know earlier.

CARISA. You are beautiful, it's true.

EGLEA. What do you mean, 'beautiful'? Wonderful! This is a delightful discovery ... (p. 506)

Self-love is her discovery: she is enchanted on meeting Azoro, the first man she sees, because he admires her, but hostilities commence when another woman, Adinia, is thrown in her path, since the two women refuse to flatter each other. Friendship between men is a more straightforward matter, but it ends when the two boys start competing for the adulation of the girls. All four are equally deceitful and self-seeking. So much so that the demonstration of 'who had first been fickle and faithless in love' is brought to an end by Hermione because she finds it 'quite unbearable', and the concluding line of the play, spoken by her, does not gloss over the problem, but tries to ensure that the spectator should mull it over further: 'We have no grounds for joking, believe me. Shall we go?' (p. 532)

The Constant Players (1757) was first produced successfully in Paris by André Barsacq in 1957 at the Théâtre de l'Atelier where, in the 1920s, Charles Dullin had introduced Pirandello to the French stage. It has become a critical cliché to call *Les Acteurs de bonne foi* a Pirandellian game of masks. In this, his last play, Marivaux reflected on the relationship between reality and fiction, the real world and the world of dreams, and also on the relationship between the actor and the part he is playing. At the start of *The Constant Players*, we drop into an improvised rehearsal of a commissioned play to be performed later that same day by non-professional actors who are also rather simple people. Merlin, the author/director/leading actor of the playlet has deliberately chosen to blur the frontiers separating fantasy from reality. His canvas is a classical Marivaudian game of love and betrayal. 'In reality' Merlin is to marry Lisette, and Blaise is to marry Colette; but he has imagined that "tis Colette who shall be in love with me and I am to play her lover. We are both agreed to observe the manner in which Blaise and Lisette respond to all the naïve expression of love we shall affect for one another. And all this to discover if it alarms them and makes them jealous.' (p. 536) At first Lisette has fun 'pretending to be another'. But Blaise has immediate misgivings: 'Ay! But what if what we plays should turn out true? Be on your guard at least! We mustn't 'ave nothing for real. 'Cos, Lord knows, I truly love Colette.' (p. 537) It soon turns out that his jealousy is not misplaced. His Colette is flattered by Merlin's compliments and Merlin is using the fiction to flirt outrageously with her. And, maybe, Blaise is again right when he suspects an ulterior motive behind the staging of the play: 'There bain't but one reason for this comedy, Miss Lisette. To see us both cast off!' (p. 545)

Nicolas Bonhôte comments: 'In Marivaux's theatre there are a great number of sincere actors – that is to say characters who play a part without knowing and without wishing to, themselves being duped by the comic action. It is such an interpenetration – to the point of confusion – of actor and character, of naturalness and artificiality that Marivaux has chosen to depict in his last work . . .' This confusion is the essence of Marivaux's dramatic world and ultimately the real source of pleasure in the theatre (even if Blaise was made terribly unhappy when he discovered that he was surrounded by people who 'only pretend to pretend').

Cited Works

Marivaux, *Théâtre complet*, 2 volumes, edited by Frédéric Deloffre, Garnier Frères, Paris, 1968

Nicolas Bonhôte, *Le Théâtre de Marivaux, Etude de sociologie de la littérature*, L'Age d'Homme, Lausanne, 1974

Henri Lagrave, *Marivaux et sa fortune littéraire*, Ducros éditeur, Saint-Médard-en-Jalles, 1970

The Double Inconstancy

Translated by Nicholas Wright

from LA DOUBLE INCONSTANCE
First performed by the Italian Comedians (1723)

CHARACTERS

SILVIA

TRIVELIN

THE PRINCE

FLAMINIA

LISETTE

HARLEQUIN

A LORD

Attendant ladies

Attendant servants

The scene is set in the Prince's palace.

The translator would like to acknowledge the help of Simon Nye.

Act One

Scene 1

SILVIA *and* TRIVELIN *enter.* SILVIA *is followed by several women; she is angry and appears to be about to leave.*

TRIVELIN. Listen to me, milady –

SILVIA. You're annoying me.

TRIVELIN. One should be reasonable, surely?

SILVIA. No, one shouldn't and I won't.

TRIVELIN. But even so, milady –

SILVIA. Even so I won't be reasonable; you can repeat your 'even so' a hundred times and I still won't want to; what will you do about that?

TRIVELIN. You ate so little yesterday that if you don't eat anything this morning you'll be ill.

SILVIA. I hate being well, and illness doesn't bother me; so you can send back every scrap of food they bring me: breakfast, lunch and dinner; and tomorrow you can do the same. I've got my anger, and my hatred of you all, and I don't want anything else until I see my Harlequin, who you stole from me. That's what I've decided; if you want to drive me raving mad, just go on saying I should be reasonable, you'll do it in no time.

TRIVELIN. Lord! I wouldn't risk it! You're a woman of your word, it's very apparent. Even so –

SILVIA. You've said it again!

TRIVELIN. I beg your pardon, the words slipped out, it won't re-occur, I shall reform completely; but I beg you to consider –

SILVIA. Don't reform: it doesn't make you any better.

TRIVELIN. – that it is your Prince who loves you.

SILVIA. I can't stop him, he's the master: but do I have to love him back? It isn't in my power to do so, so he hasn't the power to make me; it's as simple as that; a child would understand it; why can't you?

TRIVELIN. Consider that he must choose a wife from among his subjects; and he has chosen you.

SILVIA. Who told him to? He never asked me. If he'd said to me, 'Silvia, do you want me?' I'd have answered, 'No, my lord; an honest woman has to love her husband; I could never love you.' That would have been true reason; only not at all; bang, he loves me, bang, he sweeps me away and never even asks me what I think about it.

TRIVELIN. He brought you here to give you his hand.

SILVIA. What good is his hand, if I don't want to stretch my own hand out to his, to hold it? What kind of behaviour's that, to force a gift on somebody who doesn't want it?

TRIVELIN. Look at the way we've treated you over the past two days; look at the honours which surround you, at the number of waiting-women you've been allocated. Think of the entertainments we have arranged, as he commanded. What is Harlequin, compared to a Prince who so respects you that he will not even visit you until you wish to see him? And an ardent, young, delightful Prince? Where will you find another? Oh, Milady: open your eyes, behold your fortune, seize your chance.

SILVIA. Tell me, you and the others, do you get paid for this? When you try my patience with a stupid argument like that, do you believe it? Or is it your job?

TRIVELIN. It is my job. I make no higher intellectual claims.

SILVIA. For a job like yours you don't need intellect at all.

TRIVELIN. I must be doing it badly; tell me how.

SILVIA (exasperated). I will! You're –

TRIVELIN. Gently please; I'm not supposed to annoy you.

SILVIA. Then you're doing it *very* badly.

TRIVELIN. Your servant.

SILVIA. Very well, servant. First: you talk about my waiting-women. They aren't waiting, they are spying and reporting on me. You steal my lover and you give me women instead; I'm *very* grateful! Any wonder that I'm sad? What do I care for concerts, music, dancing. Do you expect me to enjoy them? Harlequin's singing is better than any I've heard so far. And I can dance for myself; I'd rather; why watch other people doing it? A decent girl in a simple village has a better life than any princess weeping in her grand apartment. I didn't ask the Prince to find me attractive; I didn't try to attract him: he saw me, not the other way round; whose fault is that? He's young and kind and decent, so you say: I'm glad to hear it; let him keep all that for people as grand as him; and let him leave me with my Harlequin, who isn't a lord any more than I am a lady; who hasn't a fortune or a palace or a glorious name any more than I do; and who loves me without any style or fancy; and who loved by me; and who I'll die of misery if I don't see soon. Oh the poor boy! What have they done to him, what has become of him? He'll be so unhappy, he'll be in despair, I know it; he's so good, so trusting! Is he being tortured?

She moves.

It's horrible. Would you do me a kindness? Go away, I can't bear having you near me. Let me endure my misery in peace.

TRIVELIN. Your compliment is brief but to the point. I wish you'd calm yourself.

SILVIA. Just go, say nothing.

TRIVELIN. Please, be calm. You asked for Harlequin: he will be here directly.

SILVIA (*with a sigh*). Will I see him?

TRIVELIN. See him, speak to him, just as you please.

SILVIA (*leaving*). I'll wait for him. But if you're deceiving me, I'll never listen or talk to any of you again.

TRIVELIN. This way.

She goes. The PRINCE *and* FLAMINIA *enter and watch her leave.*

Scene 2

PRINCE (*to* TRIVELIN). Well? what hope can you give me? What did she say?

TRIVELIN. Oh nothing, my lord, which I would willingly waste your valuable time repeating, nothing to deserve your curiosity.

PRINCE. Tell me anyway.

TRIVELIN. Oh! It was all very inconclusive, you'll be bored; but since you wish it: she referred to her lingering fondness for her lover; and her inclination to rejoin him; and her less than overwhelming desire to make your acquaintance; and her positive wish for you to stay away from her; and as for the court in general she feels violent hatred. I think that sums it up; it's not encouraging, and if I may venture a thought the most practical course might be to pack her off home.

The PRINCE *reflects sadly on this.*

FLAMINIA. It's no use telling His Highness this; I've already done so; we must persevere: Silvia's love for Harlequin must be destroyed; let's think of nothing else.

TRIVELIN. There's something very odd about her; turning down what she's turned down! It isn't natural, it isn't feminine; she is a species hitherto unknown to us. Were she a normal woman we would have made some headway; she has brought us to a halt; which tells us that we're dealing with some strange phenomenon.

PRINCE. We are; it's what I love about her.

FLAMINIA (*laughs; to the* PRINCE). My lord, don't listen to his strange phenomena; they're all very well in fairy-tales. I know my sex; the only phenomenal thing about us is our vanity. Silvia, it appears, is not ambitious; but she has a heart, and vanity is the consequence of the heart. I'll use her vanity to make her see her duty as a woman. It won't be difficult. Are they bringing Harlequin?

TRIVELIN. At any moment.

PRINCE (*worried*). But Flaminia; if she sees him she might love him all the more.

TRIVELIN. If she doesn't, she'll go mad: I have her word for it.

FLAMINIA. He is essential, as I've told you.

PRINCE (*to* TRIVELIN). I want him stopped; promise him anything: money, land, a title, as long as he marries any *other* woman.

TRIVELIN. We can always have the fellow dealt with if he doesn't agree.

PRINCE. That isn't possible; the law which forces me to marry one of my subjects also says that it can't be done by violence.

FLAMINIA. True, but don't let it worry you; I'll solve the problem amicably. Silvia knows you, but she doesn't know that you are the Prince, is this correct?

PRINCE. As I have said: one day, when hunting, having lost sight of my hounds, I found her outside her cottage; I was thirsty and she offered to fetch me a glass of wine: I was dazzled by her beauty and simplicity, and confessed it to her. By my appearance she took me for a cavalry officer from the Palace. I saw her five or six times more, keeping up the pretence but, though she treated me with the greatest kindness, I could never persuade her to give up Harlequin, who several times arrived while I was trying to do so.

FLAMINIA. The fact that she is ignorant of your rank will be extremely useful to us; and they've told her that you won't be visiting her just yet; I'll do the rest, and you must do exactly as I say.

PRINCE. I will. Win her heart and you will find no limit to my gratitude.

He goes.

FLAMINIA. Trivelin, tell my sister that she's late, as usual.

TRIVELIN. There is no need, she is here. Good day to you. I must find Harlequin.

Scene 3

LISETTE. Here I am, reporting for duty. What are my orders?

FLAMINIA. Come a little closer; let me look at you.

LISETTE. Enjoy the view.

FLAMINIA (*having looked at her*). Mm, you look pretty today.

LISETTE (*laughs*). I know I do; but why this sudden interest?

FLAMINIA. Take off that beauty-spot.

LISETTE (*resisting*). I won't! It was prescribed for me this morning after a two-hour consultation with my mirror.

FLAMINIA. Take it off!

LISETTE (*taking out her mirror-box and putting the spot inside*). Poor little thing! Have you no pity on it?

FLAMINIA. I know what I'm doing. Now, Lisette: you're a great beauty.

LISETTE. There've been few complaints.

FLAMINIA. You like being found attractive?

LISETTE. It's my little weakness.

FLAMINIA. Could you get a young man to fall in love with you, by letting him think his feelings were returned? A modest, unaffected approach is needed. Could you manage it? It's in an excellent cause.

LISETTE. If that's the plan, my beauty-spot's essential.

FLAMINIA. Do forget it; it's not necessary. We're dealing with a simple country fellow, who knows nothing of the world beyond his village. He thinks that women like us are forced to do things modestly, like country women are; oh, they have very different notions; they'd be shocked by what we get away with. So you can happily throw your beauty-spot away; make up for it with your behaviour, with the way you talk to him. Now, what will you say?

LISETTE. I'd say – what would *you* say exactly?

FLAMINIA. Listen to me: you must avoid coquettishness. For example, there's a look on your face which seems to beg for approval; you must wipe it off. The manner which you cultivate is lively, yet at the same time absent-minded. It's affectionate, casual, dainty; in your eyes one sees a longing to provoke, or to make one sorry for you, or hand out punishment or lark about; your head is high, your chin is pertly jutted forward, all for the sake of seeming fun, and possibly more than that, and certainly youthful. In your conversation, you use all the latest catchwords, all the small-talk, decorated with a joke or two; now these little tricks are fine when you're a woman of the world; they're seen as marks of elegance; they drive men mad, if only briefly; you must put these pleasures behind you; the man in question wouldn't approve of them; his palette is too refined; he's like somebody who all his life has only drunk water: he wouldn't appreciate wine or *eau-de-vie*.

LISETTE (*astonished*). My charms don't seem as charming as you say they are, once you've pulled them to bits.

FLAMINIA (*naively*). They weren't designed for sober analysis; it's bound to make them look absurd. They're *man-traps*, and as such they're very effective.

LISETTE. What do I do instead?

FLAMINIA. Nothing; let your attention wander where it will, as though coquettishness weren't guiding it. Show interest in whatever interests you, don't work so hard at seeming empty-headed; and behave as though you hadn't an audience. Come, let's try it, let us test your talent. Now: look natural.

LISETTE (*turns around*). Is this right?

FLAMINIA. It still needs work.

LISETTE. For God's sake! Shall I remind you who you are, milady? It might improve both our acting. Enough, let's stop; or I'll have wasted my performance. Isn't it meant for Harlequin?

FLAMINIA. Yes.

LISETTE. But, poor man! If I don't love him I'll be cheating him. I'm a woman of honour, I'll feel guilty.

FLAMINIA. If he grows to love you, you will marry and your

fortune will be made. Will you still feel guilty? Come, dear
sister, you're no better than me. You too are the daughter of a
minor Palace servant, and you could be a lady.

LISETTE. That's my conscience settled; I could marry him and
never love him at all. Goodbye, dear sister; tell me when to
start.

FLAMINIA. I'm leaving too: here's Harlequin.

Scene 4

HARLEQUIN *looks at* TRIVELIN *and the whole apartment with
astonishment.*

TRIVELIN. Well, my lord Harlequin: what do you make of it?

HARLEQUIN *says nothing.*

It's a magnificent palace, is it not?

HARLEQUIN. Where the hell do I fit into it? Why've you brought
me here? Who are you anyway?

TRIVELIN. I am an honest gentleman; I'm your gentleman's
gentleman. I'm your servant; and we have reached our
destination.

HARLEQUIN. Honest or whatever, I don't need you. So your
services are not required. I'm off.

TRIVELIN. One moment.

HARLEQUIN. Did I hear you contradict your master? That's
disgraceful! Right, let's hear you.

TRIVELIN. I've a more important master. You are master over me
at his discretion.

HARLEQUIN. He's a very strange fellow, giving out gentlemen's
gentlemen without first asking the gentlemen.

TRIVELIN. Once you've met him you'll talk differently. There is a
matter we must discuss.

HARLEQUIN. I didn't know you and I had any outstanding business.

TRIVELIN. We must talk about Silvia.

HARLEQUIN (*enraptured and ardently*). Silvia! Oh forgive me, we've got lots to talk about.

TRIVELIN. Two days ago you lost her.

HARLEQUIN. She was stolen by a gang of thieves.

TRIVELIN. They were not thieves.

HARLEQUIN. Let's call them scoundrels.

TRIVELIN. I know where she is.

HARLEQUIN (*enraptured, caressing* TRIVELIN). You know where she is, my friend, my gentleman's gentleman, my whatever you choose to call yourself, do you? Oh, if I were rich, I'd pour my grateful millions on you! Where is she? Which way? Left, right or straight ahead?

TRIVELIN. You will meet her here.

HARLEQUIN (*enraptured, sweetly*). And now I know you, what a saint you are, what a firm fine comrade! Bringing me here to meet that – child of my soul! Tears burst from my eyes! Oh, Silvia!

TRIVELIN (*aside*). Hardly a promising start. (*To* HARLEQUIN.) There's more to tell you.

HARLEQUIN (*impatiently*). Let's find her first! Have pity on me!

TRIVELIN. You will see her: but till then I must accompany you. Do you recall a cavalry officer; one who called on Silvia half a dozen times? And whom you met with her?

HARLEQUIN (*sadly*). That man had 'scoundrel' written all over his face.

TRIVELIN. He found your mistress very charming.

HARLEQUIN. So she is, I don't need him to tell me that.

TRIVELIN. Quite so; he told the Prince.

HARLEQUIN. Couldn't he keep his mouth shut?

TRIVELIN. And His Highness, wishing to inspect her, ordered the girl to be brought here.

HARLEQUIN. Will he send her back in the proper manner?

TRIVELIN. Ah, now for the problem; he has fallen in love with her, and hopes that he, in turn, will be loved by her.

HARLEQUIN. Tell him it's very pleasant when it happens, but it isn't his turn, it's mine.

TRIVELIN. To get to the point –

HARLEQUIN (*raising his voice*). That *is* the point. He's taking something that belongs to me.

TRIVELIN. As you are aware, the Prince must choose a wife from among his subjects.

HARLEQUIN. I wasn't aware and I wasn't agog to know.

TRIVELIN. And now you do.

HARLEQUIN. And thanks for the useless information.

TRIVELIN. He loves Silvia; he desires her love before he marries her; what is the problem is her love for you.

HARLEQUIN. He ought to look elsewhere. In this case, all he'll get is the girl. I'll keep her heart. So he'll lose out and I'll lose out and all of us will be unhappy.

TRIVELIN. If you marry Silvia he'll be *very* unhappy.

HARLEQUIN (*after a moment's thought*). Not for long, though; then he'll realise he's done the decent thing, and that'll console him. If he marries her, she'll cry and cry; and so would I, except I wouldn't give him the satisfaction.

TRIVELIN. Harlequin: your duty is to your Prince. He cannot relinquish her. This adventure is predicted in his stars; so is his marriage. It is written in heaven.

HARLEQUIN. Nobody up there writes such nonsense. If my stars told me I was going to creep up on you from behind and kill you, ought I to do it?

TRIVELIN. Murder is not permitted.

HARLEQUIN. *I'm* being murdered! All because some star predicted it! When I'm dead I hope you hang the astrologer.

TRIVELIN. Good Lord, good Lord, nobody means to hurt you. We have delightful women here at Court; why don't you marry one of them? You'll find it highly advantageous.

HARLEQUIN. Marry one of them! Oh, very good, and Silvia gets so angry that she marries the Prince. D'you think I'm stupid? What are you paid to trip me up like that? I've had enough. Go away, you're a fraud, and keep your ladies to yourself. We haven't a deal, I can't afford the price.

TRIVELIN. Don't you realise that a marriage of the kind I've outlined would result in the Prince's friendship?

HARLEQUIN. Oh, that's a wonderful idea, having a friend who isn't one.

TRIVELIN. His Highness's friendship is the key to wealth.

HARLEQUIN. I don't need wealth. I'm healthy, I'm a hearty eater and I earn my keep.

TRIVELIN. You don't know what you're losing.

HARLEQUIN. Then I'm not exactly losing it.

TRIVELIN. You'd have a house in town, a house in the country.

HARLEQUIN. That's a very attractive prospect! Only, when I'm basking in my country residence, who lives in town?

TRIVELIN. Good God, your servants!

HARLEQUIN. Servants! What's the point of making a fortune for the benefit of scum like that? Couldn't I live in both places at once? ·

TRIVELIN (*laughing*). Why hardly, that would defy the laws of nature.

HARLEQUIN. Well, till we've sorted out that little problem, who needs two houses?

TRIVELIN. You could travel from one to the other as you pleased.

HARLEQUIN. I see, so I give up the woman I love for the pleasure of non-stop changes of address?

TRIVELIN. Does nothing attract you? you're an odd fellow! Everyone wants a beautiful house with plenty of rooms, and lots of attendants –

HARLEQUIN. One room suits me fine. I don't intend to support a bunch of idle scroungers, and the only servant I've ever met who I could totally trust was me.

TRIVELIN. Quite true, you can't dismiss him! My little joke . . .
But come, do you not like horses? Imagine a first-class team of
your own, and a splendid carriage! Picture a mansion,
richly furnished!

HARLEQUIN. Dear friend, you must be mad if you try to compare
my Silvia with a carriage and horses or a stack of furniture.
What do we do in a house but sit and eat and sleep? Well then!
With a dozen straw chairs and a sturdy table and a bed, I'm
fully furnished. I am replete with comfort. True: I don't have a
carriage. What a relief, it can't turn over.

He points to his legs.

I use the team of horses which my mother gave me: strong,
well-trained and obedient. Who needs more? Hear this, you
parasite; give your horses to some honest labourer to grow
food with. Exercise your legs and you won't get gout.

TRIVELIN. How far do we go in our search for the simple life? Do
we not wear shoes?

HARLEQUIN (*tersely*). What's wrong with clogs? Enough, I'm
bored with your stupid stories. Where's Silvia? You promised
you'd fetch her. I don't see her. Gentlemen keep their word.

TRIVELIN. One moment. You are not attracted, then, by
honours, money, glory, credit, teams of horses –

HARLEQUIN. None of them is worth a damn.

TRIVELIN. What about food? How would you fancy a cellar filled
with vintage wines? A cook to provide you with exquisite
meals, and in abundance? What do you like to eat? What
favourite meat or fish? Imagine it! It's yours for as long as you
live.

HARLEQUIN *doesn't reply at onec.*

Have you no answer?

HARLEQUIN. This is tempting, and I don't very often turn down
food. But no! My heart is more important than my stomach.

TRIVELIN. Come, my lord Harlequin: indulge yourself for life.

It's only a matter of changing one girl for another.

HARLEQUIN. No! No, no! I'll stick to the local wine and plain boiled beef!

TRIVELIN. Think of the succulent platefuls! Think of the bottles of wine, the fine bouquet!

HARLEQUIN. It hurts me to say this, but it can't be helped. The only bouquet I want is Silvia. Will you show me her? Or not?

TRIVELIN. You'll meet her, never fear; but it's not quite time.

Scene 5

LISETTE (*to* TRIVELIN). I've been looking everywhere for you: you must attend His Highness.

TRIVELIN. An urgent summons? Goodness, I must waste no time; why don't you entertain Lord Harlequin?

HARLEQUIN. No need for that! When I'm alone I entertain myself.

TRIVELIN. Oh no, that sounds extremely tedious. Adieu. I shall return very shortly.

He leaves.

Scene 6

HARLEQUIN (*withdrawing to the corner of the stage*). No flies on her; she's here to seduce me, I'd put money on it.

LISETTE (*with charm*). Why, it's you monsieur: the gentleman who is Silvia's lover!

HARLEQUIN (*coldly*). Yes.

LISETTE. She's very attractive.

HARLEQUIN (*in the same tone*). Yes.

LISETTE. The whole world loves her.

HARLEQUIN. Then the whole world's wrong.

LISETTE. But why, if she deserves it?

HARLEQUIN (*tersely*). She is devoted to myself.

LISETTE. I don't doubt it; and I forgive it.

HARLEQUIN. Why does it need forgiving?

LISETTE. I only meant that now I've met you I'm a little less surprised at her determination.

HARLEQUIN. What surprised you?

LISETTE. Why, she's turning down a delightful Prince.

HARLEQUIN. Delightful, is he? What if he is, does that make me any less delightful?

LISETTE (*with a sweet look*). But he *is* a Prince.

HARLEQUIN. That's no advantage, not with women.

LISETTE (*pleasantly*). I'd like to believe it. But the Prince has lands and loyal subjects; and nice as you are, you don't.

HARLEQUIN. You're making too much of them. Having no subjects means I haven't got responsibilities. If times are good I'm happy, if they're bad at least I don't get grumbled at. As for lands, however much land we've got, we use the same amount of space to move about in, and it doesn't improve our looks that I'm aware of. So there's nothing to be surprised at.

LISETTE (*aside*). What an awful man! I pay him compliments and he argues back!

HARLEQUIN (*asking her what she said*). What's that?

LISETTE. I'm a little upset. Your appearance led me to expect a pleasant talk.

HARLEQUIN. Appearances are deceptive.

LISETTE. Yours is. How dangerous it is to trust one's first impression!

HARLEQUIN (*defensive*). Oh, very well said; except I didn't choose my physiognomy.

LISETTE (*looks at him astonished*). But now I look at it again, I think my first impression might have been correct.

HARLEQUIN. However I look, that's me. It's what I am; it can't be helped, this is it.

LISETTE (*as though annoyed*). You've persuaded me.

HARLEQUIN. Does it bother you?

LISETTE. Why do you ask?

HARLEQUIN. I'd like to know.

LISETTE (*with a natural air*). I'd be a fool to tell you. A girl should know when to keep her mouth shut.

HARLEQUIN (*aside*). No chance of that. (*To her.*) How sad it is you're such a flirt.

LISETTE. Me?

HARLEQUIN. You.

LISETTE. I've never heard of a woman being spoken to like that. You've insulted me.

HARLEQUIN (*innocently*). Not at all: what's wrong with seeing what's put in front of you? I'm not wrong for calling you a flirt; you're wrong to be one.

LISETTE. How do you know what I am?

HARLEQUIN. Because you've talked in pretty phrases for an hour; because you're talking the long way round to say you love me. Listen: if you love me, fine; get away as fast as you can and let it pass, because I'm spoken for. Besides, I hate it when a girl is forward. I like to be forward myself, it's better that way round. That's how I am. If you don't love me, bah!, miss. Bah! bah! bah!

LISETTE. What nonsense! What ideals!

HARLEQUIN. How can the boys at Court put up with such behaviour? And it makes a woman look so nasty!

LISETTE. Poor boy, you're delirious.

HARLEQUIN. You mentioned Silvia: she's a woman a man can love. If I told you about our love you'd learn a little respect for modesty. You should have seen, in the first few days, how she'd move away with a start when I got too near to her; then she moved away more gently; then, little by little, she stopped

withdrawing; then she watched me secretly, then blushed and
felt ashamed when I saw her doing it; then, seeing her shame,
I felt as proud as a king; then I caught hold of her hand – she
didn't stop me – then she got embarrassed again and then
I spoke to her; she didn't reply though she had plenty to say;
then her looks grew talkative, though she still didn't speak;
then all of a tumble words spilled out, unplanned, unthought,
because her heart was racing ahead of her. She bewitched me,
I was a man possessed. And that's what I call a woman; but you
aren't like Silvia.

LISETTE. You make me scream with laughter. I could listen all
day.

HARLEQUIN. I'm bored with making you laugh at your own
expense. Goodbye. If people were all like me you'd catch a
snow-white blackbird quicker than a man.

Scene 7

TRIVELIN *enters.*

TRIVELIN (*to* HARLEQUIN). You're going?

HARLEQUIN. Yes. This young lady's after me and it's out of the
question.

TRIVELIN. Come, let's take a stroll until our lunch is ready; it
might change your mood for the better.

Scene 8

FLAMINIA. Are we any further? How is his heart?

LISETTE (*annoyed*). I've had a vile experience.

FLAMINIA. He responded badly?

LISETTE. 'Women who flirt are ugly, bah! bah! bah!' that's what he's like.

PRINCE. I'm sorry, Lisette; but don't be too distressed about it. You did what you could.

LISETTE. My lord, if I were a conceited woman I'd be devastated. He's proved that people can dislike me. Woman don't need such proof.

FLAMINIA. Come, it's my turn to try.

PRINCE. You'll never win Harlequin. I shall never win Silvia.

FLAMINIA. Let me explain, my lord. I've seen Harlequin, and he's pleasant enough. I'm determined to make you happy and I promise you I'll succeed; you have my word; whatever you say I won't go back on it. Oh, you don't know me! What? Can Harlequin and Silvia resist me? Do you honestly think, my lord, that I could fail with those two innocents? Me, a stubborn, determined woman? I'd be denounced by every woman in the land, I'd have to go into hiding. My lord, you can plan your wedding, you can arrange it all with confidence, I guarantee you will be loved, I guarantee you will be married. Silvia will give you heart and hand. She will say 'I love you', I can hear it now. I see you at the altar. Harlequin and I are marrying too. You are showering wedding-gifts on us. There, it's over.

LISETTE (*incredulously*). Over! When it hasn't even started!

FLAMINIA. Quiet, you fool.

PRINCE. You give me hope; but where's your evidence?

FLAMINIA. I'll provide the evidence; I have ways; I'll start by calling Silvia; it's time for Harlequin to meet her.

LISETTE. If they're left together you'll get evidence all right.

PRINCE. That's what I'm afraid of.

FLAMINIA (*casually*). Good. We agree, except in one small detail: whether I'm right or wrong. I insist they meet; I shall expose their love to a number of dangers; this is the first.

PRINCE. Indulge your fantasy.

FLAMINIA. Here's Harlequin; let's withdraw.

Scene 9

HARLEQUIN *and* TRIVELIN *enter, followed by a train of valets.*

HARLEQUIN. And something else I've been meaning to ask you:
    why is it that wherever we go these great big chaps in fancy-
    dress come lolloping after?

TRIVELIN. The Prince, who likes you, has begun to show his
    generosity. He's ordered these men to walk behind you as a
    mark of honour.

HARLEQUIN. Oh, I see. It means I'm honourable?

TRIVELIN. Absolutely.

HARLEQUIN. Then tell me. Those men following me: who
    follows them?

TRIVELIN. Nobody.

HARLEQUIN. What about you, don't you have followers either?

TRIVELIN. No.

HARLEQUIN. So none of you have honours?

TRIVELIN. No. We don't deserve them.

HARLEQUIN (*angrily wielding his stick*). Out! Get out! And take
    that scum away with you!

TRIVELIN. What do you mean?

HARLEQUIN. Get out! I don't like men who haven't got honour
    and don't deserve it!

HARLEQUIN *hits him.*

TRIVELIN. Ah ha, a slight misunderstanding –

HARLEQUIN. I'll speak up then.

He hits TRIVELIN *again.*

TRIVELIN (*fleeing*). Stop it! Stop it at once!

HARLEQUIN *chases the valets off.* TRIVELIN *hides in the wings.*
HARLEQUIN *returns to the stage.*

Scene 10

HARLEQUIN. Phoo! Exhausting work, dismissing one's servants. What a ridiculous way to make an honest man feel honoured, putting a team of thugs behind him. It makes him a laughing-stock.

He turns round and sees TRIVELIN *returning.*

It's you, my friend; I thought I explained myself.

TRIVELIN (*from a distance*). Please listen. Though you hit me, I forgive you. You're a reasonable man.

HARLEQUIN. As you can see.

TRIVELIN (*still from a distance*). When I say we don't deserve to have people following us, I don't mean we're dishonourable. It's just that only persons of importance, very rich people, peers, receive that kind of honour. If it sufficed to be a decent person, then I flatter myself there'd be an army of men behind me.

HARLEQUIN (*putting back his stick*). Now I see. Why the devil don't you talk properly? I wouldn't have put my arm out if you did, and you wouldn't have those bruises.

TRIVELIN. You hurt me.

HARLEQUIN. I was trying to. Still, it was only a mix-up. I attacked you and you didn't deserve it. Aren't you relieved? Don't worry, I understand. Honour is given to rich and powerful people, not to decent folk.

TRIVELIN. Correct.

HARLEQUIN (*disgustedly*). So being honoured isn't worth very much, if all it means is that you don't deserve it.

TRIVELIN. It is possible for the two to go together.

HARLEQUIN. Do me a favour; leave me alone. Then passers-by will see at once that I'm a gentleman; and I'd prefer it to being mistaken for a lord.

TRIVELIN. Our orders are to stay with you.

HARLEQUIN. Then take me to Silvia!

TRIVELIN. Have no fear, she will come in due course . . . Good God, she is here. Good day to you, friend. Adieu.

TRIVELIN and the followers leave. FLAMINIA *and* SILVIA *enter.* SILVIA *rushes forward joyfully to greet* HARLEQUIN.

Scene 11

SILVIA. He's here! Dearest Harlequin, it's you! Poor darling, how relieved I am!

HARLEQUIN (*overwhelmed with joy*). Me too! I'm so happy, I could die!

SILVIA. Gently, my little boy, gently! How he loves me! How happy I am to be loved like this!

FLAMINIA (*looking at them both*). You make an enchanting sight, dear children. Constant love, is anything better? (*Quietly to them.*) I'd be in peril of my life if anyone heard me; but I admire you with all my heart, and pity you.

SILVIA (*to her*). Your heart is good to us. Oh Harlequin, how often I've sighed!

HARLEQUIN (*takes her hand*). Do you still love me?

SILVIA. Do I love you? How can you doubt me? Oh what a question!

FLAMINIA (*to* HARLEQUIN). I can assure you of her feelings; I saw her in despair, in tears because you weren't beside her; even I was moved. I longed to see you reunited. Now you are. Goodbye, dear friends, I have to leave you. Something's touched me very deeply. I'm reminded of a man I loved, who died. He looked like Harlequin; I'll never forget him. Silvia, adieu. They've made me spy on you, but you can trust me. Love your Harlequin, he deserves it. (*To* HARLEQUIN.) And whatever happens, think of me as a friend who wants to help you. I'll do all I can.

HARLEQUIN. Go, miss. You're a good girl. I'm your friend too.
I'm sorry your lover died, I'm sorry to make you sad. I'm sorry
for all of us.

FLAMINIA *goes*.

Scene 12

SILVIA. Ah, my dear Harlequin!

HARLEQUIN. Yes, my love?

SILVIA. We're so unhappy!

HARLEQUIN. Why don't we stay in love for ever? Then the
present won't seem so bad.

SILVIA. But will our love survive it? That's what worries me.

HARLEQUIN. I'm trying to give you courage, but I've none
myself. (*He takes her hand*.) My dearest treasure, it's a full
three days since I last looked in your beautiful eyes: make up for
it now.

SILVIA. I've such a lot to tell you. I'm afraid of losing you.
I'm afraid they'll hurt you out of spite or envy. I'm afraid
that now you've been away from me for three days you'll get
used to it.

HARLEQUIN. My dearest, can a man get used to misery?

SILVIA. I don't want you to forget me, but I don't want you to
miss me so much·that it makes you unhappy. I'm so in love
I can't say what I want, I'm lost in the way I feel. Everything
makes me sad.

HARLEQUIN (*cries*). Hi, hi, hi, hi.

SILVIA (*sadly*). Don't cry, you'll make me cry as well.

HARLEQUIN. How can I stop when you're as sad as this? You
wouldn't make me cry if you really loved me.

SILVIA. I do, I do. Stop doubting. If I feel unhappy I'll hide it.

HARLEQUIN. Hide it from me? I'll see through it at once. You've
got to promise me you aren't unhappy.

SILVIA. Yes, little boy, I do. But you must promise that you love me.

HARLEQUIN (*stopping short to look at her*). Silvia, I'm your lover, you're my mistress. Remember it, it's the truth. As long as I live it will be carved in stone: unshakable. I'll die saying it. What do you want me to swear by? Anything! Give me an oath!

SILVIA. You've said enough. I don't swear oaths. I have the word of a man of honour, he has mine. I'll never go back on it, what could make me? Is there a handsomer man? Or a girl who could love you more than I do? That's all we need: ourselves, and the way we are. Why swear an oath?

HARLEQUIN. We'll say the same in a hundred years.

SILVIA. Yes, yes.

HARLEQUIN. There's nothing to fear. We can be happy.

SILVIA. Though we're suffering at the moment.

HARLEQUIN. This won't last. When it's over we'll enjoy our happiness all the more.

SILVIA. I'd enjoy it more without the suffering.

HARLEQUIN. We can deal with suffering; we can dream it away.

SILVIA (*looking at him tenderly*). What a dear little man, what hope.

HARLEQUIN (*looking at her*). You're all I care about.

SILVIA. The things you say: where do you find them? There's nobody in the whole wide world like you. And nobody loves you as much as I do, Harlequin.

HARLEQUIN (*jumps for joy*). Those words are sweet as honey!

FLAMINIA *and* TRIVELIN *enter*.

Scene 13

TRIVELIN. I'm sorry to interrupt you but your mother is here, Miss Silvia. She demands to see you.

SILVIA (*looking at* HARLEQUIN). Harlequin, come too, I haven't any secrets from you.

HARLEQUIN. Yes, my love.

FLAMINIA (*approaches them conspiratorially*). You've nothing to fear, my children. Silvia dear, receive your mother alone; it's more appropriate. You two can see each other whenever you want to, take my word for it. Don't you believe me? Am I your friend?

HARLEQUIN. You are.

SILVIA (*to* HARLEQUIN). Adieu, little one, I'll come back soon.

She goes.

HARLEQUIN (*to* FLAMINIA, *stopping her as she is about to go*). Dear friend, why don't you talk to me while she's gone? I might get bored on my own, and you're the only person here I can bear to be with.

FLAMINIA (*as if in confidence*). Dear Harlequin, I enjoy your company too; although I'm worried that our friendship might give rise to comment.

TRIVELIN. My lord Harlequin: lunch is ready.

HARLEQUIN (*sadly*). I'm not hungry.

FLAMINIA (*affectionately*). Eat, if only for my sake. Really, you ought to.

HARLEQUIN (*gently*). Do you think so?

FLAMINIA. Yes.

HARLEQUIN (*to* TRIVELIN). Well, what's the soup like?

TRIVELIN. Marvellous.

HARLEQUIN. Silvia likes a bowl of soup. I'll wait for her.

TRIVELIN. I think she's eating with her mother. The decision is yours, but if I were you I'd leave them to it. Don't you agree? You'll see her once you've eaten.

HARLEQUIN. Fine. Although my appetite's a trifle nervous.

TRIVELIN. The wine is chilled and the roast is ready.

HARLEQUIN. This is upsetting. Beef, is it?

TRIVELIN. Game.

HARLEQUIN. What, nice and juicy? Oh, how difficult. Game's no
    good when it's cold.

FLAMINIA. Harlequin, drink my health.

HARLEQUIN. Come drink to mine. Let's drink to our friendship!

FLAMINIA. I accept! I can't stay long, though. Half an hour and
    that's my limit!

HARLEQUIN. Good. I'm grateful.

Act Two

Scene 1

FLAMINIA *and* SILVIA *enter.*

SILVIA. Yes, I trust you; you seem to wish us well; besides, you're the only person here I can bear to be with. Everyone else is against me. Where's Harlequin?

FLAMINIA. He'll come. He's eating.

SILVIA. There's something frightening about this place. I've never seen women so polite, or men so friendly and open. Their manners are gentle; they're always bowing and paying each other compliments and treating each other as friends. You'd think they were the best people in the world, with the kindest hearts and the quietest consciences. But they aren't; there isn't one who hasn't come up to me and said: 'Mademoiselle, take my advice. Give up Harlequin and marry the Prince.' They do it in a practical way, with no embarrassment, as though they were prompting me to do a good deed. I tell them: 'Harlequin has my word of honour. What about duty, decency, trust?' Their faces go blank, they don't know what I'm talking about, it's as though I were speaking Greek. They laugh in my face, and say I'm talking like a child and that a grown-up woman ought to be more reasonable. It's wonderful! Be cheap, deceive the people around you, break your promises, cheat and lie: those are the duties of important people in this horrible place. What sort of creatures are they? Where do they come from? What are they made of?

FLAMINIA. The same as everyone else, dear Silvia. Don't be

shocked. They think that marrying the Prince would make you happy.

SILVIA. But shouldn't I be faithful? Isn't it my duty as a decent gril? And how can I be happy if I forget my duty? It's my constancy that makes me attractive. And they've the cheek to tell me to throw it away, to hurt myself, to give up everything that gives me happiness, and then to despise me when I don't.

FLAMINIA. What do you expect? That's how they think. They want the Prince to be happy.

SILVIA. Why doesn't he choose a girl who's willing? What nonsense, wanting a girl who doesn't want him. What can he get from it? Everything he does is wrong, plain wrong. The concerts, the plays, the dinners which look like wedding-banquets, the jewels he sends me; they must cost him a fortune. He's throwing his money away, he's ruining himself, and all for nothing. If he offered me a row of dress-shops, I'd prefer a waistcoat button that Harlequin gave me.

FLAMINIA. I believe you. This is what love is like. It's how I felt when I was in love and I remember it well, right down to the button.

SILVIA. There's only one man who could tempt me away from Harlequin. He's an officer of the Court who came to see me half-a-dozen times. He's as handsome as a man can be, and I was sorry that I couldn't love him. I felt pity for him. I could never pity the Prince.

FLAMINIA (*smiling secretly*). Oh, Silvia! I assure you if you met the Prince you'd pity him just as much.

SILVIA. Well, he should try to forget me, send me away, see other girls. There are girls at Court who have a lover, just the same as I do, but it doesn't stop them loving everyone else. They find it easy; it's impossible for me.

FLAMINIA. Dear child, is anyone here your equal, can they even approach you?

SILVIA (*modestly*). I'm not as pretty as some of them. Even the girls who are plain make better use of their looks. I've seen ugly women who make their faces up so cleverly it deceives the eye.

FLAMINIA. You're what you are. That's what's so charming about you.

SILVIA. Oh, I'm nothing to look at, and my conversation's dull; I stand there stuck in one place while they go skittering round the room, full of life, making love to the men with their eyes. They're bold and free and they don't hold back. They're much more attractive than someone like me, who can't look people in the eye, who feels ashamed to be beautiful.

FLAMINIA. This is what the Prince finds so intriguing. Yours is a simple beauty: it's true and unaffected. And believe me, you needn't be so flattering about the women here. They won't do the same for you.

SILVIA. What do they say about me?

FLAMINIA. They gossip. They make catty remarks. They tease the Prince and ask him how he's getting on with his rustic virgin. 'That's a very common-or-garden face she's got,' one of them said the other day, 'And a lumpy figure.' Then they all joined in. One criticised your eyes, another your mouth. Even the men agreed. I was furious . . .!

SILVIA. The men as well! How foul! To pander to the women, to deny their feelings!

FLAMINIA. Oh, they found it easy enough.

SILVIA. I hate those women! If I'm unattractive, why is it me the Prince is fond of? Why not them?

FLAMINIA. They think his fondness is a passing whim, and that he'll be the first to laugh, once he's got over it.

SILVIA (*piqued, looks at* FLAMINIA *for a moment*). It's lucky for them I'm so in love with Harlequin. If I weren't, I'd like to prove them wrong.

FLAMINIA. It'd serve them right! I said to them: 'I know what you're doing! You're trying to get her sent away; because she'd only have to change her mind and the Prince wouldn't look at any of you.'

SILVIA. That's their plan, I see! Well then, it's up to me to stop them.

FLAMINIA. We have company.

SILVIA. I think it's him: the officer I told you about. It is! Isn't he handsome?

Scene 2

The PRINCE *enters, disguised as an officer of the Palace, with* LISETTE, *who is disguised as a Court lady. Seeing* SILVIA, *the* PRINCE *greets her shyly.*

SILVIA. What a surprise! Or did you know I was here?

PRINCE. I knew, mademoiselle. Though, since you told me never to visit you, I am here only because this lady asked me to be her escort. She has the Prince's leave to call on you, and pay you homage.

LISETTE *says nothing, but scrutinises* SILVIA *carefully. She and* FLAMINIA *exchange looks.*

SILVIA (*sweetly*). I don't mind seeing you; but I'm very depressed. As for this lady (*To* LISETTE.) I thank her for her homage. I don't deserve it. But since she wants to pay it, let her. I'll return it as well as I can. If I'm clumsy, she'll just have to forgive me.

LISETTE. Forgive you? But of course! One can't expect the impossible.

SILVIA (*curtsies angrily; aside*). 'Expect the impossible'! What does she mean by that?

LISETTE. How old are you, my child?

SILVIA (*piqued*). I don't remember, mother dear.

FLAMINIA (*to* SILVIA). Well done.

The PRINCE *affects to be surprised.*

LISETTE. I think she's annoyed!

PRINCE (*to* LISETTE). Madame, what are you doing? You said you wanted to pay her homage, not insult her.

LISETTE. I didn't want to cause offence. I was curious about this girl who's so adored, who stirs such passion. I wanted to learn her secret. They say she has a certain homespun wit, which can be very amusing in an obvious way. Let's hear it.

SILVIA. It isn't worth the trouble; yours is much more obvious.

LISETTE (*laughs*). Ha ha! We asked for coarseness and we got it!

PRINCE. Go, madame.

SILVIA. I've had enough! I'll lose my temper if she doesn't leave us.

PRINCE (*to* LISETTE). You will regret this.

LISETTE (*leaving scornfully*). Good day to you all. To see the Prince entangled with a woman like this is a sweet revenge.

Scene 3

FLAMINIA. What arrogance!

SILVIA. I'm outraged! Obviously they only brought me here so they could laugh at me. What right have they? I'm just as good as she is!

FLAMINIA. The insults of a jealous woman ought to please you. They are compliments.

PRINCE. Dear Silvia: she deceived the Prince and deceived me too. Believe me, I'm in despair about it. You know the respect I feel for you; you know my heart. I've come to feel the pleasure of being near you, to look once again at someone dear to me, to honour my queen. But I must be careful not to be discovered, not to be overheard by her, and not to bore you.

FLAMINIA (*to the* PRINCE, *in a natural tone*). There's no harm done; to see her is to love her, didn't you know?

SILVIA (*to* FLAMINIA). But I'd prefer him not to love me. It upsets me that I can't return it. If only he were a man like all the rest, I could say whatever I wanted. He's too likeable. I'm worried I might upset him.

PRINCE. How kind you are, Silvia! What can I do to deserve those words, except to love you for ever?

SILVIA. Love me then, you're welcome, if you don't mind being disappointed. I can't say better than that. Your only drawback is that Harlequin came first. If only I'd known that you were coming on after, I'd have waited. You were unlucky, I was too.

PRINCE. Flaminia, be the judge: could a man stop loving Silvia? Could there be a girl with a sweeter nature? No, I'd rather have her pity than the love of any other woman.

SILVIA (*to* FLAMINIA). Flaminia, be the judge, you see what he's like. How does one deal with a man who's always grateful?

FLAMINIA (*to* SILVIA). Silvia, he has reason on his side. You're enchanting. If I were in his place I'd do the same.

SILVIA. Don't encourage him. He doesn't need to be told I'm pretty, he's convinced already. (*To the* PRINCE.) Listen: learn to love me without getting so worked-up. And help me be revenged on that insulting woman.

PRINCE. I'll do it at once. As for me, whatever you decide, I know my future: I shall love you for the rest of my life.

SILVIA. I knew I could rely on you. I know what you're like.

FLAMINIA. Go, monsieur, and tell the Prince about that woman's behaviour. Silvia must be respected, and the whole Court must know it.

PRINCE. I shall report back soon.

Scene 4

FLAMINIA. Harlequin seems to have been detained at lunch. While I find him, why don't you try on that new dress they made you? I'm longing to see you in it.

SILVIA. It's a beautiful cloth, and I know it'll suit me. But I can't touch it. The Prince wants me in exchange and, once we've started bargaining, we'll never stop.

FLAMINIA. Wrong, my dear. When you leave, you can take it with you. You've misjudged him.

SILVIA. Very well. But he mustn't complain that I've taken presents and not been grateful.

FLAMINIA. He'll complain unless you take enough.

SILVIA. I'll take everything he's got on offer, then he can't complain.

FLAMINIA. And I shall take complete responsibility. Off you go.

Scene 5

FLAMINIA. It's falling into place. Here's Harlequin. I can't be sure, but I suspect that if the little fellow took a liking to me, I might pounce.

HARLEQUIN *enters, followed by* TRIVELIN.

HARLEQUIN (*laughing*). Ha ha! Hello, dear friend!

FLAMINIA. Good day to you, Harlequin. Tell me why you're laughing, I might join in.

HARLEQUIN. It's because my servant, Trivelin – not that I'm paying him – has been showing me round the house, through all the rooms, all packed with people ambling up and down, chattering, making deals, like they would in a public market.

You'd expect the master of the house to throw them out, these
visitors who never say hello, and stare at him while he eats his
lunch but never buy him a drink to wash it down with. I was
watching it all, enjoying myself, when I saw some scoundrel
pull the back of a lady's dress up. I thought he was playing a
joke, so I said 'Hey! Stop it, it's rude!' The lady turned round
and said, 'Don't worry, he's only giving me a bon-bon.' 'I see,'
I said. 'But that's no way to give a bon-bon; it should go in your
mouth.' 'Oh, that comes later' said the scoundrel, and he burst
out laughing. So did she and so did the people round us. I joined
in, and had a good laugh to keep them company; and now I'm
wondering what the joke was.

FLAMINIA. It was nothing. Merely that what surprised you is an
everyday occurrence amongst our ladies.

HARLEQUIN. Oh, I see, it was another mark of honour?

FLAMINIA. Yes, exactly.

HARLEQUIN. Then I'm glad I laughed. It was a mockery of honour.

FLAMINIA. You've cheered up. It's good to see you happy. Did
they give you enough to eat?

HARLEQUIN. Ah! God help me, what superlative meat, what a
wonderful stew. The cook's a genius. I couldn't resist, I ate the
lot. If you get ill I'm not responsible, I drank your health, and
Silvia's all through the meal.

FLAMINIA. What? You remembered me?

HARLEQUIN. A friend once made is always remembered, most of
all at meal-times. As for Silvia – is she still with her mother?

TRIVELIN. My lord Harlequin, must you persist in thinking
about her?

HARLEQUIN. Keep your mouth shut when I'm talking.

FLAMINIA. Trivelin, you spoke out of turn.

TRIVELIN. Out of turn?

FLAMINIA. He's talking about the woman he loves; don't interfere.

TRIVELIN (*with irony*). You serve your Prince most conscien-
tiously, Flaminia.

FLAMINIA (*as though alarmed*). Harlequin, he's threatening me.

HARLEQUIN (*angry*). Let him try! (*To* TRIVELIN.) Now listen: I am the master here. You told me so, I didn't ask to be. Informing is beyond the bounds of your engagement. If you try, or if there's any problem for this honest woman here I'll twist off your ear and have it pickled.

TRIVELIN. I'm a civil servant; I have duties!

HARLEQUIN. Not one ear, both! Now go!

TRIVELIN. I forgive you, in the public interest; but Flaminia, you'll regret this, see if you don't!

    HARLEQUIN *makes as though to turn on him, but* FLAMINIA *stops him.*

Scene 6

HARLEQUIN. Appalling! I find the only person here who listens to reason and we can't even talk without that creature sticking his ear in. Dear Flaminia, let's converse, let's talk about Silvia. When I'm parted from her, yours is the only company I'm at ease in.

FLAMINIA (*innocently*). Thank you. I'll do everything I can to make the two of you happy. When you're sad, or if anyone hurts you, Harlequin, I suffer too.

HARLEQUIN. What a wonderful woman you are! Your sympathising makes my sorrow easier to bear.

FLAMINIA. Who wouldn't sympathise? Who wouldn't be concerned about you? Harlequin, you undervalue what you are.

HARLEQUIN. I probably do, I've never had it valued.

FLAMINIA. If only you knew the pain it gives me to be so powerless! If only you could read my heart.

HARLEQUIN. I never learned to read. You'll have to read it to me. God, I'm miserable. I wish it would stop. I hate upsetting you like this. It'll pass, you'll see.

FLAMINIA (*sadly*). I won't see anything, Trivelin will inform on me, they'll take me who knows where? Harlequin, this may be the last time you and I talk. My happiness will be ended.

HARLEQUIN. The last time – ! All I owned in the world was a mistress, and they stole her. If they steal you too I'll never endure it. Do they think my heart is made of iron? Are they trying to kill me? Are they savages?

FLAMINIA. You must remember your Flaminia, who only wanted to bring you happiness.

HARLEQUIN. Dear woman, my heart is yours. Tell me what to do. Let's think. You think, I can't when I'm upset like this. Loving Silvia is all that matters to me, and so is your friendship; but our friendship mustn't affect my love for you, for *her* I mean. I'm confused.

FLAMINIA. And I'm unhappy. Since I lost the man I loved, I've never known peace except with you. I feel I can breathe once more. He was the image of you. It's as though he were here beside me. I've never known a man as kind as either of you.

HARLEQUIN. Poor girl! How sad it is I'm in love with Silvia. If I weren't, your lover's image would be yours to keep. I'd give him willingly. Was he a handsome fellow?

FLAMINIA. Don't you remember? He was just like you, he was your double.

HARLEQUIN. Did you love him a lot?

FLAMINIA. Look at yourself. As much as you deserve to be loved, I loved him.

HARLEQUIN. I've never met a woman with such answers; there's no limit to your friendship. I've never imagined I was handsome. Tell me, if you loved a man who was a copy of me, then the original version might deserve a little something.

FLAMINIA. I would have loved you more; but I was never pretty enough for you.

HARLEQUIN. By God! You look so beautiful when you say that.

FLAMINIA. You've disturbed me; I should leave. I hate to leave you now, but what if I stayed? Harlequin, adieu, I'll see you when they let me. I don't know where I am.

HARLEQUIN. I feel the same.

FLAMINIA. I like your company too much.

HARLEQUIN. It's yours whenever you want it; see me whenever you feel inclined, and I'll do the same for you.

FLAMINIA. I daren't. Goodbye.

HARLEQUIN (*watching her go*). That girl's too good for here. If the worst were to happen, if I lost Silvia, in my misery she'd be the one I'd turn to.

Scene 7

TRIVELIN *enters, followed by a* LORD.

TRIVELIN. Lord Harlequin, would there be any risk involved if I returned? I worry about my back. You wield your wooden spoon so vigorously.

HARLEQUIN. I'll be good to you if you behave yourself.

TRIVELIN. A noble peer wishes to talk with you.

The LORD *approaches and performs several bows, which* HARLEQUIN *returns.*

HARLEQUIN (*aside*). I've seen him before.

LORD. I come to beg a favour of you. But I hope I don't incommode you, Mr Harlequin?

HARLEQUIN. I'm easy either way, so far. (*Seeing the* LORD *replace his hat.*) What about mine, does it go back on?

LORD. Whether you wear it or not, you do me honour.

HARLEQUIN. I'll take your word for it. (*He puts his hat back on.*) What can I do for you? Come to the point and don't waste time on empty compliments, I shan't return them.

LORD. Empty? They are tokens of my esteem.

HARLEQUIN. They're pigfood! And another thing, I know where it was I saw you. You were hunting, on a horse, and playing the trumpet. And I raised my hat to you and you have still to return that greeting.

LORD. What! Didn't I even tip my hat?

HARLEQUIN. You didn't touch it.

LORD. Didn't I see you were a gentleman?

HARLEQUIN. Of course you did! But you hadn't come to beg a favour, so you didn't bother with me.

LORD. My behaviour is a mystery to me.

HARLEQUIN. Then it can't be held against you. How can I help?

LORD. I am counting on your generosity. My case is this: I had the misfortune to speak flippantly of you in the Prince's presence . . .

HARLEQUIN. More mysterious behaviour?

LORD. . . . and the Prince was angry with me.

HARLEQUIN. Oh, he doesn't like slanderers?

LORD. No.

HARLEQUIN. Oh ho! Very good. He's an excellent man. I'd like him very much indeed if only he hadn't kidnapped my mistress. And what did he say, did he call you an insolent oaf?

LORD. He did.

HARLEQUIN. That seems fair enough. What's the complaint?

LORD. More is to follow. 'Harlequin,' he said, 'is a decent man; I respect him, and I intend to show him honour. His frankness and simplicity are qualities I'd like to see more widely emulated. It wounds me to intrude upon his love. I only do so since the love I feel is irresistible.'

HARLEQUIN. My God! I'm much obliged. I'm very impressed. I've quite forgotten to be angry with him.

LORD. He ordered me to leave his presence. My friends tried to pacify him.

HARLEQUIN. He should have thrown them out. He should have known them by the company they keep.

LORD. He did, they were dismissed.

HARLEQUIN. And so he swept the rubbish out of the Palace, did he? God bless him.

LORD. None of us may reappear until you ask him to forgive us.

HARLEQUIN. Then you can pack your bags, the lot of you. *Bon voyage!*

LORD. What! Won't you plead for me? I'm ruined unless you agree. How can I exist at Court if I'm barred from the royal presence? I shall have to live on my country estate. I shall be exiled.

HARLEQUIN. Exiled? What's the problem in being exiled if it just means staying at home and not going out to eat?

LORD. That is the problem.

HARLEQUIN. Living in peace and quiet with four square meals a day, is that it?

LORD. Absolutely. Why do you ask?

HARLEQUIN. Not joking, are you? Slanderers get exiled?

LORD. Very often.

HARLEQUIN (*jumps for joy*). That's it! I'll slander the first man I see! So will Silvia, so will Flaminia!

LORD. Why?

HARLEQUIN. Because I want to be exiled! Punishment here's a damn sight better than being rewarded!

LORD. Be that as it may, spare me the punishment. The slander in my case was nothing.

HARLEQUIN. What was it?

LORD. It was trivial, I assure you.

HARLEQUIN. Prove it.

LORD. I remarked that judging by appearances you were an honest man, without a trace of malice, trustworthy and decent.

HARLEQUIN. Did you indeed? That's serious. I see what you mean by slander. 'Honest' I suppose means simple-minded, in comparison with a wit like you. Do you have to make these shallow judgements? What was the rest? That can't be everything!

LORD. I said that when you spoke you made the people who heard you laugh.

HARLEQUIN. They do the same for me, I'm getting my own back. Is that all?

LORD. Yes.

HARLEQUIN. This is absurd! You shouldn't be exiled, there are many more deserving cases.

LORD. Never mind that. Prevent it if you please. People like me can only survive at Court. If we want to be respected, or defeat our rivals, we must please the Prince and cultivate the friendship of important people.

HARLEQUIN. I'd rather cultivate a marrow-patch; something always comes up, if only a turnip. And I bet it's difficult to win these people's friendship, let alone keep it.

LORD. True, their favour is capricious. But one can't be seen to jib at it. One is tactful, one accommodates, one gives way. It is through them that one takes revenge on others.

HARLEQUIN. What a ridiculous hoo-hah! You stand there getting hit on the one side, all for the sake of hitting the man on the other. It's pride gone mad! And this degrading posture is the mark of the ruling class!

LORD. It comes with practice. Listen: you could get me back into favour with no trouble at all. You know Flaminia, don't you?

HARLEQUIN. She's my bosom friend.

LORD. The Prince is well disposed to her; she is the daughter of one of his officers, and I had hoped to make her fortune by marrying her to a wealthy cousin of mine, my ward, who lives in the country. Tell the Prince: he'll approve the plan. And he'll approve of me for thinking of it.

HARLEQUIN. Leave her out of this; and leave your cousin out as well. I don't like people marrying off my friends, forget it.

LORD. But I thought –

HARLEQUIN. You thought too much.

LORD. I'll drop the plan.

HARLEQUIN. You better had. I'll do what I can for you, but wealthy cousins won't be any part of it.

LORD. I'm greatly obliged. I await the consequences of your

promise. Good day to you, Mr Harlequin.

HARLEQUIN. Your servant.

The LORD *goes, with* TRIVELIN.

Blow my boots! I've influence here; they'll do as I tell them. But I needn't tell Flaminia about that cousin of his.

Scene 8

FLAMINIA *enters.*

FLAMINIA. Dear friend, I bring you Silvia, she's on her way.

HARLEQUIN. Why didn't you come straight back? We could have chatted while we waited for her.

Scene 9

SILVIA *enters.*

SILVIA. Harlequin! What a beautiful dress I've just tried on! You'd have thought me very pretty in it, ask Flaminia. Oh! If I were to wear that dress I'd knock those women off their feet; I'd like to hear them call me clumsy then. The people who made that beautiful gown are artists.

HARLEQUIN. What inspired them? You, your beauty.

SILVIA. If I'm beautiful, it's to match your goodness.

FLAMINIA. At least I have the pleasure of seeing you happier now.

SILVIA. Why not? There's no one bothering us. I like it here as much as anywhere. Places are much the same; there's no such thing as a place you can't be in love in.

HARLEQUIN. Also, here, if people insult us they get forced to apologise.

SILVIA (*happily*). I've found that too. There's a woman who didn't think I was attractive. She was told to come and beg forgiveness. I'm waiting for her now.

FLAMINIA. If anyone annoys you, you must tell me.

HARLEQUIN. Flaminia loves us like her brother and sister. (*To* FLAMINIA.) That's how we feel too.

SILVIA. Oh, Harlequin. Imagine who I've met: the officer who called on me at home. He's tall and well turned-out and very attentive to me. I want you to be friends with him. He's good in the same way you are.

HARLEQUIN (*casually*). Yes, whatever you like.

SILVIA. After all, what does it matter if he loves me a little? People in love make better company than those who haven't any interest in us, don't you agree?

FLAMINIA. Without a doubt.

HARLEQUIN (*cheerfully*). Let's add Flaminia. She's got an interest in us. Then we'll be a foursome, that's much neater.

FLAMINIA. Harlequin, that's an unforgettable mark of friendship.

HARLEQUIN. Now we're a team, I suggest we all three go and look for something to eat.

SILVIA. But, Harlequin, we can see each other whenever we want to. Let's not tie each other down. If you want to eat, go and eat. And I'll stay here.

HARLEQUIN *signals to* FLAMINIA *to follow*.

FLAMINIA. I'll come with you. Look: here's company for Silvia.

Scene 10

FLAMINIA *and* HARLEQUIN *go*. LISETTE *enters with some*

women, as witnesses of what she is about to do. They remain behind
SILVIA. LISETTE *curtsies grandly.*

SILVIA. Don't curtsy so elaborately, madame, or I'll have to do the same for you, and you seem to think I'd find it difficult.

LISETTE. Whatever you do is perfect, so they tell me.

SILVIA. That won't last. I'm not trying to be approved of. It embarrasses me to be pretty, especially when I look at someone who isn't.

LISETTE. Oh what a state I'm in!

SILVIA. What a tragic sigh! And all because of a little village miss! You can't be trying. Where's your mean little tongue? What's stopping it? Doesn't it like being made to behave itself, is that the trouble?

LISETTE. I can't bring myself to speak.

SILVIA. Be quiet then. Because even if you cry all day it won't affect my face. Pretty or not, this is how it's going to stay. What more do you want from me? Haven't you been nasty enough for one day? Oh, all right, finish up.

LISETTE. Spare me, mademoiselle. The way I treated you has put my family in danger. The Prince has forced me to apologise. Don't ridicule me while I do so.

SILVIA. I've stopped. I won't make fun of you again. I know it's hard to take a little teasing when you're used to people bowing and scraping to you. I resented you and it made me spiteful. But I'm sorry for you. I forgive you. Why were you so unpleasant?

LISETTE. I thought the Prince had certain feelings towards me. I thought I wasn't undeserving of them. But I realise now that men aren't necessarily attracted by refinement.

SILVIA (*sharply*). No, they like plain, bad-mannered girls, is that what you mean? That's my attraction, is it? Your jealousy has addled your brain!

LISETTE. I admit I'm jealous. But since you aren't in love with the Prince, why don't you help me to win him back? He

doesn't dislike me, and I'm very well placed to cure him of his
love for you, if only you'll let me do so.

SILVIA (*piqued*). I think you'll find his love's too serious for *you*
to cure.

LISETTE. I doubt it. After all, I don't lack beauty, nor a certain
degree of style.

SILVIA. Let's talk about something else. I've heard enough about
your shining virtues.

LISETTE. A strange reply. Never mind, we'll see in a day or two
who calls the tune.

SILVIA (*sharply*). We'll hear some very funny tunes indeed.
By God! I'll speak to the Prince. I've been so angry with him
that he hasn't dared visit me. I'll tell him to pluck up his
courage and do so, and we'll see what happens.

LISETTE. Adieu, mademoiselle. We'll each of us do whatever we
can, you may be sure of that. I've carried out my orders, insofar
as they affect you. Please forget whatever has passed between us.

SILVIA (*brusquely*). Go away, go away, I've wiped you from my
mind!

LISETTE *goes*.

Scene 11

FLAMINIA *enters*.

FLAMINIA. Silvia, what's the matter? You're upset.

SILVIA. I'm furious! That rude woman who's just gone out had
come to ask my pardon. And without exactly saying it – that's
how horrid she is – she made me angrier than ever; saying the
only reason people like me is because I'm ugly, that she's
prettier, that she's cleverer, that the Prince's love won't last,
and that she'll see it doesn't and I'll soon find out. And this was

to my face, so what's going on behind my back? Wouldn't you
be angry?

FLAMINIA (*brightly and with interest*). Listen: you'll never be
able to show your face in public till you've shut those people up.

SILVIA. I would if I could; but what about Harlequin?

FLAMINIA. I know what you mean. Your love for him is awkward.
It's as inconvenient as anyone could imagine.

SILVIA. Oh, I've always been unlucky with my friends.

FLAMINIA. If you were rejected by the Court, if you were forced
to leave it in disgrace, would Harlequin be happy about it?

SILVIA. What do you mean? Do you mean he'd love me less?

FLAMINIA. I would expect so.

SILVIA. I must think about this; I wonder: have you noticed how
off-hand he's been since we arrived? He left me alone a moment
ago to find some food: a very flattering excuse!

FLAMINIA. It struck me too. Tell me, in strictest confidence,
woman to woman: when it comes down to it, do you really
love him?

SILVIA (*casually*). Yes, of course, I love him as is right and proper.

FLAMINIA. A word of advice: you don't seem very well-matched.
You have taste and wit and a good appearance; he's portentous
and crude. He isn't your style. I don't see the attraction.
I probably shouldn't say this but I think you're making
a mistake.

SILVIA. Put yourself in my place. He was the most suitable man
in my part of the world. He lived in my village, he was my next-
door neighbour, he had a sense of humour, and so do I. He
made me laugh, he started following me everywhere, he loved
me. I got used to seeing him, I got used to being in love with
him, for want of anyone better, though I always knew how soft
he was on food and wine.

FLAMINIA. Yes, he must have cut a very romantic figure with his
glass in one hand and a pork chop in the other. What will you do?

SILVIA. My mind's so full of voices for and against that I don't
know which to listen to. On the one hand, Harlequin's been

casual with me ever since we've been here; all he's thought about is food. On the other hand, if I'm sent away from Court we'll have those women going round saying somebody told me 'You won't do, you aren't pretty enough, go home'. And then again there's that man I've only just met once more –

FLAMINIA. What do you mean?

SILVIA. I'll tell you a secret: since I've seen him again, I don't know how he's done it, but he's been so kind, so gentle, he's had such a delicate way of saying he loves me that I can't help feeling pity for him; and I can't control it.

FLAMINIA. Do you love him?

SILVIA. No, I don't think so; Harlequin's my lover.

FLAMINIA. Though the other is attractive.

SILVIA. Yes, I know.

FLAMINIA. If you married him, you'd lose your chance of being revenged; but I'd forgive you, truly I would.

SILVIA. If Harlequin were to marry another girl there'd be no problem. I'd be in the right. I'd say 'You left me, now I'm leaving you, I'm taking my revenge'. But there's no hope of that. Who'd have him, rude and boorish as he is?

FLAMINIA. I feel so close to you. Now, I've often thought of moving to the country. Harlequin is vulgar, I don't love him, but I don't dislike him. And, since this is the way I feel about him, if he agreed, I'd be prepared to disembarrass you, if it would make you happier.

SILVIA. But I can't imagine what would make me happy. It isn't one thing or the other. I'm still looking.

FLAMINIA. Today you'll meet the Prince; and here's the officer you like so much. You'd better choose sides. Adieu, we'll see each other soon. (*She goes.*)

Scene 12

The PRINCE *enters.*

SILVIA. I see you've returned. If you say you love me again I'll be more upset than ever.

PRINCE. I've come to see if the woman who insulted you has made a decent apology. As for myself, dear Silvia, if my love is oppressive to you, if my company is unpleasant, simply tell me to be quiet and send me away. I won't say a word, I'll go wherever you want, I'll suffer in silence. I'll obey you absolutely.

SILVIA. Do you see what I mean? This is what I'm talking about. How can I send you away? If I do, you'll go. If I tell you to be silent, you'll obey. You won't object, you'll do whatever I tell you. It's impossible for me to tell you anything!

PRINCE. What can I do but place my destiny in your hands?

SILVIA. What good is that? What if I made you unhappy? I couldn't bear it. If I told you to go, you'd think I hated you. If I said 'Be quiet', you'd think I had no feeling for you. And it wouldn't be true. And, once it was done, do you think I'd feel any better?

PRINCE. What do you want me to do, my beautiful Silvia?

SILVIA. What do I want? I just want somebody to tell me; you know the answer better than me. There's Harlequin who has my heart, there's the Prince who wants it, and there's you who deserve it. There are women who've insulted me, and who I want to be revenged on. There's the fact that I'll be hurt and wounded if the Prince rejects me. Harlequin upsets me, you upset me in a different way, by loving me too much. I wish I'd never met you, and I'm wretched and I'm utterly tangled up.

PRINCE. Your words cut deep; you're too easily moved by my sorrow. My love is great, but it doesn't deserve to make you sad at being unable to return it.

SILVIA. But I could. If I wanted to, I could love you easily.

PRINCE. Then you'll know the pain I feel, and give me leave to miss you till the day I die.

SILVIA (*impatiently*). I warn you, I can't stand it when you look so lovingly at me. Are you doing it on purpose? Do you call this reasonable behaviour? For God's sake, I'd much rather say I love you, than be stuck as I am. If only it were up to me, I'd stop it at once.

PRINCE. I see I'm making you impatient; you want me to go. I cannot disobey the woman I love. Silvia, adieu.

SILVIA (*sharply*). Silvia, adieu! I'll lose my temper in a moment. Where do you think you're going? Stay where you are! I hope I know my own mind better than you do.

PRINCE. I was trying to obey you.

SILVIA. What can I do? What do I do about Harlequin? Why are you not the Prince?

PRINCE (*with concern*). What difference would it make if I were?

SILVIA. Every difference. I could say the Prince had exercised his right as master; that'd be my excuse. But I could only use an excuse like that for a man like you.

PRINCE (*aside*). How easy she is to love! It's time to tell her who I am.

SILVIA. Is something wrong? Have I annoyed you? Don't think I wanted you to be the Prince because of thrones and kingdoms. I was thinking of you and you alone. If you were the Prince, then Harlequin need never know I'd chosen you out of love; that's all I meant. But perhaps it's better that you aren't the Prince. I'd be too tempted; and my loyal duty to you would be too attractive. There, I've finished.

PRINCE (*aside*). It might be better if we told her later. (*To her.*) All I ask is that you keep your feelings for me as they are. The Prince has arranged a play for your entertainment; let me accompany you. Let me see you whenever I can. After the curtain has fallen you will meet the Prince. I have been asked to say that if your heart does not respond to him, you'll be free to go.

SILVIA. My heart won't say a word. I feel I'm half-way home already. Perhaps you'll visit me there? Who knows how the play will end: perhaps you'll win me. Let's go at once, or Harlequin might find us.

They leave.

Act Three

Scene 1

The PRINCE *and* FLAMINIA *enter.*

FLAMINIA. Yes, my lord, you were right not to reveal yourself, in
spite of her tender words. The delay won't hurt, and it will give
her time to grow accustomed to her feelings. You're nearly
there, thank Heavens.

PRINCE. Ah! Flaminia, how adorable she is!

FLAMINIA. She certainly is.

PRINCE. I've never known a woman like her. When one's mistress
feels such powerful emotion that she utters the words, 'I love
you', it's enjoyable, I won't deny it. But, oh! Flaminia! That
pleasure is grey and dull compared to the pleasure Silvia's
conversation gave me, though she didn't say 'I love you'.

FLAMINIA. May I presume, my lord, to ask you what she did say?

PRINCE. It's impossible. I'm entranced, I'm ravished, I've no
other way to describe it.

FLAMINIA. It's an odd description, but it gives the general drift.

PRINCE. She said it grieved her that she couldn't love me, that
she hated making me unhappy but she had to be true to
Harlequin ... There was a moment when she almost said:
'Don't love me any more, I beg you; or you'll make me love
you too.'

FLAMINIA. That's very good! It's better than if she'd said it.

PRINCE. I'll tell you again, the love of Silvia is the only real love
there is. When other women love, their love is spoiled by
civilisation. They've had a certain education, they've learned

certain manners; these things falsify nature. With Silvia, it's her heart which speaks in all its purity; she shows her feelings as they arise. Her artlessness turns them into art, her reticence makes them truthful. You must admit it's charming. All that makes her hesitate is her feeling that it's wrong to love me without telling Harlequin. So, be quick as you can, Flaminia. Will you win him soon? I can't use violence on him, I don't want to. What does he say?

FLAMINIA. My lord, I believe he loves me with all his heart, but he's done nothing about it yet. He calls me 'friend'; he clings to the word for reassurance, and he takes his love for granted.

PRINCE. Excellent.

FLAMINIA. Next time we talk I shall enlighten him. I'll give a name to his emotions. Part of the plan is that you'll treat him gently, speak of him kindly, as we agreed. And this, I think, will bring an end to your anxieties and my hard work. I'll be victorious and vanquished.

PRINCE. Vanquished?

FLAMINIA. It's a detail not worth mentioning. I've grown fond of him, merely to add some sparkle to our intrigue. Let's withdraw, let's meet with Silvia again. Harlequin mustn't see you yet, and he's approaching. (*They leave.*)

Scene 2

HARLEQUIN, *looking a little gloomy, enters with* TRIVELIN.

TRIVELIN (*after some time*). Well? You told me to bring a pen and paper. What must I do with them?

HARLEQUIN. Be patient, menial.

TRIVELIN. For as long as you like.

HARLEQUIN. Tell me, who provides the food here?

TRIVELIN. The Prince.

HARLEQUIN. Oh, whiskers! Now I'm having second thoughts.

TRIVELIN. And why is that?

HARLEQUIN. I'm worried I might have run up a bill without knowing it.

TRIVELIN (*laughing*). Ha ha ha!

HARLEQUIN. What're you laughing at, you fathead?

TRIVELIN. At your quite preposterous notion. Harlequin, you can dine and drink without a worry in the world.

HARLEQUIN. I eat my food in a trusting spirit. Getting a bill at the end of the day would be a shock, you can take my word for it. No you can't, I'll take your word for it. Now tell me: what does one call the man who runs the Prince's business?

TRIVELIN. You mean his Secretary of State?

HARLEQUIN. Yes. I want to write him a letter, telling the Prince I'm bored, and asking him when he thinks he'll finish with us, because my father's on his own at home.

TRIVELIN. Well?

HARLEQUIN. If he wants to keep me any longer, he must fetch him here in a carriage.

TRIVELIN. Say the word and he'll dispatch it.

HARLEQUIN. Next thing, we must marry, me and Silvia, and I want the doors unlocked, so I can wander in the fields the way I'm used to. Then we'll live here, me and Silvia and Flaminia, who likes us much too much to want to leave us. And if the Prince insists on giving us a present, I can always manage something to eat.

TRIVELIN. My lord, must you involve Flaminia?

HARLEQUIN. It's what I want.

TRIVELIN (*in a displeased manner*). Hmm.

HARLEQUIN (*imitating him*). Hmm. This servant's terrible. At the double! Pen out! Write my letter!

TRIVELIN (*having prepared himself*). Dictate.

HARLEQUIN. 'Dear Sir' –

TRIVELIN. Stop, please. You ought to start: 'My lord'.

HARLEQUIN. Well, put down both and let him make his mind up.

TRIVELIN. Very good.

HARLEQUIN. 'As you know, my name is Harlequin' –

TRIVELIN. Not so fast. You'll need to say, 'Your Highness knows –'.

HARLEQUIN. 'Your Highness'? He's a giant, is he?

TRIVELIN. No, but – Never mind.

HARLEQUIN. What's all this gobbledegook? Whoever heard of writing to somebody's measurements?

TRIVELIN (*writing*). Oh, please, I'll say whatever you like. 'As you know, my name is Harlequin.' Next?

HARLEQUIN. 'I have a mistress, name of Silvia, citizen of my village and a girl of honour –'

TRIVELIN. Continue.

HARLEQUIN. '– and a very dear friend I've only just met who cannot do without us, and I can't do without her. And so, as soon as you get this letter –'

TRIVELIN (*stopping as though hurt*). Flaminia can't do without you? Ha! My pen has flown from my fingers!

HARLEQUIN. Fainting? What's the meaning of this rudeness?

TRIVELIN. Lord Harlequin, for two years, a full two years, I've nursed a secret passion for this lady.

HARLEQUIN (*drawing his stick*). Hard luck, menial. While we wait for her to hear the happy news, I'll thank you for her.

TRIVELIN. Oh, not again! I don't appreciate your thanks! What do you care if I'm in love with her? You're only a friend, friends don't get jealous!

HARLEQUIN. Wrong. My friendship is identical to love. I'll prove it.

He hits TRIVELIN.

TRIVELIN (*fleeing*). Oh, blast your friendship! (*He goes.*)

Scene 3

FLAMINIA *enters.*

FLAMINIA. Harlequin, what's going on? What is it?

HARLEQUIN. That toad just told me he's been loving you for the past two years.

FLAMINIA. It's very possible.

HARLEQUIN. And you, dear friend, how do you feel about it?

FLAMINIA. It's too bad for him.

HARLEQUIN. You're sure?

FLAMINIA. Quite sure. But would you mind if somebody loved me?

HARLEQUIN. You can do what you like, worse luck. But if they loved you, you might love them back and that would ruin our friendship, there'd be less to go round. I'd hate to lose the smallest bit of it.

FLAMINIA (*tenderly*). Harlequin, has it never crossed your mind to treat me gently?

HARLEQUIN. What? I haven't touched you! What did I do?

FLAMINIA. If you go on talking to me like this, I'll start to wonder about my feelings for you. And I can't examine them too closely, I might find out more than I want.

HARLEQUIN. You're right; don't probe. Whatever will be will be. Another thing, don't take a lover. I've got a mistress, and I'm hanging on to her, but if I hadn't, then I wouldn't look for one. As long as I'd got you, I wouldn't need one. Hell, she'd bore me.

FLAMINIA. Bore you? You tell me that, and then expect me to be merely a friend?

HARLEQUIN. Why not? What else could you be?

FLAMINIA. Don't ask me, I'd rather not know. The only thing I'm certain of is that there isn't a soul in the whole wide world I love, but you. And you can't say that. Silvia must come first, it's only right.

HARLEQUIN. Ssh! You go together, you're a combination.

FLAMINIA. I'll find her. If I send her to you, will it make you happy?

HARLEQUIN. Just as you like. Don't send her by herself, though; you come too.

FLAMINIA. I can't. The Prince has asked for me. I must see what he wants. Harlequin, adieu, I'll soon return.

The LORD *begins to enter, carrying Letters of Nobility; as she leaves,* FLAMINIA *smiles at him.*

Scene 4

HARLEQUIN. Here's that man from a while back. Welcome, your Noble Slyness! – since I never heard your name. I haven't told the Prince about you because I haven't seen him.

LORD. I'm greatly obliged to you, Lord Harlequin. Only, I'm out of trouble now. I've reinstated myself in the Prince's favour, having assured him that you'd speak on my behalf; so now I'm doubly hopeful that you'll keep your word.

HARLEQUIN. I may look stupid, but I have got standards.

LORD. I beg you, forget the past and let's be friends, especially since I bring you a present from the Prince. It ranks among the finest gifts a man could receive.

HARLEQUIN. Is it Silvia?

LORD. Since it's in this package, that would not be easy. These are Letters of Nobility, by which the Prince intends to honour you as one of Silvia's relatives, since there seems to be some tenuous family link between you.

HARLEQUIN. No, there isn't. And I won't presume to honours which I don't deserve, so take it back.

LORD. Accept it anyway, what does it matter? You'll please the Prince, and why refuse what all good people think of as the summit of their ambition?

HARLEQUIN. I'm a good person too. As for ambition, I've heard about it, but I've never seen it, and if I've got it I don't know about it.

LORD. If you lack it, this will provide it.

HARLEQUIN. Why, what is it?

LORD (aside). It's like talking to a foreigner. (To HARLEQUIN.) Ambition is one's noble pride in rising upward.

HARLEQUIN. Noble pride? This is how you talk here, is it – giving pretty names to human follies?

LORD. You misunderstand me. Pride in this case means a desire for glory.

HARLEQUIN. That meaning's just as bad: it's six of one and half a dozen of the other.

LORD. Do as I say, accept it. Wouldn't it make you happy to be a lord?

HARLEQUIN. No, and it wouldn't upset me, either. The way I feel is the way my feelings take me, it's as simple as that.

LORD. You'd find it to your advantage. Those around you would respect and fear you.

HARLEQUIN. But they wouldn't love me, not of their own free will. When I'm afraid of people, or respect them, then it takes the pleasure out of loving them. It's too many things at once.

LORD. You're full of surprises!

HARLEQUIN. It's the way I'm put together. And another thing: I'm the easiest child in the world. I don't harm anyone. And if I wanted to I couldn't, I'm too unimportant. But what if I had power, if I were a noble lord? Well then, I'm damned if I'd be good all the time. I wouldn't promise to be! I might be like the squire back home who lays about him with his riding-crop because nobody dares hit back.

LORD. And if you were beaten, wouldn't you want to beat him back?

HARLEQUIN. I'd want to pay him back with interest.

LORD. Well, since men are sometimes very wicked, you should have the power to harm them if you want to, to deter them from harming you. And to this end, accept these Letters of Nobility.

HARLEQUIN (*takes the Letters*). My God! You're talking reason! I'm an animal. No, I'm not, I'm a noble. Mm, real live parchment. Now I've got another worry, that the rats might nibble my nobility. I'll watch them. Thank you, sir, and the Prince as well. He's decent.

LORD. And I'm glad you're satisfied. Adieu.

HARLEQUIN. Your servant.

When the LORD *has gone ten or a dozen paces* HARLEQUIN *calls him back.*

Monsieur! Monsieur!

LORD. What is it?

HARLEQUIN. Does my nobility have any duties tied to it? I like to do things properly.

LORD. It's your duty to be honourable.

HARLEQUIN (*very seriously*). Did you have a special licence to be rude about me?

LORD. Think no more of it. A gentleman is generous.

HARLEQUIN. Generous! And honourable! Excellent duties. They're more noble than my noble parchment. If I fail them, am I still a gentleman?

LORD. No.

HARLEQUIN. So do a lot of nobles get reduced to the ranks?

LORD. I couldn't say how many.

HARLEQUIN. And that's all? No extra duties?

LORD. No. Though, being a favourite of the Prince, as so it seems, you'll have one further duty. You must earn his favour by submitting to him, paying him homage and obeying him at the slightest opportunity. As for the rest, I think I've covered it: be good and honest, and esteem your honour higher than your life and everything will be in order.

HARLEQUIN. Stop a moment. What's all that about, that last bit? I don't like it. Firstly, what's this honour that I've got to prefer to living? What's it consist of?

LORD. Its merit won't be lost on you. You must avenge an insult. Rather than endure it, you must die.

HARLEQUIN. That's a change. I was all set to be generous and forgiving. Now if you want me to be violent, that's a different matter. How does killing people square with keeping them alive?

LORD. You'll be generous and forgiving only as long as you aren't insulted.

HARLEQUIN. I've got it. I'm not allowed to behave better than anyone else, and if I do good in return for evil, then I've lost my honour. Lord preserve us! There's enough wickedness in the world, it doesn't need support. What a stupid system! Tell you what, we'll compromise: if anyone insults me, I'll insult him back, as long as he is smaller than me. Is it a bargain?

LORD. An insult in return for an insult cannot wash away the stain. It can only be cleansed with blood, your enemy's blood.

HARLEQUIN. Then leave the stain alone. Blood isn't water, you know, it's blood. My honour isn't up to being noble, it's too reasonable. I'm giving you back your parcel, with my compliments.

LORD. You haven't properly considered.

HARLEQUIN. Now I'm giving it back without my compliments.

LORD. Keep it. You and the Prince will settle this question. Nobody in your case will study the finer points.

HARLEQUIN (*taking it back*). I want it in writing that if the man next door is rude to me, I can make him apologise, but I needn't get killed as well.

LORD. Quite so, you'll make your own rules. Good day to you, sir. Your servant.

HARLEQUIN. I am yours.

The LORD *leaves.*

Scene 5

The PRINCE *enters.*

HARLEQUIN (*seeing him*). Who the devil's this? It's him! The
   reason that they kidnapped Silvia in the first place. Greetings
   to you, Lord Gossip. Isn't it you that advertises people's
   girlfriends? Many congratulations, mine was snapped up
   instantly.

PRINCE. No insults, Harlequin.

HARLEQUIN. Oh, you're a gentleman, are you?

PRINCE. Certainly.

HARLEQUIN. Lucky for you! If you weren't, I'd tell you what
   I think of you; then your honour might insist on being
   revenged, and you'd be dead.

PRINCE. Harlequin, calm yourself. The Prince has ordered me to
   speak to you.

HARLEQUIN. Speak, what's stopping you? But he didn't order me
   to listen.

PRINCE. Very well! Temper your speech. Recognise me as you
   should. It is your Prince who speaks to you, not an officer of the
   Palace as you thought, as Silvia still believes.

HARLEQUIN. Prove it.

PRINCE. You must believe me.

HARLEQUIN. Forgive me, Your Highness. It was me who was the
   idiot to insult you.

PRINCE. I pardon you.

HARLEQUIN (*sadly*). You do? Well, if you can forgive me just like
   that, just you make sure that I do the same for you. I can't be
   angry with a Prince, I'm not big enough. If you persecute me,
   what can I do but cry and hope you'll pity those beneath you?
   Because you wouldn't want to rule a country where the only
   happy person was yourself, I hope.

PRINCE. You never stop complaining, do you, Harlequin?

HARLEQUIN. My lord, does it surprise you? I've got a woman who loves me. You've got a palace full of women, yet you pick on mine. I am poor, my worldly goods add up to a copper or two; you are a millionaire and you snatch my purse. It's sad, admit it.

PRINCE (*aside*). Reasonable enough. I'm touched by this.

HARLEQUIN. I know you're a very good Prince, and everyone in this part of the world thinks likewise; but I'd hate to lose the pleasure of agreeing with them.

PRINCE. I've taken Silvia from you, this is true. But ask whatever you want: I offer all the riches you could wish for; only leave me the woman I love.

HARLEQUIN. Let's not start bargaining, you're bound to come out best. Just tell me, truthfully, if anyone else had taken her, wouldn't you make him give her back? Well, nobody else has done so, only you. So now you've got a wonderful chance to show that justice applies to all.

PRINCE (*aside*). What can I say to this?

HARLEQUIN. Ask yourself: 'Should I rob this little fellow of his only happiness, simply because it's in my power to do so? Being his master, shouldn't I protect him? Must he be turned away without receiving justice? If he is, won't I feel sorry about it? Who will do my princely duties if not me? I therefore order myself to give back Silvia to him.'

PRINCE. Is this all you can say? Look at the way I've treated you. I could send you home, I could keep Silvia here, I could ignore you. Yet in spite of my love for her, despite your stubbornness and lack of respect for me, I show concern for your distress; I try to alleviate it by my generosity; I've even begged you to relinquish her of your own free will. Everyone tries to persuade you, everyone blames you, everyone else is an example to you of obedience. You are the only person to resist. You call me Prince: very well then, show it.

HARLEQUIN (*still sad*). Your Highness, don't trust anyone who tells you I've been properly treated. They're lying to you. You're taking their false advice for genuine. So, however fine a

man you are, however honest, none of your actions does you
any good. If you didn't have these people around you, then you
wouldn't try to cheat me, wouldn't say I lack respect for
speaking up for what is mine by right. You are my Prince, I love
you. But I'm your subject: that deserves something too.

PRINCE. Leave me, I despair of you.

HARLEQUIN. You should pity me.

PRINCE. How can I give up Silvia? How can I win her love if you
don't help me? Harlequin, I've hurt you; but the pain you've
given me is worse by far.

HARLEQUIN. Fight it, my lord. Take a walk, take a journey.
Leave your sorrows on the open road.

PRINCE. My child, I hoped your heart would give me more.
I would have owed you more than anyone. No matter. I'd
decided to be generous to you, and your cruelty to me won't
prevent my doing so.

HARLEQUIN. Life is difficult.

PRINCE. It's true that I acted wrongly. I was unjust, and I regret it.
But you're more than adequately revenged.

HARLEQUIN. I'd like to go now. You're too miserable to be
entirely in the wrong. I'm getting worried I might see your
point of view.

PRINCE. You've earned your victory. You asked for justice, now
enjoy it, even if it costs me all my happiness.

HARLEQUIN. Now you're being so kind to me, I ought to be
kind to you.

PRINCE (*sad*). Don't trouble yourself, I beg you.

HARLEQUIN. I'm upset! Just look how desolate you are!

PRINCE (*caressing* HARLEQUIN). I'm grateful for your delicacy of
feeling. Harlequin, adieu. I shall respect you even more for
refusing me.

HARLEQUIN (*takes one or two steps towards the* PRINCE).
My lord.

PRINCE. What is it? Do you require some favour?

HARLEQUIN. No, I'm trying to decide if I should give you what you want.

PRINCE. Your heart is good, I can't deny it.

HARLEQUIN. So is yours; that's why I'm weakening. Isn't it sad how feeble decent men are!

PRINCE. I admire your sentiments.

HARLEQUIN. You should. But don't rely on them yet. I've promised nothing. There's a lot of things need sorting out first. Say we agreed, just say I gave you Silvia? Would I be your favourite?

PRINCE. Who could be my favourite if not you?

HARLEQUIN. Only I've heard that you're used to people flattering you. Now me, my habit is to tell the truth, and I don't see my good habit living side by side with your regrettable one. How will your friendship carry the strain of mine?

PRINCE. We will only quarrel if you fail to speak your mind. And one thing more: remember that I love you. This is my only advice.

HARLEQUIN. Will Flaminia be my mistress?

PRINCE. Don't say that name. You could never have caused such anguish if it weren't for her.

HARLEQUIN (*to the* PRINCE, *who is going*). That's wrong, quite wrong. She's the most wonderful girl in the world, you leave her alone! (*The* PRINCE *goes.*)

Scene 6

HARLEQUIN. It seems my friend has been betrayed by that rat of a servant. By Christ! I'll find her at once. But then what? Do I abandon Silvia? Is it possible? Can it happen? Damnit no! Most definitely not. I made a downright idiot of myself just then. And why? Because I'm sensitive to other people's problems. Still, the Prince is sensitive too. He'll understand.

Scene 7

A sad-looking FLAMINIA *enters.*

HARLEQUIN. Oh, there you are, Flaminia, I was looking for you.

FLAMINIA (*sighing*). Harlequin, adieu!

HARLEQUIN. Adieu? What does that mean?

FLAMINIA. Trivelin has betrayed us. The Prince, who knows about our conversations, has banished me. He's forbidden me to talk to you; and yet I couldn't restrain myself from seeing you one last time; then I shall flee to avoid his anger.

HARLEQUIN (*astonished and disconcerted*). A fine upstanding fellow he turned out to be!

FLAMINIA. I'm in despair! To live without you, never to see you, you who are dearest to me in all the world! The seconds are racing by. I have to leave you. Let me reveal my heart.

HARLEQUIN (*takes a deep breath*). Your heart, did you say? What about it?

FLAMINIA. It wasn't friendship that I felt for you. I was deceived.

HARLEQUIN (*breathless*). Then is it love?

FLAMINIA. The dearest, tenderest love. Adieu.

HARLEQUIN (*holding her back*). No, wait! Perhaps I was deceived as well!

FLAMINIA. What? You were mistaken too? You love me, and we're never to meet again? Harlequin, don't say another word, I'm leaving.

She takes one or two steps.

HARLEQUIN. Stop there.

FLAMINIA. Let me go. What can we do?

HARLEQUIN. Let's talk sense.

FLAMINIA. But what can I say?

HARLEQUIN. My friendship's out of the window along with yours. It's gone. I love you. That's decided. But I don't understand it. Whoo!

FLAMINIA. What an adventure!

HARLEQUIN. Luckily I'm not married.

FLAMINIA. Perfectly true.

HARLEQUIN. Silvia will marry the Prince, so he'll be happy.

FLAMINIA. I don't doubt it.

HARLEQUIN. Then, seeing that our hearts deceived us, and we fell in love by accident, let's be calm and patient and make proper arrangements for the future.

FLAMINIA (*softly*). I think I understand: you mean we'll marry.

HARLEQUIN. That's right. Now don't blame me for this. You never warned me you were going to capture me and be my mistress.

FLAMINIA. Why didn't you warn me you'd become my lover?

HARLEQUIN. How could I guess?

FLAMINIA. You should have done. You're lovable by nature.

HARLEQUIN. Let's not start finding fault. Though, if being lovable is called a fault, you're more in the wrong than me.

FLAMINIA. Marry me! I consent: but there's no time to lose. I might be ordered away at once.

HARLEQUIN (*sighing*). I'll go and talk to the Prince. Don't tell Silvia that I love you. She'll get it into her head that I've wronged her, which I haven't – you know that. I'll talk to her and I won't make any excuses, I'll just say I'm leaving her so she can make her fortune.

FLAMINIA. Very good, that's just what I'd have recommended.

HARLEQUIN. One moment! Give me your hand to kiss . . . (*After kissing her hand.*) Now who would have thought a kiss could give such pleasure? It's amazing! (*He goes.*)

Scene 8

FLAMINIA (*aside*). The Prince is right: the way these little folk make love is irresistible. Here's the other one. (*To* SILVIA, *who enters.*) What are you dreaming of, beautiful Silvia?

SILVIA. I'm dreaming about myself, and I don't understand it.

FLAMINIA. What can't you understand?

SILVIA. You know how I wanted my revenge on all those women? Now I don't.

FLAMINIA. You're not vindictive.

SILVIA. I loved Harlequin, didn't I?

FLAMINIA. So it seemed.

SILVIA. Well, now I don't think I do.

FLAMINIA. It's no great loss.

SILVIA. But what if it were? What could I do about it? My love for him arrived and then I loved him. Now that I don't, it's gone the way it came. It never warned me to expect it, and it never told me it was leaving. I don't see how I can be blamed for anything.

FLAMINIA (*aside*). Let's amuse ourselves for a moment. (*To* SILVIA.) I feel roughly similar.

SILVIA. What does that mean, 'roughly similar'? Why can't you agree? I know I'm right. And, frankly, I like people who say 'yes' or 'no', not sit on the fence.

FLAMINIA. Now why are you getting angry?

SILVIA. I've got every right to. I ask your advice and trust you, and you palm me off with 'roughly similar'.

FLAMINIA. Can't you see I'm teasing you? You deserve nothing but praise. And isn't it perfectly clear that you love that officer?

SILVIA. Who else could it be? I haven't allowed myself to love him yet, but I can't escape it. Saying 'no' to a man who asks for 'yes' all day, seeing how sad he is, hearing his miseries, constantly having to comfort him for all the pain I'm putting him through – it wears me out. The only thing to do is stop him doing it.

FLAMINIA. You'll transform the man, he'll die of joy.

SILVIA. Having him die of sadness would be even worse.

FLAMINIA. There's no comparison.

SILVIA. I'm waiting for him now. We spent two hours together, and he's promised to be with me when the Prince arrives. But I worry sometimes about Harlequin, that I'll make him very unhappy. What do you think? Tell me, but don't make me feel too guilty.

FLAMINIA. Don't worry. We'll make it up to him somehow.

SILVIA (*slightly concerned*). Make it up to him? I'm easily forgotten, am I? Has he found another mistress?

FLAMINIA. Harlequin forget you? Did I suggest he might? – I must be mad. No, no, if he doesn't despair we shall be very lucky.

SILVIA. Don't say that! 'Despair'? Now I'm confused again.

FLAMINIA. And if I told you that he didn't love you any more, what then?

SILVIA. Not love me any more? . . . You can keep that news to yourself.

FLAMINIA. Oh, very well! He still adores you and it makes you miserable, is that what you want?

SILVIA. Oh, you can laugh. You ought to be in my position, then you'd see.

FLAMINIA. Your lover has come to find you. Get it settled with him. Don't worry about anything else. (*She goes*.)

Scene 9

The PRINCE *enters*.

PRINCE. Silvia! Won't you even look at me? Whenever I approach you, you look sad. I hate to be such a nuisance.

SILVIA. Very well, nuisance: I've been talking about you.

PRINCE. You were talking about me? And what did you say, my Silvia?

SILVIA. All sorts of things! I said you still don't know what I think of you.

PRINCE. I know you're keeping your heart from me; so I know your thoughts.

SILVIA. Don't be so sure of yourself, you don't know everything. Now tell me – you're a man of honour, so you'll tell me the truth – knowing what things are like with me and Harlequin, let's say I wanted to love you. If I had my wish, would I be better off, or worse? There. I want your honest advice.

PRINCE. We aren't the masters of our hearts. If your wish is to love me, then your wish must be obeyed. That's what I think.

SILVIA. Do you speak as a friend?

PRINCE. I do, sincerely.

SILVIA. This is what I think too. We've reasoned it out together, and we're right. And I'll love you if I want to, and that's all there is to be said about it.

PRINCE. I gain nothing. I've forced you into this.

SILVIA. Don't try to guess my feelings, I know them better than you do. Now; the Prince. Since I've got to see him, when will he be here? I'll meet him and there's an end to it.

PRINCE. He'll be here sooner than I'd like and, once he is, you might stop loving me.

SILVIA. Have courage! Why be afraid at a time like this? Whatever he's promised himself, he won't find happiness.

PRINCE. I'm still afraid.

SILVIA (aside). What a man! It's up to me to get his confidence back. (To the PRINCE.) Stop trembling. Nothing will make me love the Prince, I swear it by –

PRINCE. Do not complete that vow, I beg you –

SILVIA. You'd stop me swearing my love for you? I'm very flattered!

PRINCE. Do you want me to let you swear you'll never love me?

SILVIA. Never love you? Are you the Prince?

PRINCE. Yes, Silvia. I've hidden my rank from you till now, so that your love might be an answer to mine, no more than that. I wanted to experience that love completely. Now that you know me, you are free to accept my heart and hand. Or reject them both, or one, or the other. Silvia, speak.

SILVIA. Dear Prince, what an oath I would have sworn! If what you wanted was the pleasure of my love, you have it now. You know my love is true, and so do I, and that's the pleasure.

PRINCE. We shall marry.

Final Scene

HARLEQUIN *and* FLAMINIA *enter.*

HARLEQUIN. Silvia, I heard everything.

SILVIA. Then I'm spared the pain of telling you. You must console yourself as best you can. The Prince will explain; my heart's been won; you must get used to it. This is the truth, I've lost my reason. What could you say, if you spoke? That I abandoned you? And what would I answer? Only that it's true, and that I know it already. Can't you simply assume you've said it, that I've given my answer; turn and walk away and everything's over.

PRINCE. Flaminia, I bestow Harlequin on you. I respect him and I'll make him rich. Harlequin, take Flaminia as your wife, and be assured of my goodwill for as long as you live. My Silvia, let our celebrations tell my subjects of the joy I feel; they'll be your subjects too.

HARLEQUIN. Just for the moment I can laugh at the trick our friendship played. Have patience; it will be our turn soon.

The False Servant

Translated by Michael Sadler

from LA FAUSSE SUIVANTE
First performed by the Italian Comedians (1724)

Translator's Note

This is a curious, cold, staccato play. I can imagine it set in a dark, unkempt house. The Countess doesn't give the impression that she is excited by estate management. Dogs bark in the echoing distance, the geometry of the garden is overgrown, and large heavy birds take off in the bush.

No one in the play is immediately attractive. They are either garrulous, naïve, on the defensive, drunk or nasty. They are all interested in money. The two most fragile inhabitants are the Chevalier and the Countess. The Chevalier begins by acting level-headed (1.3) but who is this supposed to impress? Two minutes at the ball with Lelio should have been enough to see through him. Is the calculation a front to conceal – spite? curiosity? a desire to stay with Lelio? The Chevalier is inexperienced but the play which follows will provide the education. This dirty apprenticeship culminates in a violent scene (2.7), in which the Chevalier is mauled by the two servants. The education of the Countess is more straightforward. She is seduced and abandoned. But the punishment involves unexpected bewilderment. Neither she nor the Chevalier are going to find it easy to love after this.

The one character who has the wit and, almost, the intelligence to rise above all this is Trivelin. But his Figaro-like bravura cannot be accommodated by either the play or the world and he explodes (Act One), burns (Act Two) and disappears (Act Three).

The abundant use of the colon and semi-colon in the play is an indication of the nature of the language, which is both self-conscious and halting, lacking in conjunction. The characters are very aware of the words they use and listen to (the essence of 'marivaudage' according to Deloffre). There is a lot of acting (I am out to impress you, to impress myself, to fool you, to fool myself) and the translator is constantly reminded that he is translating, to some degree or another, a linguistic performance. No one is ever relaxed. There is a lot of intelligence around, but the brilliance, like the silver in the cupboard, needs a clean.

What draws me to this play is its ambivalence, the strain between word and feeling, the emotional versatility which conceals the deeper, hidden hurt.

CHARACTERS

FRONTIN
} *the* CHEVALIER's *servants*
TRIVELIN

CHEVALIER

LELIO

HARLEQUIN

COUNTESS

SINGER

PEASANT

Act One

Scene 1

FRONTIN. It can't be. No! It is! Trivelin! And in person. Good Lord. How are things with you, my dear friend?

TRIVELIN. Couldn't be better, Frontin. Things couldn't be better. I've lost neither of those two essential riches which have always attended me. I'm still healthy and hungry! But what about you? Last time I saw you, you were about to make the big time in Paris. What happened? Rich and retired?

FRONTIN. Bust and ruined more like, my dear boy. But how has fortune treated you in the meantime?

TRIVELIN. In the way she normally treats men of worth.

FRONTIN. Badly.

TRIVELIN. Precisely. I do however owe fortune a debt. She has taught me to do without her. I am no longer envious. No longer forced to live in her shadow. Which suits me nicely. A man of reason could ask no more. I am not fortunate. But I am not bothered not to be fortunate. That's my school of thought.

FRONTIN. My my! I've always known you to be quick-witted. And scheming. But philosophical! You have come a long way! You've already turned your back on material things!

TRIVELIN. Hold your horses, my dear friend. Not so fast. You're making me blush. And the compliment is perhaps not wholly merited. My scorn for fortune could be nothing but a sham. Words, words, words. Worse – but this is strictly for your ears only – I wouldn't advise anyone to let their material things fall within the clutches of my philosophy. Because – and I can feel it in my fingers – I would purloin them. Oh yes, I would, Frontin. I'd purloin. Play truant from my school of thought. Deep down, man is nothing but a naughty boy.

FRONTIN. Truth sadly must out. I'm forced to agree.

TRIVELIN. This truth I would of course not normally noise abroad. But something tells me I'm preaching to the converted.

FRONTIN. One question, my friend. What's in your bag?

TRIVELIN. Bag?! This is no bag! This is luggage. This packet contains all my worldly possessions.

FRONTIN. An attractively compact, self-contained property . . .

TRIVELIN. Over the fifteen odd years that I've been making my way in this world of ours, you know the lengths to which I've gone in my attempt to settle down. It had come to my notice that scrupulous men rarely make money. So, to give myself an even chance, I laid scruples aside. If it was profitable to be honorable, then I was a man of honour. If I deemed it pertinent to be devious, then, once my conscience had heaved a deep sigh of regret, I was devious. On occasions I have indeed been rich. But how is one to lend permanence to such a situation, when our path is littered with rocks? The odd flutter, the odd fling, the odd beverage. How is one to avoid temptation?

FRONTIN. True.

TRIVELIN. What else can I say? One day upstairs. The next day downstairs. Ever prudent. Ever industrious. Befriending crooks by design and gentlemen by inclination. Respected in one disguise, horse-whipped in another. Swapping employment, clothes, lifestyle, personality. Taking risks. Making peanuts. On the surface respectable, deep down a libertine. Suspected by some, spotted by others, dubious for everyone. I owe money left, right, and centre. My debtors fall into two categories. Those who don't know they've lent me money. And those who do. And who will continue to know that I do for a long time yet. My lodgings? Anywhere and everywhere. Pavement, inn, doss-house. I've been entertained by the bourgeois and the aristocrat. Even had my own place once. And, when I fell on hard times, the halls of justice extended their welcoming arms. But these latter apartments are somewhat gloomy. So I chose not to stay too long. In all, my dear friend, after fifteen years of blood, sweat and tears, this unprepossessing packet is all I own. This is what the world has chosen to give me. Pretty mean, don't you think? My contribution deserves a larger reward. Given so much. Received so little.

FRONTIN. Don't complain, my friend. The only unhappy chapter in your story concerns your brush with the law. But none of that. You arrive at a most opportune moment. I have a proposition. But first things first. What precisely have you been doing over the last two years? Where have you just come from?

TRIVELIN. Primo. Since last we met, I entered service.

FRONTIN. Joined the army? You're not a deserter, I trust?

TRIVELIN. Wrong uniform. Domestic service, my friend.

FRONTIN. Now that is good news.

TRIVELIN. But. Before stooping to this final humiliation, I sold my wardrobe.

FRONTIN. You had a wardrobe?

TRIVELIN. I did, yes, own one or two ... suits ... which I had picked up second- ... third-hand ... and which enabled me at certain times to pass as a gentleman. I felt compelled to part with them. In order to put behind me all that might remind me of my past grandeur. If one is to renounce vanity, there's no beating about the bush. I took a decision. I burnt my boats. Took the irremediable step. Sold the lot. And drunk the proceeds.

FRONTIN. Wonderful.

TRIVELIN. Indeed, my friend. I had the courage to indulge in one or two salutary bouts of profound debauchery which served to empty my purse and to clinch my determination to pursue my course of action. Thus, as I drank myself to oblivion, I had the extraordinary pleasure of telling myself that the hand on the bottle was the hand of reason. Sublime. So. One morning I wake up. And there's not a penny left. But, being of a resourceful nature, and as there was no time to lose, I followed the advice of a passing acquaintance who led me to the house of a gentleman who was married, but who had given himself over to the study of dead languages. This situation I did not find displeasing. I am not without education myself. I thus took up residence. And, day in day out, all I heard was educated talk. My employer was very keen on certain people that he called the Ancients. And he nurtured a keen dislike for others that he called the Moderns. I had him explain all this to me.

FRONTIN. And what's it all about?

TRIVELIN. One moment. Let me get it straight. There's an Ancient ... What's his name? The Big Noise. As it were Homer. That mean anything to you?

FRONTIN. Nothing.

TRIVELIN. Pity. Homer was a man with a very distinct command of Greek.

FRONTIN. He wasn't French?

TRIVELIN. Hardly. I think he came from Quebec. Somewhere in the region of Egypt. This, of course, was all at the time of the Flood. He left us a number of most attractive satires. My master enjoyed him a great deal. As he did indeed many of Homer's contemporaries. Virgil. Nero. Plutarch. Ulysses. Diogenes.

FRONTIN. Never heard of any of them. What horrible names!

TRIVELIN. Horrible! That's because you never heard of them. Allow me to inform you that the sum total of the intelligence these names represents is greater than that contained in the Kingdom of France.

FRONTIN. It's not me who's going to prove you wrong. But what about the Moderns?

TRIVELIN. You are inciting me to digression. But no matter. Now the Moderns. How best can I put it? The Moderns are, for instance ... you.

FRONTIN. Me?! I'm Modern?!

TRIVELIN. Absolutely. Without just having been born, it would be difficult to be more Modern.

FRONTIN. And what had your master got against us Moderns?

TRIVELIN. His contention was the following. If you weren't

4000 years old, you were no one. In order to get in his good books, I started getting excited by everything old. Furniture, fashions, coins, medallions, glasses. I bought old hats. Never spoke to anyone under seventy. He thought I was the bees knees. I had the key to the cellar where he kept . . . guess what? . . . old wine! 'The Greek vintage', he called it. He used to give me the odd drop. And I took it upon myself to . . . purloin the odd bottle. My enthusiasm for things old getting the better of me, as it were. Not that I was oblivious to the charms of the young wine. That's what his wife gave me. She liked the young better than the old. That was her penchant. So, without in any way stooping to the flirtatious, I used to have a little tipple of the contemporary. Just for politeness' sake.

FRONTIN. Marvellous.

TRIVELIN. And one would think, would one not, that such conciliatory conduct would have kept me in the good books of both parties. Nothing of it. They got wise to my diplomacy. And they got shirty. The husband thought I was insulting the Ancients because I was drinking so much Modern wine, and the wife the versa because of the vice. It was no good being appallingly apologetic. They just wouldn't listen to reason. So, unable to choose between the Ancients and the Moderns, I had to pack my bag. Was I in the wrong?

FRONTIN. Not in the least. You were prudence itself. But I can't listen to you any longer. I'm being sent for the night to Paris. So, I'm looking for someone to take my place while I'm away. Shall I introduce you to my master?

TRIVELIN. With pleasure. But what kind of master is he? What I mean is, does he like eating? Because in my present condition I'm in need of good food.

FRONTIN. No problem there. You'll be serving the most considerate girl . . .

TRIVELIN. You said 'master'.

FRONTIN. I'm stupid. My mind's going. I don't know what I'm talking about.

TRIVELIN. Frontin. You wouldn't be having me on, Frontin?

FRONTIN. All right. Yes. I am. My master is my mistress. A girl dressed up as a man. I didn't mean to tell you. But it slipped out. I've boobed. Like an idiot. All I ask is that you keep quiet about it.

TRIVELIN. You know me full well to be the very incarnation of discretion. So what's the game? You and this girl up to something?

FRONTIN. Yes. (*Aside.*) I told him her sex. But I can still keep quiet about her status. (*Aloud.*) But here she comes. Step back a bit. I'll broach the matter with . . . her.

TRIVELIN *steps back and keeps a respectful distance.*

Scene 2

CHEVALIER. Well, Frontin. Have you found me a servant?

FRONTIN. Indeed I have, mistress. By chance I . . .

CHEVALIER. You're annoying me, Frontin. Let's stick to 'sir', shall we? Cut the mistress.

FRONTIN. I beg your pardon, miss. Blast. Sir. I just happened upon an old acquaintance. A most reliable person. Who has only just left the employment of a country gentleman. Who's dead. He's standing over there. Ready to step forwards and pay his respects.

CHEVALIER. I trust you weren't stupid enough to tell him who I was?

FRONTIN. On that score you can set your mind at rest. I know how to keep a secret. (*Low.*) Until it slips out. Would you be requiring my acquaintance to step forward?

CHEVALIER. Of course I would. And I'd be requiring you to leave for Paris immediately.

FRONTIN. You just have to give me the despatches.

CHEVALIER. I've changed my mind. I'm not going to give them to you. You could lose them. And my sister, to whom I was to send them, she could lose them as well. I don't want anyone to get wind of my adventure. Here's what you have to do. Listen carefully. Tell my sister she is not to worry. Tell her this. Some girlfriends of mine recently took me to a masked ball. I was wearing the disguise that I'm wearing now. At that ball I met by chance a man I'd never seen before. A man who was not supposed to be there, but to be away in the country. This man turned out to be none other than Lelio, with whom my sister's husband had contracted my marriage by letter. Surprised to see him secretly in Paris, surprised to see him in the company of another woman, I resolved there and then to use my disguise to delve more deeply into his heart and into his mind. We were a couple of bachelors on the loose so we hit it off immediately. He invited me to go with him the next day to a party in the country at the house of the woman in whose company he had arrived. She was accompanied by a relative. This is what you must tell my sister. Tell her that this is how things stand at the moment. That I have already uncovered certain things that I must pursue before making the decision whether or not to marry Lelio. Nothing could be more vital to my happiness. Leave immediately. Don't waste any more time. Your servant friend can now step forward. In a moment I shall make sure that you have already left.

Scene 3

CHEVALIER (*alone*). This encounter with Lelio was a present fate made me. A present I don't intend to squander. I am my own . . . master. No ties. No dependants. My enterprise will in no way surprise my sister. She knows the way I am. I have money.

When I marry I shall be handing over a fortune with my heart. I want to know exactly who is going to get both me and it.

Scene 4

FRONTIN. Here he is, sir. (*Low.*) Remember. Just keep the secret.

TRIVELIN. Safe in a box ready to be returned to you where and when you want it. (FRONTIN *exits.*)

Scene 5

CHEVALIER. Step forward. What's your name?

TRIVELIN. Take your pick. There's no shortage of names for servants. Bourguignon, Champagne, Poitevin, Picard. All the same to me. The name you choose to call me will be the sweetest in the world.

CHEVALIER. Cut the compliments. What's your real name?

TRIVELIN. To tell the truth, I'm loathe to tell you. You see I'm the first of my family who is not his own master. But. To wear your colours rather than mine, can you imagine anything more gallant?! I just long for your livery!

CHEVALIER. What kind of language is this? He's very strange.

TRIVELIN. None the less, sir, may I introduce myself. My name is Trivelin. A name I received quite correctly, handed down as it was from father to son. No hokey-pokey. And of all the Trivelins there ever was, this Trivelin here present, yours truly, considers himself the most fortunate.

CHEVALIER. I said, forget the elegance. All a master requires of a servant is that he should serve.

TRIVELIN. A servant! The word's a hard one. It reeks of humiliation. Couldn't we dispense with it?

CHEVALIER. You are uncommonly sensitive.

TRIVELIN. Let's come to an agreement. Let's find something more attractive.

CHEVALIER. You must be joking.

TRIVELIN. The prospect of being joined to you in servitude does, it is true, mitigate the mortification.

CHEVALIER. Listen. I shall not be requiring your services. You are dismissed. I don't want you.

TRIVELIN. You don't want me?! You can't be serious!

CHEVALIER (*low*). This man is most singular. Would you please go.

TRIVELIN. I can't. It's the sting. You stung me. I can't go until you've told me that you want me.

CHEVALIER. Will you please leave.

TRIVELIN. Where shall I wait?

CHEVALIER. Nowhere.

TRIVELIN. Look. Let's cut the patter. Time's getting on. But we're not.

CHEVALIER. May I tell you, my friend, that you are sticking your neck out.

TRIVELIN. I've got nothing else to lose.

CHEVALIER. He's getting on my nerves. I'll have to leave. (*Turns.*) Are you following me?

TRIVELIN. No. I'm following my instinct. Did I omit to tell you? I'm pig-headed as well.

CHEVALIER. Don't be insolent.

TRIVELIN. Don't be cruel.

CHEVALIER. I beg your pardon.

TRIVELIN. Cruel, I said. Like lovers say. Carry on like that and you'll see. I'll be reduced to sighs and tears. I can feel it coming on.

CHEVALIER. What am I supposed to make of all this?

TRIVELIN. Ha. Aha. Now, Chevalier. Now you're beginning to ask yourself questions. You're pausing to wonder. Your anger subsides. You're becoming reasonable. We can come to an agreement. I know we can. I am taken with a veritable desire to enter your service. Nothing can stop me now. It's in my blood.

CHEVALIER. And I am taken with the desire to treat you as you deserve. (*Hand to sword.*)

TRIVELIN. Come off it! Stop making threatening gestures. They're out of character. Let go of that sword. It's obvious you've never touched one in your life. I can tell you. There's more steel in your eyes than in this limp appendage.

CHEVALIER. He knows the secret.

TRIVELIN. Truth must out. I know what you are.

CHEVALIER. Do you?

TRIVELIN. Yes. Frontin let on.

CHEVALIER. He told you who I was?

TRIVELIN. Not who. What. He said his master was a woman. Full stop. And I believed him. I don't quibble. I take people as they come.

CHEVALIER. If the cat's out of the bag you might as well know the rest.

TRIVELIN. Fine. Why are you dressed-up like that?

CHEVALIER. My intentions are innocent.

TRIVELIN. Of course they are. If you'd have wanted to do mischief, you'd have remained a woman.

CHEVALIER (*aside*). I'll deceive him. (*Aloud.*) I'll tell you why I hid the truth from you. I am disguised because my mistress, a woman of both means and merit, has set her sights on Monsieur Lelio. Someone you will soon meet. She wants to lure him away from the Countess, the owner of this castle, and the present object of his attentions.

TRIVELIN. And what precisely is your brief with this Monsieur Lelio? Your mission seems a trifle doubtful. Sweetheart.

CHEVALIER. Not in the least. My mission is that, dressed-up as a man, I should try and win the heart of the Countess. I pass, you can judge for yourself, as quite an attractive young man. The Countess has already given me one or two lingering looks. If I can make her fall in love with me, I can prise her away from

Lelio. He would then return to Paris, where my mistress is waiting for him. She has a lot in her favour and he already knows her. Marriage would soon follow.

TRIVELIN. That accounts for the upstairs interests. Now for the downstairs. Is your heart unattached?

CHEVALIER. Yes.

TRIVELIN. Mine too. On a quick reckoning that makes both of us. Right?

CHEVALIER. Correct.

TRIVELIN. Therefore. *Ergo*. There's no reason why these two hearts shouldn't hit it off.

CHEVALIER. If you like.

TRIVELIN. And I also conclude, in an extremely judicious manner, close friends always being ready to do each other a good turn, that you give me two months' pay in advance. In recognition of the very real discretion that shall henceforth characterise the services I shall render. We'll leave aside the other domestic services I shall undertake on your behalf. With respect of those, love shall be my reward.

CHEVALIER (*gives him money*). Here. Six pounds. An advance. To keep your mouth closed. And three more. For the other services.

TRIVELIN. My principles incite me to refuse the last three. But hand them over all the same. Your very presence intimidates my ideals.

CHEVALIER. Lelio is approaching. Leave us, and wait for me at the castle gate.

TRIVELIN. Remember ... miss. I'm your servant on stage. But your lover in the wings. You can give orders in public ... But in private, the giving will be accompanied by a little taking ... (*He moves off.* LELIO *approaches.* HARLEQUIN *and* TRIVELIN *exchange greetings.*)

Scene 6

LELIO *has an absent air.*

CHEVALIER. Lelio appears to be deep in thought.

HARLEQUIN (*to* TRIVELIN). You look like someone out for a good time.

TRIVELIN. My face doesn't lie. You read me well.

LELIO (*turns towards* HARLEQUIN. *Sees the* CHEVALIER.) Harlequin . . . Ah. Chevalier. I was looking for you.

CHEVALIER. What's wrong, Lelio? You worry me. You look preoccupied.

LELIO. I'll explain the problem. Harlequin. Go tell the musicians to be ready.

HARLEQUIN. Yes, sir. (*To* TRIVELIN.) Let's go and have a drink. To speed on our friendship.

TRIVELIN. A good idea. In matters of the heart, I'm all for haste.

Scene 7

CHEVALIER. Well, my dear friend. What is it? What's wrong? Can I be of any help?

LELIO. You could be of great use to me.

CHEVALIER. Just tell me how.

LELIO. Do you count yourself a real friend?

CHEVALIER. You deserve a negative reply for even having asked the question.

LELIO. Don't be annoyed. The very quickness of your temper is flattering. Forget what I asked. I have another question.

CHEVALIER. Better luck this time.

LELIO. Are you a man of scruples?

CHEVALIER. Within reason.

LELIO. I'll describe the kind of person I'm after. Have you that misconceived sense of honour which causes fools to stumble over trifles?

CHEVALIER (*aside*). An ugly overture.

LELIO. For example. A lover who deceives his mistress, in order to get shot of her. Is he any less a gentleman in your eyes?

CHEVALIER. Look. Do you mean all you've just been talking about is infidelity?

LELIO. Correct.

CHEVALIER. About being treacherous?

LELIO. Nothing more, nothing less.

CHEVALIER. From the way you began the least I suspected was arson! Come, come, sir. To deceive a woman is an act which is in itself both disinterested and courageous.

LELIO (*smiling*). If you look at it like that, then I'm beyond reproach. In fact, and in all modesty, you see standing before you a deeply courageous man.

CHEVALIER (*as if admiring and impressed*). Let me get a good look at you. Let me observe a man who has such honourable crimes to his record. You devil! You are only to be admired for having chalked up so many dirty victories.

LELIO. I like the way you put it. Allow me to embrace you. And how many reputations have you wrecked? How many stately vessels have come apart on the reef of your affections? Naxos must be crowded with your cast-offs.

CHEVALIER. There you get me wrong. I know of no one whose adventures with women are more boring than mine. I've always had the misfortune of meeting level-headed women.

LELIO. Level-headed women?! And where in hell did you find them? That must be an extremely rare breed! What's the point of a woman being level-headed? There is no point. If a man's happy, he says so. If he's not, he lies. So as far as she's concerned, the truth makes no difference. In my own experience I've told the truth more often than I've lied.

CHEVALIER. You speak of these matters with an attractive lightness.

LELIO. Let's get down to the matter in hand. One day I'll tell you stories which will make you fall about. Now if I read things correctly, you must be the youngest of your family. With the result that you have very little money.

CHEVALIER. Your analysis is correct.

LELIO. You are good-looking. You are well built. Guess why I invited someone as charming as you to follow me here? Because I want to beg of you to make your fortune.

CHEVALIER. No need to beg. But more of my fortune.

LELIO. All you have to do is to arrange things so that the Countess falls in love with you. You then win her heart and marry her.

CHEVALIER. You must be joking. I happen to know that you are in love with the Countess.

LELIO. You're wrong. I'm not. I was, until a few days ago, when suddenly it came to my notice that it was in my interest not to be in love anymore.

CHEVALIER. You mean ... When you're in love and you no longer want to be in love, all you have to do is to switch off?! You have a very novel relationship with your heart.

LELIO. In matters of love, I do with my heart what I will. I used to be in love with the Countess. Because she is attractive. I was to marry her. Because she is rich. And because I had nothing better to do. But, recently, while I was at my country retreat, I received a letter proposing marriage with a woman in Paris whom I'd never met, but who has an annual income of 12,000 francs. The Countess has only six. So I took paper and pencil and worked it out. Twelve was unavoidably better than six. Could the love I felt for the Countess resist such overwhelming arithmetic? I would risk exposing myself to ridicule. Six must give way to twelve. Don't you agree? You're very silent.

CHEVALIER. What can I say in the face of such devastating mathematics? If you know how to count, it's obvious that you're right.

LELIO. So you take my point?

CHEVALIER. But what I don't understand is why you hesitate. If it's just a matter of ditching the Countess, where's the problem? It's simply a question of being unfaithful. All you have to do is to go and find her, show her the piece of paper and say: 'Add it up for yourself. See if I've got my sums wrong. That's all there is to it.' Maybe she'll cry. Maybe she'll have some disparaging things to say about arithmetic. She might call you a wretch, a traitor. She might even go as far as to say you are chicken-hearted. But for someone like you, for someone for whom scruples are mere trinkets, such insults can only amuse. You will listen attentively, proffer a half-hearted excuse and leave, bowing deeply, in the manner of a man who knows how to behave in society and how a gentleman, when called a heartless deceiving villain, merely turns the other cheek.

LELIO. Those insults I've indeed heard often before. And time has taught me how to bow out gracefully. The Countess would already have been gratified with my final performance if all I had to do to disappear was to be elegant. But there is a hitch. A short while ago I wanted to buy some land. The Countess lent me 10,000 francs. For which I signed a promissory note.

CHEVALIER. I see. That is another matter altogether. However deeply you bow, it's difficult to erase a debt. To be unfaithful only exposes one to reproach. To be in debt exposes one to the law. And that's a different kettle of fish. I have no remedy for that problem.

LELIO. Not so fast. The Countess is under the impression that she is going to marry me. She is merely waiting for her brother to turn up. Now, before we drew up the loan agreement, we signed a forfeit. For the same sum. The contract stipulates the following. If I break with her, I owe her both the debt and the forfeit. And I would dearly like to pay neither. If you see what I'm getting at.

CHEVALIER (aside). Oh, the honest dealer. (Aloud.) Yes. I think I begin to get the picture. This is how it goes. If I can get the

Countess to fall in love with me, you reckon she'd be happier to forgo the debt and the forfeit rather than to marry you. That would mean you'd make 10,000 francs out of her. Right?

LELIO. Correct.

CHEVALIER. Your plan is ingenious and lucrative. A jewel in your crown. And, when all is said and done, the honour you did the Countess in deigning once to love her, is well worth a mere 10,000 francs.

LELIO. I think she might find your estimation of me a little on the generous side . . .

CHEVALIER. But do you think that I could win the heart of the Countess?

LELIO. No problem. I'm sure of it.

CHEVALIER (*aside*). At least on that point we are in agreement.

LELIO. I've noticed. She likes being in your company. She speaks highly of you. Finds you have an attractive mind. All you have to do is to press home the advantage.

CHEVALIER. I can't admit to being particularly drawn to marriage with the Countess.

LELIO. Why not?

CHEVALIER. I have my own reasons. I could never love her. I could be a close friend. That would present no problem. But that's by the by.

LELIO. Who's asking you to love her? Is it necessary to love a wife? If you don't love her, too bad. That's her problem, not yours.

CHEVALIER. I was under the impression that one was supposed to love one's wife. That if one didn't it . . . soured the atmosphere.

LELIO. All the better. If the atmosphere's bad, you don't even have to see her. Which is always an advantage.

CHEVALIER. Now I get it. And I'm ready to put your plan into action. If I do marry the Countess, I'll just have to turn to Lelio for a few lessons in scorn.

LELIO. No worry on that account. Just watch me and take note. The woman in Paris, for example. Do you think I'm going to love her? For a couple of weeks at the most. After that the novelty will wear off.

CHEVALIER. Come, come. She does have an income of 12,000 pounds. Surely she deserves a month.

LELIO. Only the heart dictates.

CHEVALIER. What's she like? Any idea?

LELIO. In the letter I read that she is beautiful. But, in my present frame of mind, that makes precious little difference. If she's not ugly yet, she will be soon. Because she'll be my wife. There's no getting away from it.

CHEVALIER. But don't women sometimes . . . react?

LELIO. If she . . . reacts, then she can cool off at my country place. Which happens to be miles from anywhere. Let off steam in the desert.

CHEVALIER. I see. If you happen to own a place in the country, all's well and good. Nothing like solitude for inducing calm. And the countryside does have a certain melancholic charm. It is sad. It is quiet. The colours are so restful. There are so many pleasures to choose from.

LELIO. She can take her pick.

CHEVALIER. You really have got things nicely worked out. (*Looking off.*) But I can see the Countess. I'd just ask one thing of you. Continue to pretend that you're still in love with her. If once she doubts of your affections, her vanity will be tickled and she'd run after you. Leaving me high and dry.

LELIO. I'll play my part very carefully. And I'll leave before she gets here.

The COUNTESS *has not yet arrived.* LELIO *leaves. The* CHEVALIER *speaks as* LELIO *goes.*

Scene 8

CHEVALIER (*alone*). If I had married Lelio I would have found myself in most attractive company! To surrender 12,000 francs for the pleasure of a lonely country holiday . . . No thank you, Mr Lelio. Your price is too high. I can get better cheaper. But, as the game has begun, why stop playing? I can punish a rogue, save the Countess and enjoy myself.

Scene 9

LELIO (*to the* COUNTESS *as she enters*). I was waiting for the musicians, madame. I'll go and tell them to hurry. I'll leave you in the company of the Chevalier. He says he wants to leave us. He is uneasy in this house. I think that you intimidate him. Which, of course, is quite understandable. I don't find him at all odd. I know the effect you have. But the Chevalier is my friend and it would be a pity to see our friendship evaporate so rapidly. He'll just have to get used to braving the danger of seeing you. Try and bring him to his senses. I'll be back in an instant.

Scene 10

COUNTESS. What's this all about, Chevalier? Fancy going to such lengths! Inventing such complicated excuses for leaving us! If you told us the real reasons, perhaps we'd be more willing to let you go.

CHEVALIER. Lelio has just told you my real reasons.

COUNTESS. I beg your pardon! You mean, you really can't trust your heart in my presence?

CHEVALIER. Trust?! It's a bit late for trusting. You didn't even give me a chance to try. The deed, I'm afraid, was already done.

The malady implanted. It's now just a question of stopping its progress.

COUNTESS (*laughing*). Poor Chevalier. You really are to be pitied. I had no idea I was so contagious.

CHEVALIER. Oh, but you are. And I am only telling you what is obvious. What your mirror must tell you every morning. Your eyes are such that, in bringing me into your house, you invite a violation of the rules of hospitality.

COUNTESS. My mirror is not of the flattering kind, Chevalier.

CHEVALIER. Indeed I would defy it to flatter you! Mirrors are mean with praise. It is nature that has flattered you. Nature that has composed your features.

COUNTESS. I cannot see that these gifts have been so extravagant.

CHEVALIER. Countess, you would be doing me a great service if you would lend me your dispassionate point of view. From where I'm standing, calm is impossible.

COUNTESS (*laughing*). You are extremely gallant.

CHEVALIER. I am more than that. If I were nothing but gallant, there'd be no problem.

COUNTESS. In any event, you mustn't hesitate, Chevalier. Some love-affair is doubtless calling you back to Paris. You will only be bored if you stay here.

CHEVALIER. No. I have no loves in Paris. Unless, that is, you come with me. (*He takes her hand.*) As for boredom. If you discover how to inspire boredom in me when I'm in your presence, then please do. You would be doing me a real favour. It would even be a humanitarian gesture. But that is beyond you. You only know how to inspire love. That is your real talent.

COUNTESS. It is something I do badly.

Scene 11

LELIO. The musicians won't be ready until later, madame. But here is a village wedding come to entertain you. (*To the* CHEVALIER.) Your valet and mine are leading the dance.

Divertissement

SINGER:

This is the song of Lucas,
Who went out and bought himself Colette.
Nice shopping. Lucky lad.
I'd go for marriage myself,
If it wasn't for one problem . . .
When you marry, even the most reluctant girl
Falls, crack, into your arms.
And then . . . catch us if you can!
There's no fun to beat
The first days of marriage.
But, alas, the bliss won't last.
The heart's not up to it, and more's the pity.

A PEASANT:

What do you think, gentle Mathurine,
Of this here wedding?
Doesn't it make you think about you and me?
Doesn't it tickle your fancy?
From the way you look,
I guess you've got secret feelings . . .
Friend Lucas and your cousin,
They're both going to have a good time.
They won't care what the others say.
Come on, Mathurine,
Him and her. It could be you and me.

MATHURINE:

What a way to speak!
And what a time to ask:
'What are you going to do? What are you not going to do?'

Let's get married.
Without all this fuss. You'll be the witness.
You'll soon know whether I mean it or not.
I often go up the valley.
You know where to find me. Cunning lad.
And it's better to lie on the grass
Than in front of a notary.

DANCE:

Say what you like, say what you will,
All this and all that,
I want to have a go at marriage.
I don't care what happens,
All this and all that;
I'll be damned if I won't try!
Courage, they say, disappears,
All this and all that;
But we'd like to see for ourselves!

One day my Claudine told me,
All this and all that,
That her mother got angry and told her
She wasn't to love me,
All this and all that;
But, straightaway, Claudine says to me:
Come for a walk in those woods over there,
All this and all that;
Let's find out for ourselves.

And when we got there, she started to sing,
All this and all that:
'Shepherd, tell me your heart loves me;
And mine will also tell',
All this and all that,
'How big its love is.'
And then she looked at me,

All this and all that,
With such a look that I was done for.

Then my heart in turn sang,
All this and all that,
A song so soft,
That for pleasure she sighed and sighed,
All this and all that,
And she wanted it again and again;
All this and all that,
So I started again and sang on,
All this and all that,
Until I could sing no more.

Act Two

Scene 1

TRIVELIN. Here I am, involved in an uninvolved kind of way, in an intrigue which promises to be reasonably profitable. I've already gained some money and a mistress. A nice start. Promising a happy end. Now, given that I am of a resourceful nature, can it be expected that I fold my arms, sit back and do nothing? Surely it would be more in character if I came to the aid of my dear master-stroke-servant? If I were to tell the Seigneur Lelio that the heart of the Countess is about to be conquered by the Chevalier, he would leave for Paris even faster. For Paris where we shall be waiting for him. I've already indicated respectfully that I craved the honour of an interview. But here he is, in conversation with the Countess. I'll wait until they've finished.

Scene 2

LELIO *and the* COUNTESS *enter in conversation.*

COUNTESS. No, sir. I'm afraid I don't understand. You form a friendship with the Chevalier and you invite him to my house. And now you want me to be offhand with him. This is all very strange. You yourself were the first to say that he was a very likeable person and, in effect, my judgement is only corroborating your own.

LELIO (*repeating the words*). 'In effect'! So he has had an effect, has he? I don't know quite what to think. Apart from the fact that I would be happier if this effect didn't exist.

COUNTESS. Unfortunately it does.

LELIO. You must be joking.

COUNTESS. How do you expect me to understand your abrupt dislike for the words 'in effect'. Was I ungrammatical? Have the words been suddenly banned from the language?

LELIO. No, madame. But these words suggest that you are more than somewhat impressed by the merits of the Chevalier.

COUNTESS. Do they?! In that case you are right to criticise and your objection can be upheld. But you must admit it yourself, that there is no real harm done when one simply shows oneself sensitive to merits which are undeniable. And that's all I've done in the case of the Chevalier.

LELIO. Just a minute. 'Sensitive to'. I don't like that either. 'Sensitive' is going too far. 'Aware of' you should say.

COUNTESS. I think I would probably do best to shut up altogether and wait until you've given me a complete list of terms I can and can't use. That would doubtless be the most . . . effective. It would appear that it is only under these conditions that we can carry on a conversation.

LELIO. Please, madame. Please remember. I am in love.

COUNTESS. And you must excuse my ignorance. But I really can't see what difference there is between 'sensitive to' and 'aware of'.

LELIO. 'Sensitive to' belongs to the language of love. And this is not the kind of language you should use when speaking of the Chevalier.

COUNTESS. Listen. I'm afraid I am not at all sensitive to the kind of language you are presently using. It is cold. It is insensitive. And, to be completely honest, it is most displeasing.

LELIO (*aside*). She will return the forfeit.

COUNTESS. Let's just leave each other alone for a while. I'm saying things I ought not to. And your replies are no better. The result hardly adds up to an attractive conversation.

LELIO. Are you going to rejoin the Chevalier?

COUNTESS. Lelio. You've just been giving me a lesson. May I give you one in return? There are moments when it would be much to your advantage if you weren't here. Understood?

LELIO. Clear as a bell. You can't stand being in my presence.

COUNTESS. I choose not to reply. Because I know what you'd do. You'd just go and dismantle what I say in order to find something wrong with it.

LELIO. But I can guess what it is you're not telling me. What you want to say and daren't is that you hate me.

COUNTESS. Wrong. It's not true. But if you persist as you are now, it won't be long before I do. And, given the person you are, you will persist.

LELIO. I almost get the impression you want me to.

COUNTESS. And if I did you would be only too happy to comply.

LELIO (*seemingly angry and cut to the quick*). I am deeply disappointed, madame.

COUNTESS. And I am exerting immense self-control, sir. Immense. (*She goes to leave.*)

LELIO. Just a moment, Countess. You did once reply favourably to my attentions.

COUNTESS. Ah. Now we are getting down to the nitty gritty.

LELIO. The existence of the forfeit we both signed . . .

COUNTESS (*angry*). What of it? If you find the forfeit irksome, all you have to do is to renounce it. Why didn't you say that was the problem in the first place? You've been beating about the bush for the last half hour . . .

LELIO. Renounce it?! That would be the last thing I'd do. It is my only guarantee of our marriage.

COUNTESS. And what is marriage without love?

LELIO. I am hoping to combine the two.

COUNTESS. Then why do you behave in such a displeasing fashion?

LELIO. What have I done to displease? You will be hard put to find an answer.

COUNTESS. First. You are jealous.

LELIO. Good God. What do you expect? When you're in love . . .

COUNTESS. Oh, the fiery temperament . . .

LELIO. Can one prevent oneself from being jealous? There were times when you criticised me for not being jealous enough. You found me too docile. Now I'm touchy, and you don't like that either.

COUNTESS. That's it. Go on. Go to the logical conclusion. Tell me I'm capricious. Because that's what you want to tell me. I know you do. That's the kind of compliment which is quite to be expected in the kind of conversation with which you've been regaling me for the last hour. And after all that, he asks me why I find him displeasing. What an obtuse man!

LELIO. But I didn't say you were capricious, madame. I simply said there was a time when you begged me to be jealous. Now that I am, I can't quite fathom why you aren't delighted.

COUNTESS. And after all that, you have the nerve to continue to uphold that you are not accusing me of being capricious!

LELIO. All I ask is that you reply.

COUNTESS. No, sir. I will not. And may I inform you that what you have just said has never been said to a woman before. You are the first person I have ever met who has dared to call me ridiculous.

LELIO (looking around him). I'm looking for the person you're talking to, madame. Because you can't be talking to me.

COUNTESS. And now he thinks I'm crazy! Strange in the head! Talking to myself! Wonderful. You just go on like that, sir. You just continue in that way. You do not want to renounce the forfeit. But, according to you, I do! Is that what you're getting at?

LELIO. You are going to such lengths to avoid asking yourself a very simple question to which you can't reply.

COUNTESS. I can't contain myself. Capricious. Ridiculous. Crazy. And now, to cap it all, in bad faith. What an attractive portrait! I really didn't know you, Monsieur Lelio. I really didn't appreciate you to your full value. You've been leading me astray. So I've been making you jealous, have I? Allow me then to tell you that your jealousy is quite unbearable. It is an odious, evil jealousy which is born of a vicious, twisted mind. It has nothing to do with delicacy. It is simply an expression of those bad moods which seem to inhabit your character. That was not the kind of jealousy I was after. I was looking for that gentle doubt, which comes from an agreeable lack of self-confidence. When you are jealous in that way, may I tell you, sir, you don't go around shouting invectives at the person you love. You don't go around telling them they are ridiculous, untrustworthy and soft in the head. On the contrary. One spends one's time wondering whether one is truly loved because one has doubts as to one's merits. But you couldn't understand that. That kind of feeling is foreign to your heart. All you are acquainted with are tempers, moods and trickery. You are suspicious for no reason whatsoever. You lack respect, humility, esteem. And you build your love on a forfeit. A contract! The rights you seek to exert are repressive. A forfeit, Monsieur Lelio! Suspicions and a forfeit! Is that love? If it is, it's a kind of love which gives me shivers down the spine. Farewell.

LELIO. May I say just one thing. You are angry. But you will return to me. Because deep down you respect me.

COUNTESS. Maybe. But there are a lot of other people I respect. And I don't know what is particularly respectful about respect. You are what you are.

LELIO. To attempt to mend our relationship, grant me one thing. I am deeply attached to you. The Chevalier is in love with you. Please be a little more cool towards him. Insinuate that it would be a good idea if he left. If he went back to Paris.

COUNTESS. Insinuate that he should leave us?! You mean whisper some impolite lie in his ear which would immediately make him think that I am the most discourteous of women? No, sir. I certainly will not. And you will please withdraw your request. Doubtless I should find all this most flattering. But however subtle the flattery, when it is absurd, as is yours, it remains absurd. Allow me to insinuate that sweet lesson in your ear. Just to give you a taste of the suggestion of which you are so fond. (*She leaves.*)

Scene 3

LELIO (*remains alone for a moment. Then laughs to himself*). Cheer up, Lelio. Things are coming along nicely. You'll marry your 12,000 francs. But here comes the Chevalier's servant. (*To* TRIVELIN.) You apparently have something to tell me?

TRIVELIN. That's right, sir. You will excuse the liberty I'm taking. My present livery doesn't exactly plead in my favour. But I can assure you, deep down, under all this, there beats the heart of a real gentleman. One who has a distinct weakness for people of distinction.

LELIO. I don't doubt it.

TRIVELIN. I myself, and I say this in all modesty, once belonged to the ranks of the privileged. But life has its ups and downs, does it not? And fate has played a few dirty tricks on me. As it is wont to do. The history of the world is full of accounts of its whims. Princes and heroes, all have been buffeted on the seas of misfortune, and I am happy to count myself a traveller in such distinguished company.

LELIO. You will do me the favour of curtailing your reflections and coming to the point.

TRIVELIN. Victims of fate tend to be loquacious, sir. They like to recount their mishaps in a self-pitying fashion. But I won't say any more and will merely trust that this short preface will, saving your grace, serve to elevate me in your esteem and to lend weight to what I am about to say.

LELIO. Of course.

TRIVELIN. You are aware of the fact that, at this present moment, I am employed as a domestic in the service of Monsieur le Chevalier.

LELIO. I did know that.

TRIVELIN. But I won't be staying long in his service. We're incompatible. His personality doesn't agree with me.

LELIO. And what's wrong with it?

TRIVELIN. How different you are from him, sir. The first time I saw you, the first time I heard you speak, I said to myself now there's someone who really speaks his mind. Now there's an honest soul.

LELIO. If you start singing my praises you're going to lose the track.

TRIVELIN. You must admit, sir, that exceptional merit does deserve the occasional digression.

LELIO. Come to the point.

TRIVELIN. Just one thing. Before we begin I'd like us to agree on one detail.

LELIO. Tell me what it is.

TRIVELIN. I am poor but I am proud. These two qualities you will admit make odd bedfellows. But, strange to say, they so often find themselves cohabiting. As in my case.

LELIO. Continue. And where do pride and poverty lead us?

TRIVELIN. They lead me to tell you of the war they're fighting one against the other. Pride at first resists. But the enemy is relentless. And soon pride finds itself wavering, retreating, then fleeing, leaving the country wide open to be raped by that scavenger, poverty. Poverty which is shameless and which, as a consequence, at this very moment solicits your generosity.

LELIO. I get it at last! You're asking for money for what you are about to tell me.

TRIVELIN. Correct. Generous souls have that peculiar ability of being able to detect need, and thereby of sparing one the shame of having to expose one's penniless condition. I find that very touching.

LELIO. I will consent to what you ask. On one condition. That the secret you have to tell me is worth the money I pay for it. You have my word. Now. Tell me.

TRIVELIN. What is it that leads the lack of money to impede your natural impulsive generosity? What a pity. But never mind. Your innate sense of justice will no doubt restore what your parsimoniousness has refused me. I shall begin. You count the Chevalier amongst your most intimate and faithful friends?

LELIO. I do.

TRIVELIN. Wrong.

LELIO. Why?

TRIVELIN. You think the Countess still loves you?

LELIO. I'm certain of it.

TRIVELIN. Wrong again. You couldn't be further from the truth.

LELIO. And why is that?

TRIVELIN. You will have to face up to it, sir. You have neither a friend nor a mistress. What a wicked world we live in. The Countess doesn't love you any more. The Chevalier has stolen her heart. He loves her. She loves him. There's nothing you can do about it. I know it. I've seen it with my own eyes. And I'm telling you. You would do well to begin seeing how you can make the most of what I just told you. Both for you and for me.

LELIO. Tell me. What makes you so certain this is the case?

TRIVELIN. Because I know how to read things. For instance. I've only got to look a woman in the eyes to know exactly what her feelings are and what her feelings will be. And that to an extraordinary degree of accuracy. Everything that goes on in her heart is written all over her face and I've been a student of that writing for such a long time that I can read it just as if it was my own. Another instance, for example. Just now while you were off picking a bunch of flowers in the garden for the Countess, I happened to be mending a fence near where she happened to be and I saw the Chevalier giggling, laughing and generally gambolling around her like a little lamb. 'Oh, you are so amusing,' she says to him, smiling in a negligent kind of way at his entertainments. Now anyone else but me would have seen nothing in that particular smile. But, for me, it was a sign to be decoded. And do you know what this smile said? It said, 'I find you most amusing, Monsieur le Chevalier. I like the way you carry on. Are you sensitive to the extent to which I find you pleasing?'

LELIO. Your interpretation is interesting. But tell me something that I can readily understand. Given that I am not as learned as you are.

TRIVELIN. Then I'll give you another example, which doesn't require any special training. The Chevalier continues in a like manner, stealing kisses which are ever scolded, never avoided. 'Oh . . . leave me alone,' she says, with an indolent expression on her face, and doing nothing whatsoever to move, seemingly too lazy to put herself out of harm's way. 'Really,' she says, 'honestly . . . you don't know what you're doing,' she adds. And me? All the while mending my fence, what do I do? I decode this 'honestly' and this 'stop it', 'really'. And I read between the lines. I see what she means: 'Pray carry on, Chevalier. Don't stop whatever you do . . . Have another one. Another little peck . . . Just like the last one. Take me by surprise. Just in case anyone is watching. I'm not going to grant you anything, but if you're clever you can take what you like. That way no one could ever find fault with me.'

LELIO. Ouch. Kissing. Now that is something.

TRIVELIN. But now we arrive at the most moving moments. 'Oh,' he says in reply. 'What a pretty little hand. Allow me to admire it.' 'Oh no,' she says, 'Really, you shouldn't. I don't want you to.' Nonetheless the hand is granted. Admired. Caressed. Things take their course . . . 'Stop it! Now! Really!' And I give you a little tap on the fingers with my fan. A gallant little reprimand which says, 'Naughty boy don't you stop whatever you do.' And I snatch the fan away . . . And I continue with my thieving. The other hand comes to the rescue. Got it! Both of them in captivity. 'What are you doing? This has really gone too far. Do you know what you are saying, madame?' . . . And then they get down to it. A lot of kissing of the Countess. Tender looks from the Chevalier. Blushing. Then the Chevalier starts to get a bit heated. And the Countess to get angry without meaning it. And he throws himself before her. At her knees, he is. And she, at that moment, gives a half sigh of pleasure. He, in reply, gives a whole one. Then we have silences. Tender glances. And others which have nothing to do with tenderness. And then, 'What does all this mean, sir?' 'You understand full well, madame.' 'Rise to your feet, sir.' 'Will you forgive me?' 'I don't know if I can.' And that was the state of play when you arrived on the scene. But I think we all now know where we all stand. Don't you?

LELIO. Things, yes, are beginning to take shape in my mind.

TRIVELIN. Beginning to take shape?! How far do I have to go to persuade you? I mean, I can hardly go much further, can I? There I was, present at the birth of love. But when love's grown up into a big boy, I can hardly hang around my fence waiting for him to come down and have a little frolic, can I? And grow up he will, if he hasn't already reached the age of consent. Because growth was rapid, I can tell you.

LELIO. Wonderfully rapid, indeed.

TRIVELIN. And what do you think of the Countess, then? I mean, you'd have married her if it hadn't been for me. If you'd have seen her! The way she gives her hand to the Chevalier. Gives? Abandons . . .

LELIO. Really? You had the impression that she found all this pleasurable?

TRIVELIN. I did, sir. (*Aside.*) But he seems to be getting a certain pleasure out of it as well! (*Aloud.*) Well? Have I earned my reward?

LELIO. Without doubt. You are a villain.

TRIVELIN. 'Without doubt. You are a villain.' Odd way to begin a vote of thanks.

LELIO. The Chevalier would horse-whip you if I told him of your treachery. The beating you deserve I shall, out of the goodness of my heart, spare you. I will say nothing of all this. Adieu. You should be content with your wages.

He leaves.

Scene 4

TRIVELIN (*alone*). That's a new kind of money to me. Farewell, sir. Your humble servant. May the heavens heap upon you all the favours that she should have bestowed on me. Well I never! Fortune has played me some weird games. But never one as odd as this. To thank you for your services, I will refrain from beating you up. I suppose everything passes as money nowadays. But I don't understand. I tell him that his mistress is going to dump him. And he asks if she is finding pleasure in her new relationship. Could it be that our pretend Chevalier has been having me on? Could they be even more friendly than I thought?

Scene 5

TRIVELIN (*aside*). Let's ask Harlequin what he thinks. (*Aloud.*) Ah. There you are. Where are you going?
HARLEQUIN. To see if any letters have arrived for my master.
TRIVELIN. You look worried. What's on your mind?
HARLEQUIN. Money.
TRIVELIN. Good heavens. A most rewarding preoccupation.
HARLEQUIN. I was also looking for you. Wanted to speak to you.
TRIVELIN. And what do you want to talk to me about, my friend?
HARLEQUIN. Money.

TRIVELIN. Again? That's not a brain-box. That's a money-box.

HARLEQUIN. Listen, my friend. Where did all that money come from that you had in your pocket just now? That you used to pay for the wine. If you know how to make it, you can slip me the secret.

TRIVELIN. My dear fellow. The only secret I can tell you is how to spend it. Not how to make it.

HARLEQUIN. I've got my own secret for spending. Did my apprenticeship . . . at the bar.

TRIVELIN. True. One can use wine to achieve ruin. But the process is slow. However, if to the recipe you choose to add a pinch of the opposite sex, the efficiency is greatly enhanced.

HARLEQUIN. Ah, women! A secret ingredient sadly lacking in this place.

TRIVELIN. You won't be spending your life here. But there is something I wanted to ask you. Your master and Monsieur le Chevalier. Do they like each other?

HARLEQUIN. They do.

TRIVELIN. Indeed. Are they very fond of each other? Do they get on really well together?

HARLEQUIN. They say things to each other like 'How are you?' They say. 'And me too. I've very pleased to hear it.' Then they have lunch and supper together. After which they say 'Good night.' Then they go to bed. And they sleep. Then it's the next day. What are they supposed to do? Tear each other's hair out?

TRIVELIN. Not at all, no. It's just that I had a reason for wanting to know, with regard to an intrigue in which I am at present involved.

HARLEQUIN. You?

TRIVELIN. Me. You see, I have moved the heart of a most lovable person. And if our masters hit it off, my stay here will be prolonged.

HARLEQUIN. And where might this rare, gentle-hearted person live?

TRIVELIN. Here, I said. I can tell you. This is all very serious.

HARLEQUIN. Lucky man. Young?

TRIVELIN. Nineteen. Twenty.

HARLEQUIN. A flower. Pretty?

TRIVELIN. Pretty?! The adjective is too paltry. It doesn't do her justice. She is charming, adorable. In a word, worthy of me.

HARLEQUIN (*moved*). Ouchigoochiegoochiegoochie.

TRIVELIN. And it is from her fair hand that I received the gold coin to which you made reference. A source which makes the gift even more valuable.

HARLEQUIN (*when he hears this, he drops his arms*). This is too much.

TRIVELIN (*aside*). I'm enjoying this. I'm going to make him sick with envy. (*Aloud.*) And that's not all. The way she speaks enchants me. The way she talks about me . . . I blush to think myself so lovable. 'Will you always love me,' she says? 'Will your heart always be mine?'

HARLEQUIN (*in a dream*). Yes, my dearest!

TRIVELIN. Who are you talking to?

HARLEQUIN. To her. I thought she was asking me.

TRIVELIN (*laughing*). And even as she spoke, she was seeking to invent new ways of proving her affection. Finally from her pocket she takes out this wholly delightful gold coin that you just saw. 'Pray accept this,' she says, slipping it into my hand. I, of course, always courteous, was slow to extend my palm. 'Please take it, please,' she says. 'This is only a meagre token of the treasure I intend to bestow on you.' So I gave in. You can't refuse a token

HARLEQUIN (*throws bat and belt onto the ground. On his knees*). I beg you, my dearest companion, I crave of you the permission to be shown the merest glimpse of the regal exterior of this unique vision who gives her purse with her heart. Who knows? Perhaps she'd also slip me a token. All I ask is that I should glimpse her, worship her and die.

TRIVELIN. Unthinkable, I'm afraid, my dear child. You mustn't imagine that what befalls me will necessarily befall you.

Between the ass and the stallion falls the shadow, my friend.

HARLEQUIN. And it is true. You are one of the world's greatest steeds.

TRIVELIN. Hold your horses, Harlequin. By all means hold me in esteem, but don't try to sing my praises.

HARLEQUIN. Just a glimpse. Just one glimpse . . .

TRIVELIN. Out of the question. Which doesn't mean that I'm not very fond of you. You'll profit from my good fortune. I'll give you a bottle of Burgundy for each day we manage to prolong our stay here.

HARLEQUIN (*almost in tears*). A bottle a day. That means thirty bottles a month. To console me in my grief at not seeing her, perhaps you would advance me the first month.

TRIVELIN. No, my friend. It is my intention to accompany you in drinking each day's pay.

HARLEQUIN (*goes to leave. Crying*). So I shall never see my queen. Where are you, dear sovereign of my heart? I am going to look for you everywhere. (*Stops, less confused.*) How about a little sip of today's salary?

TRIVELIN. My master is coming. I can't. But wait for me.

HARLEQUIN *leaves, and as he leaves he begins to sob again.*

Scene 6

TRIVELIN (*alone for a moment*). I'm sending him mad. Poor lad. But he's not got enough wit to take part in our intrigue. (*The* CHEVALIER *arrives.*) Ah. There you are, my one and only Chevalier. And how fare our interests?

CHEVALIER (*as if angry*). Extremely well, thank you, Monsieur Trivelin. But I was looking for you. I wanted to tell you. You're a no good.

TRIVELIN. A no good!? You wanted to see me so much to tell me so little?

CHEVALIER. In a word. You are a scoundrel.

TRIVELIN. There you go. Falling into the same trap as everyone else.

CHEVALIER. A traitor. And I shall have my revenge.

TRIVELIN. My worth has the peculiar quality of never having been recognised by anyone.

CHEVALIER. I'd very much like to know why you went and told Monsieur Lelio that I was in love with the Countess.

TRIVELIN. What?! You mean he's been telling you what I told him?!

CHEVALIER. Indeed, he has.

TRIVELIN. You do very well to tell me. In order to pay me for my frankness, he promised to be discreet. But he hasn't been. Therefore, the debt remains.

CHEVALIER. I see. So it was in order to extract money that you went and told him, was it? Rascal.

TRIVELIN. Rascal! Look. You'd do well to erase these little niceties from your vocabulary. They are figures of rhetoric I don't much like. So I was after money. That's true.

CHEVALIER. And hadn't I already paid you?

TRIVELIN. And hadn't I already gracefully accepted what you'd given me? What are you complaining about? Is your money so exclusive? Can't your money keep company? Is it so special it can't rub shoulders with Monsieur Lelio's?

CHEVALIER. You just take great care. If you start causing problems, my mistress will see to you. Be warned.

TRIVELIN. Enough. I can feel my discretion weakening. Getting very feeble, it is. Needs to be nursed. Needs a healing kiss. Or two.

CHEVALIER. Nothing doing.

TRIVELIN. Then convert affection into something else.

CHEVALIER. Nothing doing.

TRIVELIN. I don't think you quite follow me. And I can't bring myself to explain the riddle. (*The* CHEVALIER *takes a watch from his pocket.*) Ah! Now you're warm. Now you're cold. The

word is not 'watch'. But watch is close, because of the shape,
because of the metal.

CHEVALIER. I know exactly what you want. I give in.

TRIVELIN. I'd prefer a kiss.

CHEVALIER. Take that instead. (*Gives him money.*) But control
your tongue.

TRIVELIN. Ah my dearest. You play with my heart. But when you
slip through my fingers, you do it with such grace that I just
have to obey.

Scene 7

HARLEQUIN *returns. He has overheard the end of this last scene.*
Just as the CHEVALIER *gives the money to* TRIVELIN, HARLE-
QUIN *intervenes. With one hand he seizes the money. With the*
other he takes hold of the CHEVALIER *and kisses him.*

HARLEQUIN. Got it! Got her! Oh, my love. Oh, I die. I languish.
Dearest piece of gold. It's too much. Oh, Trivelin, I am
so happy!

TRIVELIN. And I am so robbed.

CHEVALIER. I despair. My secret is out.

HARLEQUIN. Let me just get a look at you. Dearest treasure.
She's so pretty. Oh, sweetness, I'm quite losing my heart to
you. I'm coming over quite queer. Quick. A potion. A secret
ingredient. A token to put me back on my feet.

CHEVALIER. Get him off me, can't you! What the hell's all this
token business?

TRIVELIN. You know what he wants. He wants money.

CHEVALIER. If it's just money . . . In order to see this affair
through to the bitter end . . . Take him away. Take him
somewhere secret. Tell him, and give him this to keep him

quiet. (*To* HARLEQUIN.) My dear Harlequin. Don't give me away. In return I'll give you as many tokens as you like. Trivelin will see to it. Just follow him, and say nothing. If you go and open your mouth, you'll get nothing.

HARLEQUIN. Don't you worry. I'll obey. But will you learn to love me? Little man.

CHEVALIER. Doubtless.

TRIVELIN. Come on, dear boy. Remember the bottle of Burgundy? Let's go and drink it.

HARLEQUIN (*doesn't move*). Let's go.

TRIVELIN. Come on. Come on. (*To the* CHEVALIER.) You go your own way. I'll see to everything.

HARLEQUIN. What a find! I struck it rich!

Scene 8

CHEVALIER (*a moment alone*). I'll just have to take the risk. Carry on regardless. My enterprise is too enjoyable to be abandoned. Even if it is to cost me the odd 20 francs here and there. I'm not going to let up. The Countess is coming. I sense that she is generally well disposed towards me. Let us now try to translate the general disposition into a precise inclination. You look sad, madame. What's wrong?

COUNTESS (*aside*). I must probe. See what he really thinks. (*Aloud.*) I have come to pay you a compliment which I find displeasing. But I don't know how to get out of it.

CHEVALIER. Our conversation gets off to a bad start, madame.

COUNTESS. You will certainly have noticed that I take pleasure in your company here. If it was only up to me, I would have even greater pleasure in seeing you more often.

CHEVALIER. I understand. And can spare you the trouble of going any further. I shall leave for Paris immediately.

COUNTESS. Whatever you decide, don't think it's because of me, that's all I ask.

CHEVALIER. I am not asking any questions. Your orders are mine to obey.

COUNTESS. And, please, don't say that I'm giving orders.

CHEVALIER. Madame, please, you are going to excessive lengths to excuse yourself to someone who merits neither the time nor the trouble.

COUNTESS. Don't, I said. That's all. And, in truth, if you want to stay, then stay. It's for you to decide.

CHEVALIER. You risk nothing in giving me freedom of choice. You know full well the extent to which I respect your real wishes.

COUNTESS. But Chevalier . . . whims are not to be respected.

CHEVALIER. Your language is most profoundly courteous.

COUNTESS. I can think of nothing more irritating than your obstinacy in always thinking me to be courteous. I am courteous. I have to be courteous. But maybe I am courteous in spite of myself. I am a woman. Women are proud. I am telling you to stay if you want to. I can't do any more. It's now up to you to do something for yourself.

CHEVALIER (aside). Her pride is melting. I shall make her suffer. (Aloud.) Adieu, madame. I am frightened of changing my mind. I am tempted to remain but must flee before the danger of misinterpreting your frankness. Adieu. You are dismissing me, and I leave, my heart in a pitiable state.

COUNTESS (aside). Have you ever heard anything like it? His heart must be deaf to sense.

CHEVALIER (turning). All that I ask, madame, is that you wait until I have gone, before you vent your scorn.

COUNTESS. Go on, then. Leave. I can't wait. Go to Paris where you will doubtless find women who can explain themselves more clearly than me. Who know how to tell you to stay in no uncertain terms. And who don't blush. Not in any circumstances. I, on the other hand, am aware of the acceptable limits. I know how far I can go. But if you do leave, it will only be because of your relentless determination to understand everything backwards.

CHEVALIER. Would you be pleased if I stayed?

COUNTESS. Is it polite or permissible to constrain a woman in such a way? To squeeze her between a yes and a no? To confront her with some brusque alternative or other? There's nothing more hateful than a man who is incapable of taking hints. Go. Go on. I'm fed up with taking the lead all the time.

CHEVALIER (*pretending to go*). I take the hint. And my leave.

COUNTESS. He takes the hint! He takes the hint and he leaves! How sensitive! How penetratingly intelligent! I have no idea why this man pleased me in the first place. And Lelio might just as well go at the same time. I wash my hands of both of them. I no longer want to be bothered by either of them. I hate men. They are unbearable. I'm finished with them for ever.

CHEVALIER (*returning with an afterthought*). It just struck me, madame. As I'm going to Paris, perhaps I can do something for you. Do you have any wishes?

COUNTESS. I certainly do. I wish that you should wipe immediately from your mind the fact that I had ever wanted you to stay here. That's all.

CHEVALIER. But that wish only gives birth to another. It's now obvious that I must stay. And that is the wish I shall obey.

COUNTESS. Do my ears deceive me? Is this a miracle? Have you understood at last? I must say, you require a great deal of patience and kindness from those around you. It's either that or nothing.

CHEVALIER. I love you. I can't presume that you should look upon me favourably.

COUNTESS. I didn't ask you to be presumptuous, either.

CHEVALIER. In that case there's no point in me staying.

COUNTESS. No point?! But you misunderstand everything. You should listen to what people say to you.

CHEVALIER. Then why don't you say what you want more clearly? I am leaving. You call me back. I am under the impression that if you retain me, it must be for a worthwhile reason. But nothing of the sort. You retain me to tell me that you didn't ask me to be presumptuous, either. Do you think that this is a tempting prospect? Because, madame, I do not intend to live according to those precepts. I couldn't. I love you too much.

COUNTESS. This love of yours is very headstrong. Very urgent.

CHEVALIER. I am not to blame. My love is how you gave it to me.

COUNTESS. Look. What exactly do you want?

CHEVALIER. To please you.

COUNTESS. Well. Who knows? Hope springs eternal.

CHEVALIER. Hope?! I'm not venturing into the realms of hope. Hope is unchartered territory. I'd soon lose my bearings.

COUNTESS. Press on. We'll see that you don't go astray.

CHEVALIER. If your heart is my travelling companion, I'll leave tonight.

COUNTESS. I don't know. Perhaps we wouldn't travel far together.

CHEVALIER. What makes you think that?

COUNTESS. The fact that I find you . . . fickle.

CHEVALIER. You had me frightened for a moment. I thought you suspected something more serious. As for 'fickle', if that's the only thing holding you back, we can embark immediately. When you know me better, you will soon see that I am not subject to that particular weakness.

COUNTESS. Let's talk more simply. I could, I suppose, find you pleasing. I won't contest it. But is it normal that I find you . . . pleasing . . . suddenly . . . just like that?

CHEVALIER. No, it is not. But if everything has to be natural between us, if that's the criterion, then I'm not going to get anywhere. Either you give me your heart, or we call it a day. If I am to wait until I've won it, nothing will ever happen between us. I know what you are. And what I am. That's the way it is.

COUNTESS. Confide in me. I have an open mind. I will perhaps forgive you.

CHEVALIER. You should forget the 'perhaps'. What you say would be all the more gracious.

COUNTESS. Let 'perhaps' be. 'Perhaps' its a little word that's only there for the sake of decorum.

CHEVALIER. It is certainly more pleasing in your last sentence.

COUNTESS. Because I wanted to reconcile you with 'perhaps'.

CHEVALIER. Let's get down to brass tacks. Are you ever going to love me?

COUNTESS. But, when all is said and done, do you love me yourself?

CHEVALIER. I do, madame. Yes. I have taken that bold step.

COUNTESS. But you've known me for such a short period of time. I can't stop myself finding it all somewhat surprising.

CHEVALIER. Surprising? You find that surprising, do you? What else surprises you? That the sun shines in the daytime?! Quite honestly I don't quite know how to reply. Do you really think it's necessary to see you for more than a second to fall head over heels in love with you?

COUNTESS. Please. Don't get worked up. I'm quite ready to believe you. But stop picking holes in everything I say.

CHEVALIER. Yes, Countess, I love you. Compared with all the men who have ever loved, there has never been one whose love is as pure and as reasonable as mine. I swear it to you on that sweet white hand of yours. That hand which is so ready to receive my kisses. Look at me, madame. Turn your gaze in my direction. Let me see the effect I have on you. You look at me in such a way . . . Your eyes are so beautiful. Who would ever have thought that they would have alighted on me?

COUNTESS. Look, that will do nicely for today. Please, give me my hand back. That's not where it belongs. You can speak just as well without it.

CHEVALIER. You allowed me to take it. Allow me to keep it.

COUNTESS. Don't despair. I'll leave it there until you have finished.

CHEVALIER. I shall never finish.

COUNTESS. Now I've forgotten what it was that I wanted to tell you. I came to see you with a precise purpose in mind but you haven't stopped distracting me. Let's be more business-like. You are in love with me. That's all well and good. But how are we going to manage? Lelio is jealous of you.

CHEVALIER. And I'm jealous of him. We're quits.

COUNTESS. He fears that you love me.

CHEVALIER. He's wrong to fear. He should be certain.

COUNTESS. He also fears that I am in love with you.

CHEVALIER. And why shouldn't you? He is so presumptuous. You should have told him, 'Yes, I am in love with the Chevalier.' That would have put paid to his fears.

COUNTESS. Not so fast, Chevalier. To say it, I'd have to think it.

CHEVALIER. But what is this? Didn't you say just now that you would forgive me?

COUNTESS. I said, 'perhaps'.

CHEVALIER. I knew that damned 'perhaps' wouldn't leave me alone. What better can you do than to love me? Is Lelio going to come out on top again?

COUNTESS. Lelio I begin to dislike more than somewhat.

CHEVALIER. May you be quick to hate him. That way we can be alone together.

COUNTESS. He has a very strange character.

CHEVALIER. He's the most difficult man I know.

COUNTESS. He's so abrupt, so disturbed. I don't know how to behave with him.

CHEVALIER. Cleverly is the best bet.

COUNTESS. But neither my intelligence nor my heart speaks in his favour.

CHEVALIER. Then there's nothing more to be said.

COUNTESS. Do you really think that's all there is to it? I'm afraid that you are probably right.

CHEVALIER. But afterwards, how will you dispose of your heart?

COUNTESS. Is this really your business?

CHEVALIER. Is this my business, she asks me?!

COUNTESS. You will have your answer all in good time.

CHEVALIER. Is it possible?

COUNTESS. What's wrong now?

CHEVALIER. There are times when your slowness drives me to despair.

COUNTESS. But you are so impatient, Chevalier. You're not like other people.

CHEVALIER. I can tell you, madame, when someone is in love with you, he does his best to be what he can.

COUNTESS. You must wait. I need to know you better.

CHEVALIER. There's not much to learn. I'm fast and I'm passionate. That's all there is to it. Look, I can suggest a solution which won't in any way embarrass you. If you don't like me, tell me to go and I'll go. There'll be no discussion. No recrimination. If, on the other hand, there is reason for me to hope, then don't say anything at all. Don't reply. Your very silence would send me into raptures. You won't even have to open your mouth. It must be said, you could hardly express yourself in more economical a fashion.

COUNTESS. Ah!

CHEVALIER. Bliss.

COUNTESS. And now it all comes back to me. I came to see you on Lelio's request. To ask you to leave.

CHEVALIER. You can forget Lelio. He no longer matters.

Scene 9

LELIO *arrives. He signals his joy to the* CHEVALIER.

LELIO. Not so fast, monsieur. Not so fast. Forget Lelio. Did I hear you right? You don't seem to think very highly of Lelio, do you?

But, thanks to chance and to the goodness of madame, you're going to have to think again. Because Lelio, whose merit is far greater than yours, is here to stay. Lelio remains. It is the Chevalier who is going to pack his bags. What do you think of that, madame? What do you say of my dear scrupulous friend? His behaviour is most admirable, don't you think?!

CHEVALIER. And what do you find to reproach in my behaviour, Monsieur Lelio? When I became your friend, did I take an oath to close my mind and heart to beauty, grace and to all that is lovable in the world? Indeed, I did not. Your friendship is one thing. My love for madame is another. And I can do without you, believe me. So you now have a rival. What's the problem? Take things as they come. Are you really surprised if madame decides she doesn't want to shut herself away with you? It seems to me that you have more and more occasion to be surprised. You'll just have to get used to it.

LELIO. I refuse to reply. The Countess will take it upon herself to punish your admirable intentions. (*To the* COUNTESS.) Would you care to take my hand, madame? I cannot for a moment imagine that you derive much amusement from such talk.

COUNTESS (*serious, moving back*). Where do you want me to go? We can, yes, go and walk together. I'm not complaining about the Chevalier. If he loves me, I find nothing untoward in the manner in which he expresses his love. My only reprimand might concern the unworthiness of the object of his affections.

CHEVALIER. Madame, I would find more people ready to understand my inclination than your reprimand.

LELIO (*angry*). Fine. Wonderful. I see things are advancing a pretty pace. And what am I supposed to do? I don't know what you think, madame, but . . .

COUNTESS. I don't like people who lose their temper. I'll talk to you when you've calmed down. (*Exits.*)

Scene 10

LELIO (*watches the* COUNTESS *disappear. When she has gone, he bursts out laughing.*). Foolish woman. Dupe. What did you think of my performance? The jealous Lelio . . . (*The* COUNTESS *returns to see what is happening.* LELIO *low.*) She's returned to spy. (*Aloud.*) We shall see, Chevalier. We shall see.

CHEVALIER (*low*). Oh the quick-witted criminal. (*Aloud.*) Farewell, Lelio. You can be as angry as you like. I give you my word. You shall see. Adieu.

They leave in different directions.

Act Three

Scene 1

HARLEQUIN *enters, crying.*

LELIO. Why the tears? I've got to know. (HARLEQUIN *cries even more.*) What are you crying for?

HARLEQUIN. It's all done for. I'll never be happy again.

LELIO. Why?

HARLEQUIN. Because I'll never want to laugh again.

LELIO. And why don't you want to laugh again? Idiot.

HARLEQUIN. Because of the grief. That's why.

LELIO. And I am asking you a question. Why are you grieving?

HARLEQUIN. Because of the chagrin. That's what's done it.

LELIO. He won't laugh because of the grief. He's grieving because of the chagrin. Could you possibly be a little more explicit? Otherwise I'm going to lose my temper.

HARLEQUIN. I promise you. I'm telling the truth. (*Deep sigh.*)

LELIO. But you're telling the truth in such a stupid way that I can't make head or tail of it. Has someone hurt you?

HARLEQUIN. Hurt me bad.

LELIO. Did someone beat you?

HARLEQUIN. Worse.

LELIO. Worse than a beating?

HARLEQUIN. When someone who is poor loses his gold, he just dies. So I'm going to die. No getting away from it.

LELIO. What do you mean. Gold?

HARLEQUIN. Peruvian gold. That's what they told me it was.

LELIO. You had some Peruvian gold?

HARLEQUIN. Once. Yes, I did. That's what it's all about. I haven't got it anymore. That's why I'm crying. When I had it, I was all right.

LELIO. Who gave you this Peruvian gold?

HARLEQUIN. The Chevalier. He gave me a present. A token.

LELIO. A token?

HARLEQUIN. That's what I just said.

LELIO. You need patience to talk to a cretin! But I'm going to get to the bottom of this. Harlequin, dry your tears. If you're in trouble, tell me and I'll put things right. But just explain yourself. What's all this business about Peruvian gold? About a token? I don't understand. Understand? Just reply carefully to my questions. The Chevalier gave you some gold?

HARLEQUIN. He didn't actually give it to me. He gave it to Trivelin. In front of me. To be given to me. But I never got it. That crook kept it all for himself. And that's not right.

LELIO. How much gold was there? How many coins?

HARLEQUIN. I don't know. I didn't count. Forty? Fifty?

LELIO. Forty or fifty?! And why did the Chevalier give you this present?

HARLEQUIN. Because I'd asked him for a token.

LELIO. Here we go with that damned token again.

HARLEQUIN. But I did. It's true. The Chevalier gave another token to Trivelin.

LELIO. I am finding it somewhat difficult to unravel what you are telling me. But I sense there is something in all this which concerns me. Tell me this. Had you done something for the Chevalier which meant that he had to reward you?

HARLEQUIN. No. But I was jealous. The Chevalier loved Trivelin. His charms had captured his heart. He put gold in his purse. And so I wanted the same for me. I wanted to be captured by his charms. I wanted gold in my purse.

LELIO. What the hell does this rubbish mean?

HARLEQUIN. There's nothing more true than what I'm telling you.

LELIO. What's the connection between the Chevalier's heart and Trivelin? And what's this business about the Chevalier's charms?? You speak of him as if he was a woman.

HARLEQUIN. Of course I do . . . Because he's ravishing. And if you knew him better, he'd capture your heart as well. Go on. Go and see for yourself. Go and tell him. I know your secret, but I'm not letting on. You'll see if he doesn't give you a token. On the spot, there and then. Then come and tell me this is rubbish. You'll see.

LELIO. I can't make head or tail of all this. Who is the Chevalier?

HARLEQUIN. Ah. Now there's precisely the secret that can earn you a present when you keep it.

LELIO. I order you to tell me.

HARLEQUIN. If I do, I'll be ruined. He won't give me anything anymore. And I love him too much to make him angry. This darling little almost man.

LELIO. This darling little almost man! What the . . . ?! And why does he love him so much? Why do you find the Chevalier so attractive?

HARLEQUIN. Because you don't see many men like him. He's unique. The only one in the world. You'd be mad if you went looking for others. But his fancy dress hides his charms.

LELIO. His fancy dress! An idea dawns . . . which confirms certain observations. The Chevalier has such delicate features, a very particular kind of face . . . But here is Trivelin. I'll force him to tell me the truth, if he knows it. I'll get more sense out of him than out of this half-wit. (*To* HARLEQUIN.) Make yourself scarce. I'll do my best to get your money back. (HARLEQUIN *groans, kisses his hand, disappears.*)

Scene 2

TRIVELIN *enters, mind elsewhere. Then he catches sight of* LELIO.

TRIVELIN. And here he is. The man who doesn't pay. I'm

beginning to take a distinct dislike to his face. I'll walk the other side.

LELIO. Trivelin. I'd like a word with you.

TRIVELIN. With me, sir? Couldn't we put it off until another day? I've got such a headache. Don't feel up to talking to anyone.

LELIO. Don't fool with me ... People like you don't have headaches. Come here.

TRIVELIN. I've got nothing new to tell you.

LELIO (*coming over to him and taking him by the arm*). I said, come here.

TRIVELIN. All right. What's it all about? Far be it from me to reproach you for the payment you so generously made me just now. I've never received anything quite like it in my life. But it's this gift of novelty that I'd most like to see disappear from your character. I know it's only a small thing. But it's a small thing that fouls up everything else.

LELIO. Listen. You talk too much.

TRIVELIN. I told you. I'm not in a sociable mood.

LELIO. I don't care. I want you to give a clear reply to the questions I'm going to ask you. Your behaviour will determine mine.

TRIVELIN. In that case you'll be brief because I'll be short. I've only got one good answer to anything you want to ask, i.e., I don't know. Anything. Nothing. See? Thanks to me you can also be economical in your questions.

LELIO. If you tell me the truth, it will be to your advantage.

TRIVELIN. Could it be ... there's yet another beating that you are going to spare me?

LELIO (*not paying attention*). Let's put an end to this, shall we?

TRIVELIN. Fine by me. (*Going away.*)

LELIO. Where are you going?

TRIVELIN. Best way of ending a conversation is to stop talking. Most efficient way I know.

LELIO. You are beginning to get on my nerves. I am going to lose my temper. Just stand still. Listen to me. And reply.

TRIVELIN (*aside*). Who's he got it in for, this devil of a man?

LELIO. Are you muttering under your breath?

TRIVELIN. It happens sometimes. When I'm not thinking.

LELIO. For your own good, Trivelin, let's converse in a calm fashion.

TRIVELIN. Why not? Like the civilised people we are.

LELIO. Have you known the Chevalier a long time?

TRIVELIN. No. I just met him. I met him at the same time I met you.

LELIO. Do you know who he is?

TRIVELIN. He says he's a youngest son. The eldest is a gentleman. But I've never seen his birth certificate. If ever I do, I promise I'll make you a copy.

LELIO. Speak straight.

TRIVELIN. I swear I am. I give you my word. But there's no way of assuring what that's worth.

LELIO. You're hiding something. The Chevalier is travelling under an assumed name.

TRIVELIN. You mean he might be the eldest son? And I thought he was on hard times! See what people are like!

LELIO. You're playing for time. This Chevalier who isn't one, admit it, you're in love with him.

TRIVELIN. There is a general rule in human affairs that one must love one's neighbour. That's what must explain his standing in my affection.

LELIO. But this rule. It's with pleasure that you obey it . . .

TRIVELIN. You get me wrong there, sir. Nothing costs me more than obedience. In matters of, shall we say, gratuitous virtue, then I'm courage itself. But when it comes to the essential duties of life, I'm less than lukewarm. Incredible, but true. What is man? Are you not like me in this, sir?

LELIO. You're trying to fool me. You're in love with this false Chevalier.

TRIVELIN. Gently does it. Hang on a bit, sir. This is . . . getting deep.

LELIO. You know what sex the Chevalier is.

TRIVELIN. Let's get this clear. As far as I know there are just two sexes. One sex that says it is reasonable, and the other which proves that this cannot be the case. Now which of the two does the Chevalier belong to?

LELIO (*taking him by the coat*). You're forcing me to do this. Listen carefully to what I say. If you carry on play-acting I'll club you to death.

TRIVELIN. That at least has the advantage of being clear as a bell.

LELIO. Don't make me angry. I have a very serious interest in this affair. A great deal of money is at stake . . . Either you speak or I'll kill you.

TRIVELIN. You'd kill me if I don't speak?! I can assure you, sir, that if blabbermouths never died, I'd be the first to be immortal.

LELIO. All right. Talk.

TRIVELIN. You just name the subject. Big or small. All the same to me. And I'm off. (*Makes to go.*)

LELIO (*drawing his sword*). So you're still trying to get out of it? Perhaps this will help you compose your mind.

TRIVELIN (*pretending to be afraid*). Gosh. Golly. Do you know something? You'd really put the wind up me if you didn't have that look of a gentleman about you that you have.

LELIO (*staring at him*). Two-faced scoundrel!

TRIVELIN. It's my livery which is two-faced. Underneath it all, I'm as straight as they come. But once you wear this, honesty doesn't pay. It leads to neither honour nor profit.

LELIO (*puts sword back*). I'll endeavour to do without what I wanted to extract from you. But if things go wrong, we'll have an account to settle and I'll be looking for you.

TRIVELIN. Any time. Any place. I'll always pay you the respect to which you are due. You can rely on that. (*Low bow with hat.*)

LELIO (*angry*). Leave.

TRIVELIN. Precisely what I've been trying to do for the last half an hour.

Scene 3

The CHEVALIER *enters.* LELIO *in deep thought.*

CHEVALIER. The Countess is at this moment writing letters to send to Paris, my friend. She'll be down in a moment. She says she wants to take a walk with me. So I've come to ask you not to interrupt us while we're together. Go and sulk in some other corner of the garden. Like a jilted lover consumed with jealousy. In the course of this conversation, I intend to put the final touches to our grand scheme, and to bring her at last to make a decision. But as I would like everything to work out perfectly, I did think of one possible hitch. The forfeit. Is it in due form? There are contracts which are badly drawn up and which are null and void as a result. Show me yours. I know a little about law and, if anything needed adjusting, we could put it right.

LELIO (*aside*). Are my suspicions founded or not? I'll try and unmask him.

CHEVALIER. Who are you talking to? Why don't you talk to me?

LELIO. I don't have the forfeit on me. Let's speak about something else.

CHEVALIER. What's wrong? Have you got someone else in mind that you want me to marry at the same time as the Countess?

LELIO. No. I'm contemplating something more grave. I'm thinking of cutting my throat.

CHEVALIER. Heavens. When you're grave, you don't mess around. And what has your throat done that makes you so cut up about it?

LELIO. This is no joke.

CHEVALIER (*aside*). Has Harlequin told him? (*To* LELIO.) If you do happen to go through with your threat, remember to remember me in your will.

LELIO. I was thinking of taking you along with me.

CHEVALIER. But I have nothing against my throat. In all modesty, I think it's quite attractive.

LELIO. But I've got something against you. And I'd like to cut your throat as well.

CHEVALIER. Mine?

LELIO. Yours.

CHEVALIER (*laughing and giving him a friendly shove*). Go to bed. Sleep it off. You're sick in the head. Need a purge.

LELIO. Step this way.

CHEVALIER (*feeling* LELIO's *pulse*). You've been in the sun too long. Your brain's over-active. Feel your pulse.

LELIO. The reasons are much simpler. Step this way, I said.

CHEVALIER. And I said, go to bed.

LELIO. If you don't come with me, I shall think you're a coward.

CHEVALIER (*pitiful*). Poor man. After what you've just said, you can count yourself lucky I know you're not right in the head.

LELIO. You are a coward. As cowardly as a woman.

CHEVALIER (*aside*). Don't give in. (*To* LELIO.) Lelio, I said you are sick in the head. I just hope for your own sake that I'm right.

LELIO (*with disdain*). And I tell you, you lack guts. A needle and cotton would look better in your belt than a sword.

CHEVALIER. I could even thrash you with a needle, Lelio.

LELIO. If the duel was in a drawing-room.

CHEVALIER. If the duel was anywhere. You are beginning to irritate me. Let's have a closer look at you. Look at me. I persist in thinking you must have a temperature. (LELIO *looks at him.*) There is a mad look in your eyes. Maybe I was wrong. Calm down. Be at least so good as to tell me why I'm going to have to . . . see to you.

LELIO. There is a small wood over there. Follow me. It'll all come clear.

CHEVALIER. All right. Let's go. (*Aside.*) I'll call his bluff. Maybe he'll be the coward. (*They walk off together. They are on the point of disappearing.*)

LELIO (*turns, looks at the* CHEVALIER). You really are following me?!

CHEVALIER. What do you mean, am I really following you? What's going on now? Do you want to use your temperature as an excuse to back down? It's too late. Mad, sane, sick, healthy you just walk on. I'm in the mood for needlework. And when I've finished with you, you won't be needing doctors anymore. Let's go.

LELIO (*looking closely at him*). So it's not a trick?

CHEVALIER. Look. No more talking. You should be a corpse already.

LELIO (*coming back*). Calm down, my friend. Let's try and get things in perspective.

CHEVALIER (*taking him firmly by the hand*). Back down now and it's me who'll be calling you a coward.

LELIO (*aside*). It looks like I got things wrong. He is a man. A real man.

CHEVALIER (*fiery*). You are a coward. You're as frightened as a little girl.

LELIO. All right, Chevalier. I'll come clean. I did think you were a woman. It's the truth. It's your fault. You've got the kind of face that would look . . . right with make-up. Any woman would be glad to have a face like that. You're a man with a woman's face.

CHEVALIER. You're the one with a false face. Let's get back to the wood.

LELIO. No. I was testing you. For a reason I can't understand, you told Trivelin to give money to Harlequin.

CHEVALIER (*seriously*). The reason is simple. When I thought I was alone with Trivelin, Harlequin overheard me say something concerning our project that he could go and tell the Countess. That's the reason, sir . . .

LELIO. How could I guess? The way Harlequin spoke of you I thought you were a girl. You're good-looking. I was suspicious. But I give in. You may be pretty but you are also brave. Let's kiss, make up and press on with what's in hand.

CHEVALIER. When someone like me has got his blood up, it's difficult to calm down.

LELIO. Yet another thing you have in common with women.

CHEVALIER. Whatever. I don't particularly want to kill anyone. I'll forgive your error. But you must apologise.

LELIO. I am your humble servant, Chevalier, and I would beg of you to forgive my folly.

CHEVALIER. I shall choose to forget it. And I am happy that this reconciliation spares me both a tricky problem and a homicide. Our duel none the less had a positive result. I now see that if I ever do fight, it won't be the kind of duel that'll ever get me in trouble with the law.

LELIO. And your duel won't be with me. That I can assure you.

CHEVALIER. You never spoke a truer word.

LELIO (*gives his hand*). We'll swear on it. (HARLEQUIN *enters*.)

Scene 4

HARLEQUIN. Excuse me bursting in like this, Monsieur le Chevalier. It's that no-good Trivelin. He won't give me the money you gave him to give me. For no reason. I did everything you said. I didn't let on to nobody. About you being a woman. Ask Monsieur Lelio if I ever told him. I never did. And I never will.

CHEVALIER. The fool! I can hardly control myself!

HARLEQUIN. Fool?! Is that how much you love me? (*To* LELIO.) Look, sir. You listen. You see if you think I'm not right. I came in, just now, and there was Trivelin saying, 'Oh you're so pretty. My dove. Give us a kiss. No. Give us some money.' Then he held out his hand to take it. But my hand was there first. And the money fell into it. When the Chevalier sees that I'd been there all the time, he says; 'Listen. Don't tell anyone that I'm a girl.' 'No, my sweetness,' I reply. 'But in return give me your heart.' 'Take it,' she replies. Then she tells Trivelin to give me the gold. Then we go to have a drink together. Ask anyone down there, they'll tell you. And then I come back to take possession of the heart and of the gold. And all I get is to be told I'm a fool. (*The* CHEVALIER *is thoughtful.*)

LELIO. Leave us. And don't let on to anyone.

HARLEQUIN. Take care of my belongings.

Scene 5

LELIO. Well, duellist? Whose duels have little to do with swords. How are you going to get out of this?

CHEVALIER. No point in trying. It's all true.

LELIO. You look a little put out, my friend.

CHEVALIER. Me? Put out? Not in the least. And I can thank God for that. I am a woman. And pleased to be.

LELIO. Perhaps now we might know exactly what and who you're after.

CHEVALIER. You must admit, I've had bad luck. I hadn't put a foot wrong. Come on. Own up. I'd got you frightened of a coquette. That's the best bit.

LELIO. Don't change the subject. I was stupid enough to . . . open my heart to you.

CHEVALIER. That's of little importance. Given that I couldn't see anything in it which particularly attracted me.

LELIO. But, you know what I'm at.

CHEVALIER. And the last thing you wanted was to tell someone like me. Is that the problem?

LELIO. Correct.

CHEVALIER. But your plans are so fetching. I particularly went for the country retreat. And the sure-fire guarantee of instant

ugliness which would be your wedding present to your wife.
Quite something.

LELIO. You have a good memory. But let's talk of something else.
Who are you?

CHEVALIER. I am a young woman. Reasonably attractive, as you
can judge for yourself. And who intends to remain so if she can
find a husband who will spare her the pastoral prison and the
fifteen-day love-affair. That's who I am. To this portrait one
final detail. A wickedness almost as great as your own.

LELIO. Even worse.

CHEVALIER. No. You're wrong. Don't underestimate yourself.

LELIO. And what did you come here to do?

CHEVALIER. To paint your picture. So that I could take it back to
a certain woman, who would then decide what she wanted to do
with the original.

LELIO. An attractive mission.

CHEVALIER. There's nothing ugly about it. Because of what I've
done a lamb will be saved from the wolf. And 12,000 francs
will be recovered to be distributed elsewhere. Meagre results,
perhaps. But well worth the bother of dressing up.

LELIO (*intrigued*). What do you mean?

CHEVALIER. Allow me to explain. The lamb is my mistress, the
12,000 francs is her income. Which gave rise to the above
calculation. And the wolf, sir, who would have gobbled it all up,
is or was you.

LELIO. All is lost.

CHEVALIER. No. Your prey has slipped out of your clutches,
that's all. True. She was worth clinging on to. But why be a
wolf? That's your fault, not mine. We learnt that you were in
Paris incognito. We asked ourselves questions as to the kind of
man you were. We followed you and found out you were going
to a masked ball. As I am quick-witted, and not easily caught
out, I was sent to the ball, kitted up as you see me now, to try
and meet you. I arrive, do my thing, we become friends. I get to
know you. Realise that you are worthless. And I'm now going to

make my report. That's all there is to it.

LELIO. So. You are the attendant of . . . the woman in question.

CHEVALIER. At your service.

LELIO. You must admit, I am unlucky.

CHEVALIER. And I am clever. But tell me. Do you regret the ill you wanted to do? Do you repent for what didn't happen?

LELIO. Let's talk of something else. Why do you push your spite to the lengths of wanting to rob me of the Countess? Why did you go along with the part I wanted you to play?

CHEVALIER. My reasons were excellent. You wanted to use her to make 12,000 francs. Right? To that end you enlisted my help. I was going to play along until just before the denouement, when I was going to corner you, to get my share of the pickings. Either I was going to get my hands on the forfeit, saying I wanted to look at it, and then make you pay to get it back. 100 francs, in cash, or as an order made out payable to me. Otherwise I was going to threaten to tell the whole story, so that you would lose the time and money invested. It was all nicely worked out. As soon as I was paid, I was going to leave with your money plus the portrait of you I was going to take back to my mistress. Which was to earn me a further tidy little sum. The net total of all this, along with the expenses I'd put by during this voyage and my own natural good looks, would have made me quite an interesting match. If it hadn't been for the wolf. It didn't work out. It's infuriating. You on the other hand, I find pitiful.

LELIO. Now, if you wanted . . .

CHEVALIER. Go ahead. Search round for a new idea.

LELIO. You could earn even more than you ever dreamed of.

CHEVALIER. Look. Let's not be hypocritical. I'm not new to this game. I've played dirty tricks in my time. I'll come clean. Show you exactly what I'm made of. Obviously someone like you is unshockable. So let's forget trying to impress each other. Between people like us there's no point. Putting it simply, if things can be arranged so that I make a fortune, I'm ready to swear you're a gentleman. But this honour has a price. A price which we must determine beforehand. And it will cost you.

LELIO. Ask what you like of me. It's yours for the taking.

CHEVALIER. But this secret must never be let out. I want two thousand francs. I won't discuss the price. It's that or nothing. For this sum I'll leave you my mistress and I'll finish things off with the Countess. If we can come to an agreement, I'll write the letter to Paris this evening – a letter which you can dictate yourself. You can go over the top as much as you like, I'll put it all in. And once you're married, you can do as you please. I'll be rich. You too. The others can fend for themselves.

LELIO. I give you the two thousand francs. And my friendship.

CHEVALIER. That is a trifle, my friend, which I'd happily exchange for a further 50 francs if you so wish.

LELIO. A hundred.

CHEVALIER. That's more like you. But it's not worth it.

LELIO. So, tonight we write the letter?

CHEVALIER. Yes. But, when are you going to give me my money?

LELIO. Take this ring. That'll at least cover the 100 francs for the friendship.

CHEVALIER. I am more interested in the two thousand francs.

LELIO. I shall write you out a promissory note. Shortly.

CHEVALIER. Shortly! The Countess will be here very soon and I'm not going to budge unless I'm sure of what I'm going to earn. An idea. Hand over the forfeit. I'll return it when you write me the note.

LELIO. Here.

CHEVALIER. And don't try and do the dirty.

LELIO. You must be joking.

CHEVALIER. Here is the Countess. Give me a little time with her. And then come back angry. Demand that she makes up her mind. Either you or me. Go quickly. I don't want her to see us together.

LELIO *leaves.*

Scene 6

CHEVALIER. I was on the point of coming to find you, Countess.

COUNTESS. And I was worried for you, Chevalier. I was some way off, and I saw you in conversation with Lelio. He is a violent man. I would beg of you. Don't have anything to do with him.

CHEVALIER. You're right. He has been acting in a most strange fashion. Did you know that he's going round telling everyone that he's forcing you to get rid of me?

COUNTESS. If he told everyone he'd been . . . dismissed, that would be more like it.

CHEVALIER. But I promised him you would get rid of him. Help me keep my word. It's still early. He can still arrive back in Paris before sunset. Do it, dear friend. Send him away.

COUNTESS. You must be out of your mind, Chevalier. Just think of what you're saying!

CHEVALIER. You still expect reason to prevail! When I'm so much in love! Love moves too fast for reason. Can you still be reasonable, Countess? You are hurting me deeply. Your love for me must be very thin.

COUNTESS. And there you go with your madcap ways again. You know how touching you are when you're headstrong. And that's why you do it. And it is true. I do find you . . . deeply . . . amusing. You are so very different from Lelio.

CHEVALIER. And you haven't seen anything yet! But let's get back to Lelio. I told you to dismiss him before sunset. You have no alternative. Love commands. You can but obey.

COUNTESS. What if I choose to revolt? What happens then?

CHEVALIER. You wouldn't dare.

COUNTESS. I wouldn't dare! Listen to him. Just listen to the way he talks.

CHEVALIER. I'm sure you couldn't. I know you wouldn't. Because you love me too much. Your heart is mine. I can do what I will with it, just as you can do what you will with mine.

Those are the rules of the game. You can't play it any other way. You must believe me.

COUNTESS (*aside*). Have you ever heard such outrageous talk! He's so overweening. So sure of himself. I love him. He possesses my heart. And he says it like that. Matter of fact. As if there was no question about it!

CHEVALIER. There is not a shadow of a doubt in my mind. You have given me confidence. And this confidence inspires me, as you can see. And that's what makes me so sure that Lelio will leave this evening.

COUNTESS. I've never heard anything like this in my life! You expect me to tell a man that he is to leave!

CHEVALIER. And you expect me to accept your refusal to do it! As if it wasn't my due!

COUNTESS. You must be joking.

CHEVALIER. Faint-hearted lover.

COUNTESS. Petty tyrant.

CHEVALIER. And still you resist? Will you never give in?

COUNTESS. I cannot, my dear Chevalier. And I have one or two very good reasons for acting in a more civil manner towards Lelio.

CHEVALIER. Reasons! Reasons! All I hear is reason! Is this a way to talk, Madame?

COUNTESS. Don't get so het up. The fact is, simply, that I have lent him some money.

CHEVALIER. What of it? Did he write you the kind of IOU that you can't in all decency display before a court?

COUNTESS. Not at all. And I have his promissory note.

CHEVALIER. Then all you have to do is to despatch a man of law and you get your money back.

COUNTESS. That is true. But . . .

CHEVALIER. But?! What's this 'but'? Are you hiding something from me?

COUNTESS. How can I put it? To ensure that I would get my money back, I agreed to sign a forfeit for the sum.

CHEVALIER. A forfeit?! Indeed, madame! Now that really is the sign of true passion! Now that really is touching! A forfeit. The very idea moves me deeply. I don't quite know what to do with myself.

COUNTESS. This wretched forfeit. Why did I go and do it? I don't know what came over me. To be so weak with such a loathsome man. With a man I always knew I was going to end up hating. There's something about him that I've always found unsympathetic. But I didn't have the wit to heed my instinct.

CHEVALIER. And he certainly managed to make the most of your ... lack of sympathy. He even managed to turn it into something loving and tender. When you speak like that everything comes clear. I can see both of you. I can see him kneeling before you. I can see you listening to him attentively. He swears he will love you for ever. You swear the same. His lips search for your lips. They find them. They meet. I can see it all. I can hear your sighs of pleasure. Your eyes eat him up, burning, languishing, pining. This is a love that can only grow. And this love is a knife to my heart. This is a mortal blow. How can I live when haunted by these visions? Oh cruel forfeit. Will I ever forget you? How much sorrow are you to cost me? (*Aside.*) And how many crazy things are you going to make me say?

COUNTESS. You must be more courageous, sir. If you are to be haunted by these things, then, at least, see both of us as victims. I should never, never have spoken of this forfeit. Why did I ever think that you were calm and reasonable? Why did I ever set eyes on you? Do I deserve all the terrible things you say to me? Will you never take pity on me? Have I not given you sufficient proof of my love? Have you anything to fear from Lelio? Did I ever love him in the way I love you? Show me the man who is adored more than you are adored. Who can be more sure, more certain than he is to be adored for ever? And even this is not enough to persuade you! You are consumed with doubt. You won't listen to reason. You pitch headlong into despair. I am distraught. What is to become of us? How can we carry on living like this, tell me?!

CHEVALIER (*aside*). My performance is surprisingly successful. (*Aloud.*) It is true, Countess, that the pain you feel restores my calm and fills me with joy. What you have just said. How tender, how moving! I never dreamed I would hear such words. I am under your spell. Let's be happy again. Let's forget all that has been said and done.

COUNTESS. But why should I love you so much? What have you done to me?

CHEVALIER. I have done less than nothing. All this is the result of your goodness.

COUNTESS. I suppose you must be the most lovable person on earth. Or so it appears.

CHEVALIER. Compared with all that does not resemble you . . . perhaps I am. But when compared with you and your likes . . . no. And I could never return your love. In truth, I am not worthy of it.

COUNTESS. What does one have to be, to be worthy of it?

CHEVALIER. That is a question that you should not ask of me.

COUNTESS. If you love me for ever, I shall be happy for ever.

CHEVALIER. Could you bear to live with someone who would bring you so little pleasure?

COUNTESS. Be kind to me and all will be well.

CHEVALIER. Kindness. That, at least, I can promise. But Lelio must go.

COUNTESS. Because of the forfeit I would have preferred his departure to be of his own doing. It would have been 10,000 francs that I would have saved for you, Chevalier. For, ultimately, I am only doing this in your own interest.

CHEVALIER. I care nothing for all the riches of the world. All that counts is that he goes. If you are the first to break with him, I shall consider myself richly rewarded.

COUNTESS. Think carefully.

CHEVALIER. And there you go, hesitating again. You're finding it difficult to choose between me and Lelio. Is that how true love speaks? To be perfect in the eyes of a man such as I, you are still lacking in many things.

COUNTESS. All right. Then rest assured. I shall be perfect. I shall lack nothing.

CHEVALIER. But I shall always lack something for you.

COUNTESS. Untrue. I give in. I'll dismiss Lelio. You must tell me what I am to say.

CHEVALIER. Will you tell him to leave? Like that. Immediately. With no fuss.

COUNTESS. Yes.

CHEVALIER. Then, no, my dear Countess. You must not. You must not send him away. It is sufficient for me that you agree that you would. I have put your love to the test. I shall push your goodness no further. It would be cruel. It is now up to me to take care of you, when you have forgotten yourself because of me.

COUNTESS. I love you. There is nothing else to say.

CHEVALIER. To love me is not enough, Countess. You have perhaps used these very words to Lelio. Is there no way of distinguishing me from him?

COUNTESS. What else is there that I can say?

CHEVALIER. 'I adore you.' If you weren't to tell me today, you would tell me tomorrow. Give in to my little whim. Grant me an advance. Tell me.

COUNTESS. I so much want to tell you. I shouldn't. I should die of shame. As should you, for ever having asked.

CHEVALIER. Once you have told me, I shall beg forgiveness.

COUNTESS. My resistance is weakening.

CHEVALIER. Come, dearest love. Grant me this little favour. You have nothing to fear from me. Just let these words slip from your beautiful lips. Shall I kiss them to lend courage?

COUNTESS. Enough! Will you never be satisfied? I shall not always complain. But all in good time . . .

CHEVALIER. You are moved. Tender. Don't lose the chance. All I desire is a word. Shall I help you? Let's say it together.

Chevalier, I adore you.

COUNTESS. Chevalier, I adore you. He does what he will with me.

CHEVALIER (*aside*). How weak our sex is. (*Aloud*.) My dearest
heart. You give me such pleasure. Once more.

COUNTESS. As you wish. But you are to ask nothing more of
me afterwards . . .

CHEVALIER. What do you fear that I might ask?

COUNTESS. How am I to know? There seems to be no end to your
desires. You must be calm.

CHEVALIER. I shall obey you. I am not a hothead. I respect your
person. And nothing could bring me to violate this respect.

COUNTESS. I am ready to marry you. Is that not enough?

CHEVALIER. If the truth were known, it is more than I ask.

COUNTESS. I am ready to swear that I will be faithful to you for
ever. And I am ready to forgo the 10,000 francs. Without regret.

CHEVALIER. No. You will not have to lose them. If you take care
to do as I say. Lelio will doubtless soon be here to urge you to
make your choice. It is essential that you consent to marry him.
I want you to see exactly the kind of man he is. If you agree to do
as I say, the forfeit is safe, and you will see the real Lelio. But
here he comes. I have no time to explain any further.

COUNTESS. I shall do as you say.

Scene 7

LELIO. You will, madame, excuse me for interrupting your
conversation with the Chevalier. Rest assured, I am not
coming to complain or to reproach. And I will be brief. Not that
we're lacking in topics of conversation. There is a lot we could
speak about. The indifference, for instance, that you show
towards me since this gentleman, who is not my equal . . .

CHEVALIER (*aside*). In that he's not mistaken.

LELIO. Allow me to finish. My reproaches are well founded. But the fact is that you don't seem to like me. I've promised not to make a fuss. And I shall keep my promise, however painful it is. When you think of all I'm dying to tell you. Why do you find me so hateful? Why do you run away when I approach? What have I done? You're driving me to despair.

CHEVALIER (*laughs*). Hahahahahahha!

LELIO. Laugh, Monsieur le Chevalier. But you have chosen your moment badly. And I shall soon choose another in order to reply to you.

CHEVALIER. Don't get angry, Lelio. You were going to be brief, that's all. I will be brief, you said. And you can't stop talking. And still you're getting nowhere. I find that funny.

COUNTESS. Calm down, Lelio. And tell me clearly what it is that you want.

LELIO. I beg of you to come to a conclusion. Which of us do you want? Choose between monsieur and myself. But make a decision, madame. My heart can no longer bear the strain.

COUNTESS. You are in a nervous state, Lelio. But in the circumstances one can understand and forgive your nervousness. I am more sensitive to you than you think. Chevalier, we have spent a very pleasant time together. We have even been flirtatious. But this must now come to an end. You did speak to me of love. But I would be more than a little displeased if all this was serious. I am to marry Lelio. And I am now ready to marry Lelio. (*To* LELIO.) Can you still find reasons to criticise?

LELIO. Indeed not, madame. What you have just said is much to my advantage. And if I dared . . .

COUNTESS. Please do not thank me, Lelio. I am quite certain of the real joy I am bringing you. (*Aside.*) He's as pale as a ghost.

VALET. This letter has just arrived by the post, madame.

COUNTESS. Thank you. Will you both excuse me if I step aside a moment to read it? It is a letter from my brother.

Scene 8

LELIO (*to the* CHEVALIER). What the hell's going on? She took me at my word! What do you say to all this?

CHEVALIER. Me? Nothing. I must be dreaming. I'll try and wake up.

LELIO. Now I'm in a fine mess. She gives me her hand. Which I have been passionately asking for. And which happens to be the last thing in the world that I want. You wouldn't by any chance be fooling around with me, would you?

CHEVALIER. What are you going to invent next? I swear, if I haven't been doing my best for you, then I'm no servant. What just happened can only have been caused by one thing. In the course of our conversation she started to suspect me of having someone else in Paris. When she asked, I just laughed it off. But she was serious. And at that point you came in. What followed was just the result of her bad temper. But clouds pass. I'm sure she's in love with me.

LELIO. And I'm sure I'm in a very difficult situation.

CHEVALIER. If she persists in wanting to marry you, the only way out I can see is to tell her that you accept. But that you don't love her. Try and disguise the insult. Make it elegant. Then tell her that, if she refuses marriage on those conditions, the forfeit is her affair.

LELIO. There's a lot that's strange in what you say.

CHEVALIER. Strange! Since when have you been so fastidious? You're surely not going to back down now, just because of one final villainy that is going to save you 10,000 francs? 'I don't love you any more, madame. Nonetheless, I am ready to marry you.' You don't fancy it? Then you pay the forfeit. Just make up your mind. Your money or my wife.

Scene 9

COUNTESS. Lelio, my brother will not be arriving as soon as I expected. So there's no point in waiting around. We can conclude our affair as soon as you wish.

CHEVALIER (*low, to* LELIO). Be brave. One more lie and you're home and dry.

LELIO. The thing is, madame, in all honesty, my heart no longer seems to be in quite the same condition as it was before.

COUNTESS. What is this? What do you mean? Don't you love me any more?

LELIO. I didn't exactly say that. But my preoccupations have somewhat tampered with my inclinations.

COUNTESS. Then what was all that shouting and crying about? Can your despair suddenly have vanished into thin air? Was it all play-acting? I was under the impression that, unless I did something fast, you were at death's door. 'You must make up your mind, madame. The waiting is intolerable . . .'

LELIO. Put it like this. I thought, at that time, that there was no danger you might accept. So I was risking nothing.

COUNTESS. What an excellent actor you are. And the forfeit? What of the forfeit?

LELIO. We shall abide by the terms of the forfeit. And I shall have the honour of marrying you.

COUNTESS. What?! You'll marry me! But you don't love me!

LELIO. Love has nothing to do with it, madame. Don't let that come between us.

COUNTESS. Come, come, sir. I despise you. And will have nothing to do with you.

LELIO. Then what of the forfeit, madame? Are you ready to assume the consequences?

COUNTESS. Lelio. Think of what you are saying! What of your integrity?

CHEVALIER. I don't think he's ever heard that word before,

madame. It isn't in his dictionary. But it's certainly wrong to allow a wretched forfeit to come between you. Look. Don't worry about it any more. There. (*Tears up forfeit.*) That's put paid to it. (*He laughs.*)

LELIO. Traitor!

CHEVALIER (*still laughing*). Don't despair, Lelio. There's still the girl in Paris. The one with 12,000 francs. They told you in a letter she was beautiful. But they told you wrong. Because here she is. (*Takes off disguise.*) My face is the very image of hers.

COUNTESS. No. I . . . !

CHEVALIER. This change of sex is a bitter blow to your most tender feelings, my dear Countess. Had I been able to keep you company, doubtless we could have gone far together. So much love for nothing . . . But, in exchange, you have saved a large sum of money. I can tell you all the details of the trap that was set for you.

COUNTESS. I know of no trap sadder than the one you set for me.

CHEVALIER. You'll get over it. A pleasant prospect is no more. But I had excited these feelings in you only for your own good. You must look upon the present pain as a punishment for your fickleness. If you deserted Lelio, it was for the wrong reasons. You were seduced, not intelligent. In that you were at fault. As for you, Monsieur Lelio, here is your ring. You gave it to me quite readily. And just as readily I now give it to Trivelin and Harlequin. Here. (*Throws it at them.*) Sell this and share the proceeds.

TRIVELIN }
HARLEQUIN }   Money at last!

TRIVELIN. The musicians have just arrived for the festivities.

CHEVALIER (*to* LELIO). Stay for the celebrations, as you're still here. You can leave afterwards. That pleasure, at least, you can have for nothing.

Divertissement

    This love which consumes our hearts,
    This magic charm,
    This sweet pleasure of loving,
    Is the most treasured gift that heaven can send us.
    So why resist?
    Surrender to the spell,
    And in its throes,
    Swear to your loved one that you will burn for ever.
    But if the fire goes out
    There's not a moment to lose.
    Be heartless. Betray without remorse.
    Declarations must not be made
    To someone you no longer find pleasing.
    It is to Love alone that we owe allegiance.
    It is to Love alone that we shall be forever faithful.

    To swear to love all one's life,
    Is not a painful shackle.
    Do you know what it means?
    It's not some Phyllis or Sylvia
    Who can command our constancy.
    We are only always faithful
    To the one we love.

    Lovers,
    If your heart of hearts
    Was to be brought before us, undisguised.
    What should we do? How should we choose?
    To do without is too austere.
    Should we do without marriage?
    We need it too much.

Ladies, you will doubtless conclude
That all men are bad.
But not so fast,
And spare us your blame.
When we come to paint your portrait
It is, rest assured,
A hundred times more droll.
Of that you can be certain.

The Game of Love and Chance

Translated by John Walters

from LE JEU DE L'AMOUR ET DU HASARD
First performed by the Italian Comedians (1730)

This translation, originally commissioned by the Nuffield Theatre, Southampton, was first performed there on 20 February 1986 in a production directed by Robert Cordier. The cast was as follows:

MONSIEUR ORGON	Leon Tanner
MARIO	Nicholas Jeune
SILVIA	Lynn Clayton
DORANTE	Stephen Boxer
LISETTE, SILVIA's *maid*	Lesley Chatterley
HARLEQUIN, DORANTE's *servant*	Peter Kelly
Designer	Sarah-Jane McLelland
Lighting Designer	Robert Ornbo

The scene is set in Paris.

Act One

Scene 1

SILVIA. But I ask you once again – what business is it of yours? Why should you answer for my feelings?

LISETTE. I just thought that your feelings would be the same as anybody else's in this situation. Your father asks me whether you are pleased that he is marrying you off, whether this news gives you any joy. I tell him yes. It seems obvious, and you are perhaps the only girl in the world for whom such a 'yes' is untrue. But 'no' is unnatural.

SILVIA. 'No' is unnatural? What a foolish thing to say! Do you find marriage so very appealing, then?

LISETTE. My word, it's definitely another 'yes'!

SILVIA. Be quiet! Go and scatter your silly remarks elsewhere. And understand this – it is not for you to gauge my heart in terms of yours.

LISETTE. My heart is made like everybody else's. Why should your heart take it into its head to be made like nobody else's?

SILVIA. I tell you – if she dared, she would call me an eccentric.

LISETTE. If I were your equal, we should soon see.

SILVIA. You are doing your best to upset me, Lisette.

LISETTE. I don't mean to. But come on, what harm have I done really by telling Monsieur Orgon that you were pleased to be married off?

SILVIA. In the first place, my love, you didn't speak the truth. I am not unhappy with my maiden state.

LISETTE. That too is entirely novel.

SILVIA. You see, there is no need for my father to believe he is doing me such a great favour by marrying me off. It makes him behave with a confidence which may prove unfounded.

LISETTE. What! You will not marry the man he intends for you?

SILVIA. How do I know? Perhaps he will not suit me. That worries me.

LISETTE. They say that your intended is a real gentleman. They say he is well put together, friendly, and good-looking. They say he is as witty as you could wish, and that nobody could have a kinder nature. What more do you want? Could anyone imagine a sweeter marriage, a more ravishing union?

SILVIA. Ravishing! What nonsense you talk!

LISETTE. Why, madame, count yourself lucky that such a man should be prepared to marry according to the rules. There is scarcely a girl who wouldn't be in danger of marrying him without rules if he were to make advances. Friendly and well put together – there's enough to keep love alive. And civil and witty – that will do for entertaining society. Good Lord – everything about such a man must be good! He is both useful and pleasing. He has everything.

SILVIA. Yes – in the picture you paint of him. And they say it is a good likeness. They say. But I might not share this view. They say he is a handsome man, and that is almost a pity.

LISETTE. A pity? A pity? Now there is an unorthodox thought, to be sure!

SILVIA. It is a very sensible thought. Handsome men are only too ready to be conceited, I have noticed.

LISETTE. Oh, he is wrong to be conceited, but he is right to be handsome!

SILVIA. They also say he is well put together. But let that go.

LISETTE. Oh yes, indeed – that is forgivable!

SILVIA. Handsome? Good-looking? I can do without such luxuries.

LISETTE. Good gracious! If I ever marry, these luxuries will be my necessities.

SILVIA. You don't know what you are saying. In marriage, you have to deal more often with the man of reason than the man of passion. In short, all I ask of him is a kind nature, and that is more difficult to find than people think. His nature is much praised, but who has lived with him? Men are wont, are they not, to give out a false image of themselves, especially if they are clever. Why, I myself have seen those who seemed the nicest people you could imagine with their friends – the soul of sweet reason and good humour. Their very faces seem to vouch for all the good qualities we think we find in them. 'Monsieur Such-and-Such seems a real gentleman – so courteous and reasonable.' That's what people used to say all the time about Ergaste. 'And so he is,' others would reply, 'his face tells not a word of a lie.' I have said it myself. Oh yes, a lot of trust you can put in that face! So gentle, so considerate, it seems, and a quarter of an hour later it disappears and gives way to a brooding look, brutal and barbarous, which strikes dread into an entire household! Ergaste got married. His wife, his children, and his servants only ever see that dark face, whilst everywhere else he parades that kindly look we see him wear – like a mask he puts on whenever he goes out of the house.

LISETTE. What a weird fellow with his two faces!

SILVIA. And there's Leander. People are happy with him when they see him, are they not? Well, let me tell you, at home he is a man who says not a word, who neither laughs nor scolds – a frozen, solitary, unapproachable soul. His wife does not know him, she has no dealings with his mind. She is married only to a shape who emerges from an inner room to come to table, and withers all around him with a chilling apathy and torpor. Now there's an entertaining husband for you!

LISETTE. I freeze to hear you speak of him. But how about Tersander?

SILVIA. Oh yes, Tersander! The other day he had just lost his temper with his wife. I happened to call. I was announced, and I saw a man who came to welcome me with open arms, as calm and cheerful as you like. You would have said he had just been having the most light-hearted conversation – the laughter still lingered round his mouth and eyes. The traitor! That's what men are like. Who would ever dream that his wife is to be pitied? I found her utterly despondent, her face leaden, her eyes fresh from weeping. I found her as I shall be, perhaps. There is my future portrait. At any rate, I am not going to risk becoming a copy of it. I pitied her, Lisette. What if you should come to pity me? That is a terrible thought, don't you agree? Just think what a husband is!

LISETTE. A husband is a husband. You shouldn't have ended with that word – it reconciles me to all the rest.

Scene 2

ORGON. Ah, good morning, dear girl. Will the news I bring you bring you pleasure? Your intended comes here today. His father informs me of it in this letter. You make no answer? You look sad, and Lisette lowers her eyes. What does this mean? Tell me, Lisette – what is it all about?

LISETTE. Sir, a face to make you tremble, another to chill you and kill you, and a frozen soul which keeps itself apart. Also, the portrait of a despondent woman with a leaden face and swollen eyes who has just been weeping. There, sir, is the subject of our meditation.

ORGON. What does this jabberwocky mean? A soul? A portrait? Explain yourself. I don't understand a word.

SILVIA. I was talking to Lisette about the misfortune of a woman mistreated by her husband. I referred to Tersander's wife whom I found the other day in great distress because her husband had just been picking a quarrel with her, and I was offering my reflections.

LISETTE. Yes, we were talking of a face that comes and goes. We were saying that a husband wears a mask for the world and a grimace for his wife.

ORGON. From all that, my child, I gather that marriage alarms you, the more so as you do not know Dorante at all.

LISETTE. In the first place, he is handsome, and that is almost a pity.

ORGON. A pity? Are you out of your mind? A pity!

LISETTE. I only say what I am taught. It is madame's thesis – I am studying with her.

ORGON. Come, come. All this is out of place. My dear child, you know how much I love you. Dorante is coming here in order to marry you. During my recent journey in the provinces I arranged this marriage with his father, who is my oldest and dearest friend. But it was on the condition that the two of you should like one another, and that you would have complete freedom to discuss this between you. I forbid you any subservience towards me. If Dorante does not suit you, you only have to say so, and he leaves. He leaves equally if you should happen not to suit him.

LISETTE. It will all be decided through a love-duet. An operatic morsel – You want me, I want you, send for a lawyer quickly. Or else – Do you love me? No. Neither do I. Haste, haste to horse!

ORGON. For my part, I have never seen Dorante – he was away when I visited his father's house – but from all the good things I have been told about him, I have little fear that either of you will dismiss the other.

SILVIA. I am deeply sensible of your kindness, father. You forbid me all subservience, and I shall obey you.

ORGON. I order you to do so!

SILVIA. But if I dared, I would suggest to you, in respect of an idea which has just come to me, that you grant me a favour which would set my mind perfectly at rest.

ORGON. Say on. If it is something feasible, I grant it you.

SILVIA. It is eminently feasible, but I fear it may be an abuse of your kindness.

ORGON. Very well, abuse it. Why, in this world we must be too kind in order to be kind enough.

LISETTE. Only the very kindest man could say that.

ORGON. Explain your idea, my child.

SILVIA. Dorante is coming here today. What if I could see him, examine him a little without his knowing who I am? Lisette is clever, sir – she could take my place for a little while, and I would take hers.

ORGON (*aside*). It's an amusing idea. (*Aloud.*) Let me reflect a little on what you say. (*Aside.*) If I let her do it, something quite unique is bound to happen. Something she isn't expecting herself. (*Aloud.*) Very well, my child, I grant you this disguise. Are you quite sure you can keep up yours, Lisette?

LISETTE. Me, sir? You know me. Just you try it on with me, and show disrespect if you dare to this one's dignity. Here is a sample of the fine airs with which I will await you. What do you say, eh? Can you still see Lisette?

ORGON. Good Lord! I am completely taken in myself at present. But there is no time to lose. Go and arrange your dress to suit your role. Dorante might catch us unawares. Hurry, and let the whole household be informed.

SILVIA. I don't need much more than an apron.

LISETTE. And I am going to doll myself up. Come and do my hair, Lisette, to get used to your chores. A little more attention to your duty, if you please!

SILVIA. You will be satisfied, Marquise. Let's go!

Scene 3

MARIO. My dear sister, I congratulate you on the news I have just heard. We are to see your lover, they say.

SILVIA. Yes, dear brother. But I have no time to stop. I have serious business. Father will tell you about it. I must leave you.

Scene 4

ORGON. Do not divert her, Mario. Come, you shall hear what is afoot.

MARIO. Well then, what is the latest, sir?

ORGON. I must begin by enjoining discretion upon you with regard to what I am about to tell you.

MARIO. I shall be guided by you.

ORGON. We shall be seeing Dorante today. But we shall only be seeing him in disguise.

MARIO. In disguise! Is he coming to a masquerade? Are you arranging a ball to greet him?

ORGON. Listen to this passage in his father's letter. Mmm . . . 'I do not know moreover what you will think of a notion my son has got into his head. He agrees himself that it is peculiar, but his motive is forgivable and even shows some delicacy. The fact of the matter is that he has asked me to allow him to make his first appearance at your house in the guise of his valet, who for his part will play the role of his master.'

MARIO. Oho! That will be most entertaining!

ORGON. Listen to the rest . . . 'My son fully realises the seriousness of the agreement he is to enter into, and says that he hopes to use this brief disguise in order to catch something of the character of the bride-to-be, to get a better understanding of her, so that he may then decide upon his future action in accordance with the freedom we have agreed to leave them. For my part, trusting entirely what you have told me about your lovely daughter, I have agreed to everything, taking the precaution of warning you, even though he has asked me to keep it a secret from you. In this respect you must deal as you think fit with the bride-to-be . . .' That is what his father writes. But that is not all. What has happened now is that your sister, uncertain in turn about Dorante – of whose secret she knows nothing, by the way – has asked me if she may play the same charade, precisely so that she may observe Dorante as Dorante wishes to observe her. What do you think of that? Have you ever heard of anything so distinctly unusual? Mistress and maid are even now dressing up. What do you advise, Mario? Shall I tell your sister or not?

MARIO. Heavens, sir, since that is the way things are going, I would not wish to disturb them, and I would respect the idea which has come to each of them. They must be brought to speak to one another often in these disguises. Let us see if their hearts do not inform them of each other's true worth. Perhaps Dorante will take a fancy to my sister even if she is a maidservant, and that would be delightful for her.

ORGON. We shall see how she gets out of the tangle!

MARIO. It is a business which cannot fail to amuse us. I want to be there at the beginning and spur them both on.

Scene 5

SILVIA. Here I am, sir. Am I ill-looking as a chambermaid? And you, brother, you know what is afoot, it seems. How do you find me?

MARIO. My word, sister, the valet is already as good as yours, but you could equally well steal Dorante from your mistress.

SILVIA. To be frank, I would not object to attracting him in the character I am playing. I would not mind subjugating his reason and dizzying him a little with the distance that will separate him from me. If my looks can bring that off, I shall be well pleased with them. Besides, it would help me in fathoming Dorante. As for his valet, his sighs do not alarm me, they will not dare come near me. There will be something in my look to inspire more respect than love in that rascal.

MARIO. Come, come, sister! Gently does it. That 'rascal' will be your equal.

ORGON. And will not fail to fall in love with you.

SILVIA. Very well – the honour of being loved by him will not be without its uses. Valets are by nature indiscreet, love is a chatterbox, and I shall make him the chronicler of his master.

A LACKEY. Sir, a servant has just arrived who asks to speak with you. He is followed by a bearer bearing a suitcase.

ORGON. Let him come in. It is probably Dorante's valet. His master has perhaps stopped off at the coach office on business. Where is Lisette?

SILVIA. Lisette is dressing. In front of her mirror she finds us very ill-advised to hand over Dorante to her. She will soon have done.

ORGON. Quiet now! Someone is coming.

Scene 6

DORANTE *enters as a valet.*

DORANTE. I am looking for Monsieur Orgon. Is it not to himself that I have the honour of paying my respects?

ORGON. Yes, my friend, it is indeed him.

DORANTE. Sir, you have no doubt received our news. I follow Monsieur Dorante who is following me. He has sent me ahead

of himself to assure you of his respect in anticipation of
assuring you of it himself.

ORGON. You perform your errand most graciously. Lisette, what
do you think of this fellow?

SILVIA. Me, sir? I say he is most welcome, and full of promise.

DORANTE. You are too kind. I do the best I am able.

MARIO. He is a passable-looking fellow, at any rate. Your heart
had better behave itself, Lisette.

SILVIA. My heart! Now there's much ado, to be sure.

DORANTE. Do not be upset, mademoiselle. Monsieur's words
flatter me more than I do myself.

SILVIA. This modesty is to my liking. Continue in this vein.

MARIO. Very good! But this name of mademoiselle by which he
calls you seems to me very solemn. Between people like
yourselves, the style of address should not be so stilted, or you
would be forever on your guard. Come now, do not be so stiff
with one another. You're called Lisette, and you, my fellow,
what's *your* name?

DORANTE. Bourguignon, sir, at your service.

SILVIA. Very well then, Bourguignon let it be.

DORANTE. All right – Lisette, then. But I shall none the less
remain ever your loyal and devoted servant.

MARIO. 'Ever your loyal and devoted servant'! That's still not
your style of speech. You must say 'Yours with love and
kisses'!

ORGON. Oho!

SILVIA (*aside to* MARIO). You are making mock of me, dear
brother.

DORANTE. So far as that kind of familiarity is concerned, I await
the orders of Lisette.

SILVIA. The ice is broken then. (*To* DORANTE.) Do as you like,
pet, since it amuses these gentlemen.

DORANTE. Thank you, honey – I respond at once to the honour
you do me.

ORGON. Take heart, my little ones – if you start loving one

another, you will soon be rid of these formalities.

MARIO. Steady now! As for their loving one another, that is a different matter. Perhaps you do not know that I who am speaking to you have my own designs on Lisette's affections. True, she offers me no hope, but I do not want Bourguignon poaching on my preserves.

SILVIA. Well, if that's the way you are going to take it, then *I* want Bourguignon to love *me*.

DORANTE. You do yourself wrong to say 'I want', lovely Lisette. You have no need to command in order to be served.

MARIO. Now there's a pretty compliment you must have stolen somewhere, Monsieur Bourguignon.

DORANTE. You are right, sir. I found it in her eyes.

MARIO. Be quiet! That's even worse. I forbid you to have so much wit.

SILVIA. It isn't at your expense. And if he finds it in my eyes, he only has to take it.

ORGON. You will lose your case, my son. Let us withdraw. Dorante will be arriving – let us go and tell my daughter. And you, Lisette, show this fellow his master's apartment. Goodbye, Bourguignon.

DORANTE. Sir, you do me too much honour.

Scene 7

SILVIA (*aside*). They are having their little game, but never mind, let's turn everything to advantage. This fellow is not stupid, and the maid who gets him is not to be pitied. He is going to flirt with me. Very well, let him – it may be instructive.

DORANTE (*aside*). This girl is amazing! There is not a woman in the world would not be honoured by her face. Let's make her acquaintance. (*Aloud.*) Since we are on a friendly footing and have foresworn formality, tell me, my little Lisette, is your mistress your equal? She is very bold to dare to have a personal maid like you.

SILVIA. Bourguignon, that question tells me that, in accordance with custom, you have come intending to murmur sweet nothings to me. Is that not true?

DORANTE. My word, I came with no such plan, I must tell you. Valet as I am, I have never become very intimate with ladies' maids – I have no taste for below stairs wit. But in your case it is a quite different matter. Why, great heavens, you subdue me! I am almost shy. My friendliness is afraid to be tame with you. I keep wanting to take my hat off to you, and when I try to be free and easy with you, I feel as though I am acting. In short, I long to treat you with marks of respect which would make you laugh. What kind of servant are you then, who seem like a princess?

SILVIA. Well, all you say you have felt on seeing me is precisely the story of all the valets who have seen me.

DORANTE. Upon my word, I should not be surprised if it were also the story of all the masters.

SILVIA. It's a pretty remark, but I tell you again, I am not made for the flatteries of those whose wardrobe looks like yours.

DORANTE. You mean my clothes do not suit you?

SILVIA. No, Bourguignon. Let's leave love alone, and be good friends.

DORANTE. Is that all? Your little treaty is only made up of two impossible clauses.

SILVIA (aside). What a man for a valet! (Aloud.) It must, however, be honoured. I was once told that it would only ever be my fortune to marry a man of quality, and I have sworn since then never to listen to any other.

DORANTE. Good Lord, that is strange! As you have sworn concerning men, I have myself sworn concerning women. I have vowed that I would only ever seriously love a girl of quality.

SILVIA. Do not deviate from your plan, then.

DORANTE. Perhaps I am deviating from it less than we think. You have an air of great distinction, and it is possible to be a person of quality without knowing it.

SILVIA. Oh oh oh! I would thank you for your praise, were it not made at my mother's expense.

DORANTE. Well, then – avenge yourself on *my* mother, if you find I have the face for it.

SILVIA (*aside*). And he would deserve it too. (*Aloud.*) But that is not what is at issue. Enough of this banter – prophecy promises me a man of quality for my husband, and I will not budge from that.

DORANTE. Good Lord, if I were such a man, the prophecy would threaten me; I should be afraid to verify it. I have no faith in astrology, but much faith in your face.

SILVIA (*aside*). And still he continues. (*Aloud.*) Will you end this please? What does the prophecy matter to you since it excludes you?

DORANTE. It did not foretell that I would not love you.

SILVIA. No, but it said that you would gain nothing by it. And I confirm it for you.

DORANTE. You are absolutely right, Lisette. This pride suits you perfectly, and even though it puts me in the dock, I am still delighted to see it in you. I hoped to find it from the first moment I saw you – it was the one grace which you still seemed to lack, and I am happy to lose by it since you gain by it.

SILVIA (*aside*). Truly, here is a fellow who takes me by surprise in spite of myself. (*Aloud.*) Tell me, who are you, you who speak to me in this way?

DORANTE. The son of worthy folk who were not rich.

SILVIA. All right, I genuinely wish you a better situation than you have, and I would like to contribute to it. Fortune has dealt shabbily with you.

DORANTE. Upon my word, love has dealt more shabbily. I would rather be allowed to ask for your heart than have all the goods in the world.

SILVIA (*aside*). Merciful heavens, here we are in a full-scale lovers' conversation. (*Aloud.*) Bourguignon, I cannot be angry with the things you say to me, but I beg you, let us change the subject. Let us speak of your master. I think you can manage without talking love to me.

DORANTE. *You* could manage without making me feel it.

SILVIA. Oh, I shall get angry! You try my patience. Once again, just leave your love.

DORANTE. Just leave your face, then.

SILVIA (*aside*). I think he amuses me finally. (*Aloud.*) Very well, Bourguignon, you don't want to stop? Am I going to have to leave you? (*Aside.*) I should have done so already.

DORANTE. Wait, Lisette. I did want to speak to you about something else, but I cannot remember what it was.

SILVIA. And I had something to say to you, but you have made me lose my thoughts as well.

DORANTE. I remember asking you whether your mistress was your equal.

SILVIA. You get back on your tracks by means of a detour. Goodbye.

DORANTE. No, no, I promise, Lisette – it is just my master I am concerned with now.

SILVIA. Very well, then, I wanted to speak to you about him too, and I hope you will be happy to tell me confidentially what he is like. Your attachment to him gives me a good opinion of him. He must have some merit, since you serve him.

DORANTE. You will surely allow me to thank you for what you are saying there?

SILVIA. Will you please take no notice of my carelessness in saying it?

DORANTE. Yet another of those replies which carry me away! Do as you will, I cannot resist you, and I am most unfortunate to find myself held prisoner by all that is most lovable.

SILVIA. And *I* would like to know how it comes about that I am kind enough to listen to you, for that is certainly very strange.

DORANTE. You are right. Our encounter is unique.

SILVIA (*aside*). In spite of everything he says to me, I have not left, I am not leaving, I am still here, and I am answering him. Truly this goes beyond mere banter. (*Aloud.*) Goodbye.

DORANTE. Let us finish what we wanted to say.

SILVIA. Goodbye, I tell you. No more mercy. When your master arrives, I shall try, on my mistress's behalf, to know him for myself, if it is worth it. Meanwhile, you see this apartment: it is yours.

DORANTE. Ah, here is my master.

Scene 8

HARLEQUIN. Ah, there you are, Bourguignon! Have you been well received here, you and my suitcase?

DORANTE. We could not possibly have been badly received, sir.

HARLEQUIN. A servant out there told me to come in here. He said my pa-in-law and my missus would be informed.

SILVIA. You mean Monsieur Orgon and his daughter, I suppose, sir?

HARLEQUIN. Well, yes, my pa-in-law and my missus, as good as. I've come to wed, and they're waiting for me so they can get married. It's all agreed. We've only to go through the ceremony, and that's a mere trifle.

SILVIA. It's a trifle well worth thinking about.

HARLEQUIN. Yes, but once you've thought about it, you don't think about it any more.

SILVIA (*aside to* DORANTE). Bourguignon, it seems to me that social distinction is cheaply bought where you come from.

HARLEQUIN. Hey, gorgeous, what are you saying to my valet?

SILVIA. Nothing. I am just telling him that I am going to bring Monsieur Orgon down.

HARLEQUIN. Why don't you say my pa-in-law, like I do?

SILVIA. Because he isn't – yet.

DORANTE. She is right, sir. The marriage has not taken place.

HARLEQUIN. Well, I'm here to make it take place.

DORANTE. But wait until it *has* taken place.

HARLEQUIN. Good Lord, what a lot of fuss about becoming a pa-in-law yesterday or tomorrow.

SILVIA. Indeed, what great difference is there between being married or not? Yes, sir, we are quite, quite wrong, and I shall speed to acquaint your pa-in-law with your arrival.

HARLEQUIN. And my missus too, please. But before you go, tell me something. You're a bit of all right, aren't you – are you the chamber-maid?

SILVIA. As you so rightly say.

HARLEQUIN. That's a bit of all right. I'm very glad. Hey, do you think I'll go all right here? What do you think of me?

SILVIA. I think you'll go all right.

HARLEQUIN. Good. That's great. You hang on to that feeling. I'm sure we'll find a slot for it.

SILVIA. You are very modest to find it pleasing, but I must leave you. They must have forgotten to inform your pa-in-law of your arrival, for he would certainly have come, and I am going to look for him.

HARLEQUIN. Tell him I am really looking forward to meeting him.

SILVIA (*aside*). How strange is fate! Neither of these men is in his rightful place.

Scene 9

HARLEQUIN. Well, sir, so far so good. The maid fancies me already.

DORANTE. What a cretin you are!

HARLEQUIN. What do you mean? My entrance was really rather nice.

DORANTE. You promised me solemnly not to indulge in your crass fooleries. I gave you such clear instructions; I told you only to be serious. I must have been out of my mind to trust you.

HARLEQUIN. I'll do even better later. If it's not enough being serious, I'll turn on the melancholy. I'll even cry, if need be.

DORANTE. I don't know where I am. This business is making my head spin. What must I do?

HARLEQUIN. Isn't the girl very nice, then?

DORANTE. Be quiet. Here comes Monsieur Orgon.

Scene 10

ORGON. My dear sir, a thousand pardons for having kept you waiting. But I have only just this moment learnt that you are here.

HARLEQUIN. Sir, a thousand pardons are far too many. You only need one when you've only made one mistake. Anyway, all my pardons are at your service.

ORGON. I shall try not to need them.

HARLEQUIN. You're the boss, and I'm your humble servant.

ORGON. I am delighted to see you, I assure you, and I was really looking forward to meeting you.

HARLEQUIN. I would have come straight away with Bourguignon,

but you know how it is when you've just done a journey, you
don't feel very well put together, and I was very glad to be able
to turn up in a more palatable condition.

ORGON. You have succeeded very well. My daughter is dressing.
She has been a little indisposed. Whilst we wait for her to come
down, will you take some refreshment?

HARLEQUIN. Oh, I've never been known to refuse a drop of
booze.

ORGON. Bourguignon, you look after yourself, my boy.

HARLEQUIN. He's a choosy fellow, you know. He'll drink your
best.

ORGON. He need not stint himself.

Act Two

Scene 1

ORGON. Well, Lisette – what do you want with me, dear?

LISETTE. I need to speak to you for a moment.

ORGON. What is it about?

LISETTE. I want to tell you how things stand. It is important that you should be informed so that you have no cause for complaint against me.

ORGON. This is serious then?

LISETTE. Yes, very serious. You agreed to Mademoiselle Silvia's disguise, and to begin with I thought it of no consequence; but I was wrong.

ORGON. Of what consequence is it, then?

LISETTE. Sir, it is difficult to praise oneself, but in spite of all the rules of modesty, I have to tell you that if you do not sort out what is happening here, your intended son-in-law will have no heart left to give to your daughter. It is time for her to declare herself. It is becoming urgent. If another day goes by, I cannot answer for what will happen.

ORGON. And how does it come about that he will want no more to do with my daughter once he knows her? Do you mistrust her powers of attraction?

LISETTE. No, but you mistrust mine too little. They are making headway, I must warn you, and I do not advise you to let them.

ORGON. Allow me to compliment you on it, my dear Lisette. (*He laughs.*)

LISETTE. There we are – you think it's a joke, sir. You are making fun of me, and I'm very sorry for you, because you're the one who'll pay for it.

ORGON. Don't you worry your head about it, my girl. Just you carry on.

LISETTE. I tell you again – Dorante's affections are moving fast. Look, at the moment he is very fond of me; by this evening he will be in love with me. He will adore me by tomorrow. I do not deserve it, it is in very bad taste. You may say what you like about it, but it will none the less be so. Do you understand? By tomorrow I guarantee myself adored.

ORGON. Well, what does it matter? If he loves you so much, why, let him marry you!

LISETTE. What! You wouldn't prevent him?

ORGON. No, upon my word as a gentleman, if you bring him to that point.

LISETTE. Sir, take care. Until now I have done nothing to enhance my attractions, I have simply let them do their own work, I have spared his sanity. But if I set about it, I will bowl him over. He will be beyond all help.

ORGON. Bowl him over, lay him waste, consume him with fire. And then marry him. I will let you if you can.

LISETTE. On that basis, my fortune is as good as made.

ORGON. But tell me, has my daughter spoken to you? What does she think of her intended?

LISETTE. We have scarcely found a moment to speak to one another, for her intended haunts me. But at a quick glance I would think she was not very happy. I find her serious and thoughtful, and I fully expect her to ask me to discourage him.

ORGON. And I forbid you. I am avoiding discussing it with her. I have my reasons for prolonging this disguise. I want her to examine her future husband at greater leisure. But what about the valet? How is he behaving himself? Is he taking it into his head to fall in love with my daughter?

LISETTE. He is something of an eccentric. I have noticed that he plays the man of importance with her, just because he is well put together. He looks at her and sighs.

ORGON. And that annoys her?

LISETTE. Well . . . she blushes.

ORGON. Come now, you must be mistaken. Being ogled by a valet cannot embarrass her that much.

LISETTE. Sir, she blushes.

ORGON. It must be with indignation then.

LISETTE. If you say so.

ORGON. Very well, when you speak to her, tell her you suspect this valet of trying to prejudice her against his master. Do not worry if she gets cross – it is my business. But here is Dorante – he seems to be looking for you.

Scene 2

HARLEQUIN. Ah! At last I find you, most wonderful lady! I have been asking for you everywhere. Humble respects, dear pa-in-law, or very nearly so.

ORGON. Greetings. Goodbye, dear children. I leave you together. It is good that you should love one another a little before getting married.

HARLEQUIN. I'd be quite happy to do both jobs at once, sir.

ORGON. Do not be impatient. Goodbye.

Scene 3

HARLEQUIN. He tells me not to be impatient, madame. It's all very well for him to talk, the old fellow.

LISETTE. I find it hard to believe that it hurts you so much to wait, monsieur. You are only pretending impatience out of gallantry. You have barely arrived here, your love cannot be very strong. At the very most, it can only be in its infancy.

HARLEQUIN. You are mistaken, oh wonder of our age! A love such as ours does not stay long in the cradle. My love was born at your first glance, your second gave him strength, and the third made him a big boy. Let us try to marry him off as soon as possible. Look after him, since you are his mother.

LISETTE. Do you find him mistreated then? Is he so forsaken?

HARLEQUIN. Until he is fixed up, just give him your lovely white hand to keep him amused.

LISETTE. There you are then, impatient little fellow, since there is no peace if you are not kept amused.

HARLEQUIN (*kissing her hand*). Dear trinket of my soul! That delights me like delicious wine. What a shame to have only an egg-cupful.

LISETTE. Now, now, that's enough! You are too greedy.

HARLEQUIN. I ask only for something to keep me going until I can live.

LISETTE. Should we not retain some sense of reason?

HARLEQUIN. Reason? Alas, I have lost it. Your eyes are the villains who have stolen it.

LISETTE. But is it possible you can love me so much? I cannot convince myself it is so.

HARLEQUIN. I care little for what is possible, but I love you like a lost soul, and you will see from your mirror that that is only right and proper.

LISETTE. My mirror would only serve to make me more incredulous.

HARLEQUIN. Oh my most adorable sweetie! Your humility would merely be a hypocrite.

LISETTE. Somebody is coming. It is your valet.

Scene 4

DORANTE. Could I speak to you for a moment, sir?

HARLEQUIN. No. Cursed be the entire *corps de valets* who cannot leave us in peace.

LISETTE. See what he wants with you, monsieur.

DORANTE. I only want to say one word to you.

HARLEQUIN. Madame, if he says two, his dismissal will be the third. (*To* DORANTE.) Come, what is it?

DORANTE (*to* HARLEQUIN). You impudent rascal!

HARLEQUIN (*to* DORANTE). These are insults, not words. (*To* LISETTE.) One moment, my queen.

LISETTE. Go ahead.

DORANTE (*to* HARLEQUIN). Rid me of all this. Don't give yourself away. You must appear serious and thoughtful, even unhappy, do you understand?

HARLEQUIN. Yes, my friend. Do not trouble yourself. Now leave us.

Scene 5

HARLEQUIN. Ah, madame, without him I was going to say such fine things to you, and now I shall only find trivial ones, apart from my love which is extraordinary. But, speaking of love, when will yours keep it company?

LISETTE. We must hope that that will happen eventually.

HARLEQUIN. And do you think it will happen soon?

LISETTE. The question is rather abrupt. Do you realise that you're embarrassing me?

HARLEQUIN. I cannot help it. I am on fire, and I'm sounding the alarm-bell.

LISETTE. If I were allowed to reveal myself so quickly . . .

HARLEQUIN. I believe you can with a clear conscience.

LISETTE. The modesty of my sex will not allow it.

HARLEQUIN. Then it isn't the modesty that's fashionable these days. That has quite different ideas about what it will allow.

LISETTE. But what are you asking of me?

HARLEQUIN. Just tell me a little bit that you love me. Look, *I* love *you*. Be my echo, princess, repeat it.

LISETTE. He is insatiable. Very well, monsieur, I love you.

HARLEQUIN. Very well, madame, I am dying, my happiness overwhelms me. I am afraid I may run mad with it. You love me! That is amazing!

LISETTE. I too would have good grounds for being amazed at the swiftness of your declaration. Perhaps you will love me less when we know one another better.

HARLEQUIN. Ah, madame, when we reach that point, I shall lose a lot. The discount will be considerable.

LISETTE. You credit me with more quality than I have.

HARLEQUIN. And you, madame, do not know mine. I should only be talking to you on my knees.

LISETTE. Remember that we do not choose our situation in life.

HARLEQUIN. Fathers and mothers do as they think fit.

LISETTE. As far as I am concerned, my heart would have chosen you whatever your social condition had been.

HARLEQUIN. It has a wonderful chance to choose me again.

LISETTE. May I flatter myself that you would be the same towards me?

HARLEQUIN. Ah! Even if you had been only a serving-wench going down to the cellar with a candle in your hand, when I saw you, you would still have been my princess.

LISETTE. May such fine sentiments prove enduring.

HARLEQUIN. To strengthen them on both sides, let us swear to love one another always, in spite of all the spelling mistakes you may have made concerning me.

LISETTE. I have more to gain than you from such a vow, and I make it with all my heart.

HARLEQUIN (*falls to his knees*). Your kindness dazzles me and I prostrate myself before it.

LISETTE. Please stop. I cannot bear to see you in that position, and I should be ridiculous to leave you in it. Stand up. Oh! Now somebody else is coming!

Scene 6

LISETTE. What do you want, Lisette?

SILVIA. I need to speak to you, madame.

HARLEQUIN. Wouldn't you just know it! Look, sweetheart, come back in a quarter of an hour. Go on! Where I come from, chambermaids don't come in unless they're called.

SILVIA. Sir, I have to speak to madame.

HARLEQUIN. What a pig-headed creature it is! Queen of my life, send her away. Go away, girl. We have been orderd to love one another before we get married – do not interrupt us when we are at the job.

LISETTE. Can you not come back in a moment, Lisette?

SILVIA. But, madame . . .

HARLEQUIN. But! My blood will boil in this 'But'.

SILVIA (*aside*). Oh, the vile man! (*Aloud.*) Madame, I assure you it is urgent.

LISETTE. Allow me to deal with it then, monsieur.

HARLEQUIN. When the devil drives . . . and her too! Give me patience! I'll go for a walk until she's done. Ah! What fools our servants be!

Scene 7

SILVIA. I find your behaviour amazing – making me suffer the vulgarities of that animal. Why didn't you send him packing?

LISETTE. Now look here, madame. I cannot play two roles at once. I have to appear either as mistress or as servant. Either I obey or I command.

SILVIA. Very well. But since he is no longer here, listen to me as your mistress. You can see that that man definitely does not suit me.

LISETTE. You haven't had the time to examine him very much.

SILVIA. Are you crazy with your examining? Is it necessary to see him twice to see exactly how unsuitable he is? To put it briefly, I want nothing to do with him. Apparently my father does not approve of my repugnance – he avoids me and says not a word. This being the case, it is up to you to ease me gently out of difficulty by cleverly letting this young man know that marrying him is not to your taste.

LISETTE. I cannot do it, madame.

SILVIA. You cannot? And what prevents you, pray?

LISETTE. Monsieur Orgon has forbidden me.

SILVIA. He has forbidden you! I do not recognise my father in such a proceeding.

LISETTE. Positively forbidden.

SILVIA. Well then, I must give you the job of telling him of my distaste, and assuring him that it is beyond all persuasion. I cannot believe that after that he will want to take things any further.

LISETTE. But, madame, what is it you find so unpleasant, so repellent, about your intended?

SILVIA. I do not like him, I tell you – any more than I like your lack of commitment.

LISETTE. Give yourself time to see what he is like. That is all you are being asked.

SILVIA. I hate him enough already, without spending time learning to hate him more.

LISETTE. His valet acts very important – he wouldn't by any chance have tried to turn you against his master, would he?

SILVIA. Hmph! Stupid girl! His valet has nothing to do with this!

LISETTE. It's just that I don't trust him – he's always quibbling.

SILVIA. Enough of your character-sketches – we do not need them. I take care that this valet speaks to me little, and in the little he has said to me, he has never said anything which was not extremely sensible.

LISETTE. I think he is the kind of man to have told you all sorts of unsuitable stories just to show off his brilliant wit.

SILVIA. Obviously my disguise exposes me to hearing pretty compliments. Who have you got it in for? Why this obsession with attributing to this fellow an aversion in which he has no part? Because, after all – you force me to come to his defence – just because you want to make me out to be an idiot for listening to his stories, there is no call to set him at odds with his master or make him out to be a treacherous rogue.

LISETTE. Oh, madame, since you take that tone to defend him, and since this even makes you angry, I have no more to say.

SILVIA. Since I take that tone to defend him? And what tone do you take to say that? What do you mean by this remark? What is going on in your mind?

LISETTE. I say, madame, that I have never seen you as you are now; and that I cannot understand why you are being so sharp. Very well, if this valet has said nothing, then that's all right – there is no need to leap so angrily to his defence. I believe you, and it's all over. I am the last person to be opposed to the high regard in which you hold him.

SILVIA. What a trouble-maker she is! Just see how she twists things! I feel an indignation . . . which . . . brings me close to tears . . .

LISETTE. But what for, madame? What hidden meaning do you hear in what I say?

SILVIA. Me hear hidden meanings! Me scold you on his behalf! Me hold him in high regard! Are you so lacking in respect for me? High regard, great heavens, high regard! How do I answer that? What does it mean? Who do you think you are talking to? Who is safe from what is happening to me? What have we come to?

LISETTE. I have no idea. But it will be a long time before I recover from the astonishment you have caused me.

SILVIA. She has a way of saying things which drives me distracted. Please go away. I find you unbearable. Leave me. I will take other steps.

Scene 8

SILVIA (*alone*). I am still shaking from what I heard her say. How insolently servants treat us in their minds! How such people degrade you! I do not know how I shall recover from it. I dare not think of the words she used, they still make me afraid. It is a valet we are talking about, a servant! Such a thing is unheard of! I must push aside the idea with which that insolent girl has blackened my imagination. Here is Bourguignon, here comes the very object of . . . the very person for whom I am in such a passion. But it is not his fault, poor boy, and I must not take it out on him.

Scene 9

DORANTE. Lisette, my love, however distant you feel from me, I am bound to speak to you. I think I have to complain about you, my darling.

SILVIA. My dear Bourguignon, please let us not speak so affectionately to one another.

DORANTE. Whatever you wish, my love.

SILVIA. But you have not stopped doing it.

DORANTE. Nor you, my love – you called me 'My dear Bourguignon'.

SILVIA. That just slipped out.

DORANTE. Well, I think we should speak as we can. There is no point in standing on ceremony for the short time we have for seeing one another.

SILVIA. Is your master leaving us, then? That would be no great loss.

DORANTE. Nor of me either, I suppose? I am simply completing your thought for you.

SILVIA. I would complete it myself if I wanted to. But I am not thinking about you.

DORANTE. I never lose sight of you, love.

SILVIA. Look, Bourguignon, once and for all – whether you stay, go away, or come back, should all be a matter of complete indifference to me, and indeed it is. I wish you neither well nor ill. I neither hate you nor love you. Nor shall I love you unless my wits begin to turn. That is the present state of my feelings; my reason allows no other, and I should not even need to say it to you.

DORANTE. My unhappiness cannot be imagined. You may have taken away my peace of mind for ever.

SILVIA (*aside*). What a strange fancy he has got into his mind! He makes me feel very sorry for him. (*Aloud.*) Come back to your senses. You are talking to me, and I am answering you. That is a great deal. It is even too much, believe me. If you were less ignorant about things, truly you would be happy with what I am doing. You would find I was behaving with unparalleled kindness – with a kindness I would want to blame if I saw it in another girl. But I do not reproach myself for it – my heart tells me deep down that what I am doing is to be praised. It is out of generosity that I am speaking to you. But that must not last. Such generosity is good only in passing, and I am not one to be able to reassure myself for ever of the innocence of my intentions – in the end, there would be no rhyme or reason to it. So let us end this, Bourguignon. Let us end it, love, I beg you. What does it mean? It is a mockery. Let it be no more spoken of.

DORANTE. Oh, my dearest Lisette, I am so unhappy!

SILVIA. Let us get back to what you wanted to say to me. When you came in, you were complaining about me – what was it about?

DORANTE. Nothing. A trifle. I wanted to see you, and I think I just used the nearest excuse.

SILVIA (*aside*). What can I say to that? I could be angry, but it would not change a thing.

DORANTE. Your mistress, as she was leaving, seemed to be accusing me of having spoken to the detriment of my master.

SILVIA. She is imagining it. If she mentions it again, you can straightforwardly deny it. I will take care of the rest.

DORANTE. Oh, that is not what is concerning me.

SILVIA. If that is all you have to say to me, we have no more business together.

DORANTE. At least leave me the pleasure of seeing you.

SILVIA. A fine pretext he offers me there! I should stay to amuse Bourguignon's passion! The memory of all this will surely make me laugh one day.

DORANTE. You are right to mock me. I do not know what I am saying, or what I am asking. Goodbye.

SILVIA. Goodbye. You are taking the right course ... But,

concerning your goodbyes, there is one thing I still have to
know. You said you ~~and your master~~ are leaving. Was that
serious?

DORANTE. For my part, either I leave or my wits will turn.

SILVIA. I certainly wasn't stopping you in order to get a reply like
that.

DORANTE. And I have committed only one fault – not leaving as
soon as I saw you.

SILVIA (*aside*). Every moment I need to forget I am listening to
him.

DORANTE. Dear Lisette, if only you knew the state I find myself in.

SILVIA. Oh, it isn't as strange as mine, I assure you, love.

DORANTE. What can you reproach me with? I do not seek to stir
your feelings.

SILVIA (*aside*). I would not be so sure of that.

DORANTE. And what could I hope for in trying to make you love
me? Alas, even if I did come to possess your heart . . .

SILVIA. May heaven preserve me from it! If you did come to
possess it, you would not know. I would even manage not to
know myself. Why, the very idea of it . . .

DORANTE. Is it really true then that you do not hate me, nor love
me, nor will love me?

SILVIA. Without any difficulty.

DORANTE. Without any difficulty! What is so dreadful about me,
then?

SILVIA. Nothing. It is not that which spoils you.

DORANTE. Well then, dearest Lisette, tell me a hundred times
that you will not love me.

SILVIA. Oh, I have told you enough! Try to believe me.

DORANTE. I absolutely must believe you. Take away all hope
from a dangerous passion, save me from the effects I fear from
it! You neither hate me, nor love me, nor will love me.
Overwhelm my heart with this certainty. I am acting in good
faith; give me some help against myself. I need it, I ask for it on
my knees.

He falls to his knees. At this moment, ORGON *and* MARIO *enter but do not speak.*

SILVIA. Aha, this is it! this was the only detail missing from my little adventure. How wretched I am – it is my own indulgence which has brought him to this posture. Stand up, Bourguignon, I implore you – somebody might come. I will say whatever you like. What do you want of me? I do not hate you. Stand up. I would love you if I could. I do not dislike you. That will have to be enough for you.

DORANTE. What, Lisette, if I were not what I am, if I were rich, of honourable rank, and loved you as much as I do love you, would your heart lose its aversion towards me?

SILVIA. Most certainly.

DORANTE. You would not hate me? You would suffer me?

SILVIA. Gladly. But stand up.

DORANTE. You seem to be saying it seriously, and if it is so, then I shall surely lose my mind.

SILVIA. I say what you want me to say, and still you do not stand up.

Scene 10

ORGON (*coming towards them*). It is a great pity to interrupt you, my children, when things are going so wonderfully well. Take heart, we are almost there!

SILVIA. I cannot prevent this fellow from getting down on his knees, sir. I am not in a position to command his respect, am I?

ORGON. The two of you go together perfectly. But I need a word with you, Lisette, and you shall continue your conversation after we have left. Is that to your liking, Bourguignon?

DORANTE. I will withdraw, sir.

ORGON. Off with you, then, and try to show a little more

consideration than you do when you talk about your master.

DORANTE. Me, sir!

ORGON. Your very self, Monsieur Bourguignon. You do not exactly shine with respect for your master, they say.

DORANTE. I don't know what they mean.

ORGON. Well, goodbye, goodbye, you can defend yourself some other time.

Scene 11

ORGON. Well, Silvia, are you not going to look at us? You seem quite embarrassed.

SILVIA. Me, father? What reason would I have for embarrassment? I am in my normal state, thank heavens. I am terribly sorry to have to tell you that it is your imagination.

MARIO. There is something, sister, there is something.

SILVIA. Something in your head, brother, granted. But as for in mine, there is only amazement at what you are saying.

ORGON. So it is this fellow who has just left who inspires you with such extreme antipathy towards his master?

SILVIA. What? Dorante's servant?

ORGON. Bourguignon the ladies' man.

SILVIA. Bourguignon the ladies' man – I did not know he had that title. He does not speak to me of his master.

ORGON. And yet it is claimed that he is discrediting him in your eyes. That is what I was anxious to discuss with you.

SILVIA. It is not worth it, father. Nobody but his master himself has given me the natural aversion which I have for him.

MARIO. Good heavens, it's no good saying that; your aversion is too strong to be natural. Somebody must have helped it along.

SILVIA. How mysteriously you say that! And who is this

'somebody' who has 'helped it along'? Come on, tell me.

MARIO. What a temper you are in, sister! How you fly off the handle!

SILVIA. The truth is I am utterly weary of my role, and I would already have unmasked myself had I not feared to upset my father.

ORGON. Do not do any such thing, my child. I came here to say just that. Since I indulged you by allowing you your disguise, you must please indulge me by suspending your judgement of Dorante until you see whether the aversion you have been given towards him is justified.

SILVIA. Are you not listening to me, father? I tell you, nobody gave it me except himself.

MARIO. What about that prattling fellow who just went out of here – didn't he do just a little to spoil your fancy for him?

SILVIA. I find your remarks very offensive! Spoilt my fancy for him! Spoilt my fancy! I am having to suffer some very strange expressions. All I hear are things which are unheard of, a manner of speaking quite undreamt of. I 'seem quite embarrassed', 'there is something', and then there is 'Bourguignon the ladies' man' who has 'spoilt my fancy', It all means whatever *you* like, but *I* don't understand a word of it.

MARIO. But, really, you are the one who is being strange. Who have you got it in for, then? How does it come about that you are so much on your guard? What plan is it that you suspect us of?

SILVIA. Keep at it, brother! What fate decrees that you cannot say a word to me today that does not scandalise me? What kind of suspicion do you expect me to have? Are you seeing things?

ORGON. It is true – you are so wrought up I no longer recognise you. It must have been such perturbations which made Lisette speak to us as she did. She accused this valet of not having spoken to you in favour of his master. And furthermore, she said this to us: 'Madame defended him to me so angrily that I am still quite astounded.' We scolded her about this word 'astounded'; people of her sort do not understand the repercussions of a word.

SILVIA. Impertinent hussy! Could anyone be more detestable! I freely admit, I did get angry out of a sense of justice for this fellow.

MARIO. I see no harm in that.

SILVIA. Could anything be simpler? What! Because I am fair-minded, because I want nobody to be hurt, because I want to save a servant from the wrong that could be done to him in the eyes of his master, they say I have rages and fits of temper which they find astounding! Then almost at once a trouble-maker starts bandying words; someone has to get angry, someone has to silence her and take my side against her, because of the repercussions of what she says. My side! So I need to be defended, to be justified? So what I am doing can be misinterpreted? But what am I doing? What am I accused of? Tell me, I implore you; this is serious. Am I being played with? Am I being mocked? My mind is not at peace.

ORGON. Come now, gently does it.

SILVIA. No, sir, gentleness is out of place here. What! Astounding? Repercussions? Ha! Why don't they explain themselves? What do they mean? The valet is accused, but quite wrongly. You are all mistaken. Lisette is mad, he is innocent, and there's an end of it! Why speak to me of it again? I am utterly outraged!

ORGON. You are holding back, my dear girl – you would very much like to scold me as well. But let us do better than that: only the valet is suspect here – all Dorante has to do is to send him packing.

SILVIA. Oh, this wretched disguise! Above all, keep Lisette away from me. I hate her more than Dorante.

ORGON. You will see her if you want. But you must be delighted that this fellow might be leaving, for he loves you, and that is most certainly bothersome for you.

SILVIA. I have no cause for complaint about it. He takes me for a servant, and speaks to me in that kind of tone. But he does not say what he likes to me, I keep good control of that.

MARIO. You are not as much the mistress as you say you are.

ORGON. Did we not see him get down on his knees in spite of you? To make him stand up, were you not obliged to tell him that you did not dislike him?

SILVIA (*aside*). Rage chokes me!

MARIO. What's more, when he asked you if you would love him, you had to say 'Gladly' with great tenderness – otherwise he would still be there.

SILVIA. What a felicitous footnote, dear brother! But as the action displeased me, so the replay is not to my liking. No, but seriously, when will it end, this little game with which you are entertaining yourselves at my expense?

ORGON. The only thing I demand of you, dear girl, is that you do not decide to refuse him until you are fully conversant with the facts. Wait a little longer – you will thank me for requesting this extension, I promise you.

MARIO. I predict that you will not only marry Dorante, but do it willingly. But, Father, I ask for mercy for the valet.

SILVIA. For mercy – why? *I* want him out.

ORGON. His master shall decide. Shall we go?

MARIO. Goodbye, sister, goodbye. No hard feelings!

Scene 12

SILVIA (*alone*). Oh, how my poor heart aches! What is it that mingles with my present confusion to make this whole business so distressing? I distrust every face, I am content with nobody, I am not content with myself.

DORANTE. Oh, I was looking for you, Lisette.

SILVIA. It was not worth finding me; I am avoiding you.

DORANTE (*preventing her from leaving*). Stay a moment, Lisette. I have to speak to you for the last time. It is a matter of great importance concerning your masters.

SILVIA. Then go and say it to them. I never see you without you upsetting me. Leave me.

DORANTE. I can say the same. But listen to me, I tell you. You are going to see a great change come over things through what I am about to tell you.

SILVIA. Very well, speak then. I am listening to you, since it is decreed that my indulgence towards you will be everlasting.

DORANTE. Do you promise me absolute secrecy?

SILVIA. I have never betrayed anyone.

DORANTE. If I am about to share this secret with you, it is purely because of the high esteem in which I hold you.

SILVIA. I believe you, but try to esteem me without telling me – it sounds like another pretext.

DORANTE. You are mistaken, Lisette. You have promised me secrecy, so let's get to the point. You have seen me in a state of great agitation. I could not prevent myself from loving you.

SILVIA. Oh, here we go! Well, *I* shall prevent myself from hearing you! Goodbye.

DORANTE. Wait. It is no longer Bourguignon who speaks to you.

SILVIA. Oh? Who are you then?

DORANTE. Oh, Lisette, this is where you are going to understand the anguish my heart has had to suffer.

SILVIA. I am not speaking to your heart, but to you.

DORANTE. Is there nobody coming?

SILVIA. No.

DORANTE. The state things have reached forces me to tell you. I am too much a man of honour to let them develop any further.

SILVIA. Very well, then.

DORANTE. I have to tell you that the man who is with your mistress is not what he is thought to be.

SILVIA (*sharply*). Who is he, then?

DORANTE. A valet.

SILVIA. So . . .

DORANTE. I am Dorante.

SILVIA (*aside*). Ah, now I see clear into my heart.

DORANTE. In this costume I sought to discover something of your mistress before marrying her. My father, as I left, gave permission for what I have done; the reality of it seems like a dream. I hate the mistress I was meant to marry, and I love the servant who was meant to find in me only a new master. What must I do now? I blush for her to say it, but your mistress has so little taste that she has fallen for my valet to the point where she will marry him if she is allowed. What course do I take?

SILVIA (*aside*). I won't tell him who I am. (*Aloud.*) Your situation is most certainly quite novel. But, sir, I must first ask you to excuse any unfitting remarks I may have made in our conversations.

DORANTE (*sharply*). Be quiet, Lisette! Your apologies distress me. They remind me of the distance which separates us, and make it all the more grievous for me.

SILVIA. Is your fancy for me serious, then? Do you love me that much?

DORANTE. Enough to renounce any other engagement, since I am not allowed to join my destiny with yours. And in this state the only sweetness I could savour was to believe you did not hate me.

SILVIA. A heart which chooses me in my present condition is most certainly worthy of being accepted, and I would gladly repay it with my own, were I not afraid of launching it upon a commitment which would do it harm.

DORANTE. Are you not captivating enough already, Lisette? Must you speak to me with such nobility as well?

SILVIA. I hear someone coming. Be patient still in the matter of your valet. Things will not go quite so fast. We shall meet again and find ways of getting you out of difficulty.

DORANTE. I shall follow your counsels. (*He goes out.*)

SILVIA. Well! I very much needed *him* to be Dorante.

Scene 13

MARIO. I have come to see you again, sister. We left you in a state
of anxiety which upsets me. I want to get you out of it. Listen
to me.

SILVIA. Oh, really, brother, there is some quite different news!

MARIO. What is it?

SILVIA. It isn't Bourguignon after all; it's Dorante.

MARIO. Which one are you talking about?

SILVIA. About him, I tell you. I have just this minute found out.
He has just gone out. He told me himself.

MARIO. Who did?

SILVIA. Don't you understand me?

MARIO. Hope to die if I do.

SILVIA. Come on, let's go out of here. Let's go and find my father,
he must be told. I shall need you too, dear brother. All kinds of
new ideas are coming to me – you must pretend to be in love
with me as Lisette. You already have pretended a little as a joke,
but above all you must please keep it secret.

MARIO. Oh, I shall do that all right, because I don't know what it is.

SILVIA. Come on, brother, come on. Let's not waste any time.
Nothing quite like this has ever happened before.

MARIO. I pray to heaven she is not delirious.

Act Three

Scene 1

HARLEQUIN. Alas! Sir, my most esteemed and honoured master,
I implore you . . .

DORANTE. Again?

HARLEQUIN. Have pity on my good fortune. Do not put a jinx on
my happiness; it is cruising along so smoothly, do not block off
its route.

DORANTE. Come on, you wretch, are you making mock of me?
You deserve a good beating, a hundred of the best!

HARLEQUIN. I don't refuse them if I deserve them, but when I
have had them, allow me to go away and deserve some more.
Would you like me to fetch the stick?

DORANTE. Rascal!

HARLEQUIN. Rascal, if you like. But that is not incompatible with
making my fortune.

DORANTE. What a scoundrel! What idea has he got into his head
now?

HARLEQUIN. Scoundrel is still all right, it suits me just as well. A
rascal is not dishonoured by being called a scoundrel, but a
scoundrel can make a good marriage.

DORANTE. What! You insolent fellow! You want me to deceive a
gentleman by allowing him to believe something that isn't
true? You want me to allow you to marry his daughter in my
name? Listen – if you mention such a piece of impertinence to
me again, you are out on your ear just as soon as I have warned
Monsieur Orgon what you really are. Do you understand?

HARLEQUIN. Let's come to an agreement. This young lady

adores me, she worships me. If I tell her I am really a valet and, in spite of that, she is still partial to a slice of marriage with me, won't you allow the violins to play?

DORANTE. As soon as you are recognised for what you are, I am no longer concerned.

HARLEQUIN. Good. I am going straight away to reveal my true colours to that kind and generous girl. I hope we aren't going to fall out over a few bits of braid, and that her love will let me get to the table even though fate has only placed me by the sideboard.

Scene 2

DORANTE. Everything that happens here, everything that has happened to me, is unbelievable. But I would like to see Lisette. She promised to make approaches to her mistress to get me out of difficulty – I should like to know how she fared. Let's see if I can find her alone.

Enter MARIO.

MARIO. Wait, Bourguignon. I want a word with you.

DORANTE. What can I do to serve you, sir?

MARIO. You are flirting with Lisette?

DORANTE. She is so lovable it would be difficult not to talk love to her.

MARIO. How does she receive what you say to her?

DORANTE. Sir, she makes mock of it.

MARIO. But you are a man of wit. Are you not being hypocritical?

DORANTE. No, but what is it to you? Just supposing Lisette had a penchant for me ...

MARIO. A penchant for him! Where do you find your expressions?

Your language is very high-faluting for a fellow of your sort.

DORANTE. Sir, I cannot speak otherwise.

MARIO. It must be with such little delicacies that you are wooing Lisette, trying to imitate a man of quality.

DORANTE. I assure you, sir, I am not imitating anybody. But I suppose you did not come here simply in order to ridicule me? You have something else to say to me? We were talking about Lisette, about my partiality for her and the interest you might have in it.

MARIO. Good God! I do believe there is already a hint of jealousy in your answer. Just calm down a little. Well, you were saying – supposing Lisette had a penchant for you. What next?

DORANTE. And why should it be necessary that you be apprised of it, sir?

MARIO. Ah, this is it. The fact is, in spite of the way I joked about it earlier, I should be very angry if she loved you. The fact is, without any further argument, I forbid you to make any further approaches to her. It isn't that I have any real fear that she might love you – I believe her heart would be above such a thing; it's just that I find it distasteful to have Bourguignon as a rival.

DORANTE. My word, I believe you; for Bourguignon – however much he may be Bourguignon – is not happy that you should be his.

MARIO. He will learn patience.

DORANTE. He will have to. But, sir, do you love her a great deal then?

MARIO. Enough to contemplate a serious attachment as soon as we have taken certain steps. Do you take my meaning?

DORANTE. Yes, I think I see the picture. I suppose then on that basis that she loves you.

MARIO. What do you think? Am I not worth her love?

DORANTE. Presumably you do not expect praise from your own rivals.

MARIO. It's a sensible reply, and I forgive you for it. But I am greatly mortified not to be able to tell you that she loves me. And I am telling you this not in order to let you know, as I am sure you realise, but because I have to tell the truth.

DORANTE. You amaze me, sir. Does Lisette not know of your designs, then?

MARIO. Lisette knows all the good I wish her, and appears untouched by it, but I hope that reason will win me her heart. Goodbye; leave without fuss. Her indifference towards me, in spite of all I can offer her, must console you for the sacrifice you will be making. Your livery is not right for tilting the balance in your favour, and you are in no position to compete with me.

Scene 3

MARIO. Ah, there you are, Lisette.

SILVIA. What is it, sir? You seem somewhat agitated?

MARIO. It is nothing. I was just having a word with Bourguignon.

SILVIA. He looks sad. Have you been scolding him?

DORANTE. Monsieur informs me that he loves you, madame.

SILVIA. That isn't my fault.

DORANTE. And forbids me to love you.

SILVIA. Does he forbid me to seem worthy of your love, then?

MARIO. I cannot prevent him from loving you, lovely Lisette, but I don't want him to tell you.

SILVIA. He has stopped telling me. He simply repeats it now.

MARIO. At least he will not repeat it when I am present. Leave us, Bourguignon.

DORANTE. I am waiting for her to order me to.

MARIO. Again!

SILVIA. He says he is waiting. You must have patience.

DORANTE. Do you feel some attraction towards monsieur?

SILVIA. What? Love? Oh, I don't think it will be necessary to forbid me that.

DORANTE. Are you not deceiving me?

MARIO. Really, this is a fine role I am playing here! Will he please leave! Who am I talking to?

DORANTE. To Bourguignon, that's all.

MARIO. Very well, will he please go away!

DORANTE (*aside*). I am so unhappy.

SILVIA. He is getting angry. You had best give in.

DORANTE (*to* SILVIA). Perhaps you ask for nothing better.

MARIO. Come, let's have no more of this.

DORANTE. You had not told me about *that* love, Lisette.

Scene 4

SILVIA. It would be very churlish of me if I did not love that man, you must admit.

MARIO (*laughing*). Ha, ha, ha.

ORGON. What are you laughing at, Mario?

MARIO. At Dorante's anger. He has just gone out. I made him leave Lisette.

SILVIA. But what did he say to you in the little chat you had alone with him?

MARIO. I have never seen a man more perplexed, nor in a worse temper.

ORGON. I am not sorry he has been caught in his own trap. Besides, looking on the good side, nothing could be more flattering or more helpful to him than all that you have done up to now, my dear girl. But enough of that.

MARIO. But where exactly is he up to, sister?

SILVIA. Alas, dear brother, I must confess I have some cause for contentment.

MARIO. 'Alas, dear brother,' she says! Do you detect that note of sweet peace in what she says?

ORGON. What, dear girl? You hope he will go so far as to offer you his hand whilst you are in your present disguise?

SILVIA. Yes, my dear father, I hope so.

MARIO. What a minx you are with your 'my dear father'! You've stopped scolding us now, have you? You're sweet-talking us instead.

SILVIA. You don't let me get away with anything.

MARIO. Oh, I'm just taking my revenge. Just now you were quibbling with me about my expressions. I have to have my turn at teasing you a little for yours. Your joy is every bit as entertaining as your anxiety was.

ORGON. You will not have to complain of me, dear girl. I agree to whatever you want.

SILVIA. Oh, sir, if you knew how great will be my obligation to you! Dorante and I are made for one another. He must marry me. If only you knew how grateful I shall be to him for what he is doing today, how my heart will keep the memory of the excess of tenderness he is showing me. If you only knew how ravishing this will make our union. He will never be able to remember our adventure without loving me, and I shall never think of it without loving him. By letting me have my way, you have sealed our happiness for life. It is a unique marriage. It is a story whose very telling is heart-warming. It is the most extraordinary stroke of fate, the happiest, the most . . .

MARIO. Ha, ha, ha, what a gasbag of a heart you have, sister! What eloquence!

ORGON. Your celebration is certainly quite charming, especially if you bring your business to a conclusion.

SILVIA. As good as done. Dorante is defeated. I await my prisoner.

MARIO. His chains will be more gilded than he expects. But I think his soul is in torment, and I pity his suffering.

SILVIA. What it is costing him to make up his mind only makes him more estimable in my eyes. He thinks he will grieve his father by marrying me; he believes he will betray both birth

and fortune. These are weighty matters for reflection, and I
would be delighted to triumph over them. But I have to seize
my victory, and not simply let him give it me. I want a battle
between love and reason.

MARIO. And may reason perish in the struggle!

ORGON. In other words, you want him to feel the full force of the
folly he will think he is committing. That is self-esteem carried
to a pitch of insatiable vanity!

MARIO. That is a woman's self-esteem for you. And it is all of a
piece.

Scene 5

ORGON. Hush, here comes Lisette. Let us see what she wants
with us.

LISETTE. Sir, you said just now you were handing over Dorante
into my hands, leaving me to decide his fate. I have taken you at
your word, I have worked on him as if for myself. And you will
see I have done a good job – I have got him good and ready.
What do you want me to do with him now? Is madame
surrendering him to me?

ORGON. Tell me again, my child – do you lay no claim there?

SILVIA. No. I give him to you, Lisette. I hand over all my rights to
you, and I shall never claim any share in a heart which – to
borrow your expression – I have not got good and ready
myself.

LISETTE. What! You are quite happy for me to marry him? And
monsieur is quite happy too?

ORGON. Yes. Let him sort it out with you –

MARIO. I give my consent too.

LISETTE. Mine too, and I thank all of you.

ORGON. Wait. I just make one slight condition in order to

exonerate us from what might happen. And that is, that you tell him a little who you are.

LISETTE. But if I tell him a little, he will know altogether.

ORGON. Well, but if he is good and ready, can he not easily bear such a shock? I do not think he is of a character to take fright at the news.

LISETTE. Here he comes, looking for me. Please be so kind as to leave me to my own devices. This, after all, is to be my masterpiece.

ORGON. That is fair enough. Let us withdraw.

SILVIA. Gladly.

MARIO. Let's go.

Scene 6

HARLEQUIN. At last, my queen, I see you and I shall never more leave you, for I have too long languished for lack of your presence and thought you were fleeing from mine.

LISETTE. I must admit, monsieur, it was a bit like that.

HARLEQUIN. What, dearest soul, sweet lifeblood of my very heart! Have you undertaken to end my life?

LISETTE. No, dear. Its continuation is too precious to me.

HARLEQUIN. Ah, how these words fortify me!

LISETTE. And you must not doubt my tenderness towards you.

HARLEQUIN. I would like to be able to kiss those little words, and pluck them from your lips with mine.

LISETTE. But you were pressing me about our getting married, and my father had still not given me permission to answer you. I have just spoken to him, and I have his consent for telling you that you can ask him for my hand whenever you want.

HARLEQUIN. Before I ask it from him, allow me to ask it from you. I would like to tender it my gracious thanks for the loving kindness it will have shown by its willingness to enter into mine, which is truly unworthy of it.

LISETTE. I do not refuse to lend it you for a moment, on condition that you will take it for ever.

HARLEQUIN. Dear plump and chubby little hand, I take you without haggling. The honour that you do me causes me no problem; all that worries me is the honour I offer you.

LISETTE. You add to my honour enough to multiply it more than I need.

HARLEQUIN. Nay! You don't understand that arithmetic as well as I do.

LISETTE. But I consider your love as a present from heaven.

HARLEQUIN. The present it has given you will not bankrupt it. It is really very mean.

LISETTE. I find it only too splendid.

HARLEQUIN. That is because you do not see it in full daylight.

LISETTE. You cannot know how much your modesty embarrasses me.

HARLEQUIN. Spare the expense of your embarrassment. It would be very shameless of me not to be modest.

LISETTE. Sir, do I have to tell you that I am the one who is honoured by your tenderness.

HARLEQUIN. Help! Help! I don't know where to put myself!

LISETTE. Once again, sir, I know myself.

HARLEQUIN. Well, I know myself too, and there isn't much to know. *You*'ll find out when you've found out. But that's the devilish thing about knowing me – you don't expect what you're going to find at the bottom of the bag.

LISETTE (*aside*). Such a degree of self-abasement is not natural. (*Aloud.*) Why do you say that to me?

HARLEQUIN. Aye, that's where the cat is waiting to be let out.

LISETTE. But what do you mean? You alarm me. Can it be that you are not . . .

HARLEQUIN. Help! Help! You're blowing my cover!

LISETTE. Let's find out what this is about.

HARLEQUIN (*aside*). Let's just set this up a little ... (*Aloud.*) Madame, how is your love now? Has he grown up into a big strong healthy fellow? Will he be able to cope when I make him tired? Is he afraid of living in a hovel? I can only offer him a humble home.

LISETTE. Ah, put me out of my misery! In a word, who are you?

HARLEQUIN. I am ... Have you ever seen counterfeit money? Do you know what a dud coin is? Well, I am rather like that.

LISETTE. Get to the point. What is your name?

HARLEQUIN. My name? (*Aside.*) What shall I tell her?
If I say 'I'm Harlequin',
She will make a fearful din.

LISETTE. Well?

HARLEQUIN. Oh 'struth! This is a tricky one to get out of! Do you have anything against soldiers?

LISETTE. Soldiers? What kind of soldiers?

HARLEQUIN. Well, for instance, a gentleman's personal ... soldier.

LISETTE. A gentleman's personal soldier! So I am not speaking to Dorante, then?

HARLEQUIN. He is my captain.

LISETTE. You ...! You ...! I'd like to hit you on the chin!

HARLEQUIN (*aside*). There's a rhyme I hadn't seen.

LISETTE. Why, you great ape! Take that!

HARLEQUIN. What a tumble I have taken!

LISETTE. It must be a whole hour I've been asking his pardon, wearing myself out grovelling to this animal.

HARLEQUIN. Alas, madame, if you preferred love to status, you would get as much out of me as out of any fine gentleman.

LISETTE (*laughing*). Ha, ha, ha, I cannot stop myself from laughing at him with his status! It's the only thing left to do. Very well, my status forgives you. It is well matched.

HARLEQUIN. Really and truly, kind lady? Oh, what gratitude my love can promise you!

LISETTE. Let's shake on it, Harlequin; I am caught in the trap. A gentleman's personal soldier is worth as much as milady's personal hairdresser.

HARLEQUIN. Milady's personal hairdresser!

LISETTE. She is my captain, or whatever the equivalent is.

HARLEQUIN. You little cheat!

LISETTE. Take your revenge.

HARLEQUIN. Why, you cheeky little monkey! It must be a whole hour she's been letting me get more and more embarrassed about my poverty!

LISETTE. Let's get down to facts. Do you love me?

HARLEQUIN. Good Lord, yes! Changing your name hasn't changed your face, and you know we did promise one another fidelity in spite of all spelling mistakes.

LISETTE. Well, there's no great harm done, let's take consolation. Let's not tell anyone, and don't give them any cause for laughing at us. It looks as though your master is still mistaken about my mistress. Don't tell him anything. Let's leave things as they are. I think I see him coming. Sir, I am your humble servant and chambermaid.

HARLEQUIN. And I your personal gentleman, madame. (*Laughing.*)

Exit LISETTE.

Scene 7

DORANTE. Well, you've just left Orgon's daughter. Did you tell her who you are?

HARLEQUIN. Good Lord, yes. Poor child! I found her heart as gentle as a lamb. She didn't make a murmur. When I told her I was called Harlequin and wore a uniform, she said 'Well, love, we all have our name and we all have our clothes. Yours didn't cost you anything.' That was nice of her, wasn't it?

DORANTE. What sort of nonsense are you telling me?

HARLEQUIN. I'll tell you what – I'm going to ask for her hand.

DORANTE. What! She's agreed to marry you?

HARLEQUIN. Ooh, she must be ill!

DORANTE. You are trying to fool me. She doesn't know who you are.

HARLEQUIN. My godfathers! Do you want to bet that I won't marry her dressed in my apron? Or in my overalls, if you make me angry. I would have you know that a love such as mine is not subject to breakage, that I don't need your glad rags to drive home my advantage, and that I would like mine back, if you please.

DORANTE. You treacherous rogue! Such a thing is quite unheard of, and I can see I shall have to have a word with Monsieur Orgon.

HARLEQUIN. What, with Dad? Oh, he's a good chap, we've got him in our pocket. He really is the best of human beings, a man made of the very best stuff. I'm sure you'll like him.

DORANTE. What a crazy fool! Have you seen Lisette?

HARLEQUIN. Lisette? No. She may have passed in front of my eyes, but a gentleman like me doesn't take any notice of a chambermaid. I leave that kind of pastime to you.

DORANTE. Go away. Your wits have turned.

HARLEQUIN. Your manners are a bit high and mighty, but that's a question of habit. Goodbye. After I am wed, we shall live on an equal footing. Your little chambermaid's here. Hallo, Lisette. May I recommend Bourguignon to you. He's quite a decent fellow.

Scene 8

DORANTE (*aside*). How worthy she is of love! Why did Mario have to get there before me?

SILVIA. Where have you been, sir? Since I left Mario, I haven't been able to find you to let you know what I said to Monsieur Orgon.

DORANTE. And yet I have not been far away. But what is there to tell?

SILVIA (*aside*). How cold he is! (*Aloud.*) I cried shame upon your valet, I cited his lack of conscience as proof of his lack of worth, I argued that the marriage could at least be delayed a little. All in vain. He didn't even listen to me. In fact, I must tell you, they are talking of sending for the registrar. It is time to declare yourself.

DORANTE. That is my intention. I am going to leave here *incognito*, and I shall leave a note which will tell Monsieur Orgon everything.

SILVIA (*aside*). He is going to leave? That is no use to me.

DORANTE. Do you not approve of my idea?

SILVIA. Well . . . not too much.

DORANTE. And yet I can see nothing better in my present situation, short of speaking to him myself, and I cannot bring myself to do that. Besides, I have other reasons which require me to withdraw. I have no more business here.

SILVIA. As I do not know your reasons, I can neither approve them nor contest them, and it is not my place to ask you what they are.

DORANTE. It is easy for you to guess them, Lisette.

SILVIA. Well, I think for instance that you feel some distate for Monsieur Orgon's daughter.

DORANTE. Is that all you see?

SILVIA. There are, of course, certain other things I could

suppose. But I am not mad, and I have not the vanity to linger over them.

DORANTE. Nor the courage to speak of them, since you would have nothing very obliging to say to me. Goodbye, Lisette.

SILVIA. Take care. I believe you do not understand me, I am obliged to declare.

DORANTE. Perfectly! And further elaboration would not favour me. Please keep it dark until I have gone.

SILVIA. What! You are leaving? Seriously?

DORANTE. You are very much afraid that I might change my mind.

SILVIA. How sweet of you to understand so readily!

DORANTE. Your answer is so spontaneous and natural. Goodbye.

SILVIA (*aside*). If he leaves, I love him no more, and I shall never marry him. (*She watches him going.*) He is stopping, though; he's thinking, he's looking to see if I turn my head, and *I* cannot call him back. Yet it would be extraordinary if he left, after all I have done! . . . Ah! It's all over. He is going. I have less power over him than I thought. My brother is a clumsy oaf! He set about it in quite the wrong way. Uninvolved people spoil everything. A fat lot of good that has done me! What a way for it all to turn out! But Dorante has reappeared – he seems to be coming back. I take it all back – I still love him . . . I must pretend to go out, so he can stop me. Our reconciliation has to cost him something.

DORANTE (*stopping her*). Stay, I beg you. I have something more to say to you.

SILVIA. To me, sir?

DORANTE. I find it hard to leave without having convinced you that I am not wrong to do so.

SILVIA. Well, sir, of what possible consequence is it to justify yourself to me? It isn't worth it – I am only a servant, and you make me very aware of it.

DORANTE. Me, Lisette! Are you in a position to complain when you see me putting up with things and say nothing about it?

SILVIA. Hmph! If I wanted, I could give you a good answer to that.

DORANTE. Do so, then. I ask for nothing better than to be mistaken. But what am I saying? Mario loves you.

SILVIA. That is true.

DORANTE. You are susceptible to his love. I could tell by the strong desire you had just now for me to go. So you cannot possibly love me.

SILVIA. I am susceptible to his love! Who told you that? I cannot possibly love you! What do you know about it? You are in a great hurry to decide.

DORANTE. Well then, Lisette, by all you hold most dear in the world, teach me how things are, I implore you.

SILVIA. Teach a man who is about to leave!

DORANTE. I shall not leave.

SILVIA. Leave me alone. Listen – if you love me, question me no further. You fear only my indifference, and you are only too happy if I stay silent. What do my feelings matter to you?

DORANTE. What do they matter? Lisette, can you still doubt that I adore you?

SILVIA. No, and you repeat it so often that I believe you. But why must you persuade me of it? What do you expect me to do with such a notion, sir? I am going to speak to you quite frankly. You love me, but your love is not a serious thing for you. What resources do you not have at your disposal for getting rid of it? There is a great distance between you and me; you will find a thousand women willing to love you, a thousand more eager to prove you susceptible, and a man of your situation cannot lack for entertainments – all these things are waiting to erase this love you unremittingly repeat to me. You will perhaps laugh at it when you leave here, and you will be right. But I, sir, if I should happen to remember it – as I fear I might – if I have been stricken, what help shall I have against the impression it may have made on me? Who will console me for your loss? Who do you think my heart will put in your place? Do you realise that if

I loved you, all the great matters of the world would be powerless to touch me? Think of the state in which I would be left. Please have the generosity to hide your love from me. I who am speaking to you would have misgivings about telling you I love you in your present frame of mind. The confession of my feelings could put at risk your very powers of reason; you can see anyway that I am hiding them from you.

DORANTE. Oh, my dear Lisette, what have I just heard? Your words have a passion which sears me. I adore you, and I respect you. There is neither rank, birth, nor fortune, which does not disappear before a soul like yours. I should be ashamed if my pride still held out against you. My heart and my hand are yours.

SILVIA. And indeed, if I were to take them, would you not deserve it? Would I not be very arrogant to hide the pleasure they cause me? And do you think this can last?

DORANTE. You love me, then?

SILVIA. No, no – but so much the worse for you if you ask me again.

DORANTE. Your threats do not frighten me.

SILVIA. And Mario? Have you forgotten about him?

DORANTE. No, Lisette, Mario no longer alarms me. You do not love him, you cannot deceive me, your heart is true, you respond to my tenderness. By the delight which has seized me I can no longer doubt it. I am sure, and you cannot take that certainty from me.

SILVIA. Oh, I shall not try – please keep it. We shall see what you do with it.

DORANTE. Do you not consent to be mine?

SILVIA. What! You will marry me in spite of what you are, in spite of a father's anger, in spite of your fortune?

DORANTE. My father will forgive me as soon as he has seen you; my fortune is enough for both of us; and worth is as good as birth. Let us not argue, for I shall not change, ever.

SILVIA. He will not change ever! Do you know you enchant me, Dorante?

DORANTE. Do not fetter your tenderness. Let it respond to mine.

SILVIA. At last I have come through to the end of it. You . . . you will not change ever?

DORANTE. No, my dear Lisette.

SILVIA. Oh, what love!

Final scene

SILVIA. Oh father! You wanted me to belong to Dorante. Come and see your daughter obey you with more joy than anyone ever had.

DORANTE. What do I hear? You her father, sir?

SILVIA. Yes, Dorante. The same idea for getting to know one another came to both of us. Apart from that, I need tell you no more. You love me, I cannot doubt it; but you in turn can judge the strength of my feelings for you, you can appreciate how highly I valued your heart by the subtlety with which I tried to win it.

ORGON. Do you recognise this letter? This is how I learnt of your disguise, which she, however, only learnt from you.

DORANTE. I cannot express my happiness, madame. But my greatest delight comes from the proofs I have given you of my tenderness for you.

MARIO. Can Dorante forgive me for the anger I aroused in Bourguignon?

DORANTE. He does not forgive you for it. He thanks you for it.

HARLEQUIN (*to* LISETTE). Joy, madame, joy! You have lost your rank, but you are not to be pitied, since you still have Harlequin.

LISETTE. A fine consolation! You are the only one who gains by that.

HARLEQUIN. I do not lose by it. Before we were fully acquainted, your dowry was worth more than you; now you are worth more than your dowry. Come on! Let's dance the night away!

Careless Vows

Translated by John Walters

from LES SERMENTS INDISCRETS
First performed by the Comédie-Française (1732)

CHARACTERS

LUCILE, *daughter of Monsieur Orgon*

PHENICE, *sister of Lucile*

DAMIS, *son of Monsieur Ergaste, suitor of Lucile*

MONSIEUR ERGASTE, *father of Damis*

MONSIEUR ORGON, *father of Lucile and Phenice*

LISETTE, *personal maid to Damis*

FRONTIN, *personal servant to Damis*

A SERVANT

The scene is set in a country house.

Act One

Scene 1

LUCILE (*sitting at a table, folding a letter; she is speaking to a servant standing in front of her*). Go and tell Lisette to come here. (*The servant exits. She stands up.*) Well, if this letter doesn't put an end to the plan to marry me off to Damis, then he must be a very strange man indeed. (*Enter* LISETTE.)

Scene 2

LUCILE. Ah, there you are, Lisette. Come here. I've just heard that Damis arrived yesterday from Paris. He's at his father's house at present. Here's a letter you must deliver to him. I hope it will result in my not marrying him.

LISETTE. What! Have you still got that notion? No, madame, I shall not do your errand. Damis is the husband your father intends for you, you have consented, everyone is in agreement. There's only a syllable's difference left between you and a wife, and I shall not deliver your letter. You have promised to get married.

LUCILE. Yes, it's true I have, out of consideration for my father, but has he really thought about it? What does a marriage like this mean? Don't you think I would be crazy to marry a man whose character is completely unknown to me? Besides, you know my feelings, don't you? I don't want to get married so soon, and perhaps I never will.

LISETTE. You? With those eyes? I challenge you!

LUCILE. What kind of argument is that? As if eyes had any say in the matter!

LISETTE. No problem there – yours condemn you to live in company. I mean, just look at yourself. It's a harsh course you've chosen to follow and you don't appreciate its difficulties – it would need a very frugal heart indeed to bear it. Spinsters are solitary creatures, and your face shows no vocation for such a life.

LUCILE. Oh, my face doesn't know what it's saying. I feel I have a fund of taste and sensitivity which would always be affronted by marriage, and I would not be happy in it.

LISETTE. Fiddlesticks! Two or three months' dealings with a husband would be enough to get rid of that kind of sensitivity. Come on, tear up your letter.

LUCILE. I tell you my mind is made up, and I want you to deliver it. Do you think I pride myself on being less susceptible than other women? No, I don't make any such boast, and I would be wrong to do so – I am an affectionate soul, though rather decorous by nature and that is why marriage would be a very bad state for me. An affectionate soul has feelings, she needs them to be returned, she needs to be loved because she loves, and a person like that in the hands of a husband never gets what she needs.

LISETTE. Lord, yes, those needs are expensive, and a husband's heart runs out of funds.

LUCILE. I know these gentlemen a little. I notice that men are kind only when they are lovers. Their heart is the prettiest thing in the world, so long as hope keeps them in suspense. Submissive, respectful, attentive – for the little love you show them, your self-love is enchanted, it is quite delightfully served, quite surfeited with pleasure. And everything works for us – folly, arrogance, disdain, capriciousness, impertinence – everything we do is right, it's the law. We reign as tyrants, and our idolaters are always on their knees. But once you marry them, once the goddess becomes human, their idolatry ends at the point where our kindness begins. As soon as they're happy, they no longer deserve to be, the ungrateful wretches!

LISETTE. That's them!

LUCILE. Well, I shall sort all that out, and the role of goddess will not bore me, gentlemen, I can assure you! What – young and lovely as I am, I should have less than six months in a husband's eyes before my face is thrown on the scrap-heap?! From being eighteen, it would suddenly jump to fifty? No, thank you very much! That would be murder. My face will only age with time, and become uglier only by lasting longer. I want my face to belong only to me, I want nobody to see what I do with it, I want it to depend only on me. If I were married, it wouldn't be *my* face any longer, it would belong to my husband – he would abandon it, it would not please him, and he would forbid it from pleasing anybody else. I would rather not have one. No, Lisette, I have no desire to be a flirt, but there are moments when your heart speaks to you and you are very glad to have your eyes free. So, no more discussion. Take my letter to Damis, and let whoever wants line up under the yoke of matrimony!

LISETTE. Ah, madame, how you delight me! What a sensible goddess you are! All right then, I won't say another word. Don't get married. My subsidiary divinity approves your attitude and will do the same. But do you hope for much from this letter I am going to take?

LUCILE. I outline my intentions to Damis, I beg him to serve them, I indicate the steps which must be taken to dissuade his father and mine from marrying us off – and if Damis is as much a gentleman as they say, I consider the matter closed.

Scene 3

Enter a FOOTMAN.

FOOTMAN. Madame, here is a servant who is asking to speak with you.

LUCILE. Let him come in.

FRONTIN (*comes in*). Madame, is this girl to be trusted?

LISETTE. What a lout, to begin by insulting me!

FRONTIN. I have the honour of belonging to Monsieur Damis, who has commissioned me to have the honour of offering you respectful greetings.

LISETTE. You have had the time to do it four times over. Come on, get it over with.

LUCILE. Let him finish. What is this all about?

FRONTIN. Don't bother checking her, madame; I'm not listening to her.

LUCILE. Tell me, what does your master want with me?

FRONTIN. He requests a moment's conversation with you, madame, before appearing here shortly with his father. I can assure you this conversation is necessary.

LUCILE (*aside to* LISETTE). Do you think I should see him, Lisette?

LISETTE. Wait a moment, madame, while I ask this prattler a few questions. Tell us, Mr Somebody, since you consider this conversation so important, you presumably know what it is to be about?

FRONTIN. My master hides none of his thoughts from me.

LISETTE. Hm, well, to judge by the repository, I don't have a very high opinion of the thoughts. Still, come here. What's it all about?

FRONTIN. It's about an answer that I'm waiting for.

LISETTE. Are you going to tell us?

FRONTIN. I'm a man, and I'm keeping quiet. I challenge you

to do as much.

LUCILE. Leave him be, since he doesn't want to tell us anything.
Go on, let your master come here.

FRONTIN. He is yours in a twinkling, madame. He's waiting for
me on one of the paths in the wood.

LISETTE. Go on then, go.

FRONTIN. You won't stop me, sweetheart.

Scene 4

LISETTE. Why didn't you tell me to give him your letter? It would
have spared you from seeing his master.

LUCILE. I have no intention of seeing him, either, but I need to
know what he wants with me, and here is my idea. Damis is
going to come here; you can wait for him whilst I withdraw into
this little room – I shall be able to hear everything from there.
Tell him I have decided on reflection that I shouldn't show
myself on this occasion, and that I beg him to be open with you
about what he wanted to say to me. And if he refuses to speak
and shows some insistence on seeing me, bring the conversation
to a close by giving him my letter.

LISETTE. I can hear someone. Hide yourself, madame.

Scene 5

LISETTE (*aside*). It's Damis ... Oh my goodness, isn't he
good-looking! Now there's a dainty temptation the devil's set
before us ... I expect it's my mistress you're looking for, sir?

DAMIS. It is indeed, and I was told I would find her here.

LISETTE. That's perfectly true, sir, but she felt she had to withdraw, and she said I should ask you on her behalf to entrust me with what you were going to say to her.

DAMIS. Why is she avoiding me? Does she not like the idea of this marriage?

LISETTE. But, sir, it really is very rash to get married so quickly.

DAMIS. Oh, very rash!

LISETTE. I see that sir thinks sensibly.

DAMIS. So I really can't see her?

LISETTE. Excuse me, sir – here she is. It's the same thing, I'm standing in for her.

DAMIS. Very well, I shall be all the freer to tell you my feelings, and you look like a sensible girl to me.

LISETTE. You look too much as though you know what you're talking about for me to disagree.

DAMIS. Let's get down to what brings me here. My father, whom I cannot bring myself to upset, because he loves me a lot –

LISETTE. Very good. Your story begins like ours.

DAMIS. – wanted to bring about the proposed marriage between your mistress and myself.

LISETTE. I like this beginning.

DAMIS. Wait until the end. So there I was with my regiment when my father wrote to tell me what he had arranged with Lucile's father – I believe that is the name of my intended?

LISETTE. My intended! Oh, that's wonderful!

DAMIS. He painted a charming picture of her.

LISETTE. That's rather commonplace.

DAMIS. That may well be, but according to his letter she is the loveliest person in the world.

LISETTE. Remember that I represent the original, and I shall be obliged to blush on her behalf.

DAMIS. My father then urges me to come to him, and tells me I could not console his declining years better than by marrying Lucile. He goes on to say that he is her father's closest friend, that in any case she is very rich, and that I shall be eternally grateful to him for making this match for me. In conclusion, he tells me that he, his friend, and his family, will be waiting for me in three or four days' time at their neighbouring country houses, and that I should show up there without fail on my return from Paris.

LISETTE. Well then?

DAMIS. I can refuse nothing to such a loving father, so here I am.

LUCILE. To get married?

DAMIS. Good Lord, no – not if I can help it.

LUCILE *half emerges from the little room.*

LISETTE. What! Really?

DAMIS. I'm speaking very seriously. And as they say Lucile is a very sensible person and must be quite indifferent towards me, I had planned to open my heart to her in order to get myself out of this business.

LISETTE (*laughing*). Hey! what reason have you for doing that? Do you love someone else?

DAMIS. Is that the only valid reason possible? I think I have equally sensible ones. The truth is I am not of an age to tie myself down in such a serious commitment. It frightens me, I feel it would limit my potential, and I like to live without restrictions, with a freedom whose worth I fully appreciate and which is more necessary to me than to other men because of my particular temperament.

LISETTE. There's not the slightest word to say to that.

DAMIS. If a husband and wife are to get on well together in a marriage, his disposition must harmonise with hers; and that's very difficult, because out of these two dispositions, there's always one that goes astray, and from what I hear, that's very much the way of a woman's disposition. I ask forgiveness of your sex for what I am saying. There may be exceptions, but they are rare, and I'm not lucky.

LUCILE *is still watching.*

LISETTE. How very nice of you to have such a low opinion of our minds.

DAMIS. But you're laughing. Do my intentions suit you, then?

LISETTE. I tell you, you are a wonderful man.

DAMIS. Seriously?

LISETTE. Quite priceless.

DAMIS. Good Lord, I find you quite delightful.

LUCILE *continues to watch.*

LISETTE. You redeem us. We absolve you even from your kindness in supposing there might be a few honourable exceptions among us.

DAMIS. Oh, I'm not taken in by them. I don't believe in them myself.

LISETTE. May heaven reward you for it. But can we trust what you are saying? Is it quite irrevocable? I should warn you my mistress is very lovely.

DAMIS. And I must warn you that I don't care in the slightest. I am proof against it. Without doing your mistress any disservice, I don't believe she can be more alarming than anyone else I've seen, and I'm quite sure her eyes will be of just the same quality as anyone else's.

LUCILE *looks.*

LISETTE. Heavens above, I hope you don't go back on your word!

DAMIS. If I were not afraid of being ridiculous, I would like to provoke you by recommending you not to go back on yours.

LISETTE. Well, then, out of all your attractions, the one which will charm us most will be your departure. Does that suit you?

DAMIS. You do me justice. For my part, I defy all your charms, and I guarantee my heart.

Scene 6

LUCILE (*coming at once out of the little room*). And I guarantee mine, sir, I promise you – for I can now boldly show myself after what you have just said. Come, sir, the worst is over, we have nothing to fear from one another. You do not care in the slightest about me, and I do not care in the slightest about you. I'm explaining myself in the same style as you, and we are both quite at ease. So let's agree on the facts. Put my mind at rest. How are we going to go about it? I have a sister who might be worth fancying. You could pretend to be more taken by her than by me. Perhaps you'll find that quite easy. I'll complain, then you'll crave indulgence, and carry on regardless. How does that method suit you? Would it be better if we complained of mutual estrangement? It shall be as you wish. You know my secret, and you are a gentleman, so let's get the matter over with.

LISETTE. We don't shilly-shally, you see. We lay our cards on the table. Are you doing the same?

LUCILE. What's that wisecrack? Are you trying to compromise me? 'Are you doing the same?' indeed! Are you trying to amuse the gentleman at my expense?

DAMIS. I find the question reasonable, madame.

LUCILE. And I say it is impertinent, sir. But she's only a silly girl.

DAMIS. I must confess, I feel somewhat disconcerted by your appearance. I expressed myself so freely just now on the subject of lovely women, and especially of you, madame!

LUCILE. Of me, sir? You surprise me. I'm not aware that you have anything to reproach yourself with. What! Would it be for vowing that I would not seem alarming? Well, that's fine – that's as if you'd paid me your respects. Good heavens, do you think my vanity is under attack? No, sir, it isn't! Even supposing I had any, what does it matter whether or not you find me alarming? One single man's opinion doesn't settle the matter – and whichever way it goes, one is worth neither more nor less as a result, one's attractions neither lose nor gain by it, it is of no significance. So, sir, no apologies. On the other hand, if you want to make some, if your sense of politeness is embarrassed by some remorse, that's no problem, you are free to do as you wish.

DAMIS. I have no doubt, madame, that whatever I might say would be a matter of complete indifference to you. No matter, I spoke ill, and I condemn myself very seriously.

LUCILE (*laughing*). Very well, then, so be it! Come, sir, you condemn yourself, and I agree. Your intended is better than anyone else you've seen until now, there's no comparison, I take the prize. Am I not right, isn't that the way it goes? I will be quite happy to pay myself all the compliments you want to pay me. There's no point in begrudging them. They are not rare; they are given away to whoever wants them.

DAMIS. It isn't a question of compliments, madame. You are far above that, and it would be difficult to pay them to you.

LUCILE. Well, my word, that's a very fine one, and you are right not to want to waste it. But let's stop there, I beg you – such an excess of courtesies would imply that I had a quite ridiculous degree of self-love. And it would be a strange thing if someone had to ask me to forgive them for not loving me. In fact, such an idea would be comical, it would embarrass me if they did love me. Thank heaven, that's not the case, however. Fortunately, my eyes are at peace, they applaud your indifference. This is what they promised themselves, and I am obliged to you for it. It's the only obligation I could have towards you which could avoid ingratitude. You understand me – you were a little afraid of the attitude I might have, but you may rest easy, sir, I'm taking my leave, I'm running away from you. I saw the danger, and now there's no trace of it.

DAMIS. Ah, madame, please forget what I said just now – it was only in jest. Of all men I am the one with least right to be so conceited, and it would be most impossible to be so with you of all women. Your face forbids such a feeling in anyone, and I would be only too despicable if I felt it.

LISETTE. Good Lord, if that's the way you're both going to take it, you won't get anywhere. I don't like all that verbiage, these eyes at peace, these gallant odes to madame's face, these vanities, these excuses, where is it all leading you? That's not the way to go about it – mind the devil doesn't lead you astray! Look, you don't want to marry one another, so let's get to the point. Confirm your resolutions this very moment in my presence by repeating a solemn vow that you will never belong to one another. Come on, madame, you first, to set a good example, and for the honour of your sex.

LUCILE. Well, that's a fine idea you've got! What a splendid solution, to be sure! You want me to go first, as if it didn't all depend on this gentleman, as if it weren't up to him to guarantee my resolution with his! If he wanted to marry me, he could easily bring it about through my father, by claiming that I had to obey him, couldn't he? So it's his resolution that matters, not mine. Mine would be an unqualified loss.

LISETTE. She's right, sir. Your word will dictate everything. So speak.

DAMIS. Me go first! That would be most unfitting of me, it would violate the duties of a gentleman, and I don't wish to lose my right to respect, thank you very much.

LISETTE. You will end up marrying her out of respect. All these arguments are pure gibberish. I come back to you, madame.

LUCILE. And I hold fast to what I have said. There is no answer to it. But let the gentleman explain himself. Let us know what he means by the difficulty he has raised – is it respect, is it consideration, is it mere banter, is it whatever you like? Will he please make up his mind – people ought to speak naturally.

LISETTE. The gentleman is telling you he is too polite to be natural.

DAMIS. It is true that I dare not explain myself.

LISETTE. He's waiting for you.

LUCILE (*sharply*). Very well, let's bring it to an end, if that's all that's stopping you, sir. Here are my feelings – I don't want to get married, and I never felt less like it than at this moment. This statement is clear and plain, and implies all that propriety requires that I should spare you. You are said to be a man of honour, sir, your character is much praised. I shall recognise the truth of all I have been told about you by the trouble you take to get me out of this business, and by the help you give me in it. Shall I just say one more thing? Perhaps my heart has been forewarned. I think that is enough, sir, and what I am saying is as good as a vow never to marry you. I will, however, make such a vow, if you deem it necessary. Will that suffice?

DAMIS. It is done, madame, and you have nothing to fear. I am not one to hound you in your present frame of mind. It excludes our getting married, and even if my life depended on it, even if my heart should miss you – which would not be hard to believe – I would sacrifice my heart and life to you, and sacrifice them to you without telling you. I make this undertaking, not with vows which would signify nothing – and yet which I do make as you do, if you insist – but because your heart wishes it and reason requires it, as do my honour and my integrity from which you demand it. And as we shall still have to see one another, and I cannot go away and leave you straight away, if – during the time when we shall still be meeting – I happened by chance to let slip some remark which might alarm you, I implore you in advance not to see anything in it that goes against my word, but to put it down to the impossibility of behaving indifferently towards someone who looks as you do. Apart from that, I ask only one favour of you, and that is that you help me to get out of your way, and do not leave me to suffer our families' reproaches on my own. It's only right that we should share them; you deserve them more than I do. You fear the spouse more than the marriage, and I only fear the latter. Goodbye, madame – I am in a hurry to show you that I am at least worth some respect. (*He starts to go off.*)

LISETTE. But you're going off without making any plans.

DAMIS. Madame told me I could pretend to become attached to her sister. It's as good an idea as any.

LUCILE (*sadly*). Besides, we shall have the time to meet again. Lisette, follow the gentleman since he's going away, and check that nobody is watching.

DAMIS (*aside, as he exits*). I am in despair.

Scene 7

LUCILE (*alone*). Oh, I have to sigh, and it won't be the last time. What a business for my poor heart! That wretched Lisette! Where did she dream up all the things she's just made us say?

Act Two

Scene 1

ORGON (*as if already speaking*). I do not praise him more than he is worth, but I do believe that so far as mind and body are concerned, it would be difficult to find anyone better than Damis. As regards quality of heart and character, they are the subject of general praise, and by the look of him he deserves it.

LISETTE. That's my opinion too.

ORGON. But does my daughter think as we do? That's why I wanted to speak to you, in order to find out.

LISETTE. Can you doubt it, sir? You know her. Would she fail to notice merit? In the first place, she takes after you.

ORGON. And yet she cannot have given Damis much of a welcome. He must have found her manner cold.

LISETTE. He may have found it temperate, but certainly not cold.

ORGON. What do you mean by temperate?

LISETTE. It's as if you were to say . . . between hot and cold.

ORGON. So why do we see Damis preferring to speak to her sister?

LISETTE. My word, Damis himself has the key to that secret.

ORGON. I think I have it too. He seems to think that Lucile is being distant with him.

LISETTE. Well, I think I have the key to another secret. I think Lucile is only behaving coldly towards Damis because he isn't very attentive towards her.

ORGON. He's only keeping his distance because he's badly received.

LISETTE. But, sir, what if he were only badly received because he's keeping his distance?

ORGON. What's all this playing with words? Speak naturally. My

daughter tells you what she thinks. Does Damis not suit her?
Because he's certainly complaining about Lucile's welcome.

LISETTE. He's complaining, you say! Sir, he's a rogue, upon my
word. I'll tell him myself he's wrong. He knows very well he
doesn't love us.

ORGON. He claims the opposite.

LISETTE. Well, where is it, then, this love that he has? We've
looked in his eyes, and there's nothing there. In his words, and
they don't say a word. In the sound of his voice, and there's no
sign of it. In his behaviour, and nothing comes out. Not a single
heartfelt impulse pierces through. Our vanity has eyes like a
hawk, and has ferreted everywhere. And then the gentleman
comes and tells us he is in love! We can tell in advance we are
going to be loved, we hear the news of a lover's heart before he
hears it himself! That's a fine story he's telling us, with his
imperceptible love!

ORGON. There's something here I don't understand. Isn't that his
valet? He seems to be looking for you.

Scene 2

ORGON (*to* FRONTIN, *who is going off*). Come here, come here.
Why are you running away?

FRONTIN. Well, sir, it's because we aren't very close friends.

ORGON. Come here anyway, never mind that.

FRONTIN. Seriously, sir?

ORGON. Come here, I tell you!

FRONTIN. Very well, sir, as you wish. I have sometimes been told
my conversation was as good as anyone else's, and I'll put my
best into it. Where are you up to? They say Burgundy's
produced a lot this year – that's very pleasing. They say that in

Constantinople the Turks –

ORGON. Stop it! Let's leave Constantinople.

LISETTE. He'll get out of there just as easily as he got out of Burgundy.

FRONTIN. I was just about to take you to Champagne in a moment. I like places where there are vineyards.

ORGON. No wandering off, Frontin, let's talk a little about your master. Tell me in confidence – what does he think of the marriage that's been arranged? Does his heart concur in our plans?

FRONTIN. Ah, sir, you're talking about a heart that's leading a sad existence. The more I look at you, the more puzzled I am. I see cruelty in your children that could not be guessed at from the gentleness of your face.

LISETTE *shrugs her shoulders*.

ORGON. What do you mean, cruelty? Who are you talking about?

FRONTIN. About my master, and the secret anguish he has suffered at your daughter's hands.

LISETTE. What an insolent fellow with his taradiddles! Tell me, what has anyone done to your master? What vexations has he had to suffer? What has he said to us up until now? What do we see of him except his farewell bows? Do you tell your love by running away? When you love an older sister, do you go and tell her younger sister?

FRONTIN. Don't you find this girl rather crabby, sir?

ORGON. Be quiet, that's enough! Everything I hear makes me think that perhaps there's just a misunderstanding here. As for my daughter, tell her, Lisette, that I should be very angry if I had to complain about her. I invited Damis and his father here because she gave me her word. Since she has seen the son, she does not dislike him, from what she says, and yet they are avoiding one another. I want to know which of the two is in the wrong, because it's time this stopped. (*He goes off.*)

Scene 3

FRONTIN *and* LISETTE *look at one another for a while.*

LISETTE. Ask me why that wretch is staring at me so much.

FRONTIN (*singing*). Tra la la la.

LISETTE. Tra la la la la.

FRONTIN. Ooh yes! There is voice, but no method.

LISETTE. Go away. What are you doing here?

FRONTIN. I am studying your feelings towards me.

LISETTE. I think you're a silly fool. There you are, your studies are over. Goodbye.

She tries to leave.

FRONTIN (*stops her*). Wait, wait, I have to talk to you about our affairs. You look as though you have good taste. I'm afraid you might fancy me, and that's the last thing we want in this situation.

LISETTE. Me fancy you! If you're afraid of that, you've obviously never met your ugly mug anywhere. Come on, speak, let's hear what you have to say to me. Hurry, or else I'll show you what my eyes can do.

FRONTIN. Ooh! Ow! That glance carried off half my heart. Have mercy, please, I beg you! Let's control ourselves, it's in our interest. I only stayed behind to tell you that.

LISETTE. What do you mean? Tell me more.

FRONTIN. You seem very well in with your mistress.

LISETTE. Mistress? I'm hers. I rule her.

FRONTIN. Good! Rank is no better observed between my master and me. Now suppose your mistress were to marry.

LISETTE. My authority expires, and the husband succeeds me.

FRONTIN. If my master took a wife, the household would fall into female hands. So it's in our interest that they both stay single.

LISETTE. And I've forbidden my mistress to do otherwise. Fortunately, her obedience doesn't cost her anything.

FRONTIN. Your little girl is of a rare disposition. My young man has a natural hatred of the conjugal knot, and I leave him to his bachelor life. Young chaps like him manage to get away with things, and it's good poaching country. Now, we have to keep our jobs. Our young folks' fathers are both afflicted with old age – it's an incurable disease and threatens to make some orphans before too long. These orphans revert to us as part of our portion. They are of an age to take up all their rights, and their rights will establish us in ours. You follow me?

LISETTE. I'm with you. There's no need for what you're saying to be any clearer.

FRONTIN. We shall each take good care of our household.

LISETTE. Oh yes – it's a light burden to carry when you love your master's good fortune.

FRONTIN. If we two were to fall in love, we wouldn't be able to fend off the love that our two orphans look like catching. They would get married, and goodbye to our rights.

LISETTE. You're right, Frontin, we must not love one another.

FRONTIN. You don't say that very firmly.

LISETTE. Well, it spoils everything if we have to hate one another.

FRONTIN. My dearest girl, let's have a row.

LISETTE. But arranged matches never work!

FRONTIN. Oh come on, let's exchange a few insults, and sour relations between love and us. For instance, I find you ugly. Well? You have nothing to say?

LISETTE (*laughing*). But you don't believe a word of it!

FRONTIN. What, sweetheart! So you think . . . ? Good grief, turn your face away, it's frightening off my insults!

LISETTE. I don't know what's become of all the ugliness in *your* face.

FRONTIN. We are ruining ourselves, my girl.

LISETTE. Come on then, let's rouse ourselves, that's all over. Look, I just can't stand you!

FRONTIN. Someone's coming. I haven't time to pay you back, but you won't lose anything by waiting, little girl!

Scene 4

PHENICE. I am very pleased to find you here, Frontin, especially with Lisette, who will tell my sister what I am about to say to you. Several times today I have avoided Damis, who persists in following me and speaking to me, engaged as he is to my sister. As he is not mending his ways in spite of all I have said to him, I am delighted that my feelings on this matter should be known. Lisette will bear witness that I ask you to report to him all you have just heard, and that I plainly ask him to leave me in peace.

FRONTIN. No, madame, I couldn't. Your commission is not feasible. I only ever report nice things to my master. And besides, it is not possible that the most charming man in the world can have bored you.

LISETTE. The most charming man in the world seems to me to be quite amazing. He is offered the loveliest girl in the world, and the gentleman is not satisfied. He must be as blind as a bat.

PHENICE. What does that mean, 'as blind as a bat'? Take it easy, Lisette – nobody is lovelier than my sister, but it isn't up to you to decide whether I'm her equal or not.

LISETTE. I am not attacking anyone, madame, but when a man gives up my mistress in favour of someone else, there can be no quibbling about him – he is a man without taste. Such things have been so ever since there were men. Yes, without taste, and if I only had a moment left to live, I would have to spend it mocking him. Without taste.

PHENICE. I didn't stop here to enter into conversation with you, but in what respect does he so deserve to be mocked, if you please?

LISETTE. My answer is to be found in my mistress's face.

FRONTIN. If madame's face were to give itself some help, you would hardly be the leading light.

PHENICE (*going off*). Your remarks are impertinent, Lisette, and someone will have to pay for them.

Scene 5

FRONTIN (*laughing*). That gave her a nice little dose of competition. Let's carry on like this, dear girl. Everything's catching fire, and the marriage will go up in smoke. Goodbye, I'm off – here's your mistress coming. Confirm her in her dislikes. (*He goes off.*)

LUCILE. What is going on here, then? You were talking very loudly with my sister, and I saw her in the distance as if she were angry. And another thing, my father is not speaking to me. What have you done? What is the reason for all this?

LISETTE. You should be happy, madame – we are getting rid of Damis for you.

LUCILE. Oh yes? It sounds to me from that as if you're up to some silly piece of foolishness.

LISETTE. Never fear. All you are asking for is a legitimate excuse for refusing him, isn't it? Well, I've been working hard to give you one, and I've done it so well that your sister is now smitten with him, and that's bound to lead to something for us.

LUCILE. My sister smitten with him! I don't see how this bizarre device can be of any use to me. My sister smitten! By what right is she? And how does it come about that she has to be?

LISETTE. Didn't we agree that Damis would flirt with your sister? Well, if she should come to fall in love with him as a result, you can withdraw without a word needing to be said. I challenge you to think of anything cleverer. Believe me.

LUCILE. Never mind praising your own cleverness. Don't give answers at a tangent to what you were asked. You are talking about Damis, don't leave him, let's finish that subject first.

LISETTE. Here's the rest. Frontin was with me, your sister saw him, she came to speak to him.

LUCILE. There's still no Damis there! I'm waiting.

LISETTE. What kind of mood are you in today, madame?

LUCILE. Oh very good! On top of everything else now, you're going to regale me with speculation about my mood!

LISETTE. Well, give me the time to answer you then. 'Frontin,' she said to him, 'your master is only speaking to me, although he is engaged to my sister. People think I've got a hand in it, I don't like that, and I want you to tell him so.'

LUCILE. Well, what does it matter to me if my sister is ridiculously vain? I shall confound her when I feel like it.

LISETTE. Don't do any such thing. I sensed all the advantage there was for you in this vanity of hers. I needled her, I wounded her pride. You would have been delighted by the way I spoke to her.

LUCILE. Not at all. I can see it from here. But let it go.

LISETTE. I laughed at her and said, 'Well, Damis is a fine one to neglect my mistress.'

LUCILE. Him neglect me? But he's not neglecting me. What gave you that idea? He's carrying out what we agreed, that's different.

LISETTE. I know that, but that secret has to be kept, so I carried on in the same way. 'He's chosen a funny way to behave,' I said. 'What's funny?' your sister asks. 'It's very amusing,' I tell her. 'You're having a joke, Lisette.' 'I'm telling you what I think, madame.' 'It's true my sister is lovely, but so are others too.' 'I don't know these others, madame.' 'You are offending me.' 'I'm not trying.' 'You're a silly girl.' 'I find that hard to believe.' 'Be quiet!' 'I am being quiet.' And with that she goes off, ablaze with rage and beauty, and looking likely to outrival you. What do you say to that?

LUCILE. What do I say? That I am forever indebted to you, that
I am comprehensively affronted, that my sister has triumphed,
that I can hear her gloating from this distance, that she must
think I am afflicted with the basest jealousy imaginable, and
that it would be impossible to be more humiliated than I am!

LISETTE. You amaze me! Didn't you tell Damis yourself to seem
to take a fancy to her?

LUCILE. You are crudely confusing different ideas, but it's only to
be expected from someone so small-minded as you. By
pretending to love my sister, Damis gave me a perfectly natural
reason for saying: 'I'm not marrying a man who apparently
loves another woman.' But refusing to marry a man is not the
same as being jealous of the woman he loves, do you understand?
It's a difference of kind, and that distinction seems to escape
you. And as a result I am betrayed, I am the victim of your
small-mindedness, my sister has gone silly, and I don't know
where I'm up to. It's all the results of your efforts, and that's
how everything gets spoiled when people have no brains. What
are you letting me in for? Must I in turn humiliate my sister –
my sister ablaze with rage and beauty?

LISETTE. You will do as you wish, but I thought the most certain
method was to involve your sister in loving Damis, and perhaps
Damis in loving her, so that you would have good reason for
being angry and refusing him.

LUCILE. What! You really don't sense your impertinence,
whichever way you take it? I mean, why do you want my sister
to love Damis? Why work so hard to infatuate her with a man
who surely will not love her? Were you asked to commit such
treachery against her? Am I her enemy to that extent? Is she
mine? Do I wish her harm? Is there any cruelty equal to the trap
you are setting her? You are ruining her life if she falls into it.
Are you so malicious, then? Or did you suppose that I was? You
fill me with real distress for her. I don't know if she ought not to
be warned. Because this business is not a game. Damis himself
may be forced to marry her in spite of himself. That would be

ruining two people at once, two destinies made tragic by my doing. It would be an eternal reproach to me, and it grieves me greatly.

LISETTE. Oh, come, madame, don't alarm yourself so. Come on, be consoled – I believe Damis does love her, and gives himself up with all his heart.

LUCILE. Oh yes, that's how it is. Because you don't know what to say any more, it costs you nothing to give hearts away, Lisette, you offer them cheap to all comers. But listen, answer me – I am asking your conscience. If Damis had to decide, do you doubt that he would prefer me to my sister? You must surely have noticed he was less distant towards me than towards her.

LISETTE. No, I didn't notice that.

LUCILE. No? Are you blind, then, as well as impertinent? At least lie without lacking respect for me.

LISETTE. It isn't that you aren't better than her, but every day we see the greater being abandoned in favour of the lesser.

LUCILE. Every day! You are very bold to put the exception in place of the general rule.

LISETTE. Oh, there's no point in all this shouting. I want no more to do with it. Find a way of coming to terms, I'm not the one who's threatened with marriage, and all you have to do is explain yourself to these people who are coming. Defend yourself as you think fit. (*She exits.*)

Scene 6

LUCILE (*alone*). Alas, you don't know the pain I'm suffering, or what particular fondness troubles me.

Scene 7

ORGON. My dear girl, Monsieur Ergaste and myself have brought you someone whose mind you must cure of an error which afflicts it. It's Damis. You know our intentions, you have consented to them, but he thinks you don't like him, and in this state of mind he hardly dares approach you.

ERGASTE. For my part, madame, inspite of all the joy I would derive from a marriage which united me more closely with my best friend, I should be extremely sorry to see it taking place if you find it repellent.

LUCILE. Up until now, sir, I have done nothing which might give rise to such an idea. No revulsion has been seen from me.

DAMIS. It is true, madame, I had the impression that I did not suit you.

LUCILE. Perhaps that was what you wanted to think.

DAMIS. Me, madame? I would have neither taste nor sense in that case.

ORGON. Didn't I say so? It's all a disagreement about finer feelings. Try to be fairer to one another. Monsieur Ergaste, people of our age merely scare off proper explanations, so let's go for a little walk. As for you, my dear children, since you do not hate one another, I give you two days to bring your discussions to an end, after which you shall be married. And it will be tomorrow, if anyone quibbles with me.

They go off.

Scene 8

DAMIS. 'Tomorrow, if anyone quibbles with me!" Well, madame, I did the best I could in what has just happened. I tried in my replies to show consideration for you sense of propriety. But what do you think of what they were saying?

LUCILE. That in fact it's starting to get difficult.

DAMIS. Very difficult.

LUCILE. Yes, I must agree, we're going to find it hard to get out of all this.

DAMIS. So hard that I wouldn't like to bet that we shall get out of it.

LUCILE. How shall we go about it, then?

DAMIS. Heavens, I've no idea.

LUCILE. You have no idea, Damis? Well, that's wonderful. I advise you to think about it, however. Because I am not required to have more imagination than you.

DAMIS. Oh, good Lord, madame, I don't ask you to have more than I have, either. That wouldn't be fair.

LUCILE. Well, be careful then. If we are both short of it, as looks very likely, I should be grateful if you would let me know where that's going to lead us.

DAMIS. I still say the same thing – I've no idea, and we shall see.

LUCILE. Is that how you're going to take it, sir? Well, then, I'll say the same. I've no idea, and we shall see.

DAMIS. Well, yes, madame, we shall see. That's all I know. What else can I answer?

LUCILE. Something clearer, more positive and precise. 'We shall see' means nothing. We shall see ourselves getting married, that's what we shall see. Are you curious to see that? Because your calmness amazes me. Where does it come from? Eh? What are you trying to say? Are you hoping that your father and mine will see that you don't like their plans? You could be mistaken there.

DAMIS. I could easily be mistaken, because they don't at all see what you just said.

LUCILE. They don't see it?

DAMIS. No, madame, they couldn't see it, that isn't possible. With some faces, it is impossible to believe that anybody could remain unaffected by their appearance. For instance, who will ever believe that I don't love you? Nobody. We may try as we might, but no amount of ingenuity can convince anyone of that.

LUCILE. That's true, you will find that everyone is blind. However, sir, since we are concerned here with serious matters, would you please cut out your 'Who will ever believe', which is not to my taste, and which sounds very much like a joke which I do not deserve. And please tell me what you mean when you say it is impossible to believe anybody could remain unaffected by certain faces. What is their effect then, I must ask you? Eh? How do they supposedly affect people, according to you? Do people inevitably fall in love with them? Have I got such a face? Can people not help falling in love with me when they see me? You are quite mistaken, sir, I must disillusion you. I have had it proved a thousand times that the opposite is true, and I do not share that view at all. In fact, I no more believe it than you do – you are only pretending to in order to amuse yourself, and you know what happens to compliments of that sort when they are scrutinised.

DAMIS. It's very easy for you to reduce them to nothing, because I'm letting you say what you want, and you can do as you like with them so long as that's the case. But I'm saying nothing, madame, I'm saying nothing.

LUCILE. 'I'm saying nothing, madame, I'm saying nothing.' You sound as though you're up to some kind of trick, with your serious manner there. What are these irrelevant remarks which I'm stupid enough to pick up? Do you want to go back on your word?

DAMIS. Didn't I tell you, madame, that things might slip out in conversation that should not alarm you? Don't worry, you have my word, and I shall keep it.

LUCILE. You have as much interest as me in doing so.

DAMIS. That's another matter.

LUCILE. I think it's the same.

DAMIS. No, madame, quite different. Because after all, I might be in love with you.

LUCILE. Oh yes, but to tell you the truth, I would be very glad to know whether that is the case.

DAMIS. Oh, that isn't possible, madame. I promised to keep quiet about that. I may be in love, and I may not. I didn't promise not to be, I only promised not to tell if I were, and to act as if I weren't. Those are the only commitments you extracted from me, and I must respect them for fear of reproach. Apart from that, I am entirely my own master, and I shall be in love with you if I want. So perhaps I am making a sacrifice, but it's my business.

LUCILE. Oh, that's very convenient indeed! Just see how lightly the gentleman treats the matter! 'I shall be in love with you if I want. Perhaps I am in love with you.' With no more bother than that. Whether I approve or not, there's no need for me to know. So I must be patient. But really, if you were in love with me, and being so casual about it, you would certainly be the greatest actor in the world, and such a role is not a very honest one to play, between you and me.

DAMIS. In the present situation, it would not be so much dishonest as exhausting.

LUCILE. Either way, that's enough. I find that such pleasantries tend to make conversation wearisome. You are bored, and so am I. Let's part company. We'll check that your father and mine are not in the garden, and then separate if they aren't watching us any more.

DAMIS. Oh, madame, we've only been together for a moment.

Scene 9

LISETTE. Madame, there is company, just arrived, in the

drawing-room with Monsieur Orgon, and he has sent me to tell you they are going to play cards.

LUCILE. Me play cards! But my father knows I only ever play with great reluctance. Tell him I should like to be excused from it.

LISETTE. But, madame, the company is asking for you.

LUCILE. Oh, let the company wait! Say you can't find me.

LISETTE. And is the gentleman coming? Apparently he does play cards.

DAMIS. Me? I know nothing about cards.

LUCILE. Right, tell my father I'm going to my room, and that I shall only appear after the game has started.

LISETTE (*going off*). What the deuce do they mean, neither of them coming?

Scene 10

DAMIS (*rather embarrassed*). So you don't like cards, madame?

LUCILE. No, sir.

DAMIS. I am very glad to be like you in that respect.

LUCILE. It's neither a virtue nor a fault. But, sir, since there's company, why don't you go? It would entertain you.

DAMIS. I'm not in a mood to look for entertainment.

LUCILE. But are you staying with me?

DAMIS. If you will allow me to

LUCILE. And yet you have nothing to say to me.

DAMIS. Well now, at this very moment I was just thinking about this business between us. It's so unusual, it ought to be unique.

LUCILE. Well, I think it is too.

DAMIS. No, madame, it isn't. It's only about six months since one of my friends and a lady he was supposed to be marrying found themselves in the same situation as you and me. Same resolution before meeting, about not getting married. Same agreement between them, same promises as I made to get him out of her way.

LUCILE. In other words, he broke his promise. That's not unusual.

DAMIS. No, madame, he kept it. But our hearts mock our resolutions.

LUCILE. Fairly often, they say.

DAMIS. The lady in question was very lovely. Much less so than you, however. That's the only difference I find in the story.

LUCILE. You are very flattering.

DAMIS. No, I'm simply a truthful chronicler. Besides, madame, I'm telling you this in good faith, simply to make conversation and with no particular motive.

LUCILE. Oh, I don't imagine any, either. But carry on. What happened between the lady and your friend?

DAMIS. He fell in love with her.

LUCILE. That was a nuisance.

DAMIS. Yes, indeed, because like me he had promised to keep quiet.

LUCILE. You're going to tell me that he spoke?

DAMIS. He was careful not to, because he'd given his word, and he saw only one course to take, which is very strange. He said to her what I said to you just now: 'I may be in love with you, and I may not.' And he added that he would only be bold enough to tell the truth when he saw she was herself a little bit susceptible. I'm only telling a story, remember.

LUCILE. I know. But it was very insensitive of your friend to suggest to a woman that she should speak first. She would have to be very hungry for love to buy it at that price.

DAMIS. The lady in question didn't consider it in the same way as you, madame. It is true that she felt some fondness for him.

LUCILE. Oh, that's even worse! What a cowardly way to abuse the weakness of her heart! It's like saying to a woman: 'Do you want to know about my love? Well, suffer the shame of confessing yours to me, disgrace yourself, and then I'll let you know.' What a dreadful thing! And what a nasty friend you have there!

DAMIS. Ah, but listen – this lady realised that this suggestion of his, however horrible it may seem to you, came only from respect and apprehension, and that his heart dared not risk itself without permission from hers. The confession of an unwelcome love would only have alarmed the lady, and made her afraid that my friend was being treacherous and trying to bring on the marriage. She realised all that.

LUCILE. Oh, don't tell me any more! I pity her, and I guess the rest. But I'm anxious to know how a woman behaves in such a case. In what terms can she express herself? I would forget my mother tongue if I had to say 'I love you' before it had been said to me.

DAMIS. He behaved more nobly than that. She didn't have to go to the trouble of speaking.

LUCILE. Well, I should think not!

DAMIS. There are ways which are as good as words. People can say 'I love you' just with a look, and say it very well.

LUCILE. No, sir, a look is still too much. I will agree that it may be returned, but not that it may be given.

DAMIS. But you, madame, would return only indignation.

LUCILE. What does that mean, sir? Is there any question of me in all this? I do believe you are amusing yourself at my expense. You find this very entertaining, I think. You certainly look as though you do. You really are quite amazing! Goodbye, sir. They say you love my sister. Please marry her, and bring the unpleasant situation I am in to an end. That is all I ask of you.

DAMIS. I shall continue to pretend to love her, madame. That is all I can promise you. (*Going off.*) How scornful she is!

Scene 11

LUCILE (*alone*). What strange inclinations we sometimes get, to be sure. How does it come about that I am drawn towards this man, when there is nothing lovable about him?

Act Three

Scene 1

PHENICE. No, sir, I must tell you, I can't stand the part you're playing with me any longer, and I find it quite impossible to understand. You only came here to marry my sister. She is very lovely, and yet you don't speak to her, all your conversations are with me. I might understand some of it if love entered into it, but you don't love me, there's no question of it.

DAMIS. And yet nothing would be easier than to fall in love with you, madame.

PHENICE. That's fine, but nothing would be more pointless, and I am not in a position to listen to you. However it may be, this kind of behaviour doesn't suit me. I have already indicated as much, I have let you know, and now I ask you as a favour to stop chasing after me. After all, I shouldn't have thought you would want to offend me.

DAMIS. Me, madame?

PHENICE. That being so, please stop, or I myself will force you.

DAMIS. You will forbid me to see you, then?

PHENICE. No, sir, but people imagine that you are in love with me. Your behaviour has convinced everybody of it, and I shall not deny it, I shall not appear displeased by it, and I may very well bring you to a point where you are obliged either to marry me in spite of your wishes, or to flee from here as someone rather reckless – and that's putting it kindly – as someone quite unforgivable who has shamelessly flouted all considerations of decency by making a fool of two girls one after the other, two girls of good family both equally able to settle on the finest of gentlemen. In other words, you risk either the sacrifice of your heart, or the loss of your reputation – two objects which are worth thinking about. But tell me, don't you really love my sister?

DAMIS. If I married her, I would not be upset.

PHENICE. Well, either I don't know anything about these things, or I believe she wouldn't be upset, either. So why don't you get together?

DAMIS. Heavens, I don't know.

PHENICE. But there's no sense in what you're saying.

DAMIS. Well, I wouldn't know how to put any more sense into it.

PHENICE. Well, it's your business, and I'll just stick to what I've told you. Here comes my father with my sister. Please leave before they see you.

DAMIS. But, madame –

PHENICE. Oh, sir! No more foolery!

Scene 2

ORGON (*speaking to* LUCILE, *as he enters with her*). No, my dear girl, I never intended to force you. Whatever you say to me, it's quite certain that you don't love him, so let's hear no more about it. (PHENICE *tries to leave.* ORGON *continues.*) Don't go, Phenice, I was looking for you, and I have something to say to you. Listen to me, both of you. Damis wanted to marry your sister, that was our arrangement. But we are obliged to change it. Lucile's heart has arranged things otherwise. She won't admit it, but that's only out of consideration for me, and I have abandoned that plan.

LUCILE. But, father, would I tell you I was in love with Damis? That would not be seemly. It's the sort of thing a well-bred girl could not say, even if she wanted to.

ORGON. Still at it! And what if I told you, my girl, that I heard from Lisette herself that you don't like him? What's the point in denying it? I absolve you from any such considerations on my account. And to bring the matter to a close, you will not marry him. Your distaste for him has been only too obvious, and I now intend him for your sister. He has given his heart to her, and she won't refuse him hers, although she too is going to tell me the opposite because of you.

PHENICE. Me marry him, father?

ORGON. There we are! I know the two of you. One would marry a man she doesn't love for fear of upsetting me. The other would refuse to marry the man she does love out of respect for her sister. You see, I know how things stand, and I know how to interpret you. Besides, I have been well informed, and I'm not mistaken.

LUCILE (*aside to* PHENICE). Don't just stand there, say something.

PHENICE. Really, I don't believe this is serious.

LUCILE. Take care what you're doing, father. You are mistaken about my sister. I can almost see tears in her eyes.

ORGON. If these girls are not mad, then I have lost my wits. Goodbye, I'm going to tell Monsieur Ergaste about the new marriage I'm planning. He's a good friend, and he won't disagree with me about it. As for you, my children, you may complain. I am in the wrong, indeed I am abusing the power I have over you. You may complain, I recommend it, and it can be very consoling. But I don't want to hear you, I would find it too affecting. Go on, leave without answering, and let me speak to Monsieur Ergaste. He's just coming.

LUCILE (*as she leaves*). I can't stand it.

Scene 3

ERGASTE. You are looking at a very worried man. My dear

friend, I see no likelihood of the intended marriage, short of doing violence to two hearts who seem not to be made for one another. I can never forgive my son for giving in so easily to Lucile's indifference. I have even gone so far as to suspect him of loving someone else, and here is his valet with whom I was talking about it. But whether I'm mistaken or whether this scoundrel doesn't want to say anything about it, all he will answer is that Lucile does not like my son, and I am in despair.

FRONTIN (*behind*). Sir, a scoundrel isn't a very nice thing to see – would you like me to go away?

ERGASTE. Wait there.

ORGON. Don't worry, Monsieur Ergaste, there's a solution for everything, and we shall not lose by it, if you are willing.

ERGASTE. Speak, my dear friend, I applaud your intentions in advance.

ORGON. We have a way out.

ERGASTE. I didn't dare suggest it, but in fact I can see one, along with everyone else.

ORGON. It simply requires a change of object. Let us substitute the younger for the older daughter, and we shall find no obstacle. It's an expedient which love seems to indicate.

ERGASTE. Between you and me, my son did seem to be inclining that way all of a sudden.

ORGON. Speaking confidentially, my younger daughter does not dislike his inclination.

ERGASTE. Nobody has failed to notice what we are discussing. Everyone is struck by a very visible fondness.

ORGON. Well, my word, let's give in to it, then. Let's marry them off to one another.

ERGASTE. You give your consent? Heaven be praised! That's what you call a true union of hearts, a real love-match, and there never ought to be any other sort. You delight me. Is it agreed, then?

ORGON. Certainly. I have just warned my daughter about it.

ERGASTE. I give you my thanks. Could you just allow me a word with this valet, and then I'll join you at once.

ORGON. I'll wait for you. Carry on.

Scene 4

ERGASTE. Come here.

FRONTIN. Here I am, sir.

ERGASTE. Listen, and remember the message I'm going to give you.

FRONTIN. I haven't a very good memory, but if you work hard you can do without.

ERGASTE. You will tell my son he is no longer promised to Lucile, and that today he is to be given the one he loves.

FRONTIN. And what if he asks me which is the one he loves? What shall I tell him?

ERGASTE. Oh come, come, he will know very well we are talking about Phenice.

FRONTIN (*going off*). You can count on me, sir.

ERGASTE. Where are you going?

FRONTIN. To deliver my message.

ERGASTE. You're in a great hurry. That isn't all.

FRONTIN. Very well, sir, as much as you like. Don't spare me.

ERGASTE. Tell him to take good care to thank Monsieur Orgon for his kindness in not being angry about this matter. Because if Damis is not marrying Lucile, I'll wager he is the one to blame. Tell him that because of this new marriage I forgive him the grief he nearly caused me, but that if he were to deceive me again, if he were to hesitate about marrying Phenice after the attentions he has paid her, if he were again to insult Monsieur Orgon in this way, then I never want to see him again in my life, and that I disinherit him. I shall not even speak to him so long as I am not pleased with him.

FRONTIN (*laughing*). I notice that you lower your voice to
pronounce the terrible word 'disinherit'. You're scared of it
yourself. A father's love is a wonderful thing.

ERGASTE. Keep your reflections to yourself, you rascal! Just do
as you're told. The rest is my business.

Scene 5

LISETTE. I was looking for you, Frontin, and I was waiting for
Monsieur Ergaste to leave you so that I could talk to you, and
find out what he was saying to you. Things seem to me to be
going badly. My mistress is not looking kindly on me. Do you
know what it's all about? . . . Please answer!

FRONTIN. The fear of being disinherited robs me of speech.

LISETTE. What do you mean?

FRONTIN. Of being disinherited, I tell you, or of marrying
Phenice.

LISETTE. What? Marrying Phenice! Oh, Frontin, what have we
come to? So that's why Lucile received me so well just now.
She knew I had told her father that she didn't love Damis, and
that Damis was coming out in favour of her sister. Now they
want him to marry her. I didn't foresee that happening, and
I reckon I am in disgrace. Lucile seemed too upset – she is
apparently not indifferent to your master, and I shall lose
everything if she sends me packing.

FRONTIN. Whichever way you turn, it looks like starvation diets
for us.

LISETTE. That's what comes of not just letting things go their
own way. I believe our master and mistress would be in love
with one another if we hadn't interfered. A curse upon our
ambition to govern our households.

FRONTIN. Oh, it's all very well saying that, my child, but any kind of government is profitable, and it wasn't a bad idea to try and keep them single. The worst thing I find is that I am in love with you, and you haven't come off any better.

LISETTE. Oh, why didn't you have the wit to fall in love with me straight away? I would have made Lucile change her mind.

FRONTIN. I'll tell you where we went wrong – we didn't realise what was bound to happen between people as splendid as us. But listen, sweetheart, is there really no way out of this mess? Like you, I suspect that our master and mistress don't really hate one another deep down, and all we would have to do is to get them to admit it. Then we should be out of trouble. Let's try and do them that service, then.

LISETTE. We've done a good job of souring things. Never mind, here comes your master. Let's try and win him over with a nifty change of attack.

Scene 6

DAMIS. Ah, there you are, Frontin. Hello, Lisette. What message have you for me from my father, Frontin? He has just told me that you have something to say to me on his behalf, but he didn't want to explain.

FRONTIN. Yes, sir, it's just two or three little items that I was telling Lisette. They aren't really very interesting.

DAMIS. Tell me about them without counting them.

FRONTIN. You must excuse me, arithmetic helps. The first is that he wants to hear no more about you.

DAMIS. Who? My father?

FRONTIN. Himself. But that's not the most important. The second is that he is disinheriting you.

DAMIS. Me! But such a thing is inconceivable.

FRONTIN. He didn't ask me to make you conceive it. Finally, the third is that the first two are cancelled if you marry Phenice.

DAMIS. What! They want to force me –

FRONTIN. Be careful, sir, let's not get confused, let's speak precisely. My message makes no mention of forcing you. Your liberty is not under attack, you see. You are free to choose between Phenice or your ruin, and your choice will be respected.

LISETTE. Isn't that nice of them! Because they think you're fond of her, they expect you to marry her without hesitation after the way you have apparently refused her sister.

FRONTIN. But deep down we don't really refuse this sister. Isn't that so, sir?

DAMIS. It would be all right if it was her.

LUCILE. Oh, sir, why didn't you say? Why didn't you confide your feelings in me?

DAMIS. But even if my feelings were what you believe them to be, don't you know what hers are, Lisette?

LISETTE. I think you might be wrong about them. She has been sad and dreamy ever since your agreement.

FRONTIN. I met her this morning stifling a sigh and wiping her eyes.

LISETTE. She used to love her sister and was always with her, but today she flees from her and turns away to avoid her. What does that mean?

FRONTIN. And she's always ready to return my greeting. Why should that be, except for the honour I have of belonging to you?

LISETTE (to FRONTIN). Perhaps you're not so very wrong. (To DAMIS.) At any rate, sir, I ask you to keep this secret. Just take advantage of it, that's all.

DAMIS. I must confess, Lisette, if you're being honest, what you are saying could augur well for me. And if I dared to suspect the slightest inclination in her heart –

FRONTIN. Would you go and give her yours? Oh, sir, that would be a wonderful present for her!

DAMIS. But listen. This is the same person who quite plainly

indicated her aversion for me the very first moment she saw
me, and who led me to suspect she loved someone else!

LISETTE. Oh, what she said then was pure bad temper,
I promise you.

DAMIS. Very well. But remember she demanded that I should not
marry her, and she asked me to promise this with all my
honour. She may even have a hand today in this new marriage
they want me to make, just so she can be sure of getting rid of
me altogether. In short, I don't know what to think about it
myself. Perhaps I'm mistaken, perhaps you're mistaken too.
Anyway, without some less ambiguous proof of her feelings,
I cannot bring myself to go back on the promises I have made
her. Not that I value them more highly than they deserve – they
would be nothing for a man who was loved. But they must be
binding on a man who is hated, when they have been extracted
from him as a guarantee against him. Whatever the case, here
comes Lucile now. I just need the slightest little welcome from
her and I shall declare myself. Her opening manner will decide
everything.

Scene 7

LUCILE. I have to speak to you for a moment, Damis. Our
discussion will be brief. I have one question to put to you, and
one word to answer me. And then I shall go away and leave you.

DAMIS. You will not need to, madame, and I shall take good care
to go away first. (*Aside.*) Well, Lisette?

LUCILE. First or last, I leave the choice to you. Are you so ill at
ease? Then go away at once. Lisette will pass on what I have to
say to you.

DAMIS (*going off*). I take this course as being the one which suits
you best, madame.

He pretends to go away.

LUCILE. Let him go! Let whoever wishes stop him!

LISETTE. Hey, you're not thinking straight. Come back, sir. Is there war declared between the two of you?

DAMIS. Madame begins by announcing that she has one word to say to me and will then go away from me. Doesn't that imply she cannot bear to see me?

LUCILE. If only you knew how I would like just to leave you there!

DAMIS. I do not doubt it, madame. But it's not now you should be running away from me. You should have done so the very first moment you saw me, when you took such a dislike to me.

LUCILE. Run away from you at the very first moment! Why, sir? That would be very uncivilised. Here, we don't flee at the sight of a man.

LISETTE. But what's wrong with the two of you? Must two people who wish one another well speak as if they couldn't bear the sight of one another? And you, sir, who love my mistress – because I bet you do love her –

She makes signs to DAMIS *as she says these words.*

LUCILE. What a silly girl you are! Come on, dreamer, go and lose your bets elsewhere! Who are you getting at?

LISETTE. Yes, madame, I'm leaving. But before I go, I have to speak. You ask me who I'm getting at. Both of you, madame, both of you! Yes, I would love with all my heart to take away from this gentleman – who has nothing to say and whose silence makes my blood boil – I would love to take away from him his scruples about the ridiculous agreement he has made with you, which I regret having let you make, and which is making you both suffer, one as much as the other. As for you, madame, I don't know how you see these things, but if ever a man had taken a vow never to say 'I love you' to me, oh then I would take a vow to cast the lie in his teeth. He would find out what respect he owed me. I would spare him nothing of all that is most dangerous, shameless, and deadly in the good old flirtatious armoury of looks, words, and glances. That's where I would put my pride, and not in holding myself painfully aloof as you are doing and saying to myself: 'Let's see what he says, let's see what he doesn't say, let him speak, let him begin, it's up to him, it's not up to me, my sex, my pride, the rules of etiquette,' and a thousand other useless ways of dealing with the poor trembling gentleman, who has the goodness to be afraid that his love might alarm and annoy you. Love annoy us! What planet are you from, then? Oh, for heaven's sake, sir, why don't you get annoyed good and proper! Do us that honour! Be brave, attack us! *That* ritual will make your fortune, and you will understand one another. Because up until now there's nothing to be seen in what the two of you are saying. There's 'yes,' there's 'no,' there's for, there's against, there's going away, there's coming back, there's calling back, there's no way of understanding it. Goodbye, I've finished. I've sorted you out, now take advantage of it. Come on, Frontin.

Scene 8

LUCILE. Gracious heaven! What impertinence! Where did she get all that from? In particular, where did she get such ideas about you? Besides, she doesn't spare me any more than she does you.

DAMIS. I am not complaining about it, madame.

LUCILE. You must excuse me, I am putting myself in your position. It's not very pleasant to hear certain things said to one's face.

DAMIS. What, madame! Is it her idea that I might love you that you find so unpleasant for me?

LUCILE. Unpleasant? I do not say her mistake is insulting for you.

My humility does not go so far. But on what grounds does this crazy girl come along and drive us into this?

DAMIS. On what grounds? That's quite simple – she imagines it would be very difficult not to love you. And if I bore a grudge against all those who suspected me of being in love with you, I should be at odds with everybody.

LUCILE. Not with me, you wouldn't.

DAMIS. Oh yes, I know that well enough! If you suspected me, you wouldn't be here. You would run away, you would abandon me.

LUCILE. What do you mean by abandon, sir? You have some very gracious expressions, which paint a pretty picture of my character. I really like the bizarre notion that it gives of my mind. No, sir, I would not abandon you, I would not believe that all was lost. I would have enough determination to cope with such an eventuality, it seems to me. Sufficient unto the day . . . One has to come to terms with things, sir, and put up with them.

DAMIS. It's true people can be hated or despised just as well from close at hand as from a distance.

LUCILE. It's not a question of what can or can't be done. I don't know what should be done in a situation I'm not in. And I believe you will never give me the trouble of hating you.

DAMIS. I shall have one cause for pleasure, however. You won't know if I deserve to be hated. In this respect, I shall always say 'perhaps'.

LUCILE. I don't like that word, sir, I've already told you.

DAMIS. I shan't use it again, madame, and if I had a list of words which offend you, I should take great care to avoid them.

LUCILE. A list is still an entertaining idea. Well, I will tell you where it is. You will find it in the rules of the consideration due to women. You will find, if you look there, that it is not good to amuse yourself with a 'perhaps', which is never going to get you very far with me or intrigue me, because I know where I stand. You only say it in jest, and such jesting is unbecoming – that is not the way men talk, their modesty is not based on such foundations. Let's talk about something else, I didn't come here for nothing. Listen, I suppose you know they want to give you my sister?

DAMIS. So I am told, madame.

LUCILE. They believe you are in love with her, but I've been thinking about your original reasons for pressing your attentions on her, and I'm afraid they might be making a mistake. So I've come to ask you the truth of the matter.

DAMIS. Why, what is it to you, madame?

LUCILE. What is it to me? Now there's a question that could only be asked by a man who has neither brother nor sister and does not know how precious they are! I am concerned about her, sir, and if you don't love her, it would be an affront to the very laws of that integrity you are so fond of, to marry her with a heart that would grow more and more distant from her.

DAMIS. Then why, madame, did you inspire them to give her to me? Because I have every reason to suspect that you are the cause of it, since it was you who first suggested that I should love her. Anyway, madame, do not worry yourself about her, I shall take care of her fate more sincerely than you. She deserves it.

LUCILE. Whether she deserves it or not, I am not asking you to sing her praises, nor have I come here to answer your imaginings. Do you love her, Damis? Tell me. Because if you don't, either don't marry her, or allow me to warn my father who believes you do and would be very upset about being taken in.

DAMIS. Well, madame, if you tell him I don't love her, if you carry out a plan which can only end by driving me away from here pursued by everybody's rage and hate, if you carry it out, then be prepared in return for me to renounce all my promises towards you and to tell Monsieur Orgon that I am ready to marry you when he wants – this very day, if necessary.

LUCILE. Oh yes, sir, so you adopt that threatening tone, do you? Well, I know how to make you change your tune. Go ahead, sir, carry on, I'm not stopping you. Get your revenge, break your promises – only someone who was in love could possibly be forgiven for forgetting such promises, but go ahead, rush in and punish yourself. You will not fail in your attempt, because I myself will help you. Oh, you will marry me, you say, you will marry me! And me too, sir, me too! I will be as vindictive as you, and we shall see which of the two of us will retract. What a wonderful compliment, to be sure! What a pretty little game to suggest!

DAMIS. Well, stop harassing me then, madame! My heart is incapable of doing you harm, but let me get myself out of all this fuss and bother I'm in. Be content with having already brought about what has happened to me – they would not be offering me your sister today if I had not said that I loved her in order to oblige you. Remember that I have served your distaste for me with an astonishing loyalty and honour, a loyalty I did not owe you, and which anybody else in my place would not have shown. Such generous behaviour deserves as its reward that you leave in peace a man who might have carried honour to the point of sacrificing himself for you. I am not trying to say that I love you – no, Lucile, be assured. But still, you don't know the truth of it, you might wonder about it. You are lovely enough anyway, and I say that without praising you. I can marry you, you don't want me to, and I'm leaving you. Really, madame, to seek so fervently to do me harm is a poor reward for a service which anyone except you would have suspected of being difficult to perform. Goodbye, madame.

He is going away.

LUCILE. But wait! Wait! Give me the time to defend myself. Is there nothing to do but go away when you've accused people of such wickedness?

DAMIS. I would say too much if I stayed.

LUCILE. Oh, you will do as you are able, but you must hear me out.

DAMIS. After what you have said to me, I have nothing to learn which could be of interest to me.

LUCILE. Nor I anything left to answer you. There is just one thing which surprises me, and I cannot fathom the reason for it, and that is that you dare to blame me for a marriage which I can see pleases you. The motive behind such hypocrisy is as incomprehensible as it is ridiculous, unless it is my sister who has put you up to it in order to hide from me how close your two hearts are together, and the part she herself has played in an engagement which I have refused and would never want. And I find her much to be pitied in not refusing it herself. (*She exits.*)

Scene 9

FRONTIN. Well, sir, where are you up to?

DAMIS (*in dismay*). I am up to the unhappiest day of my life. Leave me. (*He exits.*)

Scene 10

FRONTIN. Here's a business which looks very much like blowing away our inheritance.

Act Four

Scene 1

DAMIS. No, Frontin, there's no more to be tried in that direction. Lisette can say what she likes, but nobody could have explained themselves more clearly than Lucile did. It's all over, and it only remains for me to get out of this tangle I am in with Phenice. Is she coming soon? Did she promise you?

FRONTIN. Yes, sir, I told her you were waiting for her here, and you'll see her arriving in a moment.

DAMIS. What a strange situation is mine!

FRONTIN. My word, but I'm very much afraid Phenice might take advantage of it.

DAMIS. Is it possible she might want to marry a man she doesn't love?

FRONTIN. Oh, sir, a girl doesn't look as closely as that when she's getting married. She's too curious to be over-scrupulous. Marriage makes all men forgivable. Anyway, it's easy to put up with your face –

DAMIS. Oh, what bad timing! I think I can see my father coming. I'm off. Maybe he won't speak to you, but in any case come and look for me shortly.

Scene 2

ERGASTE. Wasn't my son with you just now?

FRONTIN. Yes, sir, he's just left me.

ERGASTE. It looks as if he was trying to avoid me.

FRONTIN. Him, sir? I think he's looking for you.

ERGASTE. You're lying.

FRONTIN. Me, sir? My character is as true as my face.

ERGASTE. That isn't a compliment to either of them. But let it go. I know you are not lacking in brains, and I know my son readily tells you what he's thinking.

FRONTIN. Well, he's not thinking much, then, because he hardly tells me anything.

ERGASTE. He loves Phenice, and he's going to marry her. And yet I notice that he's sad and dreamy.

FRONTIN. Indeed, and I'd like to have a word with him about it.

ERGASTE. Is he not contented?

FRONTIN. Ah, sir, who can be contented in this life?

ERGASTE. You scoundrel!

FRONTIN. For instance, I'm not contented to be called a scoundrel.

ERGASTE (*the first words aside*). I see I'm not going to learn anything. But tell me, did you pass on all I asked you to tell him?

FRONTIN. Word for word.

ERGASTE. What was his answer?

FRONTIN. Wait a minute! I believe you didn't tell me to remember his answer.

ERGASTE. I have resolved to let him do as he wishes, but you can warn him that I shall keep my promise if he does not behave as he should. As for you, you can be certain that I will not forget your impertinent remarks.

FRONTIN. Oh, sir, you have too good a nature to have such a good memory.

Scene 3

FRONTIN (*aside*). He really is very cross. But it was time he left – here comes Phenice.

PHENICE. Well? You told me your master was waiting here for me. I can't see him.

FRONTIN. He went away because of Monsieur Ergaste. But he's walking nearby, and I have orders to go and fetch him.

PHENICE. Go on then.

FRONTIN. Madame, do I dare flatter myself first that you might grant me a short audience?

PHENICE. Speak.

FRONTIN. In my lowly state as an underling, I watch, I examine, and on the way I see here and there some people that I don't like at all; others I take a fancy to, and I would give myself to them for nothing – and that couldn't be anything but a real gift.

PHENICE. No doubt. But what might this preamble be leading to?

FRONTIN. To preparing you for the liberty I'm going to take, madame, by telling you that you are one of those privileged persons for whom I feel this sympathetic impulse.

PHENICE. I'm much obliged to you for it. But carry on.

FRONTIN. If you knew how great an interest I take in your fate, which I see taking such an unfortunate turn . . .

PHENICE. Explain yourself better . . .

FRONTIN. You are going to marry Damis?

PHENICE. So they say.

FRONTIN. Hush! Keep it dark! I warn you that you can only marry half of him.

PHENICE. Half of Damis? What do you mean?

FRONTIN. His heart is not getting married, madame. It's staying a bachelor.

PHENICE. So you think he doesn't love me?

FRONTIN. Oh! You don't get off as lightly as that!

PHENICE. You mean he hates me?

FRONTIN. Wouldn't it be rather rude to admit that to you?

PHENICE. Well, tell me, then – he wouldn't happen to be in love with my sister?

FRONTIN. Passionately.

PHENICE. Then why doesn't he marry her?

FRONTIN. Oh, that's a whole different story, all that business.

PHENICE. Tell it me, then.

FRONTIN. Well, they began by getting off to a pretty giddy start together. They bound themselves together in some ill-judged pact about not falling in love or marrying one another, and they decided they could make the two fathers change their plans by having *him* pretend that he fancied you. Only pretend, you understand?

PHENICE. Oh, perfectly!

FRONTIN. And as the human heart is changeable, it turns out today that their hearts and their pact are not in tune with one another, and there is great embarrassment to know what to do about you. You understand? Discretion will not allow me to say any more.

PHENICE. That's quite enough already. I am in the picture. And for fear of appearing ungrateful, I will let you into a secret in return – your discretion could well earn you a beating.

FRONTIN. On that basis, please keep my secret. I can see my master. I'm going to tell him to come here.

Scene 4

PHENICE (*alone for a moment*). So I just provided them with an excuse! Oh, I intend to get my revenge, they have deserved it. But since they are in love, I want to behave in such a way that I not only scare them, but also force them together. Well, sir, what do you want with me?

DAMIS. I think you know, madame.

PHENICE. Me? No, I know nothing.

DAMIS. Don't you know that our marriage is agreed?

PHENICE. Is that all? I told you it would be. It couldn't fail to happen.

DAMIS. I didn't think things were going to go so far, and I ask your pardon for being the cause of it.

PHENICE. You are joking – I hold no bitterness towards a man who is going to become my husband.

DAMIS. Don't tease me, madame. I know you don't intend that honour for me, although I should consider myself very happy with it.

PHENICE. If you're speaking the truth, your happiness is assured. I promise I shall put no obstacle in its way.

DAMIS. Upon my word, it would be most unfitting for me to do so, either, and I would be quite inexcusable, especially after the way I have pressed my attentions on you, madame.

PHENICE. So our marriage will happen straight away?

DAMIS. Oh, good Lord, I guarantee it is done, if I am the only one preventing it.

PHENICE. I believe you.

DAMIS (*the first words aside*). What is all this talk? Let's frighten her. Listen, madame, putting all joking aside, don't depend on it. After all, anyone would take a fancy to someone who looks as you do, and I promise you I am not at all ashamed to have done so with you.

PHENICE. I must confess I flatter myself as much.

DAMIS. Oh come, no more banter between us. I shall fall in love with you, I warn you.

PHENICE. You must, sir.

DAMIS. But, madame, you will have to fall in love with me too, and you gave me to understand a little while ago that you were in love with somebody else.

PHENICE. At that time, you were marrying my sister. I wasn't allowed to see you, and I was pretending.

DAMIS (*the first few words aside*). How far is this going to take us? Once again, I ask you to consider. You are hoping perhaps that I will get you out of this, but you are mistaken. Don't expect anything from my heart, it will take you at your word, I'm only too ready to give it to you.

PHENICE. Don't hesitate, sir, give it.

DAMIS. I shall fall in love with you, I tell you.

PHENICE. Fall in love, then.

DAMIS. You want me to? Good Lord, madame, since I must admit it, I love you.

PHENICE (*aside*). He's lying.

DAMIS. You're blushing, madame.

PHENICE. It's true, I'm overcome by such a sudden declaration.

DAMIS (*the first words aside*). Better carry on. Yes, madame, my heart is yours, and I only wanted to see you in order to sound you out.

ERGASTE *and* ORGON *enter at this moment, and stop when they see* DAMIS *and* PHENICE.

Scene 5

DAMIS (*continues*). At first the circumstances in which I found myself held back my feelings, and I didn't dare speak to you about them. But since my situation has changed, and there is no longer any need for constraint, and since you approve of my love, (*He gets down on his knees.*) allow me to express my joy, and to indulge myself in the fondest of declarations.

ORGON. Monsieur Ergaste, here are lovers who will need no bidding to sign their marriage contract.

DAMIS (*gets up quickly*). Oh, I'm lost!

PHENICE (*ashamed*). What's this I see?

ORGON. Don't blush, my dear girl. Your feelings are acknowledged by your father, and you may well suffer the man you are to marry to kneel at your feet.

ERGASTE. My son, I had resolved only to speak to you at the moment of your marriage with madame. Your behaviour had displeased me, but I forgive you, and I am contented. The feelings I see in you reconcile me towards you.

ORGON. I am delighted by this youthful vitality. I am enchanted by this happy accident. We are expecting the registrar any moment, and we are going to meet some friends who are arriving from Paris. Goodbye – may you always love one another in the same way!

Scene 6

DAMIS (*aside, sadly*). Then we shall scarcely love one another at all. I'm so unhappy.

PHENICE (*laughing*). Well, Damis, what have you to say about that?

DAMIS. I have to say, madame . . . that I have just been caught kneeling at your feet.

PHENICE. It seems to have made you quite sad.

DAMIS. You don't seem too bright about it yourself.

PHENICE. I was quite stunned by it at first, I must admit. But I came to when I saw how angry you were – your vexation reassured me about the act you were putting on just now. You could well have done without the impression you've just given of your feelings, couldn't you? Nothing could be funnier, in fact – after what they've just seen, who would not wager that you are in love with me?

DAMIS (*sharply*). Well, madame, they would win their wager. I do not retract, and I will not lose my honour.

PHENICE (*laughing*). What? Your love still holds good?

DAMIS. I would sacrifice myself, rather.

PHENICE. I still find you looking a little like a victim.

DAMIS. Have it as you wish, madame.

PHENICE. Anyway, all the better for me if you love me. Because my mind is made up, and I wouldn't refuse you, even if you loved someone else, and even if I didn't love you myself.

DAMIS. And what makes you so strangely unafraid?

PHENICE. Well, if you didn't love me, our marriage wouldn't happen, because you wouldn't go that far. And if I consented, I would be giving my father a proof of my obedience that wouldn't cost me very much, and in that way I would win him over for a marriage more to my liking which might turn up soon. So you can see I have my own interest in leaving it to you to untangle this web, which you could easily do by going back to my sister. She doesn't hate you, and I believe you don't hate her, either. Otherwise, no mercy.

DAMIS. Ah, madame, where am I, then?

PHENICE. What's the matter with you? What I just told you doesn't affect you. You love me, remember?

DAMIS. But you don't love me.

PHENICE. Well, what does it matter? I have a strong moral sense, and that's enough to make me love you if I must.

DAMIS (*taking her hand, and kissing it*). By all that is dearest to you, don't leave me in the state I'm in. Don't lay yourself open to the same, I beg you.

PHENICE (*laughing*). Damis, your demonstrations of tenderness are fated today. Here comes my sister, and she's seen you kissing my hand.

DAMIS (*going off, emotionally*). I'm going. Goodbye, madame.

PHENICE. Goodbye, Damis, until we meet again.

Scene 7

LUCILE (*agitated*). I was coming to talk to you, sister.

PHENICE. And I was going to look for you for the same purpose.

LUCILE. Before anything else, just let me know one thing. Does that man tell you that he loves you?

PHENICE. Which man are you talking about?

LUCILE. Well, Damis, of course. Have you got two of them? That's the only one I know you have, and it would be better if you hadn't got that one.

PHENICE. But why? I was coming to tell you we are to be married this evening.

LUCILE. And you were coming specially to tell me that! What very touching news for a sister who loves you!

PHENICE. Really, you surprise me. I thought you would be as delighted as I am, since I'm taking him off your hands. How very much mistaken I am!

LUCILE. Oh, much more mistaken than anyone can say, that's for sure. Never had I less cause to be delighted, and you don't know what you're doing. Besides which, it isn't so very seemly for a girl to be delighted at getting married.

PHENICE. Do you expect a girl to be upset at marrying the man she loves? I'm being quite frank with you.

LUCILE. The point is, miss, you shouldn't be in love – that's not suitable, either. The point is, your peace of mind is at stake for the rest of your life. The point is, I shall plague you until you give up this love. The point is, I don't want you to keep him, and you will not keep him – I am the one who tells you so, and I am the one who will stop you. In love with Damis indeed! Marrying Damis! Ha! I am your sister, and I tell you it shall not be so. You are dealing with a friendship which will cause you any distress rather than let you fall into that misfortune.

PHENICE. Is he not a man of honour?

LUCILE. Who can tell? This man of honour does not love you, and yet he is marrying you. Is that honour, in your opinion? Could anyone treat marriage more offhandedly?

PHENICE. What! Damis, who throws himself at my feet, whom you have just found ready to do so again . . . !

LUCILE. There's a tasteful little story you're telling me – I don't advise you to tell it to anyone else but me. It's more the story of your weakness than of his bad faith, false-hearted rogue that he is!

PHENICE. But listen, how do you know he doesn't love me?

LUCILE. I'm going to tell you how I know. Look, there's Lisette going by. She knows about it, let's call her over. (*She calls.*) Lisette, Lisette, come here.

Scene 8

LUCILE. What's the matter, madame?

LUCILE. I haven't set her up, as you see. Now, Lisette, tell us quite straightforwardly what you think. We were talking about Damis. Do you think he loves my sister?

LISETTE. No, I certainly don't think so, because I know the opposite, and so do you, madame.

LUCILE (*to* PHENICE). Do you hear?

LISETTE. Just now he was bewailing the intended marriage.

LUCILE. That's clear enough.

LISETTE. And if I had any power here, he would not marry madame.

LUCILE (*to* PHENICE). Well, am I wrong to be afraid for you?

LISETTE. To tell the truth, the only person he does love here is my mistress.

PHENICE. Who doesn't love him, apparently.

LISETTE. It's up to her to clarify that point. She is fit to answer.

PHENICE. Anyone would think Lisette was sparing you.

LISETTE. Me, madame?

LUCILE. What does that mean? That's a very obscure remark. It's well known that I have refused Damis.

PHENICE. We may believe so, but we cannot be sure. Whatever the case, I am not afraid of anybody stealing him from me. Goodbye, sister, I must leave you. I think we have nothing more to say to one another.

LUCILE. You're pretty sure of yourself, aren't you, sister? We are well repaid for worrying about you.

PHENICE (*going off*). I might be caught out if I were grateful.

Scene 9

LISETTE. She's not afraid of anyone stealing him from her, she
says. Upon my word, madame, I renounce you if that doesn't
provoke you. Because after all it is time to agree that you do not
dislike Damis, all the more so as he loves you.

LUCILE. Whenever you want me to hate him, the recipe cannot
fail – all you have to do is to tell me that I love him. But that isn't
what's at issue. I want to get my own back on my sister's
impertinence and arrogance, and I can, if it's true that Damis
loves me, as you assure me. The success of the errand I am
going to give you hangs entirely on that truth which you
guarantee.

LISETTE. Go on, then.

LUCILE. All right, then, I want you to go and find Damis, as if on
your own account, do you understand? It isn't me sending you,
it's you going to him.

LISETTE. What shall I say to him?

LUCILE. Can't you guess? Obviously you aren't going to see him
in order to tell him I hate him. And you're only pretending not
to know out of mischief.

LISETTE. So I must let him understand that you love him?

LUCILE. Yes, miss, that I love him, since you force me to
pronounce a word which is disagreeable to me, and which I'm
only using now in a reasonable way. Apart from that, I can't
give you any indication of how to back up this false revelation.
You are a clever girl, you can fathom other people's feelings,
you can read their hearts. The art of persuasion will not fail
you, and I beg you to spare me from giving more detailed

instructions. There are certain turns of phrase and a certain
ingenuity that you can use – perhaps you will have noticed
some of my remarks, you will have seen me looking worried,
I will have sighed if you like. I don't prescribe anything; the
little I have said disgusts me, and I would spoil everything if
I got involved in it. Spare me as much as possible, and yet
persuade Damis, tell him to come and confess boldly that he
loves me. Say you sense that I want him to, that the promises
he has made me are nothing, as indeed they are only trifles, that
I will treat them in the same way, and so on. Go on, hurry.
There's no time to lose. But what's this I see? Here he is
coming. Forget everything I've just said to you.

Scene 10

DAMIS (*the first words aside*). May heaven favour my presence.
Let's see once again if her heart does not regret me. At last,
madame, our marriage is no longer under consideration. You
are free, and since I must, I shall marry Phenice.

LISETTE (*aside*). What is he coming to tell us?

DAMIS. Although I am denied the happiness of being loved by
you, may I at least, madame, in the absence of those feelings of
which I was not worthy, flatter myself that I may win those of
your friendship, which I now ask of you.

LUCILE. Such a consideration should not concern you today,
sir, and I would have misgivings about detaining you any
longer. Ah!

She tries to leave.

DAMIS. What, madame! Our marriage displeases you?

LUCILE. I found you did not suit me, and I must confess that if
anyone listened to me, you would not suit Phenice any better.

Perhaps I could even say what I think about it all. (*As she goes off.*) The ungrateful wretch!

Scene 11

DAMIS. Ah, Lisette, is that the person who had such a fancy for me?

LISETTE. What! You still dare to speak to me? Do you want to ask me for my friendship too? I refuse to give it you. Goodbye. (*Aside.*) Still, I'll see what we can do for him.

DAMIS. Stop! I'm dying. I don't know what's going to become of me.

Act Five

Scene 1

FRONTIN. I tell you he is in despair. He would already have disappeared if I weren't stopping him.

LISETTE. How silly people are when they're in love!

FRONTIN. It's even worse when they get married.

LISETTE. The quickest solution would be for your master to go and throw himself at my mistress's feet. I'm convinced that that would bring it all to an end.

FRONTIN. There's no way he will do that. He says he has sounded out Lucile's heart sufficiently, and that it is so ill-disposed towards him that she would probably broadcast his declaration of love in order to ruin him.

LISETTE. What an imagination!

FRONTIN. What do you expect? When you think of the danger he's in of marrying Phenice, of how impossible it is for him to refuse her with honour, and then the notion he's got of Lucile's feelings – it's all turned his head, and it would turn anybody's. You have to feel sorry for him, he doesn't see things the way we do. Unfortunately, he's a clever lad. This means he gets too subtle, his brain starts working on things. And in certain difficult situations, you know, it's only clever people who are quite incapable of having any common sense. I've experienced it so often myself!

LISETTE. Well, anyway, don't let him go away before he knows where he stands. Because I'm hoping we'll manage to sort things out for him through the obstacle we've created and the way we are getting Lucile to behave. I had no difficulty in persuading my mistress that this marriage was a real insult to

her, and that she had every right to complain about it. And
Monsieur Orgon seemed very embarrassed too by what I went
and said to him on her behalf. But what about you? What have
you said to Damis's father? Did you make him aware how very
unpleasant it was for his son to come into a house only to set the
two sisters at odds with one another?

FRONTIN. I surpassed myself, dear girl. You know my gift with
words, and how cleverly I can lie when necessary. I depicted
Lucile so hostile to my master, filling the whole house with
such murmurings, threatening her sister with such a terrible
severing of relations if she marries him! I depicted Monsieur
Orgon so distressed, Phenice so down-hearted, Damis so
dumbfounded!

LISETTE. And what did he answer to all that?

FRONTIN. Nothing. He just sighed at my story, shrugged his
shoulders, and went off to talk to Monsieur Orgon and to
console his son. *He*, by the way, has been forewarned, and is
waiting for him in a state of inconsolable grief.

LISETTE. That seems to me all we can do for your master in such
a case, and I like the sound of it. But go away now – here's
Lucile who seems to be looking for me. I've always told her that
she loved Damis without admitting it, and I'm going to change
my tune to force her to change hers.

FRONTIN. Bye. Don't forget I must marry you, or my head will
turn as well.

LISETTE. Go on, go on, your head's already taken the initiative.
There's no more to be feared for it.

Scene 2

LUCILE. Well, Lisette, have you seen my father?

LISETTE. Yes, madame, and so far as I can tell, I left him very worried about your state of mind. As for a reply, he didn't have time to give one, because Monsieur Ergaste came and joined him. He just said he would talk to you.

LUCILE. Very good. And yet the marriage preparations are still going ahead.

LISETTE. You will see what he has to say to you.

LUCILE. I shall see! Oh, that's a very good solution! How can you be so calm and collected when I'm in this situation?

LISETTE. Me calm and collected, madame? I'm perhaps even more upset than you are.

LUCILE. Listen, you would be right to be so. It's thanks to you I'm suffering this insult, and I have sad experience of the foolishness of your advice. You are not malicious, but believe me, don't ever get attached to anyone, because you're only good at spoiling things.

LISETTE. What! You think I bring you bad luck?

LUCILE. And why not? Isn't everything full of people like you? You only have to look at what's happened to me with you.

LISETTE. You don't know what you're saying, madame.

LUCILE. Oh, Lisette, you can say what you like about it, but fateful things are happening to me here, and they are in no way mine.

LISETTE. And so you assume that I have brought them upon you? But, madame, don't be so unfair. Wasn't it you who rejected Damis?

LUCILE. Yes, but who was the cause of it? Since we've been together, have you ever stopped telling me about the delights of some freedom or other which is nothing but an illusion? Who was it who advised me never to get married?

LISETTE. You wanted to be free to bestow your favours where you wished, without being accountable to anyone.

LUCILE. Who dreamt up the vows I made?

LISETTE. What do they matter to you, since they fall on a man you don't love at all?

LUCILE. And why then did you do your best to persuade me that

I did love him? Why have you repeated it so often to me that I almost began to wonder about it myself?

LISETTE. Because I was mistaken.

LUCILE. You were mistaken? I did love him this morning, I don't love him this evening. If I have no other guarantee than your profound understanding, all I have to do is trust in that and I'm well educated. However, in the confusion of ideas I get from all that, I end up in fact by losing sight of myself. No, I am not sure what state I'm in. Isn't that most unpleasant?

LISETTE. Be reassured, madame. Once again, you don't love him.

LUCILE. You'll see – she'll end up knowing more than I do about it! How do I know I wouldn't have loved him, if you had left me as I was, if your advice, your prejudices, and your false truisms hadn't infected my mind? Was it me who decided on my fate? Everyone has their own way of thinking and feeling, and I suppose I have too, but I won't say what it is, because I only know yours. I've been led neither by my reason nor by my heart, but by you. So I've never had anything but flippant thoughts, and that's what it is – you think you're making up your own mind, you think you're following your own feelings, acting according to your own lights, but it's nothing of the sort, you find you only have a borrowed mind, and you only live on the folly of those who have taken over your trust and confidence.

LISETTE. I don't know where I am!

LUCILE. Tell me, at my age, what kind of idea was it to remain single? Who is there who doesn't get married? Who goes and gets obsessed with hatred of a respectable state which everybody takes on? A girl's most natural condition is to be married. I could only renounce it by risking disobedience of my father, and I depend on him. Besides, life is full of difficulties, and a husband shares them. You can't have too much help, and you get a real friend. There was nobody better than Damis. He's a man of honour, and I have an inkling I would have liked him. It worked straight away. But unfortunately, *you* are in the world, and the purpose of your life is to be the plague of mine. Fate has placed you with me, and everything is topsy-turvy – I resist my father, I make vows, I rave, and my sister takes advantage.

LISETTE. I told you just now you didn't love Damis. Right now, I'm tempted to believe you do love him.

LUCILE. Well, how could I prevent myself with you around? Very well, yes, I do love him, miss. Are you contented? Yes, and I am delighted to love him to put you in the wrong and shut you up.

LISETTE. For heaven's sake, why didn't you say so earlier? You would have saved us all a lot of trouble – Damis who loves you, and Frontin and me who love each other and are getting desperate. But leave it to me, nothing is lost yet.

LUCILE. Yes, I love him, it's only too true, and the only misfortune I still lack is not being able to hide it. But if you let out a word about it, you can say goodbye to me for ever.

LISETTE. What! You don't want . . . ?

LUCILE. No, I forbid you.

LISETTE. But, madame, it would be a great pity. He adores you.

LUCILE. Let him tell me so himself, and I shall believe him. But come what may, I really do like him.

LISETTE. He deserves it, madame.

LUCILE. I don't know about that, Lisette, because when I think about it, our love doesn't always reflect credit on the loved one. More often, it implies criticism of the one who is in love. I am only too well aware of this. What are the great sources of our passions? Our vanity, and our flirtatiousness. That's where men most often derive all their worth. They aren't left with many admirable qualities, once you've taken away the weaknesses of our hearts. That little room where I hid while Damis was talking to you – take that away from my little story, and perhaps I wouldn't have been in love. After all, why am I in love? Because I was challenged to be found attractive, and I wanted vengeance for my face. What a fine way for loving tenderness to start! And yet that is the result of one little room more or less in my story.

LISETTE. Oh, madame, Damis has no need of that incident to be lovable. Let me take you to him.

LUCILE. You know what I have forbidden, Lisette.

LISETTE. Here comes your father, so I'm going. But you can say what you like, if Damis should find himself forced to marry Phenice, don't expect me to remain silent.

Scene 3

ORGON. My dear girl, what is the meaning of what Lisette came and told me on your behalf? What? You don't want to see your sister married, you'll never forgive her, you want to go into a retreat? You're upsetting all of us – Monsieur Ergaste, his son, Phenice, and me. And what is it about? The one man in the world to whom you are most indifferent!

LUCILE. Very indifferent, I admit. But I am not indifferent to the way my father treats me.

ORGON. But what have I done to you, my dear girl?

LUCILE. No, it's certain I have no share in the kindness of your heart. My sister carries off all your affection.

ORGON. But what have you to complain about?

LUCILE. It's not that I find anything wrong with your loving her, of course. I know she is very lovable, and I would be very upset if you didn't love her. But to love only her, to think only of her, to marry her off at the expense of what little esteem might be placed on my mind, my heart, and my character, I must confess, father, that is very sad, and it's a way of making me pay very dearly for her marriage.

ORGON. But what do you mean? All I can see is that she is your younger sister and she is marrying a man who was intended for you, but only because you refused him. If you had wanted

Damis, he wouldn't be hers, so you have no more interest in the
matter. And, basically, your heart has advised you well – you
and Damis were never meant for one another. Your sister took
a fancy to him with no difficulty, and as Monsieur Ergaste and I
wanted to unite our families, we are taking advantage of their
mutual inclination. This gets a man you don't love out of your
way, and you ought to be delighted.

LUCILE. All right, I've nothing to say, and you are the master. But
I should have married him. He only came here for me, and
everyone will be astonished at what's happened. Besides,
I myself might have wanted to get married one day, and now
I'm forced to renounce it.

ORGON. To renounce it, you say? What sort of an idea's that?

LUCILE. Yes, I am condemned to give up all thought of it. There's
no recovering from the humiliation which has come upon me
today. My heart and hand must henceforth be considered
disgraced. There's no longer any question of offering them to
anyone, or of looking for new insults. I have been disdained,
I shall be for ever, and an eternal retreat from the world is the
only course left for me to take.

ORGON. You're mad. Once again, everyone knows you refused
Damis, he himself broadcasts it, and the only risk you run in
this business is of getting a reputation for strange taste, that's
all. So calm yourself down, and don't let an ill-judged
discontent make people suspect you of feelings you don't have.
Here's your sister coming to join us. I told her to come and talk
to you, and I beg you to meet her in friendship.

Scene 4

ORGON. Come here, Phenice. Your sister has just told me the
reasons for her distaste for your marriage. Although Damis

does not suit her, everyone knows he came here for her, and she thought we could do better than to give him to you. But she's not thinking about it any more, and it's all over.

PHENICE. If my sister has any regrets, and Damis prefers her, he is still hers. I will give him up readily, and without complaint.

LUCILE. Believe me, sister, don't be so confident. If he heard you, I'm afraid he might take you at your word.

PHENICE. Oh no, I'm talking with absolute certainty. There's nothing to be afraid of – what I just said to you I've said to him a score of times.

LUCILE. Well, if you've run no risk by talking like that to him, you have some obligation towards me. My attitude has not done any harm to his devotion to you.

PHENICE. But let me flatter myself that he chose me.

LUCILE. And I tell you it is better for you not to flatter yourself about it, miss! You will be more attentive about pleasing him, and his love will need that kind of help.

ORGON. What's this argumentative tone you're both taking? Is that how you respond to the trouble I take to bring you together?

LUCILE. But you can see she's being quite unbearable about it.

PHENICE. What more can I do than renounce Damis if your heart wishes it?

LUCILE. And I'm telling you that if my heart wished it, I wouldn't need to deal with you, and that the vanity of your offers is quite pointless in relation to something I could take away from you with a look, if I wanted to. That's enough of that, let's finish.

ORGON. Well, there's a nice conversation! I thought you both had more respect for me.

PHENICE. I shall not say another word. I only came with the intention of embracing my sister, and I'm still ready to do so, if her feelings allow it.

LUCILE. Oh, that's no problem.

They embrace.

ORGON. Well now, that's what I wanted! Come, my children, make it up and be good friends. Here comes Damis, right on time.

Scene 5

DAMIS. I believe, sir, you are well convinced that I was extremely anxious to see this marriage concluded, but you know the obstacle that madame has raised, and rather than throw a family into disarray –

ORGON. No, Damis, you will not throw it anywhere. I have to tell you we are all in agreement, we all admire you, and my daughters have just embraced one another.

PHENICE. And our hearts were in it, I think.

LUCILE. Oh, the heart has no place in this. There is nothing of interest for it.

ORGON. Well, no doubt. Goodbye. I'm going to give this good news to Monsieur Ergaste, and I'll be back with him in a minute to round things off.

Scene 6

PHENICE (*laughing as she looks at them*). Ha, ha, ha! . . . How funny you both are! You stand there saying nothing, and giving me black looks . . . Ha, ha, ha! . . .

LUCILE. What is there to laugh at?

PHENICE. Oh, there's plenty for me, and there's nothing for you yet, I agree. But there will be. Come here, Damis.

DAMIS (*making as if to back away*). What do you wish with me, madame?

PHENICE. 'What do you wish with me, madame?' Are you

running away from me? There's a nice tender opening! Isn't this the man who is all eager to marry me? (*She goes to him.*) Come here, I tell you, and let me lead you. Come on, sir, pay homage to your conqueror, and kneel at her feet now . . . at her feet, I tell you. And you, sister, hold yourself a little proudly. Don't put out your hand towards him in a sign of peace, but don't withdraw it either – let it go, so that he can take it. There's my plan carried out. Goodbye, the rest is up to you.

Scene 7

LUCILE (*to* DAMIS, *who is on his knees*). But what does this mean, Damis?

DAMIS. That I have adored you from the very first moment, and did not dare to tell you.

LUCILE. This is certainly quite remarkable. But stand up so that you can explain.

DAMIS *stands up.*

DAMIS. If you knew how much I have suffered from remaining shy and silent, madame! No, I cannot express what happened to my heart the first time I saw you, nor all the despair I felt at having spoken to Lisette as I had done.

LUCILE. I wasn't expecting you to say that, because that was when you promised me to break off our marriage.

DAMIS. Madame, I promised you nothing. Remember, all I did was to defer to you because you seemed so cold towards me. All I did was to surrender to your attitude, to the respect I had for it, to the fear of displeasing you, and to the extreme astonishment I was in.

LUCILE. I believe you. But I'm just amazed at the combination of circumstances, because after all, if I had known your feelings, who knows, they might have made up my mind for me. But now, what are we going to do? It really is most embarrassing.

DAMIS. Ah, Lucile, if only my heart could soften yours.

LUCILE. You know, people are going to find our story quite ridiculous. That really upsets me.

DAMIS. I shall never belong to Phenice, I can only belong to you alone, and if I lose you, the only course left to me is to run away, never show my face again, and die of grief.

LUCILE. That would be a dreadful extremity. But tell me – my sister knows that you love me, doesn't she?

DAMIS. She must have been told, or guessed it from our conversations, and tried to encourage me to tell you.

LUCILE. Hm. If she guessed that you loved me, I am sure she must have suspected that I am responsive.

DAMIS (*kissing her hand*). Ah, Lucile, what have I just heard? What raptures have you thrown me in?

LUCILE. People will laugh at our story, but our love will console me for that. I think someone's coming.

Final Scene

ERGASTE. Come on, my son, hurry up. Fill me with joy, and come and sign your happiness.

DAMIS. Father, marriage with madame is no longer on the agenda. She never really wanted to, and my heart only belongs to Lucile.

ORGON. To Lucile?

LISETTE. Yes, sir, to her very self, and she won't refuse him. Marry them boldly. We'll tell you the rest later.

ORGON. Do you agree with what's being said, my girl?

LUCILE (*giving her hand to* DAMIS). Don't ask for any other answer, father.

FRONTIN. Well! How about it, Lisette?

LISETTE (*giving him her hand*). Don't ask for any other answer.

The Feigned Inconstancy

Translated by John Bowen

from L'HEUREUX STRATAGÈME
First performed by the Italian Comedians (1733)

A Note on this Translation

When, back in 1975, I was asked to translate *L'Heureux Stratagème*, it seemed to me that the elegance of the play's language and the formality of its characters' behaviour would find their best English equivalent in the plays of the early eighteenth century and just before, so I imagined that I was an English playwright of that period who had come across the French text, and proceeded to pirate it, as playwrights then readily did. I called my pirated version *The Inconstant Couple* in homage to Farquhar, and turned Dorante into Mr Worthy, the Marquise into Lady Fairfax, the Chevalier into Captain Fopwell and Frontin into Corporal Trim. Of these four, the Chevalier gave me most trouble because the joke is that he has a Gascon accent, and in the English tradition, accents are not particularly funny; the fun is made out of the choice and arrangement of words. If I were to concentrate on the Chevalier's regionality, I should have to make him Irish, and that would suggest a fortune-hunter. Instead I took him the other way, and made him a metropolitan fop with a commission in the army, and consequently Frontin dropped easily into the English dramatic tradition of soldier-servants. Harlequin, in English pantomime, is traditionally mute, so he became Martin, and put on a little rusticity. Blaise is rustic already, Lisette is pert and impressionable, and I left the Countess with the rank Marivaux gave her, though countesses are not as common in England as in France.

The problem with such a method is that equivalence is not fidelity. My pirate-playwright did what any playwright of talent in any period would naturally do; he let his characters grow. For them to have dramatic life they had to go their own way, and it was not always Marivaux's way. Such a version might be thought out of place in a collection of printed translations. I have, therefore, followed the text rather more closely in this version; there is still a deal of decoration, but rather less invention. *The Inconstant Couple* is, however, still available in typescript, and anyone wishing to perform either it or *The Feigned Inconstancy* should get in touch with my agent, Margaret Ramsay, Ltd, 14a Goodwins Court, St Martin's Lane, London WC2N 4LL.

John Bowen

The Inconstant Couple, with the characters' names changed back into French, was performed at the Chichester Festival Theatre in the 1978 season with the following cast:

DORANTE, *suitor to the* COUNTESS	Keith Baxter
BLAISE, *a farmer*	John Warner
HARLEQUIN, *manservant to* DORANTE	Martin Chamberlain
LISETTE, BLAISE's *daughter*	Veronica Roberts
COUNTESS	Siân Philips
CAPTAIN, *suitor to the* MARQUISE	Tim Woodward
FRONTIN, *manservant to the* CAPTAIN	Keith Drinkel
MARQUISE	Morag Hood

The play was directed by Noel Willman and designed by Bob Ringwood. The characters of the Lackey and the Notary were omitted for reasons of economy.

The stage is set in the COUNTESS's *house.*

Act One

Scene 1

DORANTE. Well, Blaise, what do you want of me? Speak, man. Sure, if you can't oblige me by telling me what you want, you'll quite put it out of my power to help you.

BLAISE. Ah! . . .

DORANTE. We begin.

BLAISE. It's as the old saw says, Your Honour, in matters of this kind, sir, as the world well knows, Your Honour.

DORANTE. What does the world know, Blaise?

BLAISE. There's no man better regarded, Your Honour, in the whole kingdom, Your Honour, or as I should say 'country', Your Honour, or 'district' might be the better word, for an obliging temper, as the saying goes, for a kind heart and a patient ear.

DORANTE. It shall be quite out of patience in a moment, I assure you. Pray come to the point.

BLAISE. Indeed, sir. If Your Honour would do me the kindness to put on Your Honour's hat.

DORANTE. But I don't use to wear a hat in the garden, Blaise.

BLAISE. And I don't leave my head without a cover, Your Honour, not in any weather, for I'm a prudent man, and there are many ills, you know, may come to a man's head on the east wind. But while Your Honour stands before me, as the world says, uncovered . . .

DORANTE. Well, if to put my hat on is the end of your petition, that's soon done.

BLAISE. Your Honour's a gentleman that has affairs of moment, as the world says.

DORANTE. And, therefore, on, Blaise, on.

BLAISE. I will, sir. I have a daughter, Your Honour. Lisette by name.

DORANTE. Blaise, I know it.

BLAISE. Now, this daughter, Your Honour, by name Lisette, being a maidservant to the Countess, your own . . . your own . . . and we shall hope, Your Honour, to drink your noble health, as the world says, when you and my lady . . .

DORANTE. We shall never be done, I see, unless I am to speak for you. Lisette, your daughter, is maid to your lady, the Countess, to whom I myself have been paying my addresses these many months. And furthermore this same Lisette is betrothed, and soon to be wed, to my man, Harlequin. This agreed, what follows?

BLAISE. You have hit it, Your Honour. Money, sir, is the root of the matter, as the world says, the branch, sir, the very leaf and twig, the flower, Your Honour. As my Lisette, sir, must be like a flower, as the saying is, on her wedding day, decked out in fine array, for without the blossom, you know, there's no fruit to follow.

DORANTE. Why, as to the fruit, I think you may leave Harlequin to take care of that, be she decked out or no.

BLAISE. And then the marriage feast, Your Honour, the baked meats, as the world says, the provender, sir, must be provided. And as to that provision, Your Honour, I'll be honest; there's none in the house, and therefore if Your Honour would do me the kindness to speak to my lady.

DORANTE. About the marriage?

BLAISE. You have hit it, Your Honour.

DORANTE. But what am I to say to your lady about the marriage?

BLAISE. Why, Your Honour, that I've no provision for it, unless her ladyship should provide.

DORANTE. I am to sue for money, Blaise, on your behalf?

BLAISE. Twenty-six francs, Your Honour, in advance of wages.

DORANTE. Why as to that, I think you will do better to accept five francs gratis from this hand, for I believe your wages are already damnably in pawn, and my credit does not stand so high these days with your mistress that I may pledge them further. Though your expectation be to drink healths at my marriage with your mistress, 'as the world says', yet may the world be mistaken; so may you. A smile, a little raillery, leave to visit daily, these are the familiarities allowed to a friend: they do not amount to the exchange of vows, nor does the devoted attention of seven months create an obligation of marriage. Your mistress, the Countess, continues to be her own mistress, and may bestow her person and fortune where she will. In truth she is today more likely to be carried off by a captain of cavalry than by these unworthy arms.

BLAISE. Why, it cannot be that a gentleman of Your Honour's own true colour, with the carriage of a prince and the generosity of a cardinal, as the world knows, may be thus cruelly used. It is not to be borne.

DORANTE. Yet I bear it.

BLAISE. When I remember, sir, how my own dear dead wife gave my lady suck, and where the milk passed in, surely some part of that sweet woman's nature must have followed it, that was always partial to Your Honour, why there's no cavalry captain, Your Honour, knowing my good Isabel, could displace Your Honour in my lady's favour.

DORANTE. Well, I so assure thee, Blaise.

BLAISE. Then if I might believe it, I should speak most strangely to my lady.

DORANTE. What woulds't thou say?

BLAISE. I have dandled my lady on this knee, Your Honour. I should say, 'What is this, my lady? What is this?' I have watched my lady grow these thirty years; I have that freedom, I have held her in these arms; she hath sniffed at gillyflowers in these arms. 'What is this?' I should say.

DORANTE. Well, you may say so, Blaise, if that be your privilege.

But meanwhile here is my man, Harlequin, with a sad face come to interrupt you.

Scene 2

DORANTE. Come, sirrah, what's the matter? You look like a cat in a hailstorm.

HARLEQUIN. Why, sir, much trouble for you, and consequently some for me, for a good servant follows his master.

DORANTE. Well?

BLAISE. There's some serious matter here, as the world says.

HARLEQUIN. If you'll prepare yourself, sir, for affliction, you'll be the more ready to bear it.

DORANTE. Come, I'm prepared.

HARLEQUIN. I've done some weeping, sir, on my way here. I shall be fit for consolation soon.

BLAISE. Oh, my sympathetic heart! I know I shall feel pity.

DORANTE. Will you speak?

HARLEQUIN. I've nothing to say, sir, except to assert before Heaven that you are ill-used, and prophesy despair.

DORANTE. To the devil with your prophecies!

BLAISE. Ill fortune rewards the bearer of bad tidings, as the saying is.

HARLEQUIN. Well, sir, just now while I was loitering in the hall, I saw – but that's of no consequence.

DORANTE. Tell me what you saw.

HARLEQUIN. A bottle, sir, carelessly laid by with the cork drawn, and lifting it up, sir, lest it should go to waste, I heard the Countess approaching, sir, in company with Captain Damis.

DORANTE. Oh!

HARLEQUIN. Not wishing to disturb them, sir, or waste the good wine, I stepped into a cupboard.

BLAISE. What delicacy!

HARLEQUIN. And carried the bottle with me to spare them the sight of it, for 'tis not genteel, sir, you know, to tipple before the ladies.

DORANTE. Forget the bottle.

HARLEQUIN. No, sir. Once I had undertaken the bottle, it was not for me to lay it by.

BLAISE. I'm sure he may forget it well enough, for 'tis all drunk up by now.

DORANTE. You saw the Countess with the Captain in the hall?

HARLEQUIN. No, sir. The keyhole was too small.

DORANTE. Then you could not be sure it was she.

HARLEQUIN. I know your lady's voice, sir, very well. And her voice, you'll allow, could not be there without her person, for the one requires the other.

BLAISE. They would be bound, sir, to be in company.

DORANTE. And what were they saying?

HARLEQUIN. Alas, sir, I can remember only their sentiments. I have quite forgot their words.

DORANTE. Their sentiments, then.

HARLEQUIN. I would need the words, sir, to express them. But the Captain and your lady were merry together, I'll take my oath on it.

DORANTE. How merry?

HARLEQUIN. Laughing. The Captain, sir, was very vigorous in his laughter.

BLAISE. Sure, that's a sign of happiness, which is a blessed state, as the saying goes.

HARLEQUIN. True. But happiness in one gentleman may import misery to another, and thus may be the case between the Captain and my master.

DORANTE. Well, leave it alone, man, if that be the sum of your disclosure. Do you remember that I bid you beseech my lady, the Marquise, that I might speak with her?

HARLEQUIN. Aye, sir.

DORANTE. And did you so?

HARLEQUIN. Why, sir, I remember that you laid that duty on me, but I cannot for my life remember whether I performed it.

Scene 3

LISETTE. Oh, sir, sir, take this as you will, sir, I must speak out. Your calmness, sir, astonishes me.

DORANTE. My calmness!

LISETTE. If you will not look to it, sir, sure my mistress will escape you. I may be mistaken, but I fear it, sir.

DORANTE. Why, Lisette, my own suspicions do that way tend, but what can I do to prevent it?

BLAISE. That's the nub of it, daughter, as the world says. What can His Honour do to prevent it?

LISETTE. It's the Captain, sir.

HARLEQUIN. My own words, sir.

LISETTE. Sure, he's a gallant gentleman, he has set out, sir, to make my lady the captive of his gallantry. As, item, sir, by being in constant company, by compliment, by whispers, sir, of such sweet lowness as they would ravish the heart and make a Spartan languish. Already, sir, I see my lady smile, which is like a dagger to my heart, sir, on account of the esteem in which I hold your qualities. Besides, if I'm to marry Harlequin, we shan't be at all conveniently settled unless you marry my lady.

HARLEQUIN. Separate establishments, sir. An inconvenience to comfort.

DORANTE. But, Lisette, your mistress avoids me.

BLAISE. To be sure, that's a sign of ill-favour.

HARLEQUIN. And what has Frontin, the Captain's man, been

saying to you, Lisette?

LISETTE. Oh, nothing but compliments as usual. But I'm sure I don't care for them, for I'm quite stern with him in my replies.

BLAISE. There's my brave girl! A stern demeanour, as the world says, is the affability of princes. Oh, you may know your worth, my girl. You may toss your head thus; you shall see her toss her head thus, Your Honour. 'Out of my way,' she shall cry, 'Paris monkey! Be off with thee, Paris Monkey!' and by my Lisette's behaviour with the man, Your Honour, shall she give your lady example in treating of the master.

DORANTE. Oh, I shall die of grief.

BLAISE. No, sir, no, Your Honour. You'll permit me, a mistake in tactics, i'faith. You'd lose all, sir, by dying.

LISETTE. She is coming this way. Retire, sir. Let me alone with her. I'll divine her intentions, and believe me, sir, you shall know all.

DORANTE. I'll leave you.

HARLEQUIN. And as for Frontin, my dear, you will remember to toss your head?

LISETTE. Oh, be off with you.

Scene 4

COUNTESS. I have been searching for you, Lisette. Were you in company here? Did I not see someone with you?

LISETTE. It was Monsieur Dorante, my lady.

COUNTESS. Well, that's strange, for it was of Dorante that . . . but no matter. What does he say?

LISETTE. Why, my lady, the gentleman says he is ill-used, and I'm sure I think so too.

COUNTESS. Then he has still the same partiality towards me?

LISETTE. Partiality, my lady! – the gentleman loves you. It is not in Monsieur Dorante to change his affections. Can it be, my lady, that you have ceased to love him?

COUNTESS. I am sure I cannot tell what you mean by this 'ceased to love'. When have I ever loved the gentleman? I may have singled him out as the object of my particular attention. I am sure one may single out any gentleman. And that may lead to love, child, but it is not love in itself.

LISETTE. My lady, I have heard you call Monsieur Dorante the most amiable gentleman in the world.

COUNTESS. And so I may.

LISETTE. I have seen you await his arrival with much impatience.

COUNTESS. But you know I am impatient by nature.

LISETTE. I have seen you quite out of temper when he did not come.

COUNTESS. Indeed, Lisette, any lady may be out of temper when a gentleman does not come. I have told you, I singled Dorante out as an object of my particular attention; I do so no longer. And I tell you now, Lisette, what I came hither to tell you, that if you should speak again with the gentleman, and he should mention any partiality that he may have for me, then you must calm his passion, girl. I do not wish the gentleman to be passionate on my account.

LISETTE. Is it the Captain, my lady, who has seduced your ladyship's good opinion from Monsieur Dorante? His manner of speech, my lady?

COUNTESS. Oh! . . . To be sure the Captain has a very fine manner of speech. To be sure.

LISETTE. Oh, my lady – you'll pardon me, my lady – but to be so inconstant!

COUNTESS. Child, child, you do not understand the world. It becomes a lady of quality and discretion to be . . . to be at times . . . a little mercurial.

LISETTE. What's that 'mercurial', my lady?

COUNTESS. Why, it's to be . . . not to be unfaithful, Lisette, for

I'm sure I should not put my good faith in jeopardy for any reason. Nor to be fickle neither, for that's too light a word. But to be ... changeable ... quicksilver, I may say, as one may choose to eat pigeons in pastry on one day, and prefer *ragoût* the next. One is not to be bound, Lisette; one is not to be bound. That is the law of the heart. It is in the nature of a woman's heart to give one's word a thousand times, and break it a thousand times, for the heart must be led by feelings, and I'm sure our feelings are not to be confined. If we do else, we break our hearts' own natural laws, and by being untrue to our own natures we deceive the world, which we should never do.

LISETTE. Is *that* the natural law of the heart? To be sure, if I could see the matter in such a light ... To be changeable in her affections, then, may be a woman's duty? I should never have thought it, my lady.

COUNTESS. But you see it now, child.

LISETTE. Oh, clearly, my lady.

COUNTESS. Dorante, child, thinks only of himself. Am I never to turn my eyes any way but his, because he loves me? Is only he to find me young and handsome? Am I to appear as a hag to all others, reserving my tenderest qualities only for him? It is a strange love, Lisette, which would lock one in a box, denying the world all pleasure in my charms.

LISETTE. Strange indeed, my lady.

COUNTESS. Oh, to be sure that is how these gentlemen would have our sex live. But one man should compose a woman's whole universe, all others quite struck out of her account and dead to her. Her court must be diminished to one courtier, her vanity to one flatterer, and in the lists of love she is to struggle beneath but one commander. Yet, though we are to give this foolish fidelity to but one man, why he himself may take his amusement as he shall choose, and then – away! What an abuse, Lisette, what an abuse to womanhood! Go, speak to him, make what excuse you will; I will not see him. Men, when they wish to leave us, find any excuse. As for the Captain, he loves me. His person and his parts do not displease me. I'll do no violence to my inclinations.

LISETTE. Oh, my lady, what have I learned today! Forsaken lovers may take their complaints elsewhere. I'm sure I'm quite cured of compassion.

COUNTESS. Do not mistake me; I have a great esteem for Dorante. But what is estimable is not always diverting. Oh, he's coming back, and I shall be plagued by his complaints. Do you but seize the moment, Lisette, and rid me of this estimable lover.

She is about to go, but DORANTE *stops her, as he enters with* HARLEQUIN *in attendance.*

Scene 5

DORANTE. Madam, I hope you will not flee my presence the moment I am arrived.

COUNTESS. Oh, Dorante, is it you? Sure, you cannot believe I fly from you, for you see I am busy about my own affairs.

DORANTE. Will you not allow me an instant of your time?

COUNTESS. It must be an instant only, for you know, sir, I expect company within.

DORANTE. Sure, your servants will inform you, madam, when the company arrives. Meanwhile I hope you will allow me to speak of my love for you.

COUNTESS. But, sir, it is a speech I know by heart.

DORANTE. Not by heart, madam. Your heart is not much concerned, I think.

COUNTESS. Well, if it be not, your speech will not make it so.

DORANTE. Why, you are driving me to despair, madam.

COUNTESS. I am sure I do not intend it, for your despairing tones, sir, and your despairing looks are not at all diverting, let me tell you.

DORANTE. Forever wounded by this most cruel raillery, madam, must I still be doomed to love you?

COUNTESS. 'Cruel raillery'! 'Doomed'? Why, you have been too often at the play, sir. This is the language of high romance.

DORANTE. Ungrateful lady!

COUNTESS. Your style will not cure me. Why, even your fellow there has caught the hang of it. He looks like . . .

HARLEQUIN. Like a cat in a hailstorm, my lady. The comparison has already been remarked.

DORANTE. Only my respect for your person, madam, gives me strength to contain my anger.

COUNTESS. And whence comes this anger, sir? Is it your complaint that you love me? Why sure, I have nothing to do with that, for I never heard yet that it was a crime to be loved. Is it that I do not love you? I take it ill, sir, that you should find that a fault in me; sure, love is not to be directed. The parliament of your own heart does not make laws for mine, and though you may sue me as your debtor, I'll not to prison, 'tis all fantasy, I owe you nothing. Oh, sigh, sir, sigh. You are the master of your own lamentation, as I am the mistress of my own composure. In truth there may have been a time when sighs and protestations of love diverted me, but that time has gone entirely. I pray you, sir, stop up this effusion of sentiment, and so farewell.

DORANTE. One word more, madam. It is true, then, that you no longer love me?

COUNTESS. Sir, I do not remember that I have ever done so.

DORANTE. Then, faith, madam, nevermore shall I.

COUNTESS. Be assured, sir, that what you now put yourself to forget was never more than a dream.

The COUNTESS *leaves.*

Scene 6

DORANTE. Oh, perfidious woman!

HARLEQUIN. Sure, sir, we have had an edifying encounter.

DORANTE. Wait, Lisette! Did you speak of me to your lady?

LISETTE. Yes, sir.

DORANTE. Oh, too well, too well now do I know her thoughts. Yet tell me, child; to what particular fault in me must I ascribe her present ill opinion?

LISETTE. I've no time, sir. My lady expects company in the house.

HARLEQUIN. Oh, sir, observe the change. As the man, sir, follows his master, so the maid her mistress.

DORANTE. Will you forsake my cause, Lisette?

HARLEQUIN. Do you also play us false, miss?

DORANTE. Speak! What reasons gave your lady to you that she should treat me so?

LISETTE. Oh, sir, reasons enough, if I was to set out the list. As, first, to be mercurial, sir, becomes a lady of quality. Second, it is the natural law of the heart to break one's word a thousand times. Third, to be young and handsome profits a woman nothing if it be all for one man and the others dead. Fourth, that we must deceive nobody, else we be locked in a box, which is an abuse to all our sex. Lastly, Monsieur Dorante, sir, that my lady holds you in most high esteem, which is not at all diverting.

DORANTE. Strange catalogue!

HARLEQUIN. I vow, sir, I've never heard ill words spoke with a worse countenance.

DORANTE. Explain yourself, girl.

LISETTE. Well, if you cannot understand me, sir, I'm sure I'm not to blame. In brief, sir, my lady singled you out.

DORANTE. Dost mean she loves me yet?

LISETTE. No, sir. It may lead to love, but it is not love.

DORANTE. This is beyond conception of understanding. Does she, then, love the Captain?

LISETTE. To be sure, sir, any lady might love the gentleman.

DORANTE. And what of me?

LISETTE. She holds you in esteem, sir. I hope, sir, you understand me now.

DORANTE. The wench enrages me. Sure, I may forget my breeding.

HARLEQUIN. And for me, Lisette my dear, you will not follow your lady's disdain so far I hope?

LISETTE. Oh, for you, Harlequin, I single you out; I single you out.

HARLEQUIN. Then you may lie in a box, miss, and so rest all chambermaids of your temper.

Scene 7

HARLEQUIN. Now, sir, you may see how we are both ill-treated.

DORANTE. My heart breaks.

HARLEQUIN. My breath stops.

The MARQUISE *arrives, surprising them.*

MARQUISE. Sure, Dorante, you suffer under some strange affliction.

DORANTE. Oh, madam, are you come? I have been betrayed, madam, quite murdered as I may say. You see here a very dagger of grief sticks from my heart.

HARLEQUIN. And I have been so stuffed with scorn, my lady, a mere castaway; I have been singled out.

MARQUISE. I see you have been with the Countess here. Who else could make such a carnage?

DORANTE. The same, madam.

MARQUISE. Then may I entreat you a moment of your time?

DORANTE. Indeed, but two hours ago I bid my man here beseech
  you to a conference.

MARQUISE. Then you may bid him further stand guard over us,
  lest our conference be interrupted.

DORANTE. Go, Harlequin. Let no one come by without warning.

HARLEQUIN. Oh, may Heaven, sir, console us, for beneath
  Heaven's eye, sir, we are here three poor wretches in need of
  consolation. My lady here is bereft of her admirer, the Captain,
  you of your lady, the Countess, and I, sir, of the dearest
  sweetest creature –

MARQUISE. Pray, fellow, do as your master bid you.

  HARLEQUIN *leaves to keep watch.*

Scene 8

MARQUISE. Well, Dorante, your man is in the right of it. We are
  both jilted, you and I.

DORANTE. As you say, madam.

MARQUISE. And are we to attempt no remedy?

DORANTE. What attempt may a man make, madam, other than
  to urge a suit already odious? I will not do it. How wretchedly
  are our fortunes mixed! Had only I loved your ladyship
  instead!

MARQUISE. Then why not do so, Dorante?

DORANTE. Had I . . . had I that good fortune, madam, to have . . .
  to have first fallen in love with your ladyship . . . but since
  I did not . . .

MARQUISE. Faith, you are not used to flattery, I see.

DORANTE. Your pardon, madam, I am in such a state of despair,
  my manners are forget. Indeed, I hold your person and good wit
  in such high esteem, madam, I am sure I must have told myself

a thousand times ... but being, as you see, in this most
damnable degree of love for the Countess ...

MARQUISE. Enough, sir; you have no skill at all in compliment,
and must injure my good opinion of myself with every word of
extenuation. And therefore, on.

DORANTE. No, madam, no; believe me. I should love you if
I could. It is my duty. If only to punish that perfidious
woman.

MARQUISE. If punishment is to be our word, sir, I have some
small score to settle of my own. But would it not be a great *coup*,
in punishing your lady, to restore her to you?

DORANTE. To restore her?

MARQUISE. More loving than before.

DORANTE. Is it possible?

MARQUISE. Do but attend, sir. First, I release you from all
obligations of love to me, even though you have told yourself a
thousand times how highly my person and good wit deserve it.

DORANTE. Pray, madam, do not mock me.

MARQUISE. Provided only that you will feign love to me, undying
love, sir, of the most passionate condition.

DORANTE. Oh ... with all my heart.

MARQUISE. And indeed, sir, you shall have your heart again,
I vow. Now, second, are you sure the Countess loved you
till now?

DORANTE. Alas, it seemed so.

MARQUISE. And she truly believed, sir, that you returned
her love?

DORANTE. Alas, she too well knew I loved her, as still I do.

MARQUISE. If she truly knew it, sir, all the better.

DORANTE. But ... for the Captain, madam ... shall he have
the freedom to pay court to my lady?

MARQUISE. If your lady thinks she loves the Captain, she is
mistaken. She does but play the coquette, and will, like some
greedy child, stretch out a hand to take the sweets from
others.

DORANTE. That may be so.

MARQUISE. And if she thinks she does not love you, Dorante, she is mistaken, I know her, as I know my sex. Therefore we must proceed with – But somebody comes. Let us confer elsewhere.

Scene 9

HARLEQUIN. Oh, how I suffer!

DORANTE. Sirrah, have you interrupted us to sigh?

HARLEQUIN. It is all I can do; my condition is so pitiable. But in truth there is a fellow yonder demands to speak with my lady. Shall I give him entry, sir, or fell him to the ground?

MARQUISE. Will you not first tell us who the gentleman is?

HARLEQUIN. No gentleman, my lady. A knave, and one who would steal from me my dear Lisette. By name, Frontin.

MARQUISE. The Captain's valet. Let him approach. I have something to say to him.

HARLEQUIN. I cannot commend your ladyship's acquaintance.

HARLEQUIN goes.

Scene 10

MARQUISE. This Frontin, sir, is a clever and complete rogue, and I have employed him as my spy upon his master and your lady. He comes here to report the progress of their courtship. But, sir, if you have not the resolution to stand by and listen, keeping your countenance even to indifference, you had better leave us.

Scene 11

HARLEQUIN *brings on* FRONTIN.

HARLEQUIN. Knave, here is my lady.

FRONTIN. I shall answer you for that word, sir, on my going hence.

HARLEQUIN. And I shall answer you, sir. I shall have my answer ready, sir.

HARLEQUIN *goes.*

Scene 12

MARQUISE. Well, Frontin, what news?

FRONTIN. My lady, may I speak?

MARQUISE. You heard me bid you do so.

FRONTIN. Before the gentleman, my lady.

MARQUISE. In complete safety.

DORANTE. Of what would the fellow speak, madam?

MARQUISE. Of the Countess and his master. Pray remain, sir; it may amuse you.

DORANTE. Most willingly, at your request, madam.

FRONTIN. It is true, my lady, that the matter may be said to concern the gentleman.

DORANTE. Oh, to be sure . . . it may.

FRONTIN. First, you must know, my lady, having received my orders in this affair, namely to undertake the office of a spy, observing all communications, conferences and confrontations between my master and the Countess, I prepared first –

MARQUISE. I pray you, abridge your report a little, Frontin, if you can.

FRONTIN. Your pardon, my lady. I shall never finish unless I
   speak by the book.

MARQUISE. Does your master still profess any love for me?

FRONTIN. Not a jot, my lady.

MARQUISE. Does he, then, profess to love the Countess?

FRONTIN. Prodigiously, my lady. 'Love', my lady, is not a word
   which may contain my master's passion. It is like a burning
   mountain, in which my poor master daily drowns, as I may say.

MARQUISE. Faith, it may be more easy to say than to perform.

DORANTE (*his air determinedly casual*). And for the Countess . . .
   she does not . . . hate your master, sirrah?

FRONTIN. The other way, sir.

DORANTE. Ah . . . the other way.

FRONTIN. A thousand miles, sir, the other way.

DORANTE. You would say that she . . . that she does return . . .
   'respond', you would say, is not too strong a word?

FRONTIN. It is too weak a word, sir. When there breathes such a
   love as has been ignited between my master and the Countess,
   there is no demand and response, sir, but only the instant
   cannonado of two beating hearts.

DORANTE (*laughing*). Ha! ha! ha! (*Aside.*) I may die.

MARQUISE (*aside*). Courage, sir . . . But what proof, Frontin,
   have you of all this?

FRONTIN. The witness of mine own eyes, my lady, the testimony
   of mine own ears, both valiant in your service. As, item,
   yesterday the Countess –

DORANTE. Oh, to the devil with this fellow's yesterdays. They
   love each other, and that's enough.

MARQUISE. Continue.

FRONTIN. Yesterday the Countess and my master were walking
   in the garden, my lady, I following, keeping due distance and
   unobserved. They enter the woods. I follow. They turn into a
   leafy glade, I into a coppice. Before me I hear a confusion of
   melodious voices. I creep, my lady, I glide from thicket to
   thicket. At last I reach them, and from my hiding-place, I hear,

I see. 'Oh, how beautiful, how beautiful!' the Captain cries.
In one hand he holds a portrait of the lady, in the other the
lady's own fair fingers, sir, are clasped in his.

MARQUISE. All the better!

DORANTE (*aside*). All the worse!

FRONTIN. 'Oh, how beautiful!' my master cries, and falls, my
lady, to kissing the portrait. 'Indeed,' says the Countess, 'It has
been thought the painter caught a likeness.' 'Never!' my master
says, pushing away the portrait, 'There are a thousand charms,
madam, to be descried in your fair face, that this portrait
lacks.' 'Come, come, you flatter me,' says the Countess, though
truth to tell the sparkle in the lady's eyes gives the lie to
modesty. 'Plague take me!' says my master. 'Even I myself
degrade your beauty by putting it into mere words. Your true
likeness, madam, is limmed here,' and he strikes himself over
the heart so that one can hear the bones rattle. 'And does not
the likeness of the Marquise dwell in your heart also, sir?' says
the Countess.

MARQUISE. And he replied?

FRONTIN. That you did not dwell there, my lady.

MARQUISE. Well, then, I may dwell where I please for all of
your master. What next?

FRONTIN. 'If I had a thousand hearts,' my master cries, 'you
would overfill them. My love, madam, is superabundant, and
spills over my words, my feelings, my very thoughts.' And all
the time, my lady, he would kiss her fingers, and then the
portrait, and if she would take back her hand, he would fall to
kissing the portrait, and if she would take back the portrait, he
would be at her fingers again, and so it was between them, so
lightly done, my lady, and with such grace, it was like a ballet to
see them.

DORANTE (*aside*). A most damnable history!

FRONTIN. You spoke, sir?

DORANTE. Nothing . . . A comical story.

FRONTIN. I continue. 'Return me, sir, my portrait,' says the

Countess. 'But, Countess' – 'But, Captain' – 'But my lady –'
etc, etc. He falls on his knees. There's matter ill-writ here, my
lady. My master has a fine and elegant turn of speech; I cannot
always understand it. Then the lady says, 'To give one's
portrait, sir, is to give one's heart,' and my master replies that
he will accept of both most readily. Then says the Countess she
will not give him the portrait, but if he take it, how shall she
deny him? 'Why, so I do,' says my master, 'I have captured your
portrait, and so I capture your heart.' 'What an abuse of my
kindness to you,' she cries, and with that she lets forth a great
sigh, and my master lets forth a great sigh –

DORANTE. Aaaah!

FRONTIN. Yes, sir. Of about that quality.

DORANTE. To be sure, yes, that would be the quality of their
sighing. Would you not say so, my lady?

MARQUISE. Oh, very like. Sighs are much alike, sir, to be sure.
(*She laughs.*) Ha! ha! ha!

FRONTIN. The following morning, in the Long Gallery –

DORANTE (*to the* MARQUISE). Compel the fellow make an end, I
pray. My resolution is quite gone.

MARQUISE. Enough, Frontin. You have earned your salary.

FRONTIN. I have some choice fragments remaining, my lady, if
you will hear them.

MARQUISE. No, I have heard enough.

FRONTIN. Does your ladyship mean that my commission is
concluded?

MARQUISE. That is so.

FRONTIN. Will not the gentleman put my capacities to some
profitable use?

DORANTE. Not I.

FRONTIN. Then, sir, if there be no more in the way of business, I
take my leave.

FRONTIN *goes.*

Scene 13

MARQUISE. We cannot doubt they have some secret under-
    standing. And I must tell you, sir, our game will never hold if
    you play your part so ill.
DORANTE. Well, I confess, madam, this history has caused me
    to suffer somewhat, but I shall undertake to perform better
    hereafter. Oh, the ungrateful woman, that never gave *me* her
    portrait.

Scene 14

HARLEQUIN. Sir, a thief is coming.
DORANTE. What thief?
HARLEQUIN. A gentleman thief, sir, that has stolen away your
    lady, master to a thieving knave that is in train to steal away
    mine.
DORANTE. Out of the way.

    HARLEQUIN *goes*.

Scene 15

MARQUISE. And I also, sir, must be out of the way of this
    encounter. Though our plan be not yet fully hatched, remember
    only that you love me, and desire the world should know it. As
    for the Captain, though he may believe himself to be your rival,
    you will be indifferent to that, since you have determined no
    longer to be rival to him.
DORANTE. Trust me, madam. I shall perform my part.

    She goes off. The CAPTAIN *enters.*

Scene 16

CAPTAIN. Sir, we are most conveniently met. I'd speak with you.

DORANTE. As you will, sir. Though I pray you speak to the point, for I have business in hand.

CAPTAIN. Oh, I'll have done, sir, in the blink of an eye. For, Dorante, I am thy good friend, be sure of that, and find I have some small scruple on my conscience.

DORANTE. You? Scrupulous?

CAPTAIN. To a fault. It is but the merest shadow, you know, Dorante, upon my honour, but I am such a foolish scrupulous fellow as cannot allow even a shadow – that's to say the very shadow of a shadow upon my honour. Here is the case. I have heard – though to be sure I don't believe it – that you, friend Dorante, have some regard, it may not be too strong to say 'love', for the Countess.

DORANTE. I understand you, sir. You would prefer that I had no such strong regard.

CAPTAIN. It would be a heavy burden, sir, to the conscience of your friend. For I myself love the lady, let me tell you.

DORANTE. And does the lady favour you, sir?

CAPTAIN. Favour, sir, is not in the case. I may say that the lady is conscious of my deserts.

DORANTE. Which is to say, you please her?

CAPTAIN. Spare my modesty, dear friend. I am, as you see me, a simple soldier.

DORANTE. Modesty aside, sir, does the lady love the simple soldier?

CAPTAIN. Sir, I may say, 'Yes.' My lady's eyes speak for her in this matter. They solicit my heart; they demand an answer. Scrupulous fellow that I am, what answer may I, in honour, give? I await, dear friend, your permission to reply.

DORANTE. Oh, sir, you have it freely. If you will but return me compensation.

CAPTAIN. What compensation?

DORANTE. There are eyes, sir, which solicit, as I find, my own unworthy heart. I think you know those eyes, dear friend.

CAPTAIN. You speak, sir, of the eyes of the Marquise?

DORANTE. Those very eyes, sir.

CAPTAIN. And you suspect, sir, that I have some interest in those eyes? That holds you back?

DORANTE. I confess, a little.

CAPTAIN. I have no such interest, sir. You may advance freely.

DORANTE. I must tell you frankly, dear friend, that I intend to marry the lady.

CAPTAIN. As frankly, Dorante, let me declare my own intention of marriage.

DORANTE. To the Countess?

CAPTAIN. My posterity expects it.

DORANTE. And shall you be married soon?

CAPTAIN. Perhaps tomorrow, sir, we shall terminate virginity.

DORANTE (*embarrassed*). I am to felicitate you, sir. Greatly.

CAPTAIN (*offers his hand*). Take my hand. Are we not dear friends still?

DORANTE. Why, yes . . . Yes, indeed.

CAPTAIN. Our friendship shall be measureless. I bind myself to you for a century, Dorante, and when that's done, we shall renew the bond.

DORANTE. Oh, yes. Indeed, yes. Until tomorrow, then.

CAPTAIN. Hang tomorrow! 'Tis for an age, I tell you, past, present, and future; I shall be yet your servant, and you mine, before the world.

DORANTE. Before the world. Indeed, before the world. Farewell.

DORANTE *goes*. FRONTIN *arrives*.

Scene 17

FRONTIN. I have delayed my coming hither, sir, until the gentleman's departure.

CAPTAIN. Why do you come at all, fellow? I am in haste to rejoin my lady.

FRONTIN. Wait, sir! Faith, we deal with serious matters here. I have spoken with the Marquise, sir, and made my report.

CAPTAIN. Very well. You've told the Marquise in plain terms that I love the Countess, and she loves me. How did she respond? Tell me, and be done.

FRONTIN. She said that it was well for you, sir.

CAPTAIN. It is well in truth, Frontin, and shall be well, and so farewell.

FRONTIN. Sir, sir, this is not the way. The lady's passion for you, she avows, is dead.

CAPTAIN. And what care I for that?

FRONTIN. It must be revived, sir. Only when the lady is once more monstrously in love with you, may she in honour be discarded.

CAPTAIN. What nonsense, man! Though I die in one lady's heart, I am resurrected in the heart of another. So let it be. I have died, and am reborn.

FRONTIN. Bethink you, sir, your new life may be a short one. Was it not by a sudden caprice of your lady that Monsieur Dorante himself suffered his present death?

CAPTAIN. No, Frontin, the caprice was mine. In the lists of love, it was I gave Dorante a fall, as I have done to so many other cavaliers. Your apprehensions are ill-founded. I have been received, *cap-à-pie*, into the heart of my lady, and there she will guard me well.

FRONTIN. It is a heart, sir, in which love, I think, may make camp for a season, but does not dwell for ever.

CAPTAIN. Why, sirrah, that is my own way. My capacity and

appetite for love may not be exhausted by one lady. Wish your master a better fortune, know him better, and – hark you – mistrust him less.

FRONTIN. It is a prescription I have followed before, and it has done nothing for me. But here is Lisette, sir, come to seek you. Now let me beg you use your favour with the mistress to commend your servant to the maid.

Scene 18

LISETTE. My lady asks for you, sir.

CAPTAIN. And you see I run to her side, Lisette. But do you mark my fellow, Frontin, here? Here's a man enslaved by your dark eyes, child, in a very passion of love for you; he has confessed so to me, Lisette. Sure, you can't be so hard-hearted as to spurn a poor fellow who worships you.

LISETTE. Had he made his confession to me, sir, I should have known better how to absolve him.

FRONTIN. I am in a passion of love for you, Lisette. Now you have my confession, you know as much as I.

LISETTE. Take courage; young man; you will lose nothing by it. It may be you know more than you think. I'll tell my lady you're coming, sir. Farewell, my penitent.

FRONTIN. Farewell, my angel.

Scene 19

FRONTIN. Your fortune, sir, wears a joyous aspect. Be sure the Countess loves you. You are a true gentleman of fashion, and as for me, why I'm your man, and that's enough to further my advancement.

CAPTAIN. Sirrah, I guarantee so much.

FRONTIN. Thus may a mouse behold a lion in pride,
Grasp tight his tail, and so to glory ride.

Act Two

Scene 1

DORANTE. Sirrah, a word with you.

HARLEQUIN. Oh, sir, a dozen.

DORANTE. Have you nothing better to do, man, than to run after my lady's maid?

HARLEQUIN. If the game's afoot, sir, the hunter must be nimble, and with such a plump little partridge, sir, on the run before me . . .

DORANTE. Tell me, Harlequin, do you wish to remain in my service?

HARLEQUIN. Why, sir, your service is my own. I serve myself by serving you. Though if I had but myself to serve, I'd serve nobody, sir, save myself alone, yet as I am called to service, sir, I'll serve no master in the world but you.

DORANTE. If that be so, I'll give you this command. Break off with Lisette.

HARLEQUIN. A fine jest, sir!

DORANTE. No jest. Close your account with her.

HARLEQUIN. But, sir, my account is not open. There has been no entry in the ledger.

DORANTE. I do not jest, Harlequin.

HARLEQUIN. But, sir, although you yourself have renounced the fair sex, as any fine gentleman may do by way of pleasantry, I am a mere servant, sir, and prone to lechery. Besides, the wench is already promised to me in marriage, and may slip quite away unless I can contrive to hold her.

DORANTE. You shall utter no further word to her; you shall avoid her very presence. Those are my commands.

HARLEQUIN. Though the mistress may forsake your company, sir, yet must not I in logic forsake the maid.

DORANTE. Did you not tell me just now that a good servant follows his master? Besides, the Countess may suspect I do but use your conversation with Lisette to spy out her own conference with the Captain. Therefore, forsake Lisette. You shall have recompense for the sacrifice.

HARLEQUIN. The sacrifice will kill me, and what use then is recompense?

DORANTE. Why, you shall have another partridge to chase, fellow. What think you to the Marquise's maid, Eglantine?

HARLEQUIN. Why, she's an eglantine, sir, a very briar-rose, that would tear a fellow's flesh before one could get a handful of hers.

DORANTE. Eglantine is a fine wench, sirrah, and her father farms his own two acres.

HARLEQUIN. My love, sir, is altogether given to Lisette.

DORANTE. Well, I tell you, you must make a choice here. Take your leave of my service or take the briar-rose.

HARLEQUIN. How can I choose, sir, when I've no knowledge of either?

DORANTE. You shall have knowledge of your dismissal today, if I observe but one word pass between yourself and Lisette. Dolt, can you not see, your coolness will but serve to make her regret you?

HARLEQUIN. Regret me? Lisette? Is it to say, sir, she will by this means love me more?

DORANTE. Be off with you. The Marquise comes this way.

HARLEQUIN. I obey, sir. Provided that my dear Lisette regrets me.

DORANTE. One word more. I don't choose the Countess shall know I have bid you break with Lisette, for I gave my consent to the match, and should now show ill in forbidding it. You may say, therefore, only that you prefer Eglantine to Lisette, whom you no longer love, and since the Marquise has set her mind on the match, your best happiness is to fulfil my lady's design.

HARLEQUIN. It shall be as Your Honour desires. The villains in this case shall be the Marquise and myself, she that would give me Eglantine, and I that would take her. Only Heaven shall know the bitter truth. (*He begins to go.*)

DORANTE. And that's as I would have it, sirrah.

HARLEQUIN (*returns*). But she will regret me? (HARLEQUIN *goes.*)

Scene 2

MARQUISE. Have you instructed your servant, Dorante?

DORANTE. He has his orders, madam.

MARQUISE. Sure, it is a small matter, but small matters being gathered together may yet do much, and we may touch the Countess thus through her maid.

DORANTE. Indeed, madam, I begin to believe already that we may succeed. I came from the Countess just now, my love for her and my reproach being alike concealed, and maintained so cool a composure as to disturb her strangely.

MARQUISE. Hold to that, sir, and you'll enjoy the pleasure of awakening in hers the distress you have felt in your own heart.

DORANTE. I shall be resolute, madam, until I see her weeping. Then I may break.

MARQUISE. You may break then, sir, if you will; the trick will be done.

DORANTE. And the Captain, madam? Has he noticed nothing amiss?

MARQUISE. Speak no more of that gentleman, sir, if you wish to

please me. We shall endeavour to undo him, and thereafter he
may go hang. But I have sent one of the Countess's people to
ask her if she will see me, and I see him returning with her
reply.

A LACKEY *enters.*

Well? Shall I speak with your mistress?

LACKEY. My lady, she is coming.

LACKEY *leaves.*

MARQUISE. I pray you, sir, leave me. We should not be seen
together.

DORANTE. Indeed, madam, I have a small plan of my own,
of which I'll speak hereafter.

MARQUISE. Do nothing that would spoil our strategem.

DORANTE. Trust me.

DORANTE *leaves.*

Scene 3

COUNTESS. My dear Marquise, I am come myself in haste to find
you, for since you have asked me so particularly for a meeting, I
am sure it must be of some grave consequence.

MARQUISE. Dear Countess, I shall not long detain you. I have
only one question to put to you, and that I know you will
answer truthfully, for you are the most sincere and honest of
women, and would never hold a secret from a childhood
friend.

COUNTESS. Faith, I think you rather describe the qualities you
hope to find in me, my dear, than those I have, and hope by your
panegyric to flatter me into frankness.

MARQUISE. That aside, will you be frank?

COUNTESS. Well, I shall begin by being so, and tell you truthfully that I do not know.

MARQUISE. If my question be, 'Does the Captain love you?', will you be honest in your reply?

COUNTESS. Indeed no, my dear, for I've no wish to fall out with you, and I'm sure you would hate me were I to tell you the truth.

MARQUISE. But, my dear, if I give you my word that I shall not hate you, what then?

COUNTESS. My dear, you could not keep your word, and therefore I myself dispense you from the promise. There are some feelings stronger than our control of them.

MARQUISE. But why should I hate my dear friend?

COUNTESS. Has it not been rumoured, my dear, that the Captain has been in love with you?

MARQUISE. To be sure, those who believed so may have had some reason for their belief.

COUNTESS. Come, be as frank with me. Have not you yourself believed so?

MARQUISE. I confess it; I have.

COUNTESS. And if I were to answer you, 'Yes, the Captain loves me.' You would not advise me to such an answer, my dear.

MARQUISE. Oh, is that all? Believe me, I had rather lose a mere cavalier than a good friend. I pray with all my heart that the gentleman should love you.

COUNTESS. Then you may give Heaven thanks, my dear. Your prayer is answered.

MARQUISE. I am glad of it. Most heartily.

COUNTESS. Yet one must say, the gentleman was in the wrong, for you are so agreeable and charming a lady, he should have had eyes for no other; he is much to blame. But perhaps he was less attached to you, my dear, than was believed?

MARQUISE. No, he was much attached to me, but I do not blame him, for though my person and my temper be as agreeable as you would make them by your praise, yet you are far more worthy of love than I, my dear, as who knows better than yourself?

COUNTESS. Your compliment, my dear, takes on a jealous tone, but you are not to be blamed for it. I knew that you would break your promise; forgiveness does not rise so high. I deserve your spite.

MARQUISE. I? Jealous?

COUNTESS. Come now, confess; the compliment was barbed. You would say I am a coquette.

MARQUISE. I could not dream, my dear, of saying so.

COUNTESS. My dear Marquise, there may be many matters spoke which have not first been dreamed of.

MARQUISE. Why then, if we are to be frank, have you not in truth played the coquette, at least a little?

COUNTESS. Faith, yes. But that little is not enough. Why balk, madam? Go further. Dub me coquette outright if you will, for I am sure you are so as much as I.

MARQUISE. I have not given the same proofs of it.

COUNTESS. You speak truth there, madam. Only what succeeds is proof; lack of success keeps coquetry hid. Your unsuccessful coquette has this advantage; she may retreat with discretion, a little humiliated to be sure, but at least unknown.

MARQUISE. I shall succeed when I wish, madam; you shall see it is not so difficult. As for the Captain, can you believe you would have held his heart so long, if I set so little store by it?

COUNTESS. I shall not haggle, madam, over the sum the gentleman's heart may fetch at market. It is but your self-esteem is wounded and cries out in hurt.

MARQUISE. Yet dare I wager I shall not come off the worse in this adventure. Will you engage?

COUNTESS. Sure, you cannot hope to regain the gentleman. You may have him, madam, if you can.

MARQUISE. You speak out of true love, I see, that would so readily give him away.

COUNTESS. A hit, madam; I avow. Yet you teach me but to love the gentleman more that he may the better resist you. He shall have strength for two.

MARQUISE. He shall need none, madam. I leave him to you. Farewell.

COUNTESS. But why? Let us dispute our conquest amiably, and she who carries off the prize shall earn no odium from the loser. I vow I shall fight under no other condition, for you know I cannot bear reproach from any person, and least of all from you.

MARQUISE. Are you so sure you have the victory?

COUNTESS. You have played a poor game, my dear. I should have played a better in your place.

MARQUISE. Do you believe, my dear, I could not have won the gentleman back? For I have a game will match yours, do I but choose to play it.

COUNTESS. Try. Take your revenge.

MARQUISE. No, I have something better to do.

COUNTESS. Oh, to be sure. And may one ask what it is?

MARQUISE. Dorante is worth his price, Countess. Farewell.

The MARQUISE *goes.*

Scene 4

COUNTESS. Dorante? Does she think to take Dorante from me? Sure, the woman is to be pitied; she has run stark mad with jealousy.

Scene 5

DORANTE, *arriving quickly, pretends to take the* COUNTESS

for the MARQUISE.

DORANTE. Ah, Marquise! Do your scruples still trouble you? (*Perceiving the* COUNTESS.) Your pardon, madam. In my pre-occupation I fear I mistook you for my lady, the Marquise, with whom I was in talk here but a short while ago.

COUNTESS. No great harm in that, sir. But tell me the nature of your pre-occupation.

DORANTE. Nothing of consequence, madam. Some matter of my talk here with my lady, but of no consequence, I assure you.

COUNTESS. You spoke of scruples, sir.

DORANTE. Did I?

COUNTESS. With what scruples is the Marquise troubled? For she is my dear friend, sir, you know, and it concerns me to be informed what troubles her.

DORANTE. Oh, madam, some small scruples which arose during our conversation here, but of no great matter.

COUNTESS. But what was the nature, sir, of her scruples? Come, sir, you have not been used e'er now to stand silent before me.

DORANTE. Oh, madam, I see you are distressed, and by such a bagatelle; it must not be. Believe me, now I put myself to think of it, I have myself forgot the nature of my lady's scruples.

COUNTESS. I pray you, sir, remember.

DORANTE. Madam, it is so small a matter. The Marquise out of the merest curiosity bid me tell her had I still some place in your ladyship's heart.

COUNTESS. 'Bid' you, sir?

DORANTE. Bid me, prayed me, or some such.

COUNTESS. And you replied, sir?

DORANTE. Though I have faults, madam, vanity is not amongst them. Pray let us speak of more consequential matters. Has your ladyship had letters from town? There will be a post tomorrow. The Marquise has so many friends generous in letter-writing, she will know all the news.

COUNTESS. Do not think to avoid my questions, sir. Your discomposure is pitiable.

DORANTE. Sure, madam, you are not still harping on that matter of my lady's scruples?

COUNTESS. I imagined, Dorante, that I had some power yet to command your friendship.

DORANTE. Friendship, madam, is akin to love; it is given, and may not be commanded. Yet I'll allow your ladyship has some power yet over this poor heart, and though the measure has been somewhat diminished of late, I am not to blame for that. Therefore, madam, lest your ladyship's importunities should diminish the sum still further, I'll take my leave, and go seek the Marquise as I have intended.

DORANTE *goes*.

COUNTESS. Sure, the poor gentleman is not himself today.

Scene 6

The CAPTAIN *enters, to find the* COUNTESS *thoughtful*.

CAPTAIN. Does my lady dream?

COUNTESS. Sir?

CAPTAIN. Why, it seemed to me, madam, as I approached that you were in some rapture of private contemplation. Do I dare to hope I was the subject?

COUNTESS. I was thinking of the Marquise, sir, and Dorante, who are both fallen into some strange affliction of the mind. And therefore we must put off our wedding.

CAPTAIN. Put it off, madam? But for how long?

COUNTESS. Oh, a fortnight will do.

CAPTAIN. It is to say a century.

COUNTESS. You have not observed their sufferings, sir, as I have.

CAPTAIN. Faith, you are too nice, madam, in your observations.

COUNTESS. I tell you, sir, the poor creatures are deranged. You would not push them to the end? What need have we to hurry?

CAPTAIN. Why, this need, madam, that I shall perish meanwhile in the waiting. If their cure requires a sacrifice, I hope I am not to be the lamb.

COUNTESS. Sir, sir, these be two desperate souls; you cannot wish to reduce them further. If in the past they have flattered themselves we loved them, have we not given them some small cause so to abuse their own good sense? I do not use, sir, to do ill to any fellow-creature; no more, I hope, do you. Though you are a soldier, and must be resolute, I do not bèlieve you hard-hearted. The Marquise and Dorante are your good friends, as they are mine. Shall we not at least allow them time to become accustomed to the proposition of our marriage before we plunge in and perform it?

CAPTAIN. Dearest madam, I have told you I cannot live in this prospect of postponement. My devotion to your person is so entire, delay must kill me.

COUNTESS. Sir, be moderate, I beg.

CAPTAIN. Moderation is not in my nature, madam. Faith, it is not in the nature of true love; the heart, madam, is not a moderate organ. Let us arrange this accommodation at less cost to ourselves, I pray, for I never yet heard it was the fashion to put oneself to death for the consolation of one's friends. Besides, it is put about that the two are already come to an arrangement with each other.

COUNTESS. An arrangement, sir?

CAPTAIN. An arrangement, madam.

COUNTESS. Of what sort?

CAPTAIN. Of the heart, as I hear.

COUNTESS. You have there a fine figure of speech, sir, 'an arrangement of the heart'. Speak more plain, I pray. Do you tell me they love each other?

CAPTAIN. One might say ... a certain tenderness, madam; one might say that, I'm sure.

COUNTESS. And what's this 'tenderness'? Fie, fie! 'tis some chimerical piece of tattle you would have me believe for truth, sir, with your 'it is put about' and your 'as I hear' and your talk of tenderness. You would have me believe, sir, that they, who have made the strongest avowals of love to us, are now become so indifferent as to fall in love with each other, and so, sir, you would evade postponement.

CAPTAIN. I did not say they were in love, madam; I did not categorically say 'love'.

COUNTESS. You would have me believe, then, that they console each other, no more than that?

CAPTAIN. Not a whit more.

COUNTESS. I would have some proof, sir.

CAPTAIN. If I furnish you with such a proof, madam, shall we be married instanter?

COUNTESS. If I might be sure, sir, that those two poor creatures had found tranquillity. But who could so assure me?

CAPTAIN. Why, madam, you must know what I had forgot to tell you, that the Marquise has seduced the rogue Frontin, my fellow, to spy out all that has concerned the secrets of our two hearts.

COUNTESS. How shall that serve your point, sir?

CAPTAIN. If it do not, I'll perish with what grace I can, for I scorn to win your favour by a lie. Frontin must by now have made his report to my lady. I've not seen the rogue since, and know not how she received it. Be there love between the Marquise and Dorante, Frontin has had occasion by now to have observed it, and shall tell us all. We'll question him.

Scene 7

CAPTAIN. Come hither, fellow. Have you made your report to your paymistress, the Marquise?

FRONTIN. Aye, sir. My lady was in company here with Monsieur Dorante, and so I found them.

CAPTAIN. Tell us how they received your report. My lady here has the most gentle heart in the world. It is her fear that Dorante and the Marquise may have been thrown into despair by your intelligence, though for myself, I swear, I believe they may be already in some way to console each other. Therefore tell us exactly how matters stand between 'em; do not fear to prove your master in error. Only this tenderness of heart in my lady prevents our immediate marriage. You understand me?

FRONTIN. I understand you exactly, sir. My lady may marry you in the most absolute confidence. I saw no sign or shadow of despair between the parties.

CAPTAIN. Now you see, madam, you may run down your flag with all good will, and this night surrender to me your precious citadel.

COUNTESS. Not so fast, I beg; the articles of surrender are yet to be concluded. Despair wears many faces, sir. I am not yet convinced your servant is practised in the discovery of it.

FRONTIN. You will excuse me, my lady. From your true body-servant despair cannot be hid. It is our common encounter, for though a gentleman of fashion may conceal from all others the ravages of ill fortune, be they at love or at the tables, yet from his *valet-de-chambre* they cannot be hid. We have the infallible eye, my lady.

CAPTAIN. Faith, madam, the fellow speaks the truth, for I myself met Dorante not long ago, and speaking – as my heart was full – of my great love for your ladyship, received but this reply, 'Ah, is it so? Then guard her well.'

COUNTESS. A lover may feign indifference, sir, before his rival.

CAPTAIN. But, madam, he was laughing. And in the most profound contentment.

COUNTESS. Profound contentment! In a man who loved me! 'Tis not to be borne.

CAPTAIN. Excepting only that profound contentment, madam, in which *this* happy soul is steeped by knowing its love to be returned.

COUNTESS. Oh, let that be, sir. For, truth to tell, I believe Dorante's heart to be more capable of passion than your own, though I say it but in passing. Count it not a fault, sir. A man loves as he can, and it is in Dorante's nature to love more deeply than any man, else I'm sure I should not pity him so. Laughing, say you? As for your fellow here, I'll have more grounds for certainty than the mere assurance of a *valet-de-chambre*. For if the Marquise and Dorante care so little for us and so much for each other, 'tis strange they should pay him to spy out all our actions.

FRONTIN. But very ill, my lady. To be sure, the Marquise has paid me but little for my labours, and truth to tell she's in arrears.

COUNTESS. A fine example, sirrah, of kitchen reasoning that because my lady may be illiberal to you, she must be indifferent to me.

FRONTIN. And Monsieur Dorante, my lady, did not care to employ me at all.

COUNTESS. Now, sirrah, tell me straight, and make an end. What have you seen? What do you know?

CAPTAIN (*aside to* FRONTIN). Don't overdo it, Frontin.

FRONTIN. Item: the Marquise and Monsieur Dorante, my lady, being in company, addressed this question to me: 'Are they, perhaps a little in love?', referring, my lady, to yourself and my master. I was categoric in my reply. I replied that my master is most prodigiously in love with you, my lady, and that his love is as prodigiously returned.

COUNTESS. Hum! And what said they to that?

FRONTIN. The Marquise, my lady, yawned. Monsieur Dorante took snuff.

COUNTESS. Leave us, sirrah; you're a fool. Your man has a most superficial observation, sir, and I'll have none of it.

FRONTIN. I say, my lady, that they are in love, and they themselves have bid me make it known to your ladyship.

COUNTESS (*laughs*). Themselves? Why did you not tell me so before, sirrah, fool that you are? (*To the* CAPTAIN.) You see, sir, their motive in this. They wish to make us jealous, and why should they do that, pray, but for spite, and what else will provoke spite, sir, but the pangs of despised love? 'Tis clear enough. Their pretended love is all for show.

CAPTAIN. Their passion mounts, madam, and in earnest. I am convinced.

COUNTESS. Your estimation is exaggerated, sir.

FRONTIN. Faith, my lady, now I begin to see matters in a clearer light. This pretended unconcern was but to give you pain. When Monsieur Dorante glanced idly at his watch, 'twas not to know the time, but to conceal despair.

COUNTESS. That was not the most profound contentment, sir.

CAPTAIN. Did we but know the motive, madam, for this glance, our estimation of the gentleman's feelings might be more exact.

FRONTIN. As, item: when the gentleman opened his snuff-box, he took snuff with two fingers only, my lady, and both were trembling. And when he laughed, only his mouth, my lady, expressed amusement, the remaining features, anguish.

COUNTESS. He was not laughing, sir, in his heart? Do you agree?

CAPTAIN. Indeed, madam, now I put myself to it, perhaps I recall a sigh or so, perhaps a shake of the head; perhaps he was not forward in rejoicing at our marriage. But even so, madam, what a compassion is this in you that so blights my fortune!

COUNTESS. Do not alarm yourself, sir. Though I may feel compassion, yet Dorante has behaved far too ill to deserve it, and shall receive none. But now here comes my lady, the Marquise, bearing down upon us. Sure, she will tell us of some deep engagement she has with Dorante. Do but listen.

Scene 8

MARQUISE. Your pardon, madam. I fear I interrupt some conference. I come but to tell you that I have heard how, out of a nice consideration for my feelings, your generosity has moved you to postpone your match with this gentleman. I am much obliged to you, madam, but there is no need to postpone, I assure you, on my account. The ceremony was to be tomorrow, as I have heard. I pray you, do not wait so long; let it be this very day. You shall see, I can be as solicitous for your happiness as you for mine. Farewell.

COUNTESS. My dear . . . a moment. I have heard some idle talk of an arrangement between yourself and Dorante. Indeed, it is reported that you begin to be a little in love with one another. I would rejoice if it were so.

MARQUISE. You may rejoice indeed, madam. It is so.

COUNTESS (with a laugh). In truth?

MARQUISE. In very truth, madam. Therefore, hasten to your own wedding. Farewell.

The MARQUISE *goes.*

Scene 9

COUNTESS (laughing). It is the merest pretence; my lady dies of spite. Oh, a slighted vanity, sure, may tempt a woman into some strange roles, yet I think her ladyship was somewhat overparted, for you saw well enough she could not sustain the pretence.

CAPTAIN. Your judgement is exact, madam.

FRONTIN. Just such a fluttering, my lady, did I mark not two hours gone on Monsieur Dorante's lower lip. (*To the* COUNTESS.) But, sir, will you not speak for me to my lady about Lisette, her maid?

COUNTESS. What does your fellow say of Lisette?

FRONTIN. A small petition, my lady, if you will allow it. The mere removing of Lisette, my lady, in the way of matrimony from Monsieur Dorante's servant, Harlequin, to me.

CAPTAIN. Merely that, madam.

COUNTESS. And does Lisette consent to the match?

FRONTIN. Oh, the removal, my lady, will be entirely to her taste.

COUNTESS. Well, Frontin, you have given me an idea, for though I never make mischief, you know, you see that the Marquise is not so nice in her behaviour; she would deceive us, which is a sin, and must be punished. It is true that I have promised Lisette to Dorante's servant, Harlequin; he and I have agreed so. Yet that was a bargain made when Dorante vowed his love to me, and if my lady will have it that he is now grown indifferent, we may hold the bargain broken, and you shall succeed. Yes, fellow, you shall marry Lisette; I shall tell her so myself, and we shall see how indifferently Dorante will receive the news of the match. He should be so, if my lady speaks the truth, and I am sure I hope he is so, but if he be not, here's a means to know it. If Dorante does not complain, then the Marquise is right; he has forgotten me, and I shall be rid of a troublesome admirer. Go, Frontin. Find Lisette and her father, and bring them hither. I'll speak to them.

FRONTIN. The discovery will not be difficult, my lady, for here they come.

Scene 10

COUNTESS. Come hither, Lisette. And you, Blaise, also. You
know that your daughter was to have married Monsieur
Dorante's man, Harlequin. But if you will be guided, good
Blaise, by your mistress's liking, you will marry your daughter
to Frontin here instead. What do you say?

BLAISE. Aye, my lady. You say truth, my lady; it is not good to
treat one thus. I come to you, my lady; I stand before you in
your presence. I cry outrage, my lady. 'Is it good? Is it good?'
I cry.

COUNTESS. Sure, the man is deranged. And why does your
daughter weep?

LISETTE. My father will tell you, my lady.

BLAISE. It is the man Harlequin, my lady. His Honour Monsieur
Dorante's man, a very malapert rascal, my lady, a villain or
knave, as the world says. Which is not to say, my lady, that it is
the man's own design to be a villain. It is my lady the Marquise
and his master have put him to it, being the very controllers and
managers of Harlequin's will, for I'm sure he loves my
daughter, as she, poor girl, loves him. And they might be
married tomorrow, my lady, if there were no impediment.

COUNTESS. What impediment?

BLAISE. As, item, my lady, Eglantine, the Marquise's chambermaid, my lady, promised to Harlequin by my lady.

COUNTESS. Curious proceeding!

BLAISE. And what's more, my lady, she says they shall be married
in Paris, which is a low trick, my lady, to break my poor
daughter's heart and make a blot, my lady, or stain, as one
might say, or stigma upon our good name and yours, my lady,
in consequence of which, my lady, I come for justice.

COUNTESS. And you shall have it, Blaise. Captain, this changes
our arrangement here; Frontin is to dream no longer of my
maid. Come, Lisette! Cease your lamentation! The Marquise

may make what proposal she will with her chambermaids and her Eglantines, thinking to attack me through my servants, yet shall she find I am the one shall settle the account. Dorante has no active part in this; you may believe me. I know him; he has too gentle a heart, and only carelessness has led him into complaisance. The Marquise shall see I have more credit with him still than she imagines. Therefore, weep no more, Lisette, and we shall see what may be done.

LISETTE. But even Harlequin, my lady, though I'm sure he was fathoms deep in love with me before, is become as cold as ice. Though I may stand in his way, he will not see me, that once would run after me the length of two orchards and a hayfield if I but winked an eye.

BLAISE. A young maid, my lady, that would have become a very woman by marriage, now cut off for ever from that happy state.

COUNTESS. The matter can be remedied. I have told you that I intend so.

FRONTIN. This remedy, sir, may be good medicine for the old gardener, but it is poison to me unless you prescribe an antidote.

CAPTAIN. Dear madam, the divine melody of your voice, though expressed in words of great import, is yet a little beyond this poor understanding. Sure, the matter here may be less than you would make of it. Come, Lisette, let us bring this strange adventure into the air. You will not tell us, I hope, that you care naught for my good Frontin here, for I am sure you incline already a little towards him.

LISETTE. I did incline a little towards him, sir, when I was sure that Harlequin loved me. But now Harlequin grows cold, that inclination, I find, has quite melted away.

CAPTAIN. What reason can convince a woman's heart?

COUNTESS. Well, sir, I may say that Lisette's heart has reasons enough, which merit more than your quizzing. 'Tis a simple proposition, sir, though it be outside your understanding.

There was a man who loved her, and he tells her now that he loves her no longer; therefore is her heart wounded, and she weeps. 'Twould be the same, I make no doubt, with you and me if we but stood in the same case. Go now, child. Go, Blaise. Your business lies now in my hands, and I shall bring it to a happy conclusion. Go, Frontin.

BLAISE. Faith, my lady, I should have quarrelled else with my poor girl's tormentors, though they stand high above me. I fear no man, my lady. I should speak out.

COUNTESS. You may rest your case with me. I'll speak with Monsieur Dorante presently.

Scene 11

COUNTESS. Dorante, a word with you, I pray. I'd speak with you on the subject of my lady, the Marquise.

DORANTE. With all my heart, madam.

COUNTESS. With all your heart, then, sir. What plot has my lady in hand for today?

DORANTE. My lady, the Marquise, does not plot, intrigue or cabal with any person, madam. She is no politician, but the most candid of her sex.

COUNTESS. Oh, I may hope, sir, to persuade you to change your estimation of the lady.

DORANTE. Nay, madam, you yourself above all others well know my lady's prudence and her tender heart.

COUNTESS. Do not flatter the lady further, sir, I pray; you are too obstinate in your commendation. This tender-hearted and prudent lady, out of the merest jealousy and for no other reason than that the Captain here has quite fallen out of love with her, which can hardly be imputed to my blame, this lady, I say, now sets herself to plague me, finding it not too far below her dignity to set your valet and my chambermaid at odds, only because she well knows I wished them to be married and had concerned myself in the affair. This lady, sir, whom you commend to me so highly, throws across the poor fools' path some Eglantine, some slut of her own, some wild briar, I say, to blight the fond love of these two innocent creatures. And what I find most strange, sir – I must tax you with it roundly – is that you yourself take some part in the plot.

DORANTE. But can you truly believe, madam, that my lady the Marquise, your friend since childhood, would go about so to vex you? No, no, madam; you are mistaken; my lady exerts herself only to do good. It is Harlequin who has complained that Lisette slights him, turning her favours all another way towards the Captain's man. And so, madam, finding the poor fool forlorn, the Marquise proposes instead Eglantine, her maid, Harlequin accepts with gratitude, and so the matter rests. In truth, madam, the well-being of our servants must even be the concern of us to whom they minister, as is shown by your ladyship's own concern for Lisette.

CAPTAIN. Sure, madam, I'm persuaded there's no malice in the case. May not we three generals now make peace, and leave our subalterns to pursue the squabble on their own?

COUNTESS. Let us alone, sir, I pray. You may give your opinion when it be demanded. Dorante, the intrigue displeases me. I flatter myself I need say no more, sir.

DORANTE. A moment, madam, if you will allow me. Perhaps my fellow may be close by. Harlequin!

COUNTESS. Why do you call, sir?

DORANTE. I intend sending the fellow for my lady. I have only to send in your name, madam, and I am sure my lady will be here directly, and you may settle the matter together.

COUNTESS. We have no need, sir, of the Marquise to settle what may be more conveniently settled between us two. It is to you I speak, sir; I tell you what I desire. I hope I may do so without leave of the Marquise.

DORANTE. Indeed you may, madam, but I may not. My lady has made the offer; Harlequin has accepted. Were I now to order him to refuse, it would be a great slight to my lady, which the esteem I have for her would never allow.

COUNTESS. Sir, you must slight the lady or myself, it seems. Do you hesitate between us?

DORANTE. I would not slight either, madam, if I might avoid it.

COUNTESS. Have regard, sir, I pray, not to the immediate inclination of today, but to your long tomorrow. How shall you stand in my favour if you disoblige me now?

DORANTE. It is because I look to future time, madam, that I hesitate. How shall I stand with my ladyship tomorrow in disobliging her today?

CAPTAIN. Before God, madam, what a state of passion are we got into over this backstairs affair?

COUNTESS. Your pardon, sir, if I have seemed passionate, for sure I did not intend it, since the matter concerns me so little, and is but for my maid.

DORANTE. Even so small a concern of yours with my affairs, madam, must and does honour me. It shall always be my pleasure to oblige you. If I can.

COUNTESS. Meanwhile, sir, I have no further cause to detain you. Captain, your hand.

CAPTAIN (*gives her his hand*). It is yours, madam. I pray you, never return it to me.

DORANTE. My intention in coming hither, madam, had been to put one question to you.

COUNTESS (*returns to him*). Sir?

DORANTE. I have heard, madam, that you are to marry this gentleman. When shall we have the joy to see you both united?

COUNTESS. Perhaps you may have that joy this very evening, sir.

CAPTAIN. Oh, madam! Oh divine lady, oh Aphrodite, as one may say, to this poor Paris! I faint with delight, madam, at this joyful intelligence.

DORANTE. Indeed, sir, you are much to be felicitated, yet no
   gentleman breathes who more deserves such happiness.

COUNTESS (*aside*). The man is unworthy of my respect hereto!

DORANTE (*aside*). I'll swear the lady blushes.

COUNTESS. Is that the sum of your questions, sir?

DORANTE. It is, madam.

COUNTESS (*to the* CAPTAIN). Come, sir.

Scene 12

MARQUISE. Dear madam, Blaise your gardener tells me I have
   incurred your wrath, and here I am come in a hurry to beg your
   pardon. Though I am sure, madam, ignorance and not malice
   was to blame, yet here I have brought Harlequin with me to
   make a public reparation. For when I promised Eglantine to
   you, Harlequin, how could I know it would displease my lady?
   Therefore I tell you now in her presence that you may no longer
   count upon my promise; it is quite revoked.

HARLEQUIN. Then I release you from your promise, my lady,
   with all good will, for I've heard that Blaise will cry a breach
   upon me in the courts, so if I can find a notary directly, I'll
   honour the breach, and the courts may go whistle.

COUNTESS (*to* FRONTIN). Call back your man, sir. (*To the*
   MARQUISE.) And for you, my dear, pray keep your promise.
   The fellow shall marry your maid, and I myself shall pay the
   expenses of the wedding.

HARLEQUIN. My lady!

COUNTESS. Do not thank me, Harlequin.

HARLEQUIN. My lady –

COUNTESS. No more words, sirrah; it is settled.

DORANTE. You have leave to go, Harlequin.

HARLEQUIN (*going*). Have I no way to avoid this briar-patch? It is
you, Captain, are the cause of all our troubles, for you have set
all loves to somersaults. If you had not thrust in between, my
master and I would have been married together, he to his
Countess, I to my lovely Lisette, master and mistress, maid and
man, as Providence intended. And now my master will wed the
Marquise, so I am to be bedded with a briar. Alas! Alas!

The MARQUISE *and the* CAPTAIN *both laugh.*

COUNTESS (*laughing also*). If these extravagances amuse you, tell
the fellow to come closer. We shall have a fine play here.

CAPTAIN. It is the very dementia of love.

DORANTE. Away, you impertinent scoundrel!

HARLEQUIN *leaves.*

MARQUISE. Then we may be good friends again, my dear?

COUNTESS. The best in the world. When have we been other?

DORANTE. My lady, I have just now received a piece of the most
happy news. The Countess and this gentleman are to be
married – perhaps – this very evening.

MARQUISE. Ah! So soon?

CAPTAIN. Nay, it is not soon enough.

DORANTE. Your impatience, sir, is a sign of true gallantry. But,
madam, you and I should leave these lovers alone together.
These be precious moments. There is so much to say, so much
to do before this wedding, and you and I, madam, you know,
have business of our own.

MARQUISE. My dear, let me embrace you before I leave. And,
Captain, well you know that I rejoice at your great happiness.

Scene 13

COUNTESS. I see very well you are regretted, sir. The lady sets a
high value on you still.

CAPTAIN. Why, she may set none at all, and what care I? I am on fire, madam, for this evening.

COUNTESS. It may be, sir, that you should bank your fire a little.

CAPTAIN. Bank my fire, madam? What mean you by that? I am a creature of fire; I must have leave to burn.

COUNTESS. Well, I would not have you burn out all at once. This evening may be too soon.

COUNTESS. Surely, madam, you will not change your mind again?

COUNTESS. I am not changeable, sir; changeability is beneath me. I have a design. It is to . . . but I'll consider of it further.

CAPTAIN. Will you not tell me, madam, what you intend?

COUNTESS. I pray you, be not disquieted. Farewell, sir! Do not follow me. (*She goes, then returns.*) For this little while, we must avoid each other's company. When I have need, I'll send for you. Farewell.

The COUNTESS *goes.*

CAPTAIN. Now stands my state in peril, as I find.
　　　　　This way and that the motions of her mind!
　　　　　Sure, she's more woman than all womankind.

Act Three

Scene 1

CAPTAIN. But I must see your mistress, girl. I pray you carry in my message directly.

LISETTE. I cannot burst in upon my lady, sir. It is the time of repose with her.

CAPTAIN. Repose! Does your mistress repose upright, girl?

FRONTIN. Why, sir, we may say she does, for when I was upon the terrace not long ago, I saw her walking in the gallery.

LISETTE. There are many ways of reposing, sir; my lady has her own. Sure, sir, I might know yours if you would but repose yourself a little.

CAPTAIN. Do not be pert, Lisette; it doth not become you.

FRONTIN. The girl *is* become pert, sir. I have marked it.

LISETTE. No, sir, it is a question which concerns me, for when I know the arrangements you intend for your own repose, sir, I may be able to effect my own.

CAPTAIN. The wench no longer affects my cause. She is not friendly; I do suspect it.

FRONTIN. I have a suspicion of that nature, sir, which grows, even as it is formed, into the most prodigious certainty.

LISETTE. Your observation has not lost its keenness, sirrah.

CAPTAIN. Did I not say so? The girl's unfriendly. Lisette, I am in a maze. How can you wish me evil, child, when I have ever wished you good? When my heart inclines so amiably towards you, how can yours be so hard? How comes it, Lisette, we two are thus at variance?

LISETTE. Variety is the spice of life, sir; I have heard my father say so.

FRONTIN. And will you tell me you and I shall be at variance, Lisette?

LISETTE. Only if you love me. But if you love me not, we're in agreement.

CAPTAIN. Tell me the truth, girl. Will you not take my part and commend me to your mistress?

LISETTE. Only to her indifference, sir.

FRONTIN. A touching service!

CAPTAIN. Why, I begin to believe you do not speak me fair before her.

LISETTE. Oh, ill, sir. I must tell you the truth, sir; I abhor deception. I speak very ill of you before her, for my plain desire is, my lady shall not love you.

FRONTIN. The wench is frank, sir; we may say as much.

CAPTAIN. Come, Lisette! We must be friends.

LISETTE. I do not allow the obligation, sir.

CAPTAIN. But, girl, you must. I wish you to be my friend, and you must be my friend. Plague take it! You shall love me; I undertake to make you love me; you have my promise on it.

LISETTE. You will not be able, sir, to keep your promise.

FRONTIN. Let me remind you, sir, there are some friendships stand at so high a value, they must be bought, and therefore –

CAPTAIN. Girl, I would not buy your friendship.

LISETTE. To say true, sir, it is not for sale.

CAPTAIN (*presents his purse to her*). Here! take it; keep it if you will.

LISETTE. 'Twould be only to steal your money, sir.

CAPTAIN. Take it, I tell you, and in return tell me but this: what is your mistress's purpose?

LISETTE. I am not privy to her purpose, sir, but if you will, I'll tell you what I would have her do, for that I do know. Are you curious, sir?

FRONTIN. It is not worth the money, sir; we know already.

CAPTAIN. Has she not some design?

LISETTE. Sir, who has not a design? Even I, sir, have a design, which is to leave you, if you yourself have not a design to leave me.

CAPTAIN. The wench is impertinent, Frontin. Let us leave her; we demean ourselves by dallying here. We shall return soon enough, and you shall hear how I commend your conduct to your mistress.

FRONTIN. Farewell, delicious enemy; farewell, little dancing heart! Though you waver in every wind, you shall find your Frontin faithful. Farewell!

LISETTE. What an impertinent ill-favoured fellow!

CHEVALIER *and* FRONTIN *leave.*

Scene 2

HARLEQUIN. Dear Lisette, though I have stamped myself all over with signs of importance, so that I have as many seals as a fob-watch, yet will not my master see me. I hang about at the edge of his eye like an undelivered package.

LISETTE. You must speak to him. And let it not be in the presence of my lady, the Marquise.

HARLEQUIN. My Lady Misfortune! Oh, alas, Lisette, though I've given you my heart, sure there's no profit in the gift for you and me. I have forgiven you all the slights you put on me, yet though forgiveness be a Christian act, it avails me nothing, for the devil has hold of me and will marry me to Eglantine. I feel his teeth are in my very coat-tails, Lisette.

LISETTE. Go back to Monsieur Dorante. Tell him I am waiting here for him.

HARLEQUIN. He'll not care; he won't come. If you were the Countess herself, you might go whistle.

LISETTE. There is no time to lose. Therefore make haste.

HARLEQUIN. I cannot make haste. I am numb. I am overwhelmed with despair.

LISETTE. Your skull's more numb, sirrah, than your legs, I think. If you love me, you'll put them to use. But wait! Here comes your master with the Marquise. Detain him until I return.

LISETTE *leaves*.

Scene 3

The MARQUISE *and* DORANTE *enter.*

HARLEQUIN. Sir, I must speak with you.

DORANTE. Then speak.

HARLEQUIN. I cannot speak, sir. Before my lady.

DORANTE. Then you may stand silent, sirrah, for I have no secrets from this lady.

HARLEQUIN. To be sure, sir; no, sir; you have not, sir. It is I, sir, has the secret, which my lady should not know.

MARQUISE. Is it, then, a great mystery, Harlequin.

HARLEQUIN. It is, my lady. It is Lisette, my lady, wishes to speak in private with my master, and I hold it not good, my lady, that you should be acquainted with their confidence.

MARQUISE. Admirable discretion! I would my own secrets were kept so well. Dorante, you must see what this imports, and for my part, I'll retire. Go, Harlequin. Fetch Lisette here. She shall speak in secret with your master.

HARLEQUIN *leaves*.

Scene 4

MARQUISE. We may expect Lisette speaks for her mistress.

DORANTE. Indeed, madam, it is a sign of her ladyship's distress that she should send her maid to speak with me in secret.

MARQUISE. And are you on fire, sir, to alleviate her distress?

DORANTE. You would not have me cruel.

MARQUISE. We are close to the end, sir. If you weaken now, we'll lose all. Do not deceive yourself. This perturbation is still equivocal. Do not take it for a manifest sign of love, for jealousy may wear the same distracted aspect, and for mere jealousy, sir, if you will go about to alleviate that, she'll make sport of us both. All our preparations are made. We must go together to the very gate of marriage, as we have resolved. Until we are in train to sign the contract, you'll not know for certain whether my lady loves you.

DORANTE. And if even then, madam, the answer be not clear?

MARQUISE. Love has his own sign manual, sir, as pride has his. Love sighs for what is lost; pride scorns what is refused. Wait for the sigh, sir, or for the scorn, and hold fast to that proof for your own love's sake. Meanwhile, cut short this conference with Lisette, and come again to find me.

DORANTE. Your proof is more hard to bear than the old Trial by Ordeal.

MARQUISE. And will you shrink from it?

DORANTE. No, madam, for my own reason tells me well enough that you are right. I shall endure the ordeal, I promise you.

MARQUISE. My own part in this comedy is not altogether to my liking, and will become less so, I know well, as we draw towards the end, for my courage must grow the greater as yours runs out. Yet what you must do for love, so must I for vengeance.

The MARQUISE *leaves.*

Scene 5

HARLEQUIN *arrives with* LISETTE.

DORANTE. Well, Lisette, I have no time to dally here. You see
  well enough I have been with my lady the Marquise till now,
  and any conference between you and me would not be proper
  as my affairs stand at this time.

LISETTE. Why, how do they stand, sir?

DORANTE. I am to be married. No more than that.

HARLEQUIN. Oh, sir, let it be less than that, I pray.

LISETTE. Married, sir? Not to my lady, the Marquise?

HARLEQUIN. Never!

DORANTE. Hold your tongue, sirrah. Now, Lisette, do not detain
  me here, but tell me what you want.

LISETTE. Oh, sir, gently; gently, I pray. Allow me time, sir, to
  collect my breath. Oh, sir, how you have changed!

HARLEQUIN. And if he has, my girl, 'twas not my master's faith
  first failed, but no matter.

LISETTE. Have you forgotten, sir, I am my lady's maid? Have you
  forgotten my lady?

DORANTE. No, I honour her, and I respect her still. But unless
  you come to the point, girl, I must leave you.

LISETTE. My point has passed, sir; it has gone already. Ah, men!
  Thus with respect-you-this and honour-you-that they play
  us false.

DORANTE (*going*). Farewell.

HARLEQUIN. Run after him.

LISETTE. Wait, sir! Wait!

DORANTE. Your observations on my sex, girl, are misplaced. I
  blush for your mistress, who has trained you ill.

HARLEQUIN. Lisette, confess they are ill-placed and pert.
  Do not make my master blush, or we shall lose all.

LISETTE. It is for my mistress I come to find you, sir. She would speak with you.

DORANTE. How? At this moment?

LISETTE. Directly, sir.

HARLEQUIN. The sooner the better.

DORANTE. Did I not bid you hold your tongue, sirrah? Have you made up your quarrel, then, with Lisette?

HARLEQUIN. There never was a quarrel, sir, but what you yourself made between us.

DORANTE. That's your own affair. As for me, Lisette, tell your mistress that I beg her we may hold our conversation at some other time. Make me ten thousand apologies; beseech me ten thousand pardons. My reasons are good. She shall know them and herself approve them.

LISETTE. Sir, she must and will speak with you.

HARLEQUIN (*falls on his knees*). Oh, see me here, kind master, on my knees.

DORANTE. I do. Get up, man.

HARLEQUIN. Your lady, the Countess, is quite reformed, sir, believe it. Her mind is altogether altered. She will speak you the fairest words, sir, a very turtle; I know it.

DORANTE. I bid you get up, fellow. Lisette, in one word I tell you this. Such a conference with your lady, to whom once I avowed my love, must be a cause of unease in that lady to whom now my love is vowed. Your mistress is too reasonable not to know so, and too gentle to give unease to my lady, her good friend. There is no matter of sufficient import between herself and me would tempt me into such an action.

LISETTE. No matter except that she loves you, as I believe, and always will.

HARLEQUIN. How tender that might have sounded without the parenthesis!

DORANTE. 'That she loves me, and always will!' Oh, that's too much. And if you would say you speak on her behalf, girl, and know what you say, then I tell you your mistress goes too far. Your mistress does not love me; she has turned me off, and you yourself have told me as much on this very spot. Well, that is past; I am not worthy of her love. But that she, with a light heart, sending me word here by some pert chambermaid, should now essay to engage me again in a game designed only to put me at odds with the Marquise, ah, that's too much! No, I will not see your lady, nor speak with her, save in the presence of the Marquise to whom I am now bound. You may tell her that, miss.

DORANTE *goes*.

HARLEQUIN (*following him*). Oh, sir, sir, amble in the leafy glades of your own true inclination, sir; do not climb the rocky road of mere duty. Oh, I'll be a dog and bay the moon, but you shall hear me.

Scene 6

LISETTE (*alone*). Well, well, though one may never say so, it is true my lady has deserved this.

The COUNTESS *enters*.

COUNTESS. Lisette! Is he coming?

LISETTE. No, my lady.

COUNTESS. No!

LISETTE. The gentleman prays you excuse him, my lady.

COUNTESS. How dare he! For what reason?

LISETTE. For this reason, my lady, that if he meets you now in private that would give unease to the Marquise, to whom he is to be married, my lady.

COUNTESS. Married! What are you telling me? To the Marquise? He!

LISETTE. Yes, my lady. And he says you are too reasonable and gentle, my lady, to give unease to your good friend.

COUNTESS. I cannot understand you, girl, and what I hear defies all reason and belief. Sure, it is not of Dorante you speak at all, but of some other gentleman.

LISETTE. It is he in truth, my lady, but truth to tell, he's not himself. He no longer loves you.

COUNTESS. But that is false, Lisette. Foolish girl, I should never accustom myself to such an idea; no one could persuade me. Lisette, my heart and reason both reject it. Dorante loves me; he is not changeable.

LISETTE. Your heart and reason are alike mistaken, my lady, and your case is worse than I have made it. The gentleman so little loves you that he believes your desire to speak with him is but to make mischief between himself and the Marquise.

COUNTESS. Oh, to the devil with your eternal Marquise! She doesn't exist, your Marquise; why will you be forever chattering about her? There is no Marquise in the world could efface my picture from my Dorante's heart.

LISETTE. She is a lady born to please.

COUNTESS. 'Born to please'? Have you run mad?

LISETTE. No, my lady. But though her looks be not your looks, yet I have heard them praised. Add to that your ladyship's own inconstancy, and they may cause Dorante's loyal heart to change.

COUNTESS. But, Lisette, I am not inconstant. May I die if I have ever felt the least inconstancy.

LISETTE. It is from you yourself, my lady, that I have the word. First, did you not say that you could not be inconstant because you did not love Dorante, secondly that it was natural, and could not be a sin, last that it is a woman's duty to break one's word a thousand times? So I have learned from you yourself, my lady, and so I have acted, and bitter indeed has been the consequence.

COUNTESS. I was wrong, child, I admit it. I spoke of inconstancy, and did not truly know it.

LISETTE. But, my lady, why should you have been so set on

turning the gentleman off?

COUNTESS. Child, I know not. I know only that I love him, and am become a prey to grief in losing him. I have treated Dorante ill, child; I agree. I have done the most monstrous wrong to him, and so to myself and you. My fault has been great, both in itself and in its consequence.

LISETTE. Did I not tell you so, my lady? But it was you who persuaded me to the same behaviour.

COUNTESS. Oh, miserable self-love! Oh, miserable love of being loved! These have been my undoing. I set myself out to please the Captain, though he is not worth the pain of pleasing. But I must have another ribbon in my cap, another captive as tribute to a beauty which in truth I lack, Lisette, for there is no true beauty but in the soul; without that, all is ugly. Oh, folly! folly! I have won the Captain indeed, but at the cost of losing Dorante.

LISETTE. A poor exchange!

COUNTESS. I have gone out to win a man whom it is my very nature to despise, had I but taken nature for my guide – a ridiculous fop who hath a thousand times been the butt of mine own raillery, and who now occupies the place of the most amiable gentleman in the world. This is not beauty's tribute; it is the coquette's punishment.

LISETTE. Oh, do not squander time, my lady, in mere private penitence. Monsieur Dorante does not know you still love him. He is your prize. Do not relinquish him to the Marquise, but exert yourself, my lady, to recover him. Address yourself to the gentleman's mercy. Confess that you have wronged him, and his vexation is just. That may yet do well.

COUNTESS. But, Lisette, of what ill phrases do you make use, girl? Address myself to his mercy? – sure, if the gentleman should feel mercy, it is for him to show it, not for me to sue for it. Confess that I have wronged him? – why, you and I between us may say as much and mean it too, but are we to say there has been no wrong on his part? I say there has, and much wrong too. Did I set out to lose the gentleman? You know well that was never my intention; we may say he lost himself. On provocation, sure. I have been cold to Dorante; I have shown favour to the Captain. But it is a man's part to bear misfortune with fortitude, and the gentleman has not done so. How could one imagine he would abandon me at the first chill breeze? We may agree to some small touch of fickleness in my behaviour, but 'twas rank cowardice in him. Was there any man ever trusted as I have trusted Dorante, was any man esteemed as I have esteemed him, to be steadfast in adversity, strongest when I was weakest, most loyal when I was most inconstant? Ah, blind trust! Misplaced esteem! And you would have me beg pardon of such a perfidious gentleman?

LISETTE. How shall I answer you, my lady?

COUNTESS. Because I trusted him, his jealousy and his complaints did not derange me. I defied his love ever to grow less. If I gave him pain, what risk was there in that to me? It pleased me to observe his pain, for that very pain proved the intensity of his love, so that daily I grew more secure. Might not the fool see that my ill-treating him was but the expression of the trust I had in him? And yet he leaves me! Oh, it is inexcusable!

LISETTE. Oh, my dear lady, calm yourself, I pray, unless you would have your Lisette share your tears. Let us work together to restore Monsieur Dorante's proper regard for your ladyship; only to rail at him will avail us nothing. And if your ladyship would please to begin by breaking with the Captain. Twice already he has asked to see you, and I have sent him away.

COUNTESS. Have I not forbid that importunate man to come to me until I shall send for him? How dare he disobey?

LISETTE. What shall you do with him, then, my lady?

COUNTESS. Oh, hate him, to be sure. What else is he fit for? Yet, it may be that I should see the fellow, for I may be able to put him to use. Let him come to me. Find him and bring him hither.

LISETTE. But here comes my father. Let us first find out what brings him to us.

Scene 7

BLAISE. There is an irruption, my lady, broke into the garden.

COUNTESS. What, Blaise? What?

BLAISE. A notary brought from town, my lady, and with him his clerk, a little scurvy fellow that has never seen white bread but at the sacrament, and would marry you to a pagan for ten pence, and half the money down. And this notary, my lady, is a great gaunt fellow in black wings and a white wig.

COUNTESS. Wings, fellow?

BLAISE. A gown, my lady, or some such stuff, which hangs from his shoulders like the devil's own black wings, as we may say, to bear away poor sinners.

COUNTESS. A notary in my house? Do they wish to marry here?

BLAISE. They do, my lady, no doubt of it. They say that they will make a contract of marriage for four, by which your former suitor, Monsieur Dorante, shall be bound to the Marquise, and you yourself, my lady, to your new gallant. What a conclusion are we come to here! I am like to burst with rage like the frog in the fable. How say you, my lady?

COUNTESS. I am lost in this. It is a nursery-tale.

LISETTE. A tale to frighten children!

BLAISE. Before God, my lady, Marquise or no, she has no right to practise such knavery upon a person of your ladyship's quality. I am your gardener, my lady; I am your true servant. With my good rake, my lady, I shall remove this notary and his parchments like weeds from your parterre.

COUNTESS. Speak, Lisette! Why do you not advise me? I am incapable of decision, girl. They will marry here, unless I take order to prevent it. This is no longer a question only of Dorante, for I detest him, but they place a public slight upon me.

LISETTE. Faith, my lady, did the gentleman place such a slight upon me, I should think so little of him, I should let him go.

COUNTESS. How may I let him go, girl, if I love him?

LISETTE. But you tell me, my lady, you detest the gentleman.

COUNTESS. Does that prevent my loving him? And truth to tell, why should I destest him, girl? The gentleman believed that I had wronged him, and you yourself have told me that I did so. And you were right; it was I abandoned a faithful suitor. I must find him; I must tell him of my true feelings.

BLAISE. Faith, my lady, though I am but an old country fellow, I have stood highly in the gentleman's esteem. Give me but leave to go to the gentleman. I shall stand before him; I shall speak my mind.

COUNTESS. I'll write to him, Lisette. Honest Blaise here shall carry the letter. But hark you, Blaise, the Marquise must not know of it.

LISETTE. Let it be done, my lady.

COUNTESS. As for the letter, why I recollect that I have one even now upon me, writ but a little while ago, which this irruption had caused me quite forget. Here, Blaise! Take it! Only remember that the Marquise must not see you deliver it.

BLAISE. She shall not, my lady. And while the gentleman reads over what your ladyship has writ, so shall your honest Blaise reinforce your ladyship's sentiments with the most monstrous remonstrations.

BLAISE *goes*.

Scene 8

COUNTESS. Heaven grant it may do something.

The CAPTAIN *enters with* FRONTIN.

CAPTAIN. Faith, madam, what becomes of true love here? I find you do not deal justly with me. You have bid me wait until you yourself shall summon me, but I wait and wait, madam, and I find you do not summon me at all, and I must summon myself to wait upon you.

COUNTESS. Why, sir, I have sent to summon you even now.

CAPTAIN. You have employed a tardy messenger, madam, let me tell you, or one that has gone a deuced roundabout way. But that's all one. For I have news, madam, which concerns us both, and therefore am I come in haste to impart it. What say you to this? Dorante and the Marquise are in your garden. They have drawn up a contract of marriage, and are in train to wed instanter. Surely you and I, madam, should take good advantage of the occasion, for there's a notary standing with his clerk, the most starveling little fellow with no more stomach than a titmouse. 'Twould be a fine conceit, and the prettiest sight in the world, that we four should stand up together.

COUNTESS. But that is not my design, sir.

CAPTAIN. You would say, not to be married, madam?

COUNTESS. I would say, not to be married to you, sir. My design for you is more particular. I shall reconcile your love to the Marquise.

CAPTAIN. But it is you, madam, whom I love.

COUNTESS. And it is I, sir, who no longer love you. Forgive me that I speak thus bluntly, but 'twere better you were undeceived.

CAPTAIN. A fine piece of raillery, faith! Though a little out of season.

COUNTESS. No raillery, sir.

CAPTAIN. Dear heart, do not jest, I pray. If you pursue the jest further, I am like to faint with terror.

COUNTESS. Come, sir, this is no great surprise; admit it. You know well how I have delayed our match, forever putting off and putting off, and though now I put it off for ever, that's but a matter of degree.

CAPTAIN. Madam, I should have reached the pinnacle of happiness this very evening.

COUNTESS. Why, sir, if you must reach that pinnacle this

evening, have I not told you it is my design you should be reconciled with your old love, the Marquise, and there's a lawyer in the garden, you say; the thing is not impossible.

CAPTAIN. There is no question – faith! – of such a reconciliation.

COUNTESS. You are mistaken, sir; you shall admit as much.

CAPTAIN. I have no community with my lady, the Marquise; we are not birds of the same feather.

COUNTESS. Yet you have loved the lady, sir, I think, and she you. My intention is that you shall love each other again, as much as before, and therefore have I undertaken your mutual reconciliation.

CAPTAIN. It is a whim; it will pass.

COUNTESS. It is my will, sir; it will endure.

LISETTE. It is my lady's will, sir. She is not changeable when her mind is set. I assure you.

CAPTAIN. Frontin, Frontin, I am in a maze. Where are we?

FRONTIN. We are in a winding country lane, sir, with high hedges. I fear we shall find no good way out.

LISETTE. No, sir, but you may find your way back well enough, and return with all speed whence you came.

COUNTESS. No, Captain, I'd not have you retreat at once. I have sent my gardener, Blaise, on an errand which may concern you. I pray you wait a while.

Scene 9

HARLEQUIN *enters*.

HARLEQUIN. Oh, my lady, my master and the Marquise have sent me hither to ask if they may speak with you, though in truth, my lady, it be but to pronounce my doom and yours, for I cannot marry my dear Lisette as long as my master does not marry you.

COUNTESS. Then let them come to me. (*To* LISETTE.) He has not received my letter.

HARLEQUIN. They are about to enter, my lady; they are at the door.

COUNTESS. What I'll say to them, Captain, shall pluck you from your high hedges. You shall be content; I'll answer for it.

CAPTAIN. I pray you, madam, make me no more promises. I have been once a dupe already.

Scene 10

The MARQUISE *enters with* DORANTE.

MARQUISE. Well my dear, though I find you here with the Captain, I do not see that you prepare for your wedding. When will you raise him to that pinnacle of happiness to which his noble spirit so aspires?

COUNTESS. His happiness is in your gift, my dear.

MARQUISE. Mine, my dear?

COUNTESS. You may raise him if you will or dash him down. I hope you will not be so cruel as to choose the latter.

MARQUISE. Oh, if it be for me to give permission, my dear, be assured he has already taken it; you shall marry him at once for all of me. And may I hope, my dear, you will give us the pleasure of joining our marriage with yours, so that we may all stand up together?

COUNTESS. Yours, my dear?

MARQUISE. Mine, my dear?

COUNTESS. But with whom, my dear? Is there some gentleman will join us whom you are to marry?

MARQUISE (*indicating* DORANTE). If there be, my dear, he has not far to come, for here he is.

DORANTE. It is true, madam; I have that honour. She who is my
lady and your childhood friend is pledged to me in marriage.
Too well I apprehend your generous spirit, madam; you will
share our joy, I know. And as we are at your house, we come to
ask if we may be married here.

COUNTESS. The honour would be too great, sir. Moreover I may
believe that Heaven has reserved another fate for you.

DORANTE. How am I to understand this?

CAPTAIN. Believe me, sir, it does not surpass understanding. It is
no more than to say, sir, that my lady lays the pieces out
another way. I am to fall into the court of the Marquise, and
you to the Countess.

MARQUISE. Nay, sir, let us stay as we are.

COUNTESS. I pray you, madam, let me speak. I hope you will not
deny me a hearing. First, I address myself to you, Captain, for
there is much of which I must disabuse you and all present. You
have believed I loved you, and God knows I gave you cause, for
the good reception you had of me must have so persuaded you.
Yet you were deceived. My love was truly given then, as it is
now, to this gentleman, and the welcome I gave to your
addresses was no more than a pretence put on to prove his love.
It has cost you dear, I know, for the false love I showed you
engendered a true love in you, and of that true love I availed
myself, for it served my plan. So I have used you, sir, to your
distress and now mine.

Wherefore I must beg you, my dear Marquise, for the
Captain's pardon. Sure his heart has been a little wayward
from that tender regard in which once he held you; that is the
truth, and one must tell it. Yet his fault is excusable, for he was
tempted. And as for me, his temptress, I have told you it was not
for mere coquetry I robbed you of the gentleman, far less from
vanity, for I acknowledge honestly that it was not my charms or
any good parts in me which seduced him, but only cunning and
device. I was not more worthy to be loved than you, my dear,
but as he thought more ready, for I set out to please him, and

my apparent predisposition to him was a great bait, and so was the gentleman caught. And therefore pardon him, I pray, and restore him to your favour.

As for you, Dorante, you have given but a poor proof of constancy in love. My test was all in vain, and that over-delicate sensibility in me which led me to impose it has been ill-satisfied. Yet it may be that the part you have played in this masquerade has been put on more out of resentment than a lukewarm love. I confess, sir, that I have pushed matters further than I should. If you have felt resentment, 'twas I gave you the occasion, and I am to blame as much as you, for it may have been you truly believed I loved the Captain. I will not, cannot judge you harshly, sir. I close my eyes to your conduct, and I pardon you, as this lady and gentleman will, I hope, pardon me.

MARQUISE (*laughs*). Ah, madam, you have left it too late to put all to rights with one speech like the old god in the play. If I do not flatter myself, the gentleman who loved you once, loves me now; there is no call for pardon or a general post. Indeed, if pardon is our word, let it be on your own side, my dear, and pardon the nuptials we are met to celebrate.

COUNTESS. Dorante, you will lose me for ever if you hesitate even for a moment between us.

CAPTAIN. I pray you, let me speak. First, I address myself to you, my lady Marquise. I am a soldier, madam, and a man of fashion. I have seen love and war, and must bear the fortunes of both without complaint. Though I have lost you, yet I'll own it was myself to blame, for (to be sure I don't know how) I find myself deficient in that quality of constancy so admired by lovers. I do not speak to disparage your abundant merits, madam, which well deserved my love, but as inconstancy is my fault, so honesty is my virtue; what is the truth, I must speak out. I left you.

So might I say to you, my lady Countess, in reprisal, 'Though you have deceived me, yet have I in as full a measure deceived you.' Though your professed love to me was but a counterfeit, yet was I unworthy even of that counterfeit. I was below it. My person and my parts, though they may stand comparison, I may say, with those of any gentleman, yet are not as high as you have esteemed them. Therefore, do not withdraw your counterfeit. I'll take it for true coin, and so we'll on together.

COUNTESS. You make take it for what you will, sir; 'tis counterfeit none the less.

CAPTAIN. You will excuse me; I am at my peroration, madam, I confess I love you a little less than I loved my lady Marquise. You'll allow me, madam, I set the matter out plain; it is my way. *Imprimis*, the Marquise had the most complete possession of my heart. I was a fool in love, as one may say; I would treasure her very breath to put it in my pocket for a keepsake. But my nature is inconstant. Therefore, *secundis*, I turned to you, madam, and to be sure you'll agree I've loved you well enough, for truth to tell there's much in your manner reminds me of the Marquise. There it is; you and I have had a tenderness for each other, and that's enough for matrimony. We may rub along, you know, well enough.

For you, dear friend Dorante, let well alone, I beg. Sure it distresses the Countess that you desert her colours; it is a pique to vanity; she would believe you hold her charms inferior. 'Come back! Return!' she cries. It is the siren's song, Dorante. Close thine ears, dear friend. Do but heed her, your ship will be split. Oh, Dorante, Dorante, if you have no wax for your ears, look but into (*Indicating the* MARQUISE.) these eyes; they are your antidote. There is safe harbour. There you may live out your days in peace and love. Believe me, friend, but for this cursed inconstancy of mine, I would have fought for those eyes. The last drop of my blood should have been poured out in their service. You and I should have met in the field, dear friend, and you may thank Heaven for your good fortune that we have not.

DORANTE. I do, sir.

CAPTAIN. My lady the Marquise is of all women the most estimable, the most worthy of respect and love, and it is you shall have her. My own ruin, I say, is boundless, and 'tis I myself have been the cause of it. Of all mankind the most ungrateful, the most disloyal, the most foolish. I am that unhappy he.

MARQUISE. I can add nothing to the definition, sir; you have said it all.

COUNTESS. I do not deign to reply, sir, to what you have said on my account; it is the merest spite that pricks you on to sting your benefactress. Dorante, I have told you what I intend. If you will desert me now, why there's no more to say.

MARQUISE. Come, my dear, this gentleman and I love each other in good faith. There is no remedy; what can't be mended must be endured. There was no deception on our part, and no inconstancy neither. He and I had been turned off and quite forgotten; we had the right to make a match between ourselves. Will you not try, both of you, to forget us again? You know well enough how to do it, and it should be more easy this time than the other.

She summons the NOTARY.

Come, sir. Here is a document which must be signed. Dorante, will you entreat the Countess to honour us by witnessing the contract?

COUNTESS. What? So soon?

MARQUISE. Yes, my dear, if you will.

COUNTESS. I spoke to that gentleman, madam, not to you.

DORANTE. Yes, madam.

COUNTESS. You would have me witness your contract of marriage with the Marquise?

DORANTE. Yes, madam.

COUNTESS. I would not have believed it.

MARQUISE. If you would only honour us, madam, in this respect, I'm sure we'll gladly do the same for you. (*To the*

CAPTAIN.) And you, sir, also if you will.

CAPTAIN. I . . . I have a stiffness in my fingers, madam.

MARQUISE (*to the* NOTARY). Give my lady the pen, sir.

COUNTESS. Quickly!

She signs, then throws away the pen.

Oh, faithless! Faithless!

She swoons in LISETTE's *arms.* DORANTE *throws himself at her feet.*

DORANTE. Oh, my dear lady!

MARQUISE. Yes, sir, you may surrender now. She truly loves you.

HARLEQUIN. Oh, Lisette, do our fortunes take a turn?

LISETTE. They do.

COUNTESS. What? . . . What? . . . My Dorante at my feet?

DORANTE. More fathoms deep in love, madam, than ever I was before.

COUNTESS. Oh, rise, sir! Rise! And do you truly love me again?

DORANTE. I have never ceased from doing so.

COUNTESS. And my lady?

DORANTE. 'Twas but a conspiracy between us. It is to her I owe your heart, if you will restore it to me.

COUNTESS. Sir, you know too well it is yours already. Oh, I breathe again! What torture, sir, you have inflicted upon me! How have you feigned indifference for so long?

DORANTE. Love gave me strength, madam. Only in the hope of regaining your favour could I maintain so desperate a deception.

COUNTESS (*to the* MARQUISE). Oh, dear friend, let me embrace you!

The COUNTESS *and* MARQUISE *embrace.*

MARQUISE. And are we truly friends again, my dear?

COUNTESS. Most truly, my dear. From this day forth, sweet moderation and content shall be the duty I owe you, and if you shall see me in a wayward way, I hope you'll chide.

MARQUISE. Well, Captain, you must take your sword to some other battlefield, you see. There's no prize here for you.

COUNTESS. Nay, my dear, you must oblige me. I intercede this time in earnest for the gentleman. He has quite lost his inconstancy: I'll stand surety for it. To turn him off now, my dear, would spoil the pleasure, and mar the kindness you have done me.

MARQUISE (*to the* CAPTAIN). Well, sir, I'll make trial of your new-found constancy. You shall have six months, and then we'll see.

CAPTAIN. I ask no more than a term, madam. You may leave the rest to me. (*The* COUNTESS *and* MARQUISE, CAPTAIN *and* DORANTE, *all leave.*)

Final Scene

FRONTIN. And shall you be married, then, Lisette, to your Harlequin after all?

LISETTE. My heart tells me 'Yes', sir.

HARLEQUIN. And my heart tells me 'Yes', sir.

BLAISE. And my will tells me 'Yes', sir. And there's provision in the house.

FRONTIN. Then I shall give thee six months, Lisette. I ask no more than a term.

Though now our parts be played, our partners made,
True love triumphant, fickleness dismayed,
Sure there's no state in Nature but do change.
Time stales all loves. Fancy must have his range,
And discontent to constancy succeed.
The loftiest appetites decline to greed,
And we shall follow where our masters lead.

Harlequin's Lesson in Love

Translated by Donald Watson

from ARLEQUIN POLI PAR L'AMOUR
First performed by the Italian Comedians (1720)

CHARACTERS

FAIRY

TRIVELIN, *the Fairy's servant*

HARLEQUIN, *a young man carried off by the Fairy*

SILVIA, *a shepherdess, loved by Harlequin*

A SHEPHERD, *in love with Silvia*

COUSIN, *Silvia's cousin, also a shepherdess*

A DANCING MASTER

Troupe of dancers and singers

Troupe of elves

Scene 1

The FAIRY's *garden.*

TRIVELIN (*to the* FAIRY, *who is sighing*). Madame, you are love-
sick. And I regret to say you are likely to be love-sick for a long,
long time unless you use your reason as a cure. Will you allow
me to express an opinion?

FAIRY. Speak.

TRIVELIN. The young man you have carried off from home and
family is dark and handsome and well-built, the most charming
you could hope to find. When you saw him he was sleeping in
the wood, the sleeping figure of love personified. So I'm not
surprised you were taken by such a sudden passion for him.

FAIRY. To love what is lovable, is there anything more natural?

TRIVELIN. Oh, I don't deny it. However . . . before the start of this
adventure you seemed to be in love with the great Merlin,
the magician.

FAIRY. Well, one has driven out the other. That too is part
of nature.

TRIVELIN. Nature in the raw! But one small observation must be
made. You have carried off this sleeping Adonis only a few days
before your intended marriage to the aforesaid Merlin, who has
your promise. This is a really serious matter and, between
ourselves, you are taking nature rather too literally. Still, never
mind, the worst that can happen is for you to be unfaithful.
That would be very naughty for a man, but in a woman it is
more acceptable. When a woman is faithful we admire her. But
there are some modest women who are not vain enough to wish
to be admired. You are one such woman. Less inclined to glory
than to pleasure, and why not?

FAIRY. Glory! In my situation! For such a trifle I would be a great fool to restrain myself.

TRIVELIN. Well said! But let us now continue. You carry the young man off into your palace and there you are, watching for the moment when he awakes. Dressed for conquest in a *déshabillé* deserving of the whole-hearted contempt in which you hold the glory of fidelity. Anticipating the handsome youth's awakening to surprise and love. He wakes and greets you with a stare – more moronic than ever graced the face of nincompoop. You draw near. He yawns, two or three times, with enormous gusto, stretches himself full length, turns over and drops off again. And that's the curious tale of an awakening, once so full of fascinating promise. Sighing with frustrated love you retire, driven away by a sonorous, well-nourished, baritone snore! An hour goes by. Again he wakes, and seeing no one near him cries out, 'Oy'. Hearing this tender greeting you fly back. Love is rubbing its eyes. You ask him, 'What do you wish, handsome youth?' 'Me supper,' he answers. 'But', you add, 'are you not surprised to see me?' 'S'pose so,' he replies. And for the whole two weeks he has been here his conversation has always been as masterful. And yet you love him. And, what is worse, you allow Merlin to think that you will marry him still, whereas you have told me your intention is, if possible, to marry this young man. Frankly, if you take them both, according to all the rules, two husbands make one has-been.

FAIRY. I will answer you in two words. The appearance of the young man in question I find quite enchanting. When I carried him off I did not know he had so little wit. I am not repelled by his stupidity. I love him for the charms he has already and for those he will acquire in time when he is graced with wit. How delicious! So charming a young man stretched out at my feet telling me he loves me. He is now the most handsome, bronze beauty in the world. How much more adorable he will be when his mouth, his eyes and all his features have been brushed with a touch of love. My tender devotion will, I hope, inspire him. Often he looks at me and every day I think the moment has arrived for him to reach awareness of himself and me. When that moment comes I shall at once make him my husband. Under my wing he will be sheltered from Merlin's fury. Meanwhile, I dare not displease the magician. He is as powerful as I am. And I shall hold him off as long as I am able.

TRIVELIN. But if the education you are trying to give this young man fails to make him more loving, or more witty, then you will marry Merlin?

FAIRY. No! For even if I married Merlin I should never have the strength to let the other go. If ever he came to love me, married though I might be, I must confess to you, I know I could not trust myself.

TRIVELIN. That I can well believe, even had you not told me. A tempted woman is a fallen woman. But I can see our handsome moron approaching with his dancing master.

Scene 2

Enter HARLEQUIN, *hanging his head, or in any other silly posture he likes, together with his dancing master.*

FAIRY. How now, sweet youth! You look sad. Is there something that displeases you?

HARLEQUIN. I dunno! (TRIVELIN *laughs*.)

FAIRY (*to* TRIVELIN). Pray don't laugh. It offends me. I love him. Let that suffice for him to be respected.

During this time HARLEQUIN *is catching flies. The* FAIRY *continues addressing herself to* HARLEQUIN .

Would you like to take your lesson now, darling child?

HARLEQUIN (*as though he has not heard*). Eh?

FAIRY. Would you like to take your lesson now? – for love of me?

HARLEQUIN. No.

FAIRY. What! Do you refuse me so small a thing? I who love you so?

HARLEQUIN *sees a large ring on her finger: he goes up and takes her hand, looking at the ring, raises his head and starts laughing idiotically.*

Would you like me to give it to you?

HARLEQUIN. Yes, ta.

FAIRY (*pulling the ring from her finger and offering it to him. As he grabs it rudely, she says to him.*) My dear Harlequin, when a lady offers something to a handsome boy like you, you should kiss the hand when you accept it.

HARLEQUIN *then seizes the* FAIRY's *hand and kisses it greedily.*

(*To* TRIVELIN.) He doesn't understand. But at least his misunderstanding brings me pleasure. (*To* HARLEQUIN.) Now kiss your own hand.

HARLEQUIN *kisses the back of his hand.*

The FAIRY *sighs and, giving him her ring, says.*) Here it is. Now, in return, have your lesson.

The DANCING MASTER *teaches* HARLEQUIN *how to bow.* HARLEQUIN *enlivens this scene with any relevant tricks his genius may think up.*

HARLEQUIN. I'm bored.

FAIRY. Well, that's enough now. We'll try and entertain you.

HARLEQUIN (*jumping with joy at the proposed entertainment and laughing*). Entertain me! Entertain me!

Scene 3

Enter a troupe of SINGERS *and* DANCERS. *The* FAIRY *sits* HARLEQUIN *down beside her on a bank of grass. During the dancing,* HARLEQUIN *whistles.*

SINGER (*sings to* HARLEQUIN).
  Dark and handsome! Cupid's calling.

HARLEQUIN (*standing up, idiotically*). I can't hear him. Where is he? (*He calls out.*) Oy! Oy!

SINGER (*continues to sing*).
  Can't you hear his caterwauling.

HARLEQUIN (*sitting down again*). Well, let him shout a bit louder.

SINGER (*indicates the* FAIRY *to* HARLEQUIN).
  Look at this lady, here beside you,
  See the flashing of her eye.
  Without an answer she will die
  And henceforth Cupid will deride you.

HARLEQUIN (*looking at the* FAIRY's *eyes*). Well, I'm blowed. That's funny.

LADY SINGER (*a shepherdess, approaches* HARLEQUIN *singing*).
  Love comes clad in every hue.

HARLEQUIN. Teach me, tell me more.

LADY SINGER (*continues to sing looking at him. She points to the male* SINGER.)
  But your innocence appals me
  When I think of how he enthrals me,
  For my Atys knows more than you.

FAIRY (*standing up, to* HARLEQUIN). Dear Harlequin, do you find no inspiration in these songs of love? What do you feel?

HARLEQUIN. I feel . . . a growing need . . .

TRIVELIN. That means he's sighing for his supper. But here is a peasant who wants to entertain you with a village dance. After that we'll go and eat.

PEASANT *dances.*

FAIRY (*sitting down again and making* HARLEQUIN *sit down. He goes to sleep. When the dance is over she pulls him by the arm and says as she gets up*): You've gone to sleep again? What do we have to do to amuse you?

HARLEQUIN (*waking up, weeping*). Boo-hoo-hoo! Daddy, I can't see my mummy any more.

FAIRY (*to* TRIVELIN). Take him away! Perhaps in eating he will consume his sorrows too. I shall leave you for a moment. When he has had his supper let him wander where he will.

They all go off.

Scene 4

The scene changes and shows several sheep grazing in the distance. SILVIA *enters, dressed as a shepherdess and carrying a crook, she is followed by a* SHEPHERD.

SHEPHERD. Lovely Silvia, you're avoiding me.

SILVIA. What do you expect me to do? You always talk to me about the one thing that annoys me. You always speak to me of love.

SHEPHERD. I speak to you of what I feel.

SILVIA. Yes, but *I* don't feel anything.

SHEPHERD. That's what brings me to despair.

SILVIA. It's not my fault. I know each of our shepherdesses has a shepherd who won't leave her. They tell me they're in love. They sigh for love and find all their pleasure in it. But it only makes me unhappy. Ever since you told me that you sighed for love of me, I have done all I could to sigh for you as well. For I should like to be contented, like the others. If I knew love's secret, well then I'd make you happy straight away, for I'm good and kind by nature.

SHEPHERD. Alas! The only secret I know is that I love you.

SILVIA. Your secret doesn't seem to help me much, because I don't yet love you and it makes me very angry. What did you do to make yourself love me?

SHEPHERD. I looked at you, that's all.

SILVIA. See the difference! The more I look at you the less I love you. Oh well, never mind. Perhaps it will come one day. But don't pester me. Just now, for example, if you stayed here I would hate you.

SHEPHERD. I'll go away, then, as that's what pleases you. But to console me give me your hand, so I can kiss it.

SILVIA. Oh, no. They say that's giving favours, and it's not honest to do that. It's true too, the other girls are never seen doing that.

SHEPHERD. No one can see us.

SILVIA. I agree, but as it's wrong I don't want to do it, whether it brings me pleasure, like the others, or not.

SHEPHERD. Farewell, then, lovely Silvia. And think sometimes of me.

SILVIA. Yes, yes, I will.

Scene 5

Enter HARLEQUIN *when* SILVIA *has been alone for a few minutes.*

SILVIA. How that shepherd irritates me with his love! Every time he speaks to me he makes me feel so cross. (*Then, seeing* HARLEQUIN.) Why, who's that coming? Oh, heavens, what a handsome boy.

HARLEQUIN *enters, playing with his kite until he reaches* SILVIA's *feet. At that point, while playing with the kite, he drops it and as he bends to pick it up he sees* SILVIA. *He stays bent, frozen with amazement. Little by little in jerky movements he straightens up. When he is quite straight again he looks at her. She, in confusion, makes as if to withdraw. He stops her.*

HARLEQUIN. You're in a great hurry!

SILVIA. I'm going away, because I don't know you.

HARLEQUIN. You don't know me! Never mind! Let's get to know each other, shall we?

SILVIA (*still confused*). All right, then.

HARLEQUIN (*approaching her and revealing his happiness in little laughs*). How pretty you are.

SILVIA. You're very kind.

HARLEQUIN. Oh, no, I'm telling the truth.

SILVIA (*laughing a little in her turn*). You're very pretty, too.

HARLEQUIN. I'm glad you think so. Where do you live? I'll come and see you.

SILVIA. I live close by. But you mustn't come. It's better we always see each other here, because there's a shepherd who's in love with me. He would be jealous and would follow us.

HARLEQUIN. A shepherd who loves you!

SILVIA. Yes.

HARLEQUIN. What a cheek! How dare he! I don't want him to. And do you love him?

SILVIA. No, I was never able to.

HARLEQUIN. That's good. We must never love anyone but us. See if you can.

SILVIA. Oh, there's nothing easier than that.

HARLEQUIN. You mean it?

SILVIA. Oh, yes, I never tell a lie. But where do *you* live?

HARLEQUIN (*pointing*). In that big house.

SILVIA. What! With the Fairy?

HARLEQUIN. Yes.

SILVIA (*sadly*). I have never had any luck.

HARLEQUIN (*sadly too*). What's the matter, dear?

SILVIA. It's just that that Fairy is more beautiful than I am, and I'm afraid we won't stay friends.

HARLEQUIN (*impatiently*). I'd rather die than that. (*Then tenderly.*) Come along, little heart, don't be sad.

SILVIA. Will you always love me, then?

HARLEQUIN. As long as I live.

SILVIA. It would be such a shame if you deceived me. I'm such a simple girl. But my sheep are straying! I'd be scolded if one of them got lost. I'll have to go. When will you come again?

HARLEQUIN (*upset*). Oh, I'm so angry with those sheep.

SILVIA. So am I. But what can I do? Will you be here later?

HARLEQUIN. Without fail. (*As he says this, he takes her hand and adds.*) Oh, what pretty little fingers! (*He kisses her hand and says.*) I've never had a sweet as sweet as that.

SILVIA (*laughing*). Well, adieu! (*And then, aside.*) Now I am sighing for love, and I never learnt the secret.

As she goes she drops her handkerchief. HARLEQUIN *picks it up and calls her back to return it.*

HARLEQUIN. Sweetheart!

SILVIA. What is it, my love? (*Then, seeing her handkerchief in* HARLEQUIN's *hands.*) Oh, my handkerchief. Give it to me.

HARLEQUIN (*holds it out, then pulls it back; hesitating, at last he keeps it and says*). No, I want it. To keep me company. What do you do with it?

SILVIA. Sometimes I wash my face with it, or use it to dry myself.

HARLEQUIN (*unfolding it*). And which part do you use, so that I can kiss it?

SILVIA (*going off*). All over. But I must hurry. I can't see my sheep at all. Adieu! See you soon.

HARLEQUIN *waves to her as he capers grotesquely about, then exits.*

Scene 6

The scene changes to the FAIRY's *garden.*

FAIRY. Well, has our young man supped yet?

TRIVELIN. Yes, supped enough for four! When it comes to appetite he's beyond compare.

FAIRY. Where is he now?

TRIVELIN. I think he's flying his kite in the meadows. But I have some news for you.

FAIRY. Really? And what is that?

TRIVELIN. Merlin has been to see you.

FAIRY. I am delighted that I did not meet him, for it is most trying to feign love for someone when one feels nothing for him.

TRIVELIN. Truly, madame, it is a great pity that this little innocent has driven him from your heart. Merlin is transported with joy. He is expecting to marry you at any moment. 'Can you imagine anyone more beautiful than she?' he said to me just now, while looking at your portrait. 'Ah, Trivelin! What pleasures await me!' But I can see he will only taste these pleasures in imagination. That is cold comfort when one has had the promise of warm reality. He will be back. How will you extricate yourself from this affair?

FAIRY. So far I can see no alternative but to deceive him.

TRIVELIN. And do you feel no twinge of conscience?

FAIRY. Oh, I have too many other things on my mind to play at consulting my conscience over trivialities.

TRIVELIN (*aside*). There speaks the heart of a true woman for you.

FAIRY. I can't wait to see Harlequin again. I shall go in search of him. Why, here he is, coming in our direction. What do you say, Trivelin? It looks to me as if his bearing is better than usual.

Scene 7

HARLEQUIN *arrives holding* SILVIA's *handkerchief. He is looking at it and gently rubbing his face with it.*

FAIRY (*still speaking to* TRIVELIN). I am curious to see what he'll do when he's by himself. Come close to me. I am going to turn my ring to make us both invisible.

HARLEQUIN *comes to the front of the stage holding* SILVIA's *handkerchief and jumping up and down. He lies down and rolls all over it. And all this in high spirits.*

(*To* TRIVELIN.) What does all this mean? It appears odd to me. Where did he find that handkerchief? Could it be that he has found one of mine? Oh, if that were so, Trivelin! All this posturing would be a good omen.

TRIVELIN. I'm willing to wager it's some rag that stinks of civet.

FAIRY. Oh, no! I wish to speak to him. But let us move off a little to pretend we've just arrived.

She moves a few paces away, while HARLEQUIN *walks up and down, singing.*

Good day, Harlequin!

HARLEQUIN (*sweeping his foot back into a bow and sticking the handkerchief under his arm*). Your very humble servant.

FAIRY (*aside to* TRIVELIN). What's all this strange behaviour! All the time he's been here he has never said as much to me before.

HARLEQUIN (*to* FAIRY). Madame, I wonder if you'd mind being so kind as to tell me how one feels when one really loves someone?

FAIRY (*enchanted, to* TRIVELIN). Trivelin, did you hear that? (*To* HARLEQUIN.) One always wishes to be with the person one loves, dear, for one cannot bear to be separated from him; one is distraught when one cannot see him, in short, one is swept away by joy, by impatience, and often by desire.

HARLEQUIN (*jumping with joy and as if aside*). That's me! That's me!

FAIRY. And do you feel all that I'm telling you?

HARLEQUIN (*with an air of indifference*). No, I was just wondering.

TRIVELIN. He's just not telling.

FAIRY. It's true he's not telling. But what he says is not to my liking. So, my dear Harlequin, you were not referring to me?

HARLEQUIN. Oh, I'm not such a ninny. I don't tell what I'm thinking.

FAIRY (*sharply and passionately*). What does this mean? Where did you find that handkerchief?

HARLEQUIN (*looking at her fearfully*). I found it on the ground.

FAIRY. Who does it belong to?

HARLEQUIN. It belongs to . . . (*Then, stopping himself.*) I have no idea.

FAIRY. There is some wretched mystery behind all this. Give me the handkerchief.

She snatches it from him and after looking at it with vexation, adds, aside.

It does not belong to me and he was kissing it! No matter. We'll hide our suspicions from him and we will not intimidate him, or he will never reveal a thing.

HARLEQUIN (*humbly approaching her, hat in hand, asking her to return the handkerchief*). Have charity. Give me the handkerchief back.

FAIRY (*concealing her sighs*). Here you are, Harlequin. I won't take it from you as it gives you pleasure.

As HARLEQUIN *receives it he kisses his own hand, bows to her and goes.*

(*Watching him.*) You leave me! Where are you going?

HARLEQUIN. To sleep beneath a tree.

FAIRY (*gently*). Run along, then.

Scene 8

FAIRY. Ah, Trivelin, I'm lost!

TRIVELIN. I confess to you, madame, I can make neither head nor tail of this adventure. What can have happened to the little pest?

FAIRY (*in despair and passionately*). He's found his wits, Trevelin, and I'm none the better for it. I am more fond than ever. Oh, what a bitter stroke of fortune. How delightful he appeared to me just now, the ungrateful creature! Did you notice how he's changed? Did you see the way he spoke to me? How subtle his expression had become? And these graces have not been acquired through me. Already he is blessed with delicacy of sentiment: he contained himself. He dare not name the owner of the handkerchief, aware I would be jealous. Oh, why did he have to fall in love to find such wit so soon? How unfortunate I am! Another will hear him say the 'I love you' I have so longed to hear, and I am sure he will be worthy of worship. I am in despair. Let us go, Trevelin. Now we must discover my rival. I shall follow him and survey all their most likely meeting-places. You must search, too. Go at once. I languish.

Scene 9

The scene changes to a meadow with distant sheep grazing.

SILVIA. Stay a moment, cousin. I shall soon recount my story to you and you can give me your advice. Why, this was where I met him. How strange! As soon as he approached, my heart told me that I loved him. How wonderful that is. He came up to me. He spoke to me. And do you know what he said? He said he loved me too. I was happier than if I'd been given all the sheep in the hamlet. Really, I'm not surprised that all our shepherdesses should be so pleased to fall in love. I find it so delightful I wish I'd done nothing else since I was born. But that's not all; he will soon be back again. He has already kissed my hand and I know he will want to do so again. You have had so many lovers. Give me your advice; should I let him do it?

COUSIN. Be sure you do not, cousin. Be very strict with him. Nothing so keeps a lover's love alive.

SILVIA. What! Is there no more pleasant way of doing so than that?

COUSIN. No. And you mustn't be always telling him you love him, either.

SILVIA. How can I help it? I'm still too young to know how to curb my tongue.

COUSIN. Do the best you can. But someone's waiting for me. I can stay no longer. Adieu, cousin.

Scene 10

SILVIA (*after a moment*). How worrying it all is! I'd just as soon not be in love at all as be obliged to be so strict. And yet she said it was that which kept love alive. How very strange. They really ought to change such an inconvenient method. Whoever invented it did not love as I do.

Scene 11

HARLEQUIN *appears*.

SILVIA (*seeing him*). Here comes my lover. How hard it will be to contain myself.

As soon as HARLEQUIN *sees her he runs up to her, jumping with joy. He caresses her with his hat, to which he has attached the handkerchief. He moves all round her, sometimes he kisses the handkerchief, sometimes he caresses* SILVIA.

HARLEQUIN. So there you are, little heart!

SILVIA (*laughing*). Yes, my beloved.

HARLEQUIN. How pleased are you to see me?

SILVIA. Enough.

HARLEQUIN. Enough! That's not enough.

SILVIA. Oh, yes it is. There's no need for more.

HARLEQUIN (*now takes her by the hand,* SILVIA *seems embarrassed.* HARLEQUIN, *still holding her hand, says*) But I don't want you to talk like that. (*He tries to kiss her hand as he says these words.*)

SILVIA (*withdrawing her hand*). Well, I won't have you kissing my hand.

HARLEQUIN (*angry*). Oh, you won't, will you? You're just a little flirt. (*He weeps.*)

SILVIA (*tenderly, taking him by the chin*). Don't cry, little lover, don't cry.

HARLEQUIN (*still moaning*). You promised we'd be friends.

SILVIA. Yes, and I've kept my promise.

HARLEQUIN. No, you haven't. When you love someone you don't stop him kissing your hand. (*Offering her his hand.*) Look, here's mine. You see if I'll do what you did.

SILVIA (*recalling her cousin's advice and as if aside*). Oh, my cousin can say what she likes, but I can't keep it up. (*Aloud.*) There, there, my love. I'll let you kiss my hand as you want it so much. To make you feel better. Kiss it. But listen, don't start asking me how much I love you, for I'll never tell you more than half of what I feel. That won't alter the fact that underneath I love you with all my heart. But you're not meant to know, because that would stop you being friends.

That's what I've been told.

HARLEQUIN (*in a doleful voice*). Whoever told you that was telling you a lie. Just talk, they don't understand about us. When I kiss your hand and you tell me you love me, my heart beats faster. And that proves these things help to make us friends.

SILVIA. I think you may be right, because I feel more and more friendly too. But never mind. As it's meant to do no good, let's strike a bargain, in case something goes wrong. Every time you ask me if I feel friendly towards you, I'll say to you: 'Not really'. But, of course, that won't be true. And when you want to kiss my hand, I'll pretend I don't want you to, although in fact I do.

HARLEQUIN (*laughing*). Oh yes! That will be funny! I'd like that. But before we start the bargain, let me kiss your hand as much as I like. And this won't be a game.

SILVIA. That's fair. Kiss it.

HARLEQUIN (*after kissing her hand again and again, he stops and thinks about the pleasure it gave him and then:*) Oh, but sweetheart! What if we both regret our bargain?

SILVIA. Well, even if we do regret it, we're still the masters, aren't we?

HARLEQUIN. That's true, sweetheart. So it's agreed then?

SILVIA. Yes.

HARLEQUIN. What fun it's going to be. Let's try it, to see. (HARLEQUIN *is now joking, and asks her for fun.*) Do you love me very much?

SILVIA. Not very much.

HARLEQUIN. This is only for a joke, you know. Otherwise . . .

SILVIA (*laughing*). Of course it is!

HARLEQUIN (*still continuing the joke, laughing*). Ha! Ha! Ha! (*And then, still joking.*) Give me your hand, my sweet.

SILVIA. I don't want to.

HARLEQUIN (*smiling*). But I know you really want to.

SILVIA. Even more than you. But I don't want to say so.

HARLEQUIN (*still smiling, then changing his manner, sadly*).

I want to kiss it, or I'll be cross.

SILVIA. Are you joking, my love?

HARLEQUIN (*still sad*). No.

SILVIA. What? You really mean it?

HARLEQUIN. I really mean it.

SILVIA (*offering her hand*). Take it, then.

Scene 12

FAIRY (*arriving in search of them, aside, as she turns her ring*). Ah! Now I see the cause of my misfortune.

HARLEQUIN (*after kissing* SILVIA's *hand*). I was joking after all.

SILVIA. I can see you caught me! But it was to my advantage too!

HARLEQUIN (*still holding her hand*). Those are words it gives me real pleasure to hear.

FAIRY (*aside*). Oh! Heavens above! What a speech! I must appear. (*She turns her ring.*)

SILVIA (*frightened to see her, cries out*). Ah!

HARLEQUIN (*the same*). Ouch!

FAIRY (*to* HARLEQUIN, *emotionally*). You have learnt a great deal already.

HARLEQUIN (*embarrassed*). Oh yes! But I didn't know you were there.

FAIRY (*gazing at him*). Ungrateful wretch! (*Then, touching him with her wand.*) Follow me!

After these words, she touches SILVIA *too, but without saying anything.*

SILVIA. Mercy upon us!

The FAIRY *then goes off with* HARLEQUIN, *who marches mechanically in front of her, in silence.*

Scene 13

SILVIA (*alone, still and trembling*). Oh! What a wicked woman.
  I'm still trembling with fright. Alas! Perhaps she is going to kill
  my lover. She will never forgive him for loving me. But I know
  what I shall do. I shall go and summon all the shepherds from
  the hamlet, and lead them to her. That's what I'll do.

Whereupon SILVIA *tries to move, but she cannot take one step
forward. Then:*

Oh! That sorceress has cast a spell on my legs.

At these words two or three ELVES *come to carry her off.* SILVIA,
trembling.

Oh no! No! Please, sirs, have pity on me! Help! Help!
1st ELF. Follow us, follow us!
SILVIA. I won't, I want to go home.
2nd ELF. Off with you! (*He carries her off, shouting.*)

Scene 14

The scene changes and represents the FAIRY's *garden. The* FAIRY
appears with HARLEQUIN *marching in front of her, in the same
posture he adopted before, with lowered head.*

FAIRY. You scoundrel! In spite of all the tender love and fond care
  I have shown you I never could seem pleasing in your eyes,
  never light a spark of affection in your breast. And now some
  wretched shepherdess has worked this change in you! Answer,
  ungrateful boy! What do you find in her that charms you so?
  Speak.

HARLEQUIN (*pretending to have reverted to stupidity*). What is it you want to know?

FAIRY. I advise you not to affect a stupidity you no longer possess. If you fail to show yourself as you really are you will see me strike down the unworthy creature you have chosen.

HARLEQUIN (*quickly and fearfully*). Oh, no, no! I promise to do as you wish, I shall not lose my wits again.

FAIRY. You are trembling for her.

HARLEQUIN. That's because I don't like to see anyone die.

FAIRY. If you do not love me you will see me die.

HARLEQUIN (*cajoling her*). So don't be cross with us, then.

FAIRY (*weakening*). Oh, look at me, dear Harlequin. Relent for having brought me to despair. I shall forget on whose account you found your wits, but now you have them use them to grasp the opportunities I offer you.

HARLEQUIN. Well, now I can see how wrong I really was. You are a hundred times more lovely and more elegant than she is, it drives me mad.

FAIRY. What does?

HARLEQUIN. That my heart became ensnared by that little minx who is uglier than you.

FAIRY (*with a secret sigh*). Harlequin, would you really want to love someone who deceives you, who wanted to play a joke on you and does not want you?

HARLEQUIN. Oh, but she does, you know. She loves me to distraction.

FAIRY. All make-believe. I know it was, because she is to marry a shepherd from the village. He is her lover. If you like I shall have her brought here and she will tell you so herself.

HARLEQUIN (*clutching his chest, hand on heart*). Tick-tock, tick-tock. Oo! It makes me feel ill to hear words like that.

And then, quickly.

All right, come along, I want to know about it. For if she's deceiving me, I swear by Old Nick I'll caress you, I'll marry you before her very eyes, to punish her.

FAIRY. Very well! I shall send for her.

HARLEQUIN (*still upset*). Yes, but you are very sly. If you're there when she talks to me, you'll make faces at her, and then she'll be frightened and won't dare come out with what she really thinks.

FAIRY. I shall withdraw.

HARLEQUIN. The deuce! But you're a sorceress, you'll play some trick on us, as you did just now, and she'll be suspicious. You're here among us all, and *we* can't see a thing. Oh no! I don't want you to cheat! Swear that you won't be hiding somewhere.

FAIRY. I swear, on a fairy's honour.

HARLEQUIN. I don't know whether that sort of oath is any good. But now I remember hearing, when they used to read me stories, that you could swear by the Six or the Tix. Yes, the Styx.

FAIRY. It's all one.

HARLEQUIN. Never mind, you can still swear. As you seem to be afraid of it, it must be the best one.

FAIRY (*after a moment's reflection*). Very well! I swear by the Styx that I shall not be present, and I shall give orders that she be brought here.

HARLEQUIN. Meanwhile, I shall go walk and lament.

He goes out.

Scene 15

FAIRY (*alone*). My oath binds me. Yet I still know one way to terrify this shepherdess without being present. One resource is left to me. I shall give my ring to Trivelin, who will make himself invisible, listen to all they say and report it again to me. We'll call him. Trivelin! Trivelin!

Scene 16

TRIVELIN (*coming on*). What do you wish, madame?

FAIRY. Send that shepherdess here, I wish to speak to her. And you, take this ring. When I have left the girl, you will tell Harlequin to come and talk to her. And, without his knowing, you will follow them, to overhear their conversation, after taking care to turn this ring so that they shall not see you. Then you will tell me what they say. You understand? Be sure you do exactly as I tell you.

TRIVELIN. Yes, madame. (*He goes off in search of* SILVIA.)

Scene 17

FAIRY (*alone for a moment*). Was there ever a sadder tale than mine? I came to love more than I had ever loved before, only to find my sufferings the greater. And yet there is still some hope left to me. But here comes my rival. (*Enter* SILVIA. *She continues angrily.*) Approach, come nearer!

SILVIA. Madame, do you always wish to hold me here by force? If this handsome young man loves me, what fault is it of mine? He says I am beautiful. How can I help being so?

FAIRY (*aside, in a gush of fury*). Oh! Were I not afraid of losing everything, I could tear her apart. (*To* SILVIA.) Listen to me, my child: a thousand torments await you, if you do not obey me.

SILVIA (*trembling*). You have only to speak, alas!

FAIRY. Harlequin will appear here before you. I command you to tell him that you only wished to amuse yourself with him, that you do not love him, and that you are to be married to a shepherd from the village. I shall not appear during your conversation, but I shall be beside you, though you will not see me. And if you do not observe my orders to the letter, if you allow one word to escape you which may lead him to guess that I have forced you to tell him what I wish, everything is ready for your torture.

SILVIA. What? Should I then tell him that I wished to make a fool of him? Is that a reasonable thing to ask? He will start crying, and I shall do the same. You know that is bound to happen.

FAIRY (*angrily*). You dare resist me! Appear, infernal spirits! Bind her! And do not spare her all your torments! (*Enter* SPIRITS.)

SILVIA (*weeping*). Have you no conscience, that you ask me the impossible?

FAIRY (*to* SPIRITS). Go! Fetch the ungrateful creature that she loves, and before her very eyes, put him to death!

SILVIA (*exclaiming*). Death! Oh, madame! Fairy! You have but to send for him and I will tell him that I hate him. And I promise you I shall not weep at all. I love him too much for that.

FAIRY. If you let fall a single tear, if you fail to appear quite calm, then he is lost, and so are you. (*To the* SPIRITS.) Remove her chains! (*To* SILVIA.) When you have spoken to him, I shall have you taken home, if I have reason to be satisfied. He is coming. You wait here. (*The* FAIRY *goes off, and the* SPIRITS *too.*)

Scene 18

SILVIA (*alone for a moment*). An end to weeping, or my lover will never *believe* I do not love him. Poor boy! That would be like killing him myself. Oh! Cursed Fairy! But I must dry my eyes, for here he comes.

HARLEQUIN *now enters looking sad and hanging his head. He says nothing until he reaches* SILVIA. *He presents himself to her*

and looks at her for a while without speaking; then TRIVELIN
enters, invisible.

HARLEQUIN. Sweetheart!

SILVIA (*offhand*). Well?

HARLEQUIN. Look at me.

SILVIA (*embarrassed*). What is the good of all that? I have been
brought here to speak to you. I am in haste. What is it you want?

HARLEQUIN (*tenderly*). Is it true that you have tricked me?

SILVIA. Yes. All I have done was just for my own pleasure.

HARLEQUIN (*going up to her tenderly*). Tell me frankly, sweetheart. That scheming Fairy is not here, for she has sworn an
oath. (*And then, cajoling* SILVIA.) There, there, little heart, be
yourself. Tell me, are you really false to me? Going to be the
wife of a nasty horrid shepherd?

SILVIA. Yes, I tell you, yes. It's all quite true.

HARLEQUIN (*thereupon, weeping his heart out*). Boo hoo hoo!

SILVIA (*aside*). My courage fails me. (HARLEQUIN *weeps without
a word, and searches through his pockets. He takes out a little
knife which he sharpens on his sleeve.* SILVIA *watches him.*)
What are you going to do?

Then HARLEQUIN, *without answering, extends an arm to make
a good strong thrust and bares his chest a little.* SILVIA *is
terrified.*

Oh! He's going to kill himself! Beloved, stop! I was being forced
to tell you all those lies.

Then addressing the FAIRY *she thinks is still beside her.*

Madame Fairy, forgive me. Wherever you really are at this
minute, you can see what is happening.

HARLEQUIN (*at these words, throwing off his despair and taking
her quickly by the hand*). Oh joy! Oh rapture! Support me, my
love, I am going to faint with pleasure. (SILVIA *supports him.
Then* TRIVELIN *suddenly appears before them.*)

SILVIA (*taken by surprise*). Oh! There's the Fairy!

TRIVELIN. No, little ones, it is not the Fairy. But she gave me her ring, that I should overhear you without being seen. It would be a crying shame to abandon such faithful lovers to her tender mercies, so she does not deserve an obedient servant, as she is proving unfaithful to the most generous magician in the world, to whom I am devoted. Forget your cares. I will show you a way to safeguard your happiness. Harlequin must appear displeased with you, Silvia. And you, Silvia, must pretend to jeer at him and leave him. I shall go seek the Fairy, who is expecting me and I shall tell her that you carried out her commands perfectly in every respect. She will witness your departure. As for you, Harlequin, when Silvia has left, you will remain with the Fairy. Then, while you promise her that you have driven unfaithful Silvia from your mind, you will swear to attach yourself to her and try by some trick or other, and as though in jest, to take away her wand. And I assure you that as soon as you have seized it, the Fairy will lose all the power she has over you, and that if you touch her with her wand, you will master her completely. After that you will be able to go your ways and make for yourselves whatever destiny shall please you.

SILVIA. May heaven reward you for this!

HARLEQUIN. Oh! What an honest fellow you are! When I have that wand, I will fill your hat with farthings.

TRIVELIN. Prepare yourselves, then. I shall go and fetch the Fairy.

Scene 19

HARLEQUIN (*as if angry*). You scheming minx!

TRIVELIN (*to the* FAIRY). I think, madame, you will have reason to be satisfied.

HARLEQUIN (*still scolding* SILVIA). Clear off, you hussy! Look at her cheek and impudence! Out of my sight, blight of my life!

SILVIA (*moving away, laughing*). Ha! Ha! Isn't he funny! Goodbye, farewell! Now I shall go and marry my lover. Next time, little boy, don't believe all you are told. (*Then, to the* FAIRY.) Madame, do you wish me to leave?

FAIRY (*to* TRIVELIN). See her off, Trivelin. (SILVIA *goes off with* TRIVELIN.)

Scene 20

FAIRY. So now you see I did tell you the truth.

HARLEQUIN (*feigning indifference*). Oh! I don't care about that. She's an ugly little thing, no comparison with you. Oh yes, you know, I can see you really are a very nice person. Goodness, what a fool I was! Never mind, let her go. When we are husband and wife, we can get even with her.

FAIRY. What is this, then, Harlequin, dear? Do you mean that you love me?

HARLEQUIN. Well, who else? Really, before, I can't have been able to see straight. You see, at first I felt angry about it. But now, for all the shepherdesses in all the pastures in the world, I don't give a brass farthing. (*Then, softly.*) But perhaps you don't want me any more, because I've been such a silly.

FAIRY (*charmed*). Dear Harlequin, I shall make you my master, my husband. Yes, I will marry you and hand over to your safe keeping my heart, my treasures and my power. Does that make you happy?

HARLEQUIN (*gazing at her tenderly*). Oh, my love, how wonderful you are! (*Taking her by the hand.*) And *I* give you myself in person, and then this . . . (*This is his hat.*) . . . and then this . . . (*This is his sword. Whereupon for a joke he fixes his sword at her side and taking her wand in exchange, adds.*) And I shall wear this stick at my side.

FAIRY (*anxious on seeing him take the wand*). Give it back, my boy, give me the wand again, or you will break it.

HARLEQUIN (*retiring backwards as the* FAIRY *advances, moving round the stage quite calmly*). Take it gently, then. Gently does it!

FAIRY (*still more alarmed*). Quickly, give it to me! I have need of it!

HARLEQUIN (*now cleverly touching her with it*). Steady now! You sit there and be a good girl.

FAIRY (*falling on the grassy bank near the front of the stage*). Oh! Now I'm lost and betrayed!

HARLEQUIN (*laughing*). And I am on top of the world. Oh ho! Just now you were scolding me because I had no wits. But I have more than you have!

Then HARLEQUIN *jumps for joy, laughs and dances and whistles, sometimes running round the* FAIRY *and teasing her with the wand.*

Now Madame Enchantress, see this? (*He shows her the wand.*) Have a good look and be a good girl! (*Then he calls for everyone.*) Come on, come on! Bring my little sweetheart here! Trivelin, where are my *valets de chambre*, and all those demons too? Quick now, I give the orders, I'm in command! Or else, by the Powers-that-be ... (*Everyone rushes on at the sound of his voice.*)

Final Scene

HARLEQUIN (*running to meet* SILVIA *and showing her the wand*). Here, sweetheart, this is the contraption! Now *I'm* a sorcerer! Here, take it! You must be a sorceress too. (*He gives her the wand.*)

SILVIA (*taking the wand and hopping with glee*). Oh! My beloved! No more jealous rivals now!

Scarcely has SILVIA *said these words than some of the* SPIRITS *advance.*

A SPIRIT. You are our mistress. What do you require of us?

SILVIA (*surprised at their approach and recoiling in fright*). Here are these nasty men again, who frighten me!

HARLEQUIN (*annoyed*). By Beelzebub, I'll teach you to spring to life! (*To* SILVIA.) Give me that stick, so that I can beat them!

He takes the wand and beats the SPIRITS *with his sword; then beats the* DANCERS, *the* SINGERS, *and even* TRIVELIN *himself.*

SILVIA (*stopping him*). That's enough, now, my love.

HARLEQUIN *is still threatening everyone. He goes up to the* FAIRY, *who is lying on the bank, and threatens her too. Now it is* SILVIA's *turn to approach the* FAIRY *and greet her.*

Good day, madame. How are you feeling? Not so wicked as you were? (*The* FAIRY *casts a look of fury at them and turns her head away.*) Oh, what a nasty temper!

HARLEQUIN (*to the* FAIRY). Now, now. *I'm* the master. Come on, take that look off your face and smile.

SILVIA. Leave her alone, my love. Let's be generous. It's a noble thing to forgive.

HARLEQUIN. Then I'll forgive her. But I want to have some singing and some dancing and after that we'll go and find a castle and I'll be king.

Song and dance.

Slave Island

Translated by Nicholas Wright

from L'ILE DES ESCLAVES
First performed by the Italian Comedians (1725)

This translation was originally produced at RADA on 23 July 1986 in a production directed by William Gaskill, with the following cast:

IPHICRATE	Mark Womack
HARLEQUIN	Ross Boatman
TRIVELIN	Sam Wallace
EUPHROSINE	Rachel Joyce
CLEANTHIS	Liza Tarbuck
ISLANDERS	Margaret Shade
	Paula Stockbridge
	Paul Dixon
	Duncan Duff
	Simon Harris
	Paul Sharples
Designer	Douglas Heap
Designer's Assistant	Judith Levin
Lighting Designer	Neil Fraser
Costumes	Brenda Hawkins

The translator would like to acknowledge the help of Joyce Nettles.

The scene is set on Slave Island. Sea and rocks are represented on one side of the stage, and trees and houses on the other.

Scene 1

IPHICRATE *walks on sadly with* HARLEQUIN.

IPHICRATE (*after a sigh*). Harlequin!

HARLEQUIN (*who has a bottle tied round his waist*). Yes, sir?

IPHICRATE. Have you any idea what will happen to us on this island?

HARLEQUIN. I was picturing us as two emaciated figures dying of starvation. What do *you* think?

IPHICRATE. I think that you and I, who survived the shipwreck, ought to envy our friends who drowned.

HARLEQUIN. And you're suggesting, what, I mean I see the logic, that we jump in after them?

IPHICRATE. Pay attention: when our ship collided against the rocks, a few of our companions managed to board a lifeboat. No sooner had they done so than it disappeared beneath the waves; but the chance remains that they survived, and reached some desolate spot of this very island. What we should do, you and I, is search for them.

HARLEQUIN. Search, let's search, it'll pass the time. But first let's put up our feet and have a swig of brandy. Look, sir: rescued from a watery grave. Now what I shall do, to be strictly fair, is drink two-thirds and the rest can be for you.

IPHICRATE. There's no time to waste. I shall lead, you walk behind. If we are stranded here the consequences will be fatal.

HARLEQUIN. So I pointed out.

IPHICRATE. And I shall never return to Athens.

HARLEQUIN. That would follow.

IPHICRATE. Do you know where we are?

HARLEQUIN. Er, not precisely.

IPHICRATE. We are on Slave Island.

HARLEQUIN. Are we, indeed? Remind me where that is, and who are the slaves?

IPHICRATE. They are slaves from Greece whose ancestors, a hundred years ago, rebelled against their masters, fled across the sea and formed an island republic. This is it. There! Do you see that group of huts? That is their village. And if they find us, they will carry out their custom: which is to murder all the masters whom they come across, or to enslave them.

HARLEQUIN. Ah ha. Well, all foreign countries have peculiar habits. I'm broad-minded, if they want to massacre all employers, very good luck to them. Besides I've heard they don't do things like that to people like me.

IPHICRATE. That's perfectly true.

HARLEQUIN. Good, good, live on regardless!

IPHICRATE. Don't you understand? My freedom is in danger, perhaps even my life. Have you no pity?

HARLEQUIN. Yes, indeed, sir, gallons of it.

He drinks from his bottle.

IPHICRATE. Very well, then. Quick! Let's find our companions!

HARLEQUIN *whistles, amused.*

IPHICRATE. What?

HARLEQUIN (*laughs, then turns it into a song*). Humpety-humpety-hum.

IPHICRATE. Speak! Have you gone mad? What are you trying to say?

HARLEQUIN. Sorry, Seigneur Iphicrate, but it's such an enjoyable situation. I'm deeply sympathetic, really I am, but I just can't help it, ha ha ha! (*He laughs.*)

IPHICRATE (*aside*). Damn the fellow! I should never have told him where we are. (*To* HARLEQUIN.) Harlequin: as you know, I never object to servants enjoying themselves. But you have chosen a very bad time for it. We're leaving now. Up you get!

HARLEQUIN. Dreadfully sorry, sir, my feet hurt.

IPHICRATE. Please!

HARLEQUIN. Please? Did you say please? That's a very unusual form of persuasion. What's got into you?

IPHICRATE. All I require is for you to walk with me half a mile along the coast to find, who knows, with the greatest good fortune, our companions. And, if we succeed, we can leave together in the lifeboat.

HARLEQUIN (*sings, teasingly*).
Oh I'd love to find a little boat
And sail to Kingdom come,
A big fat girl beside me,
My hand upon her –

IPHICRATE (*suppressing his anger*). I don't understand your attitude, my dear Harlequin.

HARLEQUIN. My dear master, I'm bowled over by this deluge of obsequiousness. But what I'm used to is a whack on the head with a cudgel, and the cudgel's in the lifeboat.

IPHICRATE. Surely you've always known how much I like you?

HARLEQUIN. Yes, indeed, it's just that you were patting me on the head a bit too hard. As for your friends: God bless them. If they're dead, they're dead. If they're alive, then death will strike them in the end. I shall follow their brief careers with genuine pleasure.

IPHICRATE (*beginning to panic*). It's imperative that I find them.

HARLEQUIN (*with indifference*). Yes, very likely. That's your problem, sir. I shan't intrude.

IPHICRATE. Don't be impertinent!

HARLEQUIN (*laughing*). Oh dear, you're talking that horrible Athenian language. Sorry, but I just don't understand a word.

IPHICRATE. You know your master, don't you? And that you're my slave?

HARLEQUIN *walks away from him, then speaks more seriously.*

HARLEQUIN. I was. I don't deny it. I've no reason to deny it. Why should I be ashamed? The shame is yours. I don't hold it against you. You're not worth the trouble. I was your slave, and you

treated me worse than a slave. Like a dog. I was weak and you
were strong, so you called it 'justice'. Well, that's the way it
goes. Now you're here, you'll be up against people who are
stronger than you. They'll kill you, or they'll put you in chains,
and you know what they'll call it? 'Justice.' Then we'll see how
justice appeals to you. It might make you a better person. You
might learn what the sufferings are that people endure at the
hands of others. There ought to be a law to put everyone like
you at the bottom of the heap for a change. It'd make the world
a better place. Goodbye, dear friend. I'm off to find my
comrades: your new masters.

He starts to go. IPHICRATE, *desperate, chases him, his sword in
his hand.*

IPHICRATE. Oh ye gods! Does there exist a man more justly
provoked than I am? Wretch, you deserve to die!

HARLEQUIN. Don't strain yourself; you aren't as strong as you
were. I'm disobeying you; watch it!

He evades IPHICRATE.

Scene 2

TRIVELIN *and five or six followers enter, escorting a woman and
her servant.* TRIVELIN *indicates that his followers should disarm*
IPHICRATE; *they do, and then release him.*

TRIVELIN. Stop that at once! What do you think you're doing?

IPHICRATE. What am I doing, sir? I am punishing an insolent
slave.

TRIVELIN. Slave? You are mistaken. You will need to speak more
accurately in future.

He takes IPHICRATE's *sword and gives it to* HARLEQUIN.

Comrade, this sword is yours.

HARLEQUIN. My pleasure, sir, and a long and merry life to you.

TRIVELIN. Your name, please?

HARLEQUIN. My ah.

TRIVELIN. Name.

HARLEQUIN. Don't have one.

TRIVELIN. Could you expand on that please, comrade?

HARLEQUIN. Yes, I've only got what he calls me. Nicknames. Harlequin, or Hey-you-there. And sometimes Oi!.

TRIVELIN (*to those around him*). It's the familar crisis of identity. (*To* HARLEQUIN.) And what about him?

HARLEQUIN. Oh *he's* got a name all right. You ready? Seigneur Iphicrate.

TRIVELIN. Then I am mandated to inform you gentlemen that you will exchange these appellations. You will be Iphicrate and you are Harlequin, Hey-you or –

HARLEQUIN. Oi!

TRIVELIN. Oi!

HARLEQUIN *jumps for joy.*

HARLEQUIN. Oi? You're calling him Oi! I like it!

TRIVELIN (*to* HARLEQUIN). Take care, dear friend! Our aim is not to feed your vanity but to bruise his pride.

HARLEQUIN. Let's bruise it then! Who's first?

IPHICRATE (*glaring at* HARLEQUIN). Scoundrel!

HARLEQUIN. Is he allowed to say that?

TRIVELIN. As of this moment, the rules do permit verbal abuse. (*To* IPHICRATE.) Comrade Harlequin, you are aggrieved. I am annoying you, he is provoking you, true. We islanders understand that. Let it all out, be angry, call him whatever you like, it's all allowed for. But: the moment this transitional period is completed, you must put it behind you. You must never forget that you are Harlequin; that he is Iphicrate; and that whatever he was to you, you are to him. And vice versa. Such are the laws of our republic; it's my job to see they're followed.

HARLEQUIN. That's the most brilliant job invented.

IPHICRATE. I'll be a slave! *His* slave!

TRIVELIN. If he was yours: correct.

HARLEQUIN. I shan't be asking much of him, just total obedience: I've got treats in store.

IPHICRATE. It isn't enough, you know, just calling him names: I need a stick.

HARLEQUIN. He wants a dialogue with my back: I'd like to place it under republican protection, if that's possible.

TRIVELIN. You have nothing to fear.

CLEANTHIS (*to* TRIVELIN). Excuse me. Is it the case that slaves can put their hands up and make announcements? Thank you so much. I am a slave from the same ship as these two persons here, and I think my presence should be noted.

TRIVELIN. Rest assured it has been; you were high on the agenda when I observed this person with a lethal weapon. We shall come to you any moment. Harlequin.

HARLEQUIN (*under the impression he's being spoken to*). Hello. Oh no, I'm whatsit.

TRIVELIN (*continuing*). Please concentrate. Need I inform you as to where you have arrived and who we are? No doubt you have guessed it.

HARLEQUIN. Long live the republic!

CLEANTHIS. Yes, we're very impressed.

TRIVELIN. No interjections, please, except on points of order. Point one: the history of Slave Island. Our great-grandfathers threw off the yoke of an unjust and antiquated social system. In their righteous fury, they imposed a law which gave them the right to take the life of all representatives of the oppressor class whom chance or accident of sea led into their hands. In following years, a cooler mood prevailed. Lust for vengeance is no longer a factor. Instead we seek to correct the faults of these mistaken individuals. It is not you we shall eliminate but the anti-social aspects of your behaviour. Our method will be to put you into the role of slave in order for you to savour its unpleasantness. We shall oppress you so that your awareness of oppression is increased. We shall abuse you; and by objecting to *that*, you will see how objectionable you have been till now. Your period of re-programming will last three years, at the end of which you will be sent back where you came from, provided that your new personality comes up to scratch. If it does not, you will be detained indefinitely; this is the kindest course available; it will prevent you from repeating your crimes, and I should add that a wife from the local community is normally made available.

Those are the regulations; I must urge you to make the best of them. They are rigorous, that we readily admit; but they are there to help you, and whatever you might infer, we shall be thinking of you not as slaves, but as maladjusted members of our community. And remember, in a mere three years you will be cured: you will be rational, empathetic and humane for the rest of your life.

HARLEQUIN. This is very enlightened national health care: free, no drugs, and no invasive surgery.

TRIVELIN. Do not attempt escape. It can't be done and it would count against you. Enter this phase of your life with patience.

HARLEQUIN. It'll do him a power of good, so he can't complain.

TRIVELIN (*to* HARLEQUIN *and* CLEANTHIS). You two are now in full receipt of citizenship status: you, Iphicrate, will live in that amenity over there with comrade Harlequin, and the other young lady will live next door. You will need to change garments. Not with her, with him. Is that quite clear? Harlequin, you are invited to the leisure quarters where a light snack will be provided. You have a seven-day period of grace in which to enjoy your new position responsibly. After that you will have to make yourself useful like the rest of us.

Off you go. (*To the island people.*) Take them, please. (*To*

CLEANTHIS *and* EUPHROSINE.) You two, wait here.

HARLEQUIN *and* IPHICRATE *leave*, HARLEQUIN *performing a deep bow to* CLEANTHIS.

Scene 3

TRIVELIN (*to* CLEANTHIS). Comrade – the term is appropriate, you are one of us now – may I have your name, please?

CLEANTHIS. I am Cleanthis and she is Euphrosine.

TRIVELIN. Cleanthis? That name will do for the present.

CLEANTHIS. But I've also got lots of surnames. Would you like to hear them?

TRIVELIN. Yes, if you please. What are they?

CLEANTHIS. Here we go then: Fool, Idiot, Half-wit, Moron, Cretinous Cow, et cetera.

EUPHROSINE. Rotten little beast.

CLEANTHIS. That too.

TRIVELIN. Ah! Caught in the act! Simple enough, was it not, young lady, in the past, to insult a young woman who could not answer back. Was it not so?

EUPHROSINE. You're asking the questions, I suggest you fill in the answers too. I find this whole experience quite bizarre.

CLEANTHIS. Oh, madame! You won't be able to talk to me like you did at home. It all came naturally to you, didn't it? 'Do it like that, 'cos that's how I like it.' 'Shut your mouth.' Every word you said was like a slap in the face. You'll have to talk more properly here. (*To* TRIVELIN.) She's going to need language lessons.

TRIVELIN (*to* CLEANTHIS). Please, Comrade Euphrosine, restrain yourself. And, (*To* EUPHROSINE.) Cleanthis, it's no good looking miserable. The law is the law, and an excellent thing it is for all concerned, yourself included.

CLEANTHIS. Oh, she won't change, not really, not if I know *her*.

TRIVELIN (*to* EUPHROSINE). Now we know from the start that whenever you were tempted, in your previous incarnation, to be selfish, thoughtless and proud, you succumbed with ease. How do I know? You are a woman, women are weak, it is a fact of nature. So the best I can do for you is to suggest to Euphrosine that when she describes your misdemeanours, she takes a charitable view; so that when justice takes its course it will be tempered by her generosity.

CLEANTHIS. Oh, this is miles too subtle for me. I can't understand it. Let's talk about right and wrong, like she was so fond of doing, and then wade in.

TRIVELIN. Ah! No vindictiveness, if you please.

CLEANTHIS. Why not? It's you who started all this 'she's only a woman' business. And how she was bound to fall into temptation. Well, so am I. And if I'm supposed to forgive the appalling way she used to act, then she can forgive my sneaky vicious feelings. 'Cos I'm a woman too and I just can't help it. See what I mean? All right, who's in charge? I thought I was, I thought that was the whole idea. And this is what I've decided: I shall be foul to her, and she can make allowances. Once that's done, I just might make allowances for her. But that can wait.

EUPHROSINE (*to* TRIVELIN). Do I have to stand here and listen to this?

CLEANTHIS. It's your life's work, dear, you'd better put up with it.

TRIVELIN. Euphrosine, you will moderate your approach.

CLEANTHIS (*to* TRIVELIN). What for? When you're like me, when you've got sheer black hatred boiling up inside you, you've just got to let it out. It's horrible, but you do get rid of it. Let me tell her how I hate her for a bit and we'll soon be evens. Let me try.

TRIVELIN (*aside to* EUPHROSINE). It's part of the process. Bound to blow over. Never lasts. (*To* CLEANTHIS.) Euphrosine, I hope as your friend that when you've got this rancour out of your system it will not return. Shall we move on swiftly towards a look at the character of your ex-employer. What I would like is a verbal portrait of her, so that she gets an objective view of her defects, if such they are, in order that she can mend them. As you can see, we're trying to avoid glib condemnation. Let's get on with it.

CLEANTHIS. Ask me anything.

EUPHROSINE (*sweetly*). Do you mind if I slip away? I'd rather avoid this.

TRIVELIN. I'm afraid, dear lady, that that would make the exercise quite pointless; it is for your benefit.

CLEANTHIS. Yes, stay. You'll soon get over it.

TRIVELIN (*to* CLEANTHIS). I'd like to start by feeding the following terms into your assessment. Vanity, flirtatiousness and coyness. Do they apply to her?

CLEANTHIS. Vain, flirtatious and coy? I'd say they do for a start.

EUPHROSINE. I've heard enough. Let's stop.

TRIVELIN. Excellent! You felt a wriggle of self-consciousness. That's a very good symptom, it is a sign of life. But we have to progress beyond these abstract qualities. What we need now is detail. (*To* CLEANTHIS.) Please give examples of these negative terms.

CLEANTHIS. Where can I start? Wherever she is, whatever she does. I can't begin. I'm dazzled by too much choice. When madame is sitting quietly, when she's talking, when she glances across the room at me, when she's happy, when she's depressed; they're all the same. They're different shades of the identical colour. Her vanity is sometimes gloomy, sometimes chirpy, sometimes bursting out in a rage. When she flirts it's sometimes bright and lively, sometimes madly jealous, sometimes nosy. But vain and flirtatious always, sometimes alternately, sometimes both at once. You asked for a verbal portrait, there it is and I sign myself at the bottom. Finished.

EUPHROSINE. That was quite outrageous.

TRIVELIN. That was only the beginning.

CLEANTHIS. Was it? On we go, then. Madame wakes up. How did she sleep? Has the rest restored her beauty, cleared her skin, has it driven those little pink veins from the whites of her eyes? It has? Quick, quick: to battle! It's a glorious day. 'Run my bath!' Madame will face the world, she will go to the theatre, she will promenade, she will go to committee-meetings, with her *face*, that glorious national treasure, on display for the world to look at. Hold it up high, let the sunlight catch it! Look at it, everyone! Gleaming, radiant! All the bits and pieces still in place! Hooray!

TRIVELIN (*to* EUPHROSINE). She's doing rather well on this.

CLEANTHIS. But what if she had a terrible night? 'Oh God, what time is it? Bring me the mirror! One, two, three and *look*: 'How ghastly! Close the shutters fast!' Then looks again. Tries a different angle. Nothing works. Droopy eyes, floppy skin. There's nothing to do but cover the whole thing up. Madame will not be at home to callers. She will not be at home all day, she will draw the curtains, she will lie in the dark. But what if she has visitors who refuse to leave? Who crowd into the bedroom? And who look at her *face*, that poor little cracked antique? Who see how ugly it's got? Who will *tell their friends*? There's only one way to play it when they ask how are you. 'Dreadful. I've hardly slept for a week, I daren't go out, what's happening to me?' What this means is: 'Can we get one thing straight? I do not look like this. The face you see before you is in an interim state, it is not ready to be judged, you will not form an opinion, not till I have had a *good night's sleep*!'

That's what I had to live with. Servants understand their masters on a very deep level. We see right inside their brains and it's a horrible sight.

TRIVELIN (*to* EUPHROSINE). Be as brave as you can, and try to profit from her sketch. I find it very convincing.

EUPHROSINE. Oh my God, where am I? In some kind of institution?

CLEANTHIS. I'll cut to the end, just so's you don't get bored.

TRIVELIN. Let's hear what you've got. Madame's well up to it.

CLEANTHIS (*to* EUPHROSINE). Right. Remember that handsome cavalry officer who came round one evening? I was in the room, so you talked in whispers, thinking I wouldn't hear. Of course I did. You were giving that very casual performance of yours, madly seductive without being obvious, and the subject came up of a woman he'd been seen with. 'Isn't she adorable?' you said. 'She has the tiniest eyes!' And right on cue you opened yours as wide as you could and wiggled your head and stared at the wretched man, so he was quite transfixed by these two enormous pale blue pools in front of him. I laughed. And how he fell for it. 'I offer you my heart,' he said. 'Oh what a lovely little present, is it all for me?' 'Yes, every bit, for the naughtiest little pussy in the world.' 'Well I know you're only teasing, but I like it, tell me more,' said you, and you started to peel your gloves off, saying you wanted another pair. 'Oh what exciting hands!' he goes, snatching one of them up and sticking it in his mouth. Well, I ran and got the gloves, and put them down next to you, and of course by then you'd forgotten all about them. See what I mean?

TRIVELIN. This all sounds very accurate.

CLEANTHIS. Wait, there's more. I was talking about her to Cook one day, and I knew she was listening in. So I said, 'You must admit she's very pretty.' And for the rest of the week she was delightful to me. So I tried it again, with a different script. I said, 'You must admit she has an interesting mind.' And this time she didn't respond at all, just walked around for a week looking puzzled and hurt, as though I'd accused her of something vaguely shifty.

EUPHROSINE. I cannot stay. I cannot endure another second.

TRIVELIN. Yes, I fancy we've heard enough.

CLEANTHIS. Not yet! I haven't told you about the fainting spells she gets if anything smells of anything, even a flower. One day I put a whole vaseful next to her bed where she couldn't see them. No effect. And the very next morning, when some guests were there, she spied a rose across the room and out she went like a light.

TRIVELIN. Thank you, Euphrosine, we have all we need, and you will oblige me, please, by standing out of earshot while I talk in confidence.

CLEANTHIS (*moving away*). Well, tell her not to be so domineering, that's the least you can do. Another time I'll tell you about the way she dresses sometimes, terribly simple, just a négligé, so that she can't be accused of trying to impress. Except that, underneath it, everything's bursting forth all twice as obvious 'cos there's nothing to distract the eye. Now isn't that the height of ostentation? Saying: 'Don't worry about the *clothes*, don't *look* at the clothes, it's me that matters, me, me, me!'

TRIVELIN. I asked you to move away, now kindly do so!

CLEANTHIS. Yes, I am going. Will there be another session? I've really got the knack now. I'll tell you how she makes an entrance to her box at the theatre, brilliantly timed and looking rather dazed, as though she isn't certain where she is or what she's doing. It's an art which only very grand and confident people have, so it's absolutely riveting. And I'll show you the dead blank look she gives the women in the audience, to establish that they aren't worth knowing. Oh, all right. I'll go and sit in my hut.

Scene 4

TRIVELIN. This exercise has probably tired you, but it will do no harm.

EUPHROSINE. You people are animals!

TRIVELIN. On the contrary. We are humans with an educational flair, that's all. One last formality must be completed.

EUPHROSINE. Not another!

TRIVELIN. Oh it's nothing. I have to report not only on what is said to you, but on your response. This evocation of you, these descriptions of your calculated sexual sparring, of your vapid self-absorption, do you agree with them?

EUPHROSINE. Agree? With those incredible slanders?

TRIVELIN. They are not incredible. Please take care. If you can agree with what she said, you'll find your life here much improved. But I must say no more. Let's hope that you will in time confront yourself, and see yourself, and that you will renounce these idiocies. Which must have consumed enormous energy. And think what that energy might have achieved, if only you'd devoted it to something useful! On the other hand, if you can't agree with a word, we shall regard you as incorrigible, and your date of release will be postponed indefinitely. So, think about it.

EUPHROSINE. Date of release, you said?

TRIVELIN. Oh yes, on those conditions I've described.

EUPHROSINE. Will it be soon?

TRIVELIN. Most certainly.

EUPHROSINE. Then can't we simply assume that I've agreed and there's an end to it?

TRIVELIN. You want me to lie?

EUPHROSINE. Well, obviously. You can hardly expect me to *want* to agree to anything so revolting.

TRIVELIN. Oh, it's only a little shaming, and there's nothing wrong with that. But it's up to you. An early release in return for the truth, that's the arrangement. So, don't you think she painted a good resemblance?

EUPHROSINE. But I –

TRIVELIN. Well?

EUPHROSINE. There were things in common. Here and there.

TRIVELIN. Here and there? That will not do. Do you accept it all? Did she exaggerate? Did she let you off too kindly? Be quick, please, I've a busy morning.

EUPHROSINE. Do I have to be so thorough?

TRIVELIN. Yes, and you will be glad of it.

EUPHROSINE. Well –

TRIVELIN. Yes?

EUPHROSINE. I suppose I'm rather immature.

TRIVELIN. I'm not asking your age.

EUPHROSINE. If one moves in a certain social circle, one has to fit in.

TRIVELIN. And this is why the portrait was so very accurate?

EUPHROSINE. Well, yes.

TRIVELIN. That's just what I want to hear. And did you not appear a ridiculous figure?

EUPHROSINE. Yes.

TRIVELIN. Well done. I am happy to tell you that you have reached the standard required. You may go now; I suggest you join Cleanthis, whose original name, as you may gather, has been returned to her. And so has yours: we keep our word here. Don't be impatient, carry on being humble, and the moment you are hoping for will soon eventuate.

EUPHROSINE. I shall rely on you. (*She goes.*)

Scene 5

Enter HARLEQUIN *and* IPHICRATE, *who have exchanged clothes.*

HARLEQUIN. Yoicks, tally-ho! Greetings, my man. I'm vastly impressed by the quality of wine in this republic. I quaffed my usual glass, and being a master now I had a few more. God bless wine and all who wassail in her! God save the vintner! Bless the republic!

TRIVELIN. Very good, comrade. Carry on enjoying yourself. How is Harlequin? Are you happy with him?

HARLEQUIN. He's a decent little fellow, I'll soon knock him into

shape. He tends to be glum at times, which he's been told to
stop on pain of physical retaliation. 'Cos I want him looking
cheerful. Come on there!

He takes his master by the hand and dances him round.

Yah-hoo! Yah-hoy! Yum-pum-pum!

TRIVELIN. I'm delighted to see you in such excellent spirits.

HARLEQUIN. Well, I am, it's all this *bonhomie* what does it.

TRIVELIN. And I'm gratified you're hitting it off so well with
Harlequin. Do I take it that in his own country he gave no cause
for complaint?

HARLEQUIN. What, there? I used to curse him to hell. Hated the
beast. Only now, you see, I'm so damn happy that I don't
remember. All is forgiven.

TRIVELIN. Ah, I like this facet of your character more than I can
say. Does it suggest that you will not exploit your change in
status, that you won't abuse him?

HARLEQUIN. What, abuse him? What, that poor little mite?
Well, I might, you know, stick in a verbal pin or two, now
I'm the master.

TRIVELIN. Now that you're the master? Ah, the traditional excuse.

HARLEQUIN. Quite so, you can't have feeble, gutless, over-
sensitive masters, it would muddle the servants, so it follows
that a basically decent man who happens to be a master might
seem nasty at times.

TRIVELIN. I see your point. I know you to be basically decent.

HARLEQUIN. No, I'm just a trouble-maker.

TRIVELIN (*to* IPHICRATE). Don't be taken aback at my next
question. (*To* HARLEQUIN.) Enlighten me. What was his
conduct in his former existence? Had he any character defects?

HARLEQUIN. There's a touch of malice in that question; are you
after funny stories?

TRIVELIN. He was entertaining?

HARLEQUIN. Well he certainly made me laugh.

TRIVELIN. Amuse me, then.

HARLEQUIN (*to* IPHICRATE). Only if you laugh too.

IPHICRATE. Do you want to drive me to despair? What are you going to say?

HARLEQUIN. I'll decide that. If I upset you, well I might apologise.

TRIVELIN (*to* HARLEQUIN). Come, come, I set you a simple task. The young woman you passed on the way here answered the very same question regarding her ex-employer.

HARLEQUIN. And I'll tell you the outcome: you despised the mistress, and felt sorry for the girl who served her. Am I right?

TRIVELIN. You are.

HARLEQUIN. Here's more of the same; he won't come out any better. All he has contributed to the world, to date, is a lot of wasted money and a certain amount of bother to other people. Born without too much in the way of surplus brain, he devoted his life to the art of mindlessness, on the principle that women preferred him that way. Spent money like water. Was mean when he should be generous, generous when he should be mean. Good at borrowing, bad at paying it back. Strangely terrified of seeming clever; when it came to looking stupid – you have guessed it – confident, nay, boorish. Good at mocking decent people. Boastful. Never went to bed without a woman; yet by the following lunchtime he'd forgotten her name. Behold the man! Is he worth the trouble it takes to describe him? (*To* IPHICRATE.) No answer required. Don't worry, dear friend; I've finished.

TRIVELIN. Very adequate. (*To* IPHICRATE.) All you have to do is support his statement.

IPHICRATE. Me?

TRIVELIN. Yes, you. The lady before you did the same, no doubt she will tell you what induced her; briefly, it's to your advantage.

IPHICRATE. Ah. Then, yes, one might, I suppose, there might be somehing I could go along with.

HARLEQUIN. Rubbish, it was perfect. I've been saving it up.

TRIVELIN. It's all or nothing.

IPHICRATE. You want me to say that I'm a useless fool?

HARLEQUIN. You were one.

TRIVELIN. Have you nothing to add?

IPHICRATE. Well, yes, I'll say I'm useless, if it helps.

TRIVELIN. No, no, I want it all.

IPHICRATE. All right. I'm a useless fool.

HARLEQUIN *bursts out laughing.*

TRIVELIN. Well done. You won't be sorry you co-operated.
Gentlemen: good day. You will be hearing from me. (*He goes.*)

Scene 6

Enter CLEANTHIS *and* EUPHROSINE.

CLEANTHIS. Seigneur Iphicrate, may I enquire what is
amusing you?

HARLEQUIN. I'm laughing at my Harlequin, who's just owned up
to being a worthless oaf.

CLEANTHIS. Has he? How surprising in one so sensible-looking.
Perhaps you would look at *her*: that is the kind of witless flirt
one finds in high society.

HARLEQUIN (*looks at* EUPHROSINE). I don't see it. That's a pert
little servant's face, and its natural habitat is a housemaid's
cap. But now, madame, we have joy in our hearts and a sunny
sky above us, how shall we entertain ourselves?

CLEANTHIS. How else but in delightful conversation?

HARLEQUIN. Wouldn't that make you yawn? I'm yawning now.
I've got it! How would it be if I fell in love with you?

CLEANTHIS. Oh, very well, then. Utter a heart-felt sigh. Lay
siege to my heart, make off with it, if you can; I won't resist.

It isn't my role to do so; I shall observe your progress while you do the work. But one proviso: now we are masters, our affair must be a suitably grand one, frightfully courteous, just like fashionable lovers.

HARLEQUIN. Lovers? Good, we're off to a flying start.

CLEANTHIS. One thing I'm certain of is that you cannot pour your gallant witticisms into my ear while we are standing. So, assuming we're to stay in the open air, we shall need two seats. Our servants must get them.

HARLEQUIN. Your wish is my command. (*To* IPHICRATE.) Harlequin, quick, get me a stool and find a capacious armchair for madame.

IPHICRATE. Are you allowed to do this?

HARLEQUIN. It's required by the republic.

CLEANTHIS. I've got a better idea. What we should do is promenade up and down, our heads six inches apart, and then you casually drop into the conversation something about my eyes, you know, and how it was them first fanned the flames of passion. Don't forget, whatever you say, we're proper people now, so nothing grubby or basic. Keep it on an elevated level. Ready? Good, let's walk and talk in style.

HARLEQUIN. Remember to bat your eyelids: right, let's start, it's only having a dig at our employers. Do we need the lower orders tagging on behind?

CLEANTHIS. My dear! Of course! That's our retinue. They might stand a bit further away, though.

HARLEQUIN. I say chaps, ten paces back, please.

IPHICRATE *and* EUPHROSINE *move away*. CLEANTHIS *watches* IPHICRATE *and* HARLEQUIN *watches* EUPHROSINE. *This manoeuvre having been completed*, HARLEQUIN *and* CLEANTHIS *walk about*.

Have you observed, madame, what a lucid and painterly light the air is blessed with?

CLEANTHIS. Oh, the weather today is the loveliest weather in the world. It is what I would call a sweet and dulcet day.

HARLEQUIN. Then I am like the day, madame.

CLEANTHIS. You are? And what do you mean by that?

HARLEQUIN. My thoughts are sweet, I utter them in dulcet tones, finding myself in such proximity to your ravishing charms. (*He jumps for joy.*) Oh oh oh!

CLEANTHIS. What are you doing? You've ruined our little talk.

HARLEQUIN. I was congratulating myself.

CLEANTHIS. Well, don't. It breaks the spell. (*She continues.*) Since, dear friend, you raise the subject of my ravishing charms, I will confess I knew they had enchanted you. You're skilled at inventing compliments and you speak them winningly; but you can spare yourself the effort in future.

HARLEQUIN. I am eternally grateful.

CLEANTHIS. Next you will swear you have fallen in love with me. Say it, dear friend, come straight to the point; I can assure you that I won't believe you. You are charming enough, but an incorrigible flirt and I refuse to be deceived by you.

HARLEQUIN (*seizing her by the arm and falling to his knees*). Must I fall on my knees to prove the ardour of the passionate flames which burn within me?

CLEANTHIS. I detect sincerity in your tones! How frightful! No, don't touch me, it is out of the question that you and I should be lovers in a physical sense! Get up, I beg you! Must we ruin a beautiful friendship? What shall I do?

HARLEQUIN (*laughing, still on his knees*). Ha ha ha! Hilarious! We're as daft as our employers; but we've got more sense.

CLEANTHIS. You're spoiling it all. Stop laughing!

HARLEQUIN. Ha ha ha! Your moral scruples just don't suit the upper-class tone. We're too respectable, you and I. Do you know what I think?

CLEANTHIS. No, what?

HARLEQUIN. When you booted me away just then: it wasn't a high society come-on. It was real. Come, tell me: do you love me?

CLEANTHIS. No. We'd hardly had a chance to – What about you, do you love me?

HARLEQUIN. Not yet. I was making a tentative move in that direction when a thought occurred to me: what do you think of my servant?

CLEANTHIS. Oh he's rather my type. And what do you think of mine?

HARLEQUIN. Oh, wicked.

CLEANTHIS. Then I know what you're thinking.

HARLEQUIN. Say it. No? Then I will: you fall in love with Harlequin, and I'll do *her*. I think we can take them on, don't you?

CLEANTHIS. Oh yes, we'll be inspired by the imaginative challenge; and they'll fall for us in deadly earnest; it's all they're capable of.

HARLEQUIN. They've never been teamed up before with sensible people. We're their perfect partners.

CLEANTHIS. We're on, then. Start on Harlequin. Get him to fall for me. Oh, and tell him that if he and I get married it will help him, that they'll stop him being a slave. Though I hardly expect he'll need too much persuasion, I'm a grand society lady now. I know it's only a stroke of luck that's made me one. But isn't that true of all the others? And I look the part. I have an aristocratic jawline, so they tell me.

HARLEQUIN. My God, I'd sweep you away right now if I weren't in love with somebody more attractive. Get to work on her, will you? Make her adore me. As you can see, I'm not bad-looking.

CLEANTHIS. Oh you'll get her. I shall call her over for a quiet word. You wander round for a bit and then come back and talk to Harlequin. He's got to make the moves, you see; I don't intend to compromise my woman's modesty, or my position.

HARLEQUIN. Don't bother about them, dear girl, just act on instinct. That's how it's done in high society: straight to the point. And when it comes to talking to him, be totally blatant, none of your working-class refinement, if you please.

CLEANTHIS. Too right; I'm too important now to be polite or lady-like; it would be miles beneath me; don't I know it. You talk to him, and I shall start on Cleanthis. Off you go now.

HARLEQUIN. Concentrate on my good points. If you can't think of any, make them up.

CLEANTHIS. Everything's under control, now go away. (*She calls.*) Cleanthis! Come here. (EUPHROSINE *approaches meekly.*)

Scene 7

CLEANTHIS. In future you will come at once when I call. I don't like waiting.

EUPHROSINE. What is it?

CLEANTHIS. Listen carefully. A decent man has just confessed to me that he loves you. It is Iphicrate.

EUPHROSINE. Which one?

CLEANTHIS. Which one, which one? There could hardly be two with a name like that. The man I was talking to.

EUPHROSINE. Him? What use is his love to me?

CLEANTHIS. What use was the love of your other admirers? Have you forgotten? Or is it the word you're afraid of: 'love'? I can't believe it. Love is your greatest talent. All your life you've treated men as nothing more than creatures you could give your love to. Or isn't this person good enough for you? He doesn't bow low and wave his handkerchief about, that's true; he isn't stuffed with vapid trivialities, he's not clod-witted, isn't a gambler, nor unfaithful as far as I know, nor one of those toads who tells your intimate secrets to his drinking friends. He's none of those things. He is a man with simple manners. He is innocent of affectation. He will say he loves you for the best of reasons, purely because he does. He is a decent, honest person, neither more or less. That isn't a very exciting set of qualities, true. But use your brains. Consider where you are. He'll bring about a great improvement in your living standards here, and you will be properly grateful and appreciate him, do you understand me? Now I hope you will do what I'm asking. It means a lot to me.

EUPHROSINE (*thoughtful*). Where am I? And where will this lead me?

Scene 8

HARLEQUIN *enters, greeting* CLEANTHIS *on her way out. He grabs* EUPHROSINE *by the sleeve.*

EUPHROSINE. What do you want?

HARLEQUIN (*laughing*). Ha ha! Hasn't a certain person just been talking about me?

EUPHROSINE. Go away, I beg you

HARLEQUIN. Look into my eyes and guess what I'm thinking!

EUPHROSINE. What *you're* thinking? Whoever cares?

HARLEQUIN. Aren't you dying to know what I have to say to you?

EUPHROSINE. No!

HARLEQUIN. That's because I haven't said it yet.

EUPHROSINE (*impatient*). Oh, for God's sake!

HARLEQUIN. Now, now, now, you're only playing hard to get; you know the way I feel and you're delighted.

EUPHROSINE. Oh, how frightful!

HARLEQUIN. You think I'm an idiot, don't you? Well I am, but it won't last long. It's a form of temporary mental paralysis caused by love.

EUPHROSINE. *You* in love with *me*!

HARLEQUIN. Yes, yes! And what could be better? Faced with your merciless beauty, how can a normal man respond except by utter collapse? And all you have to do is pick him up.

EUPHROSINE. This is the worst moment of my life.

HARLEQUIN (*examining her*). Oh, what delicious hands! What appetising little fingers! Oh how happy they would make me! Oh, how my heart would jump for joy! My Queen, you will not know this, it is buried beneath my tough exterior, but I'm a deeply sentimental person. And if you only found it in you to love me, I don't know what I'd do, I would be mad as a coot.

EUPHROSINE. You're mad already.

HARLEQUIN. Mad? Why not? In such a deserving cause?

EUPHROSINE. My child, what I deserve is pity.

HARLEQUIN. Do you think I don't know that? You deserve pity, affection, pampering, honours, glories! My God, an emperor wouldn't deserve you, let alone me. The difference is, I'm here and the emperor isn't. And a nobody that you've got is better than a somebody you haven't, don't you agree?

EUPHROSINE. Harlequin, you seem to have a decent nature.

HARLEQUIN. Oh, I do, it's deeply buried under a host of superficial awfulnesses.

EUPHROSINE. Please respect my terrible misfortune.

HARLEQUIN. I do! I'm kneeling to it, look!

EUPHROSINE. I beg you: don't take such advantage of me. Think of the tragic turn my life has taken. Even if what I *was* cannot persuade you, if my birth and breeding carry no weight; then can't you at least consider what I've become? Look at me *now*: a servant, lower than the low; a creature you can do what you want with, helpless, powerless, weak. The only defence I have is my despair. I depend entirely on the pity of others, of people like you. Harlequin, look hard, look as deep as you can into my misery. You are free now, they have given you power. Does it have to be evil? I haven't the strength to go on pleading. I only know I've never harmed you. Don't increase my sufferings.

She leaves. HARLEQUIN *looks defeated; his arms droop and he scarcely moves.*

HARLEQUIN. What can I say?

Scene 9

IPHICRATE *comes on.*

IPHICRATE. I am told by Cleanthis that you have something to
tell me. What do you want? To insult me further?

HARLEQUIN. Another person wanting sympathy. Sorry, there
isn't enough to go round. Concentrate on falling in love with
Euphrosine. The new one. Those are your orders.

IPHICRATE. How can you ask this of me?

HARLEQUIN. I open my mouth and out it comes. Now do it.

IPHICRATE. They told me I'd almost served my sentence. It was a
lie. That's it. There's nothing left for me. I'll die, d'you hear me?
And you won't have to worry about your inconsiderate master.
You know who I mean? The one who thought you had a spark
of kindness in you.

HARLEQUIN. Well, now we've ironed that little misunderstanding
out we ought to get on a treat. And look, I won't have you dying
just to annoy me. It isn't allowed. Natural causes, fine,
I've no objection.

IPHICRATE. Harlequin, the gods will strike you dead.

HARLEQUIN. Oh, that's my punishment, is it, for my underprivileged existence?

IPHICRATE. For being what you've become. For your contempt
for your master. I've never been so deeply wounded. Never.
You were born in my father's house. You were brought up
there. Your father lives there still. When we left the estate, you
and I, to travel the world, he called you to his bedside and
reminded you in heart-felt tones of what your duties were. And
why do you think I chose you in the first place as a travelling
valet? It's not as though you'd ever shown the slightest talent
for it. I chose you out of a sense of friendship. I detected in you
some affection for me and it touched me.

HARLEQUIN *cries*.

HARLEQUIN. Whatever makes you think I don't still love you?

IPHICRATE. If you loved me, would you treat me so abominably?

HARLEQUIN. I'm only teasing. It doesn't mean I don't still love you, just 'cos I tease you a bit. You used to say you loved me and all the time you were hitting me on the head. You said there wasn't any contradiction. So where's the contradiction about a little bit of teasing? Tell me that.

IPHICRATE. Well, let me admit that very occasionally I was harsh.

HARLEQUIN. Too true.

IPHICRATE. But just recall how generously I made it up to you.

HARLEQUIN. That I don't remember.

IPHICRATE. And wasn't I right to correct your little problems?

HARLEQUIN. They were problems for me, not problems for anyone else, besides, the only major problem I ever had was you.

IPHICRATE. You are utterly ungrateful. What you ought to be doing is thinking about a way for me to escape and sharing my troubles and giving a good example to the natives, so they see the error of their ways and let me go. And I would thank you most sincerely.

HARLEQUIN. Oh, I know. You're only telling me what I know already: how I should treat you, what the decent course is. It's just that in Athens you never remembered. The other way round, I mean. You ask me to share your troubles: when did you share mine? My life was misery, it was misery for years and years; you've hardly scraped the surface. Oh well; I seem to have been afflicted with a nicer personality than yours. You beat me out of love, you say: if that's your story, I'll believe it and forgive you. When I teased you, I was having fun; so I suggest you have a good laugh and learn from the experience. And I'll put in a word for you with my comrades here and suggest they send you home. And if they refuse, and if you stay a prisoner, it'll be under my protection. As a friend. Because I'm not like you. I haven't it in me to be happy at your expense.

IPHICRATE *comes closer to* HARLEQUIN.

IPHICRATE. Beloved Harlequin, I only hope that fate will make it possible for me to return your kindness. You are my dear friend; forget you were my slave, and I will always remember that I was once an unworthy master.

HARLEQUIN. Oh, don't say things like that, dear master; if I'd been given your chances, I expect I'd have been every bit as bad as you; it's up to me to ask forgiveness for the horrible way I served you; when you seemed unreasonable, the fault was mine.

IPHICRATE *embraces him.*

IPHICRATE. Your generosity amazes me.

HARLEQUIN. Dear master, isn't it fun being nice to one another!

He starts taking IPHICRATE's *clothes off.*

IPHICRATE. What are you doing?

HARLEQUIN. Give me my clothes back. Here, take yours, I am unworthy of them.

IPHICRATE. Forgive me, I'm going to cry. Do whatever you want.

Scene 10

CLEANTHIS *enters with* EUPHROSINE, *who is crying.*

CLEANTHIS. Will you stop that appalling racket. Leave me alone! Don't you think I've better things to do than listen to your yowling? And tell me, Seigneur Iphicrate, what's all this? Why've you taken your old clothes back?

HARLEQUIN (*tenderly, hugging* IPHICRATE's *knees*). My clothes were too small for him, dear friend, and his were too large for me.

CLEANTHIS. This is the *most extraordinary* sight. Anyone would think you're asking to be forgiven!

HARLEQUIN. Yes, it's partly that and partly punishing myself.

CLEANTHIS. And what about our plan?

HARLEQUIN. Well, the way it turned out, I've decided to be a good person. I think that's a *very* good plan, don't you? I repent and he repents. Oh, and you repent and she does too. Imagine, a fourfold feast of repentence, floods of tears and long live the reign of virtue!

EUPHROSINE. Cleanthis, this is an excellent example to you.

IPHICRATE. An example to all of us!

EUPHROSINE. Well, exactly.

IPHICRATE (*to* CLEANTHIS). Personally it's a revelation.

CLEANTHIS. Hold it one moment. These two people took advantage of us, exploited us, despised us, and treated us with as much respect as if we were crawling maggots. Now they see what we are: kind, forgiving, full of those wonderful aristocratic virtues which they never had themselves. No wonder they're delighted. (*To* IPHICRATE *and* EUPHROSINE.) You were beggars; all you owned was silver and gold and glorious honours. Your poverty was a crime. And when you posed as rich, just tell me, what good did it do you? Where would you be today, what would happen to you, if he and I were as morally bankrupt as you two used to be? We're thinking about forgiving you, do you realise that? Do you know what it takes, do you know what you need to be to take a step like that? Wealthy? Never. Blue-blooded? Hardly. Famous? No, no, no. You were all those things and did it help you? What then? You need a kind heart. And decency and a rational brain. That's all it takes, that's all that matters. That's what makes one man high and another low; it's the only kind of social class that makes any sense.

Do you hear me, you rich people of the world? All our lives we've heard you ask for good examples. And who provided them? The poor, the oppressed, the underprivileged. They've spent their lives being exploited by you. And they've showed you tolerance, pity; all the admirable virtues. Now it's your turn. Think what you are. Confront your audacious pride. Or don't: we'll still forgive you; fools that we are. (*To* IPHICRATE *and* EUPHROSINE.) You can go now; let's hope you're thoroughly ashamed.

HARLEQUIN. Enough, dear friend; if we want to do good, we mustn't use unkind words. They're sorry for what they've done. They take us seriously. Besides, they're free of sin now, as must follow from repentence. We four have travelled the same road together. Where has it led us? Ah, to tears. Come, Madame Euphrosine, she forgives you. See, she is weeping; her bitterness will soon wash away. All will be well.

CLEANTHIS. I'm crying, all right. I can't help it, it's my hopeless generous nature.

EUPHROSINE (*sadly*). Cleanthis, dear girl, I abused my position badly.

CLEANTHIS. Yes, I don't know how you found it in yourself to do so. But it's over now. What's done is done, it's cancelled out. If you were hateful to me, well, I won't join in, you'll have to carry the burden on your own. So I release you. If there were a ship available, I would get on board with you, and we would sail into the far horizon. That's all the harm I wish you. None.

HARLEQUIN (*weeping*). What a wonderful girl! What a lovable instinct!

IPHICRATE. Are you content, madame?

EUPHROSINE (*with tenderness*). Let me embrace you, my dear Cleanthis.

HARLEQUIN (*to* CLEANTHIS). Get down on your knees: that will raise you above her level.

EUPHROSINE. Gratitude, I find, is an exhausting emotion; so I haven't the strength for the speech of forgiveness you deserve. We shall forget your days of slavery; let us think of nothing else but how to share my wealth and privilege, in equal halves, once we are back in Athens, if we ever get there.

Final scene

TRIVELIN *enters.*

TRIVELIN. What do I see? You are crying, my children, and
    hugging each other!

HARLEQUIN. You should see our inner selves; we are ecstatic; we
    are kings and queens. The war is over, peace has been declared:
    it's the reward of virtue. All that we need is a boat to hop on
    board of and a boatman to ferry us home; and if you provide
    these two essentials, comrade, you'll be virtuous too.

TRIVELIN. Cleanthis, do you share his sentiments?

CLEANTHIS. What can I do but show them even more strongly;
    then you'll see for yourself.

She kisses EUPHROSINE's *hand.*

HARLEQUIN. Quite so. Enough speeches! Here's my summing-up.

He kisses IPHICRATE's *hand.*

TRIVELIN. Dear children, you have brought me joy. Embrace me
    too! You have followed the course I hoped for. If you had not, if
    you had chosen bitter feelings and revenge, we would have
    punished you, precisely as we punished them.

    Iphicrate, Euphrosine, you have suffered a bruising
    emotional process. I have nothing to add; you have learned
    enough today. You were their masters and you acted badly.
    They forgave you. Think about this.

    Degree between man and man is given us by the gods, not as
    a set of rules to follow blindly, but to test our humanity.

    All is over; in two days' time you will embark for Athens.
    May our present jubilation, and your future happiness, wipe
    out the miseries you have suffered in the past. And I suggest
    you make a note of the date, and mark the anniversary of this
    crucial day for as long as you live.

The Will

Translated by Michael Sadler

from LE LEGS
First performed by the Comédie-Française (1736)

Translator's note

From its opening lines, this play is about money. What's at stake is about £100,000, and even if the characters are reasonably well to do, they can't and won't afford to love without it. The will, like the forfeit in *The False Servant*, gives rise to strategies. This manoeuvring is clear in the case of Hortense, but far more complex and amusing in the match of pride and misunderstanding played between the Marquis and the Countess.

The text of the play is full of ellipsis, empty of material detail (where do they come from? what do they look like?). The colour of a dress the Countess doesn't want is a surprising detail. Once again the language is staccato and low-key. The register harks back (abstract nouns representing feelings abound) and forwards (the acid directness of the emotional finance).

The editor has allowed me to include my own vision of place and climate. These are in square brackets in the text. The Countess is a lazy widow, the house is doubtless in a bad state, the servants are stroppy. How clean are these people? An odour of dead pheasant seems to hang over the proceedings.

CHARACTERS

CHEVALIER

HORTENSE

LISETTE, *the* COUNTESS*'s maid*

LEPINE, *the* MARQUIS*'s servant*

MARQUIS

COUNTESS

The scene is set in a country house belonging to the COUNTESS.

[*A broken-down conservatory attached, with difficulty and leaks, to a large and badly run country house belonging to the* COUNTESS. *Since her husband died she can't (won't) cope. Damp and moss-covered logs are badly piled next to a black grate. If you try to light a fire you get smoke but no heat. On the shelves of the greenhouse, large pots containing brutally pruned geraniums, three gnarled green fingers groping upwards through the dried earth of each pot.*

Rusty garden implements, seed-boxes for nervous sowing in moments of distracted heat, shears for castration.

It's just before Easter. A wet spring redolent with sciatica. The weather is highly changeable. Clouds scud across the sky bringing sun, gloom and rain in quick succession. Throughout the piece there are abrupt changes of light. Strictly no birdsong until the end.

On a brown iron table a fan. It belongs to the COUNTESS. *She hasn't used it for some time, having had little reason to be overwrought. She will.*]

Scene 1

[*Quiet drizzle. The* CHEVALIER *and* HORTENSE *come in from the garden. He shakes out an umbrella. Warms himself by an unlit fire. She is oblivious to the cold.*]

CHEVALIER. I'm uneasy. Your plan's too risky.

HORTENSE. There's no problem. Listen. What have the Marquis and I got in common? Nothing, apart from this dead relative. Who leaves him 600,000 francs in his will on the condition that he marries me. If he chooses not to marry me, he is bound to give me 200,000. In way of compensation. The choice is up to him. Although it isn't, is it? Because he doesn't like me. A little bird tells me he's got his eye on the Countess. Moreover

the Marquis is rich. And this inheritance is just more provi-
dential booty falling out of the sky. So, why fret, Chevalier?
Do you really think this man would prefer to marry me to save
200,000 francs when, one, I'm as cold as an iceberg as far as he's
concerned, and, two, he's in love with the Countess – who
certainly does not find him unpalatable and who is far richer
than me? [*Pause. Distractedly, she takes a small watering can.
Goes to water a plant. Nothing. She takes a stick and breaks
the ice.*]

CHEVALIER. And what makes you think that the Countess has
taken to him?

HORTENSE. A lot of small things that I notice from day to day. It's
not surprising. He's just right for her. The Countess is a very
abrupt woman. Sharp. Domineering. She likes to be first. She
likes to be on top. Not the Marquis. He's soft, passive, a nice
easy ride. They're a perfect match. She's always saying nice
things about him. He's the most pleasant companion. Easy-
going, frank but unabrasive. And he's just the right age! She's
no longer as young as she was. He's about thirty-five, forty.
They're ripe for each other.

CHEVALIER. I'm not so convinced. Don't underestimate these
200,000 francs he'll have to come up with if he doesn't marry
you. And even if there is attraction, given who they are and
what they're like, they're never going to get round to telling
each other.

HORTENSE. Of course, they are. Because I'm going to put the
Marquis in such a tight corner that he's going to have to come
clean. I want to know where I stand. It's the least he can do.
For the last six weeks we've been staying here in the country
with the Countess and do you know what he's said to me?
Nothing. Six weeks of pastoral mutism. I'm going to open him
up. And I don't intend to lose what the will promises me, even if
I don't marry him.

CHEVALIER. What if he says: 'All right. I will marry you'?

HORTENSE. He won't. Leave it to me. My guess is that he's

hoping that I'm going to refuse him. He may even go as far as to
pretend to consent to our marriage. But don't let that upset
you. You're not rich enough to marry me without these 200,000
francs. And I shall be only too delighted to bring the necessary
balance to the altar. I'm convinced that the Marquis and the
Countess are attracted to each other. Let's see what Lépine and
Lisette have to say. He's cool and clever, she's sharp. They're
both very close to their master and mistress. Once they know
that any relevant information will be duly rewarded, we're
home and dry. They're here now. Go and take a walk in the
garden. (*He sneezes.*)

Scene 2

[LISETTE *and her curls.* LÉPINE *and his crew-cut. They keep their
distance. About two and a half yards. The border between respect
and disdain. Drizzle.*]

HORTENSE. Come here, Lisette.

LISETTE. You wanted something, madame?

HORTENSE. Yes, but nothing that could in any way compromise
the loyalty you both feel, you towards the Marquis, you
towards the Countess.

LISETTE. So much the better, madame.

LÉPINE. If that's the case, you can ask what you like of us.

HORTENSE (*taking money from her pocket*). First. A little token.
For services rendered.

LISETTE (*at first refusing*). Might we first know a little bit more
about the services required?

HORTENSE. Take it in any case. You too, Lépine.

LÉPINE. I would, of course, express the same reservations as
Lisette, but innate respect for rank encourages me not to.
Thank you.

HORTENSE. No strings attached. I promise. Now, down to

business. The Marquis thinks highly of you, Lépine.

LÉPINE (*coldly*). Very highly. He knows my worth.

HORTENSE. I've noticed he confides in you.

LÉPINE. I could write his diary. Know my way about him better than he does.

HORTENSE. The same goes for you and the Countess, Lisette.

LISETTE. I do have that honour.

HORTENSE. Tell me, Lépine. I think the Marquis is in love with the Countess. Right or wrong? There's surely nothing unseemly in telling the truth about the truth.

LÉPINE. Difficult to give a straight answer here and now. Soon maybe. We're due to discuss the matter this evening.

HORTENSE [*holding a dead bloom in a small pot*]. And what do you think? [*Blows.*] Does he? [*Blows again.*] Or doesn't he?

LÉPINE. Let's say I have a hunch which shall doubtless shortly be confirmed.

HORTENSE. What about the Countess, Lisette?

LISETTE. The Countess is not in the least interested in getting married again.

LÉPINE. I beg to differ.

HORTENSE. I think they're in love. A hypothesis. Suppose I'm right. There's a problem. They're never going to get round to telling each other. But supposing Lépine incites the Marquis to open his heart . . . and supposing Lisette inclines the Countess to listen to him. What do you think? You could hardly say we were acting against nature.

LÉPINE. On the contrary.

LISETTE (*returning the money*). I'd like you to take this back.

HORTENSE. Keep it, please. But what's wrong?

LISETTE. What you want me to do is precisely what I can't do. The Countess is a widow. She's happy. At peace with things. I'm not going to upset the balance. I even pray that she can hold onto what she's got.

LÉPINE (*cold*). I, on the other hand, am going to keep this token. Why shouldn't I? I'd like to help out. The Marquis is a bachelor.

He's as celibate as a monk. But marriage is a good thing. An
excellent thing. Of course it has its ups and downs. Don't we
all? I do. My lot is sometimes a heavy one. The world's like that.
So I'll go along with you, madame. I'll play the game. Don't see
any harm in it. People marry. Always have, always will. The
only honest way out when you're in love.

HORTENSE. You surprise me, Lisette. Even more so because
I was under the impression that you two had plans.

LISETTE. Not in the least. That is, as far as I'm concerned.

LÉPINE. Odd that. Me neither. I don't feel anything for her but
respect. Which doesn't mean that she couldn't excite other
feelings. But I seem to have passed by without being ...
arrested.

LISETTE. Things are fine that way.

HORTENSE. That's all I wanted to say. Goodbye, Lisette . . . Do
as you please. All I'd ask is that you be discreet. Lépine, I accept
your offer. [*Coat. Out.*]

Scene 3

[LÉPINE *tries to start a fire with wet logs. Smoke.*]

LISETTE. We have nothing more to say to each other, Monsieur
de Lépine. I have a lot to do. Farewell.

LÉPINE. Hang on, mademoiselle. There's something I want to tell
you. I think I ought to. Something that just happened.
A mishap.

LISETTE. Tell me.

LÉPINE. I'm well brought up. You've doubtless noticed. Result?
I've never looked you straight in the face. So I had no idea what
you looked like.

LISETTE. I'm in the same boat. Worse. Here I am looking at you,
and for the likes of me I'm not sure if even now I can tell what
you look like.

LÉPINE. The lady somehow got it in her head that you and me were in love.

LISETTE. She got it wrong, didn't she?

LÉPINE. This is where the mishap comes in. What she said did make me look at you differently. My gaze alighted upon your physiognomy.

LISETTE. Charming.

LÉPINE. Not bad. Very nice. A pleasant eyeful.

LISETTE. You are a one, Monsieur de Lépine. A real one. Only as soon as men start to make passes, boredom gets me behind the knees. Would that be all?

LÉPINE. A little test. Do like I did. Look at me for once.

LISETTE. All right. And?

LÉPINE. See any difference? Listen to your heart. Not your head.

LISETTE. Nothing to listen to, I'm afraid. Apart from silence.

LÉPINE. Odd that. I've often heard other people say I was attractive. We'll have another go later. Let's get down to the matter in hand. Because there, there's no doubt, is there? My master does have a soft spot for your mistress. Only today he was confiding in me. I'm thinking about unbuttoning myself to Lisette, he said.

LISETTE. He can undo what he likes. My reply will be curt and courteous.

LÉPINE. But the Countess does like it when he's around, doesn't she? She goes all bouncy. You'd doubtless reply that the people we work for are not normal. And I'd agree. The Marquis for instance. Take him. A simple man who doesn't say much and who'd certainly never open his heart. And the Countess. No one's ever likely to get tender with her. She's allergic to compliments. She's dry, cold, all mind over matter. When she's sweet she's sour. God knows how you could talk love to that kind of woman! You'd never find a chance. Unless, of course, you slip it in unexpected, the remark I mean, *à propos* of nothing, 'Oh, incidentally, I love you . . .' That kind of thing. Love could never get through her defences. Vertical intrusion's the only answer. She'd have to be bombed. It is noised abroad that she thinks love is an adolescent trifle. But I think she's got a taste for this trifle. Thus. Hence. I suggest we start moving the two pieces over the board. What will that mean? Just that they'll love each other openly, in all simplicity, and for better, for worse, for richer . . . they'll get married. And what will that mean? That will mean that you'll get used to your new colleague, me, and that, seeing me every day, we'll get married too. What d'you think? *Que sera sera?*

LISETTE. No chance.

LÉPINE. You find the proposition displeasing?

LISETTE. Yes.

LÉPINE. A frank little piece, aren't you? But listen to Lépine. I tell you. They will get married. You should assess the advantages.

LISETTE. And I tell you, they won't. I don't want them to. You're sufficiently astute to notice that the Countess considers herself above love. I want to keep things that way, because it wouldn't be to my advantage if she remarried. My situation wouldn't be so cosy. Get me. It's by no means sure that the Countess would benefit from a change in status and it's certain that I wouldn't. I worked it out. So . . . all your dealings are not to my liking. Grit in the oil, if you see what I mean. Thus. Hence. You'll just have to forget the little 'mishap' and pass me by, avoiding arrest.

LÉPINE (*cold*). Too late. You can't undo magic. You'll have to give in.

LISETTE. Sorry. You'll just have to pine, Lépine.

LÉPINE. Your last word?

LISETTE. The matter's closed. [*Goes to leave. He catches hold of a ribbon, pulls her, she resists, he pulls harder. Holds her in a lock. Hurts her.*]

LÉPINE. Look. Excuse my fixation. You may have got things worked out. But so have I. You say they mustn't get married. I say they must. So they will.

LISETTE. Big mouth.

LÉPINE. Wait and see. And then, I love you. You say 'no', but I say 'yes'. And I'm used to getting what I want.

LISETTE. Not this time, you won't.

LÉPINE. Enough badinage. [*She rubs red wrists.*] Let's hear what my master has to say.

Scene 4

[*The* MARQUIS. *He has a nasty spot that needs squeezing. Beneath the powder a distinct whiff of stale sweat. Fortunately a breeze rattles the rusty fixtures.*]

MARQUIS [*half trips coming in*]. Ah ... There you are ... Lisette ... I'm very pleased to see you.

LISETTE. Likewise I'm sure, Monsieur le Marquis. But I was just on my way out.

MARQUIS. Oh. You're going ... Pity. I ... had something to ask, say ... Are we friends?

LÉPINE. Good question.

LISETTE. I have a great deal of respect for you, Monsieur le Marquis.

MARQUIS. Really?! That is really very nice of you, Lisette. And now you come to mention it, I'm very fond of you as well. You've always given me the impression of being an honest girl, in all ways deserving of the mistress you serve, if you get ...

LISETTE. I'm aware of my good fortune.

MARQUIS. Speaking of which, of whom, I mean, does she ever ... your mistress ... talk about me? And what does she say?

LISETTE. Nothing.

MARQUIS. Oh, dear. The thing is, between you and me, there's not another woman in the world that I ... like ... as much as her.

LISETTE. What do you mean by like? Love?

MARQUIS. Well ... Yes ... Love ... if you like. Or vice-versa. The actual noun isn't terribly important, is it? If it is a noun.

I love-stroke-like her more than anyone else. There you have it.
In a nutshell.

LISETTE. I see.

MARQUIS. She, of course, hasn't got the faintest. I never dared
broach the matter. I don't feel I've got the gift of the amorous
gab, if you see what I mean.

LISETTE. Yes. I do.

MARQUIS. So . . . I'm a little . . . confused. Your mistress is a very
level-headed woman. I'm frightened she'd take the wind out of
my sails, and, once deflated I'd be . . . stuck. Wouldn't know
what to say. I was just wondering if you couldn't . . . prepare the
ground for me?

LISETTE. I'm afraid I can't help you, Monsieur le Marquis.

MARQUIS. Oh, dear. Why not? I'd be terribly grateful. And of
course, I'd reward any effort on my behalf. (*Pointing to*
LÉPINE.) If this young man was to your liking I'd . . . fix things
up . . . Ice the cake.

LÉPINE (*coldly, and without looking at* LISETTE). Tempted? Or
perhaps you'd like time to weigh up the pros and cons?

LISETTE. No way. If ever I were to broach the matter with the
Countess I'd have to use the noun you just mentioned, which,
however innocuous you might think it to be, would doubtless
make her angry, first with me, then with you. You know what
she's like.

MARQUIS. You think there's nothing we can do?

LISETTE. I'm afraid not.

MARQUIS. What a pity. And she's always been so civil with me.
Never mind. Suppose I'd better forget the whole thing.

LÉPINE (*coldly*). Don't listen. She's having you on. Come in the
garden and have a little chat with Lépine. He'll cheer you up.

MARQUIS. Really? Let's see if you can anyway. Lisette . . . All I'd
ask is that you don't act against my interests.

LÉPINE. Don't ask her anything. Just let her be.

The MARQUIS *exits.*

Scene 5

LÉPINE. So it's war. Me against you. As long as we know where we stand. So long, sweetheart. But don't think I love you less. And remember. I've paid the first instalment. I can take you home when I like.

LISETTE. It must be said. [*Imitating upper-class accent.*] Lépine is desperately amusing.

Scene 6

[*A gust of wind blows a window open. The fire goes out. The* COUNTESS *comes to. She's just got up. Late. Gummy eyes. She spends too long in bed. On the verge of being raddled, endangered by inelegant bucolic laxity. In her hand a scruffy folder with jam on it.*]

LISETTE. My mistress. Who is not, unless I've got it very wrong, in the mood for love. Poor Marquis. His days are numbered.

COUNTESS. Have this letter sent to the post will you, Lisette? I've written ten over the last three weeks. Ten. Can you imagine? There is nothing in the world as boring as a court case. I'm not surprised so many women get married again.

LISETTE. Then why bother to go to court in the first place? Are these 1000 francs really that important? If they are, of course, then go on. Get married. It wouldn't take me long to arrange. I've already got a candidate.

COUNTESS. Who said I wanted to remarry? What are you talking about?

LISETTE. Don't get shirty. I was just being witty.

COUNTESS. Doubtless someone from Paris telling you stories. Is that it? Don't tell me.

LISETTE. Come on. You know full well who I'm talking about.

COUNTESS. Stop twittering. Listen. I've got an idea. The Marquis's valet . . . If he's at a loose end, or if the Marquis himself had something to post, he could take my letter at the same time. Have you . . . seen the Marquis? Is he up yet?

LISETTE. I've seen him. But he's not what I'd call up. Speaking of which, the husband I've got in mind for you, who burns passionately for you . . .

COUNTESS. Who is this moron?

LISETTE. Guess.

COUNTESS. If he's burning, call the fire brigade. I'm not in the least interested in this Parisian hanky-panky.

LISETTE. Paris has got nothing to do with it. Your suitor's right here on the spot. You think he's an idiot. I'd be more generous. He gives the impression of being a nice and simple man. Warm?

COUNTESS. No idea. Come on, tell me.

LISETTE. The Marquis.

COUNTESS. Which Marquis?

LISETTE. They're hardly crawling out of the woodwork.

COUNTESS. Good God! How could I ever have guessed? 'Nice . . . and simple'! If you'd have said . . . open-minded. Honest and open-minded . . . Then I might have guessed.

LISETTE. I can only describe him as I see him.

COUNTESS. You must be blind as a bat. No one would ever have guessed in a 1000 francs . . . [*Corrects herself.*] years. 'Nice and simple . . .' And who's been telling you all his lovey-dovey nonsense?

LISETTE. He has. In person. Isn't that a laugh? But don't let on. Anyway, all you have to do is to disentangle him gently.

COUNTESS. Poor chap. The last thing I'd want to do would be to do him a mischief. He is a gentleman, whose qualities I much appreciate. And if there has to be someone, I'd prefer it to be him rather than someone else. But are you certain you've got it right? Are you sure that he didn't speak of . . . I don't know . . . esteem? He certainly does hold me in esteem. And has often, and very gallantly, given me signs of this . . . esteem.

LISETTE. No. He said 'love'. He's attracted to you. And for once
he managed to say it without stuttering. Passion, if you prefer.
He sighs, languishes, pines, etc.

COUNTESS. Great Scott! Then he really is to be pitied. Poor man.
Because he's by no means brainless. And if he says it, then he
must certainly mean it. Worse. He's not the kind of person in
whose mouth the word 'love' sounds ridiculous. Only, he'll
never . . . talk to me about it, will he?

LISETTE. Rest assured there's no chance of that. Thanks to me.
I put him off completely. Told him there wasn't the slightest
hope. I trust I did well?

COUNTESS. Yes. Of course. Yes. As long as you managed to tell
him without hurting his feelings. Very delicate. You are
sometimes a little on the brusque side, Lisette, and I would like
to remain on . . . friendly terms. Perhaps we ought to have let
him have his say.

LISETTE. That's not what he wanted. He wanted me to do
it for him.

COUNTESS. Poor boy.

LISETTE. I told him that I daren't. That if I even broached the
matter with you, you'd be angry with me. And then furious
with him. In a word, you'd give him the boot.

COUNTESS. Give him the what? What an appalling expression!
Give him the boot? The boot? I wouldn't even give you the
boot, Lisette?! What made you think such a thing? Why start
lying all of a sudden? You're going to make an enemy of one of
the few men in the world I respect, and who merits my respect
to boot. Forget the boot. If only servants could learn to speak
properly. All you had to do was to tell him: 'I'm sorry,
monsieur. It's neither my place nor my business, etc., etc. I'm
afraid you'll just have to do the talking yourself.' Now you've
even made me wish he would talk to me about . . . it, in order to
repair the damage you've done. The boot. The boot. He must
feel deeply hurt.

LISETTE. But you must understand, madame. This was the

easiest way of getting rid of him. And what's the alternative?
Are you going to love him so as not to hurt his feelings? Marry
him to apologise? He's supposed to be marrying Hortense,
remember. Come on. I said nothing out of place. And I've saved
you a lot of trouble. I can see him now dreaming up the garden
path. You've still got time to slip off.

COUNTESS. Slip off? Now that he's seen me?! I certainly will not
slip off. Not after what you've just told him. Which he
doubtless thinks was prompted by me. No. I am going to carry
on treating him exactly as before. Go and see to my letter. [*She
gives her a sweaty crumpled heap.*]

LISETTE (*aside*). There's more to this than meets the eye.
(*Aloud.*) I'd prefer to stay with you. I often do. So there'd be
nothing odd. And that way we'll avoid any declaration.

COUNTESS. What a clever idea. You're going to protect me.
Wonderful. Today. Tomorrow. Always going to stay alongside
me, are you, Lisette, just in case? The idea's ridiculous! Take
the letter. I can manage, thank you.

LISETTE. I'll be back in a moment. I'll give the letter to a gardener.

COUNTESS. You'll do no such thing. This is an important letter.
I want you to take it in person. So that if by any chance we've
missed the post, then you can bring it back to me and we'll send
it by some other means. I don't trust gardeners. They're not
punctual.

LISETTE. The post doesn't leave for two hours.

COUNTESS. Will you take it, I said? What is the world coming to?!

LISETTE (*aside*). She's not playing straight with me.

Scene 7

COUNTESS (*alone*). And just why did she so much want to hang
around? I hate servants. Their very servility is insolent. They
wait. But they don't wait straight.

Scene 8

LÉPINE. Madame, the Marquis spotted you in conversation with
   Lisette, here, in the conservatory. He wondered if by any
   chance you'd be put out if he came in? He'd like a word but in
   no way wishes to be importunate.
COUNTESS. But the Marquis could never be importunate,
   Lépine. Tell him to come in. Tell him I'm delighted to see him.
LÉPINE. I'll tell him immediately. He'll be over the moon.
   One moment.

Scene 9

LÉPINE (*calls to the* MARQUIS). The Countess will graciously
   receive you, sir. (*Low.*) Come on. She was warm, almost
   tender. A flower. Go on. Move in. Pluck.

Scene 10

[*A flush of watery brightness. Then, very dark. The* COUNTESS
poised with her secateurs.]

COUNTESS. Why all the fuss, Marquis? You're very ceremonious
   all of a sudden.
MARQUIS. You are most gracious to accord me this . . . There are
   a few . . . indeed many things I'd like to . . .
COUNTESS. You seem a little dreamy, even preoccupied.
MARQUIS. Doubtless. Lots of things . . . buzzing around. [*He
   makes a buzzing sound*]. I've come to see you because I need . . .
   advice . . . a sympathetic shoulder . . . ear.
COUNTESS. Then you've come to the right person. Because you

need all you've just said, you need even less than I need to be
pleasant to you.

MARQUIS. Pleasant! By all means. You can be more than that, if
you like. It's up to you . . . I mean . . .

COUNTESS. What do you mean? Are you lacking in confidence,
Marquis? Come, come. No beating about the bush. You can ask
what you will of me, Marquis, I assure you.

MARQUIS. Can I? Heavens. Aha. I'm . . . sorely tempted . . . to
abuse your kindness . . .

COUNTESS. My only worry is that you might resist the temptation. Take the plunge. That's what friends are for. You are
too reserved.

MARQUIS. I am . . . yes . . . a shade . . . inhibited.

COUNTESS. And I'm trying to cure you of your shyness, aren't I?

MARQUIS. You are . . . aware of the . . . fix I find myself in with
Hortense. I'm supposed to marry her. If I don't, I have to give
her 200,000 francs.

COUNTESS. But she doesn't seem to have taken your fancy.

MARQUIS. Not in the least. I don't like her at all.

COUNTESS. I'm not surprised. Temperamentally you're not
suited. She's too affected.

MARQUIS. That's just it. She's too aware of being attractive.
You'd have to feed her compliments all the time and compliments are not my strong point. Coquettish women make me
feel ill at ease. When I'm with her, I don't open my mouth.

COUNTESS. She is a little like that, I agree. But then, all women
are the same . . .

MARQUIS. There I beg to differ. You are an exception. You
please . . . but you're unaware that you please. As if it wasn't
your doing. I'm convinced that you don't even know how . . .
pleasing you are. But others do. Oh, yes!

COUNTESS. Me? Pleasing?! Quite honestly I'd hazard that others
think of me as little as I think of myself.

MARQUIS. That's what you think. But I know some people who
don't let on about everything that's going on up there. [*Taps*

head. Makes buzzing noise again.]

COUNTESS. And who on earth could that be, Marquis? Friends like you, perhaps?

MARQUIS. Friends? I hardly think you could call them friends. They won't be friends for long anyway . . .

COUNTESS. I do so much appreciate the little compliments you manage to slip in by the by.

MARQUIS. Nothing's slipped in, I can assure you. Everything's said on purpose.

COUNTESS. Really? So you don't think I can keep friends? Aren't you my friend?

MARQUIS. Well. Yes. But . . . If I wasn't . . . And if I was something else. Not a friend. It wouldn't be surprising.

COUNTESS. I'd be surprised, wouldn't I?

MARQUIS. Surprised? You'd be furious.

COUNTESS. Surprised, I said. Anyway, for the sake of argument, I am willing to concede that there may be people who find me pleasing.

MARQUIS. Worse! Charming! Oh! If only Hortense was like you. I'd be only too happy to marry her. As it is, I'm finding it more than difficult to . . . get my nose down . . .

COUNTESS. I understand. But think how much worse things would be if you were attracted to a third party.

MARQUIS. But that's it. That's the problem. That's precisely what's happened.

COUNTESS (*exclaiming*). You don't mean that you are in love with a third party!

MARQUIS. Passionately . . .

COUNTESS (*smiling*). I must admit Marquis that I did have an inkling . . .

MARQUIS. But . . . you wouldn't by any stroke of luck have an inkling as to the identity of the third party?

COUNTESS. You tell me.

MARQUIS. No. Go on. Have a guess.

COUNTESS. Why should I bother guessing when all you have

to do is to own up.

MARQUIS. There's the rub. You see, you know her. She is the most . . . pleasing. The most unaffected . . . You were talking of unpretentious people? She is in a class of her own. The more I look at her the more I admire her.

COUNTESS. Then why not marry her? At once. Ditch Hortense and pitch in. I see no point in dilly-dallying. Do it.

MARQUIS. Yes. But do you just think there might be a way of not losing the 200,000 francs. I'm hiding nothing from you.

COUNTESS [*Snip-snip go the secateurs*]. Please. Talk to me as if you were talking to yourself.

MARQUIS. How beautifully put.

COUNTESS. And how deliciously frank, I do so admire your frankness, Marquis. But down to business. How can we arrange things so that you don't have to lose these 200,000 francs?

MARQUIS. As things stand, Hortense is in love with the Chevalier, who is, of course, a relation of yours.

COUNTESS. Very distant.

MARQUIS. Now. Because she loves him, I conclude that she can't give a tinkers for me. Therefore, all I have to do is to pretend to want to marry her. In which case, she'd have to refuse to marry me. So, QED I don't owe her a penny.

COUNTESS. Uuummm. You could try. But it might be risky. She's a discerning woman, Marquis. You blithely, modestly, suppose she'd turn you down. I'm not so sure. You're not to be sniffed at.

MARQUIS. Me?

COUNTESS. You.

MARQUIS. You really do . . . boost my desire to tell you everything . . . This is most encouraging!

COUNTESS [*prunes violently*]. Encouraging! Marquis, please! Listen to me. I'm out to help you in every way, nothing's going to stop me and you can count on me in any event. Would you please get that into your head, odd man that you are, and be big enough to come to the point. You want advice? I'm giving you advice. And when it comes to complimenting, all you have to do is to open your mouth and compliment. Compliments are no more complicated than anything else. Understand?

MARQUIS. You're filling me with both delight and hope.

COUNTESS. Let's look at the situation rationally. Step by step. What if Hortense accepts your proposal?

MARQUIS. What an appalling thought! In that event I'd just have to pay out 200,000 francs – provided beforehand, that is, that the person who has . . . stolen my heart as it were . . . had agreed that she was . . . happy to accept me.

COUNTESS. And do you anticipate that she's going to be that difficult? Does she know that you love her?

MARQUIS. Good Lord, no. I mean, I haven't dared tell her.

COUNTESS. It couldn't be, Marquis, could it, that you're pushing shyness to the limits of the bearable? However much I admire courteous reticence, this is becoming slightly ridiculous. You're not doing yourself justice.

MARQUIS. She's so . . . sensible. I'm frightened of her. You really think I ought to broach the matter?

COUNTESS. You ought already to have done so. Maybe she's just waiting for you to do it. And if she is sensible, what have you got to be frightened of? Modesty is, of course, admirable but modest people do speak, do propose things. So say it, Marquis. Please. Go on. Out with it. Everything will be fine.

MARQUIS. Easily said. But if you knew who it was, perhaps you wouldn't be so keen. How lucky you are. Not to be in love. To despise it, even.

COUNTESS. I beg your pardon. Me? Despise love? Love?! The most natural feeling in the world! But Marquis. Think. That wouldn't be sensible of me, would it? I've got nothing against love, it's lovers or the general run of the mill average lover that get up my nose. But I've got nothing, repeat, nothing, against the feeling itself, which is honest, permissible and involuntary. It is certainly one of the best feelings around. How could I hate it? I assure you. And there is even a man who, if he were to confess that he loved me with that frankness of yours of which I spoke earlier, I'd be happy to forgive.

MARQUIS. It is true. Things said ... openly, candidly ... do sometimes ...

COUNTESS ... please. And never offend. Is that clear? That's what I think. I'm not a heartless monster!

MARQUIS. It would be such a pity if you were. You're in such wonderful health.

COUNTESS (*to herself*). Health?! What the hell's he talking about health for?! (*Aloud.*) It's the country air.

MARQUIS. But even in town you have bright eyes and a fresh glow to your cheeks.

COUNTESS. I am in good shape, thank you. But, Marquis! Do you realise what you're doing? You're paying me a compliment!

MARQUIS. Of course, I realise it. I told you. I do everything deliberately.

COUNTESS. But don't you think you should reserve your compliments for the woman you love?

MARQUIS. You're right. But if that person were you, then you could keep them, couldn't you?

COUNTESS. I beg your pardon! 'If it were you' ... Marquis ... Are you talking about me? Is this a declaration of love?

MARQUIS. No. Not in the least.

COUNTESS. Then what put it in your head to start talking to me about my health and my complexion? I mean, your intentions could be misinterpreted.

MARQUIS. No. It's just a manner of speaking. All I'm saying is that it is a great pity that you have closed the door on love and re-marriage and that this disposition is a death-blow to my happiness, because I'll never meet a woman to whom I am as suited as I am to you. But I'm not saying anything about it because I don't want to rub you up the wrong way.

COUNTESS. But you're doing it again. This is love-talk. You are in love with me. And you're telling me in no uncertain way.

MARQUIS. And what if I am? But even if I had been and it was you, there's no reason to go and get angry like that. Everything's lost. Just let's keep calm. Let's just pretend that I didn't and haven't ever said anything?

COUNTESS. What an appalling anti-climax. You are an extremely odd man.

MARQUIS. And you're in a very bad mood. You who only a few moments ago were saying that all one has to do is to declare one's love in a candid fashion . . . Look what happens when you do . . . I'm in a pretty pickle.

COUNTESS (*low*). This is worse than when we started. (*Aloud*.) Why are you so angry? Who are you so cross with?

MARQUIS. With no one. And that's all there is to it. Pleased? You must be delighted. But I can tell you, if you're going to lose your temper with everyone who behaves like me, you're going to have your work cut out.

COUNTESS (*aside*). He really is a little weird! (*Pause*.) And who was angry with whom?

MARQUIS. No one. No one with no one. The way you turned me down was extremely pleasant.

COUNTESS. You're out of your mind!

MARQUIS. Perfect. Just wonderful. First you whisper under your breath, oh yes, I heard, that I'm weird, and now I'm a nutcase. Tremendous. A fool. A loon. But don't think I'm complaining. Oh no. I prefer things to be clear. I'm not your kind of man. That's all there is to it. No good kicking against the pricks. All I have to do now is shut up. So I'll shut up. Adieu, Countess. I trust that we shall remain none the less good friends and that you shall at least have the kindness to help me out of the mess I'm in with Hortense.

COUNTESS [*Puts down the secateurs. The greenhouse is a battlefield of castrated geraniums*]. What a novel lover. I do, I know, prize simple people. But his particular brand of simplicity is perhaps just a shade too complicated!

Scene 11

[*It is so dark, she decides to light a lamp. But wick and paper are wet.* HORTENSE *comes back in with the reluctant* MARQUIS. *He hasn't had time to get far enough up the garden.*]

HORTENSE. I grabbed the Marquis as he was going up the garden path. We have something to thrash out and there's no reason why the Countess shouldn't be present.

MARQUIS. As you wish, madame.

HORTENSE. I presume you know what I want to see you about.

MARQUIS. I'm afraid I don't. At least, I . . . can't remember.

HORTENSE. You surprise me. I was hoping that you'd have the wit to break this silence. It is extremely humiliating to have to take the first step. Have you forgotten that there is a will, a legacy which concerns us both?

MARQUIS. Ah, yes. A . . . will . . . It all comes back now.

HORTENSE. A will which, as it were, leaves me to you.

MARQUIS. That is the case. Yes. I have to marry you. Absolutely correct.

HORTENSE. Well? Have you made up your mind? I would very much appreciate a decision. It's certainly no news to you that you have a rival – namely the Chevalier, a relative of yours, madame. Now I don't necessarily like the Chevalier any more than I like you, but I certainly don't like him less than anybody else. Consequently I would be quite willing to marry him, in the event of you deciding not to marry me. The Chevalier is quite aware of the situation. But as he's just told me that for extremely urgent reasons he must know one way or the other today, I promised him I'd have it out with you. So? What shall I do? Love him or leave him? It goes, of course, without saying that if it's me that you want, I'm yours for the taking.

MARQUIS. In that case I . . . accept your most gracious offer.

HORTENSE. Are you speaking from the heart?

MARQUIS. Why shouldn't I? Are you not lovable?

HORTENSE. So you love me?

MARQUIS. I haven't said I didn't. Only just now I was . . . talking it over with the Countess.

COUNTESS. That is true. He said he was toying with the idea of marriage.

HORTENSE. And did he tell you he was in love with me?

COUNTESS. He might well have done. He intimated certain leanings, that's for sure.

HORTENSE. Then how do you explain, Monsieur le Marquis, that you've not spoken to me once over the last six weeks? Someone in love generally drops the odd hint, and in the present circumstances such behaviour would hardly have been out of place.

MARQUIS. I agree. Only. Time goes by. One is absent-minded. And then . . . One doesn't know how the other party is going to react . . .

HORTENSE. How charmingly modest. Good. That's settled. I'll tell the Chevalier.

Scene 12

HORTENSE (*under her breath to the* CHEVALIER). He's said he's going to marry me. But he hates the idea. Don't fret. It's a ruse.

CHEVALIER (*to* HORTENSE). This whole business worries me. (*Aloud.*) Ah well, madame, there goes my last hope. I suppose it was stupid to think that the Marquis could ever refuse you.

HORTENSE. Correct. I am going to marry the Marquis. The matter is settled. Destiny parts us. All along, the Marquis has been nursing a secret passion for me and it's only because he's absent-minded that he didn't tell me.

CHEVALIER. Absent-minded?! You mean he forgot?!

HORTENSE. Absolutely. But then he remembered. And told me. Having first told the Countess.

CHEVALIER. But, if you knew Countess, why didn't you tell me? I always thought the Marquis was in love with you.

COUNTESS. With me?! What next?! Why drag me into all this?

HORTENSE. Odd that. I had the same impression.

COUNTESS. You both have a very twisted sense of humour.

MARQUIS. And I'm saying nothing.

CHEVALIER. You do realise, Marquis, that you're driving me to despair.

MARQUIS. I'm dreadfully sorry. But put yourself in my shoes. There's a legacy. You know that. What else can I do? Where there's a will . . .

CHEVALIER. If it wasn't for the will perhaps you wouldn't love her as much as I do?

MARQUIS. Look. Please. I love her quite enough as it is, thank you.

HORTENSE. And I shall do all in my endeavour to be a worthy object of your passion. (*Low. To the* CHEVALIER.) Now push for a swift wedding.

CHEVALIER (*aside*). This could backfire. (*Aloud.*) In my woeful state, Marquis, I would be most grateful if you'd put an end to my misery by giving me irremediable proof of the vanity of all hope.

MARQUIS. The only proof I can give is to marry her. And I can't just marry her now, like that, can I?

CHEVALIER. I see what you mean. (*Low.*) He will marry you.

HORTENSE. You're ruining it. (*Aloud.*) I think I understand what the Chevalier wants. He still hopes beyond hope that we won't get married. Is that it, Chevalier?

CHEVALIER. No, madame. I have surrendered all hope.

HORTENSE. I don't believe you. I'm sorry, but I don't. You don't find the Marquis wholly convincing. I can feel it. And as you are leaving for Paris tomorrow, where, if necessary, you will start a new life, I quite understand that you would feel happier in your mind if the last spark of hope had been well and truly doused. That's it, isn't it? You want concrete evidence. (*Low.*) Say 'yes'.

CHEVALIER. Yes.

HORTENSE. I thought so. Monsieur le Marquis. Look, we're not far from Paris. It's still early in the day. Tell Lépine to go and fetch a solicitor. We can draw up our marriage contract and put the poor Chevalier out of his misery.

COUNTESS. I get the impression you're pushing the Chevalier into requesting something he doesn't want at all.

HORTENSE (*low, to the* CHEVALIER). Cue.

CHEVALIER. Oh the contrary, Countess. No . . . I would, yes, find a solicitor most comforting.

COUNTESS. What an odd thing to say.

HORTENSE. No, it isn't. He has to know where he stands. It's as simple as that. And he's right. He didn't dare ask. That's all. So I asked for him. Are you or are you not going to send Lépine, Marquis?

MARQUIS. If you absolutely insist. But who would have thought ten minutes ago that we would have been needing solicitors . . . I mean . . . today of all days.

HORTENSE (*low, to the* CHEVALIER). Push.

CHEVALIER. I beg of you, Marquis.

COUNTESS. Çome, come, Chevalier. Surely you can wait until tomorrow. What's all the rush? This sudden passion for proof is really a little bizarre. Personally I have no desire whatsoever to clutter up my house with solicitors. I'd like a quiet evening. Tomorrow will be perfect. There.

HORTENSE (*to the* CHEVALIER). Once more with feeling.

CHEVALIER. Countess, I beg of you.

COUNTESS. Beg of me! You must be mad! Can you really be in such a hurry to see your rival marry your mistress? Of course, if that's what you want . . .

MARQUIS. Listen. It would be most discourteous to importune our hostess any further. She's right. Tomorrow will be perfect.

HORTENSE. Then as soon as she agrees we'll send Lépine.

Scene 13

HORTENSE. Here's Lisette. [*The door opens and a vast gust of wind blows everything from left to right.*] We'll ask her to go and get him. Lisette, the marriage contract between myself and the Marquis is to be drawn up this evening. The Marquis is going to send Lépine to Paris to fetch his solicitor. Could you tell him to come and see us.

LISETTE. I'll be two seconds.

COUNTESS. One moment, Lisette. I don't want to have anything to do with this or any other marriage. Neither me nor my servants.

LISETTE. I was only trying to be helpful. All I had to do was to pop out in the garden. Nothing to it. Look. There he is on the terrace. (*Shouts.*) Lépine.

COUNTESS. Stupid cow.

Scene 14

LÉPINE. [*Enters. Door. A second violent gust of wind blows everything back into place.*] You called?

LISETTE. Quick. Saddle a horse. Ride to Paris. Fetch a solicitor. Madame and Monsieur le Marquis are going to get married.

LÉPINE (*to the* MARQUIS). A solicitor?! She telling the truth? I thought we were going hunting this afternoon. Hares, not solicitors.

MARQUIS. No, no ... It's ... now the latter which is required.

LÉPINE. I see no point in going to fetch yours. He's probably dead. Don't you remember? Running a high temperature, he was, when we left. Doctors everywhere. Going fast to his brain, it was.

MARQUIS. True. He was looking poorly.

LÉPINE. Poorly?! Hardly poorly! Deathly more like.

LISETTE (*casually*). In that case you'd better fetch madame's solicitor in his place.

COUNTESS. Would you please shut up. Because if your solicitor is dead, so is mine. He'd not been his old self for some time.

LISETTE (*casual and innocent*). But you wrote to him only recently.

COUNTESS. So? What does that prove? Do letters stop people dying? Yes, I did write to him. But he didn't reply.

CHEVALIER (*low, to* HORTENSE). Things begin to look rosier.

HORTENSE (*giving him a secret reassuring smile*). Anyway there's more than one solicitor in Paris. Lépine can find out if the dead one feels any better. We've been here for six weeks. He's had plenty of time to resuscitate. Go and write to him, Marquis. Tell him, if he can't come himself, to send a replacement. In the meantime, Lépine can get ready.

LÉPINE. Sorry, madame. No go. If I get on a horse, I'm finished. All that talk about hunting just now. Madness. I don't feel well at all. It's just come over me. I won't be running after anything today. Horses. Solicitors. You name it. Nothing.

LISETTE (*smiling sweetly*). Are you dead too?

LÉPINE (*pretending to be in pain*). No. But extremely ill. And I won't be able to go to Paris. That's all there is to it. It's only respect for present company that stops me screaming with pain. Agony, it is. Fell down the stairs yesterday. A whole flight. On my back. And if they hadn't caught me by the braces, I was off down another one. Appalling pain. Incredible.

CHEVALIER. In that case, you can take my carriage. Tell him to leave at once, Marquis.

MARQUIS. But he really doesn't look too good . . . All crumpled. Not surprising. After a flight of stairs. Ought to be in bed. But, of course, yes, you must do as they say . . . if you can.

HORTENSE. Come on, Lépine. You'll be all right in a carriage.

LÉPINE. I'll come clean. Do me a favour. I don't want to go to Paris. The Marquis is just going to sign away his happiness.

That's all. You don't love him, madame. I know you don't. This marriage would be a big mistake. I'd kick myself for ever if I'd helped arrange it. And I know what I'm talking about. There. If you think I've overstepped the mark, all you have to do is say, 'Thank you, Lépine. That will be all', and I'll leave without a word. Content to have been honest.

COUNTESS. What a wonderful servant. A bijou.

MARQUIS (*to* HORTENSE). You heard what he said. What can be done? He's as stubborn as a mule. You budge him. I can't. Even if I lose my temper, it'll make no difference. I'll just have to dismiss him. (*To* LÉPINE.) Thank you, Lépine, that will be all.

HORTENSE. We can make do without him. Go and write the letter all the same. One of my people will take it. Or someone from the village.

Scene 15

HORTENSE. Go and write the letter, I said. I'm going to write one to my family.

MARQUIS. Look. I hope you know what you're doing. Because if there's any chance you don't love me . . . Too bad. Because I'm going through with it.

CHEVALIER (*low*). You've gone too far.

HORTENSE. Sssssh. (*Aloud.*) I know exactly what I'm up to, thank you. Farewell, Chevalier. You will understand that it is no longer seemly for me to spend time in your company.

CHEVALIER. Farewell, mademoiselle. Henceforth my only companion will be the chagrin with which you leave me.

[*They both leave. A final gust moves through the conservatory like a tornado. Things fall over. No one cares.*]

MARQUIS. Good Lord. That woman's got the devil in her. Do you think she loves me?

COUNTESS. Of course she doesn't. But she's sufficiently pig-headed to marry you. Take my advice. Call the whole thing off.

MARQUIS. How about offering her 100,000 francs to split the difference? Only problem. I wouldn't have the money to hand.

COUNTESS. Don't let that stop you. I can lend it to you. I've got the money in Paris. Call them all back. I'm so pleased. This was all beginning to upset me. Quickly. Before they disappear.

MARQUIS. This really is so . . . infinitely kind of you. (*Shouts.*) Madame. Monsieur le Chevalier . . .

Scene 17

[*Door opens. Leaves everywhere. They've got used to living with the wind.*]

MARQUIS. Would you mind just stepping back inside a moment. There's something I'd like to . . . suggest.

HORTENSE. What else is there to be said?

CHEVALIER. Can there still be reason to hope?

HORTENSE. I thought you'd gone off to write a letter.

MARQUIS. All in good time. I have an offer to make. An extremely reasonable offer.

HORTENSE. An offer?! And what can that mean? Have you been having me on? Could it be that your love is not as true as you'd have me believe?

MARQUIS. Love?! Good God! You apparently don't love me at all! I find that extremely vexing.

HORTENSE. I don't love you yet. But I will. And then, if both partners are virtuous, the wife can always make do without love.

MARQUIS. The wife, perhaps. But not the husband. And certainly not me. Ultimately ... marriage would only afford us the necessary leisure for endless bickering. So I thought we might rather come to an arrangement. Let's split the difference. There are 200,000 francs at stake. I'll concede you half, even though you don't love me, and we'll have no need for solicitors and what have you, whether dead or alive ...

CHEVALIER. I breathe again.

HORTENSE. Are you in your right mind, monsieur? Do you really imagine that 100,000 francs could compensate for the disadvantage of not being married to you?! You underestimate yourself.

MARQUIS. May I inform you, madame, that I'm not worth tuppence when I'm in one of my bad moods and allow me to tell you here and now that from henceforth I always shall be.

HORTENSE. My innate sweetness will be my protection.

MARQUIS. So you refuse my offer? Fine. Let us then continue as agreed. You will be married.

HORTENSE. It seems the most obvious solution.

MARQUIS. But isn't it sickening to be compelled to share half of such a large sum of money with someone who couldn't give a tinkers for you? We shall be compelled to consult a court of law. We'll see if I can be forced into marrying a girl who doesn't love me.

HORTENSE. In that case I'll say I do love you. And who'd doubt my word once I've agreed to marry you? I'll plead that it's you who doesn't love me. Worse even. Who loves someone else.

MARQUIS. Maybe. But the identity of that someone else doesn't happen to be public knowledge. As in the case of the Chevalier.

HORTENSE. Oh no? I know who it is, monsieur.

COUNTESS. Look. Would you please put an end to this little scene.

HORTENSE. I shall marry you, monsieur. That's all there is to be said.

MARQUIS. Fine. As you wish. And, I shall marry you, mademoiselle.

HORTENSE. Wonderful. Let's get married, then.

MARQUIS. Tremendous idea. Ding dong, ding dong. Splendid. You're bound to learn to love me. But to get our marriage off to a good start, I'd be most grateful if your friendship with the Chevalier became suddenly less intimate.

CHEVALIER (*aside to* HORTENSE). This is getting out of control. And so is he . . . !

HORTENSE (*to the* CHEVALIER). Keep calm. (*Aloud.*) The Chevalier knows me well enough to understand that he'll never see me again. Adieu, monsieur. I'm going to write my letter. Make sure that yours is also ready. There's no time to lose.

COUNTESS. Listen to me. You can sign your marriage contract when and where you like but not, I'm afraid, now or here. You're not marrying each other. You're cutting each other's throats. I'd prefer to lend my house for a funeral. You can go and play out your dramas elsewhere.

HORTENSE. Fine. You have a neighbour. The Marquise. We'll do it at her place.

MARQUIS. We shall if I say we shall. Because I'm in charge. And I've never heard of this Marquise.

HORTENSE (*leaving*). That makes no difference. You'll give in, in the end. I'm going to leave you for a moment.

CHEVALIER (*leaving*). This scene has given a boost to my hopes.

Scene 18

[*Heavy rain. They raise their voices.*]

COUNTESS (*stopping the* CHEVALIER). Just a minute, Chevalier. I'd like a word. Have you ever in your life seen anything like this? You love Hortense. Hortense loves you. This marriage must appal you. I mean, I'm not pining for Hortense and even I feel horrified.

CHEVALIER (*hypocritical*). It is indeed atrocious, unheard of . . .

MARQUIS. You can say what you like. She's going to be my wife. But, and here's the clever bit, I'm going to be her husband. Aha. That's going to give her something to think about. Today the contract, tomorrow the wedding, tonight locked up in her room. That's the way it is. She's put me in one of my moods. I'm not going to budge an inch.

COUNTESS. I, on the other hand, think we should call the whole thing off. I tell you, a sensible solicitor, once he learnt what was going on, would refuse to have anything to do with this whole business. If I was their mother I'd lock them both up in their rooms. Can Hortense really be ready to throw her life away for such a paltry sum? You, Chevalier, with your innate gentleman-liness, can't you . . . intervene? Make her listen to sense – if only because you love her. I'm sure all this wheeler-dealing is on your behalf.

CHEVALIER (*to himself*). There's nothing to be lost in remaining firm. (*Aloud.*) What do you want me to do, Countess? I can't see any way out.

COUNTESS. I beg your pardon. My hearing must be going. I surely can't have heard what you just said.

CHEVALIER. I said, I am powerless to do anything. Indeed it is precisely my love which prevents me from intervening.

COUNTESS [*hitting one or two pots with her fan*]. Would you be so kind as to unravel the reasons which sustain this position.

CHEVALIER. My one desire is for Hortense to be happy. If I marry her, she won't be. I simply don't have enough money. However sweet our love, it would inevitably go sour. She would regret having married me, regret not having married the Marquis. That is a risk I daren't take.

COUNTESS. [*beheading a geranium*]. I choose to disregard what you've said. These can't be your words coming out of your mouth?

CHEVALIER. Yes, they are, madame.

COUNTESS. Then what a mean mercantile little man you are,

cousin! A perfect match for Hortense. A marriage of small minds! What an appalling way to love.

CHEVALIER. I assure you, cousin, my reasons are born of tenderness.

COUNTESS. Tenderness! The word is soiled by its mere passage through your mouth.

CHEVALIER. But . . .

COUNTESS. You disgust me. We are unfortunately related – but I'd prefer it not to be noised abroad. You should be ashamed of yourself. I happen to have an idea of your present financial position. You are sufficiently well off, let me tell you, to go without this miserable little pittance which is at stake – a sum which you can moreover only win by means of trickery. To think I once had a good opinion of you! How penny-pinching and sordid! And you dare to say you are in love! A very shrivelled kind of love, Chevalier. Would you please go. I have nothing else to say to you.

MARQUIS (*abruptly*). And I nothing more to fear from you. The letter is going to leave immediately. You have just three more hours to spend in the company of Hortense. After that, curtains.

CHEVALIER. Rest assured. Before the ink is dry on the contract I'll be gone. As for you, Countess, once you have had an honest look at the situation, I think you might be just a little less hard on your cousin. (*Exit.*)

COUNTESS. I certainly will not. I have never in my life despised anyone so much.

Scene 19

MARQUIS. Well. Phew. Poor old me . . .

COUNTESS. Marquis, please. Get rid of her. Give her the 200,000 francs

MARQUIS. When I can keep them by marrying her? Not on your life. I'm damned if I'm going to put myself out of pocket to that extent. I'd have the devil of a job rounding up 200,000 francs.

COUNTESS (*casually*). Haven't I already told you that half of that sum is ready and waiting? As for the other half, we'll just have to see.

MARQUIS. But when you borrow money you have to pay it back. Of course, if you hadn't rejected me, things would be different. But as there's absolutely no hope on that front, I might just as well hang on to this little miss. Anyway, she's becoming rather expensive to spurn.

COUNTESS. Expensive! Be careful or you'll start talking like everyone else! Surely you, of all people, are not going to stoop to small-mindedness. Expense mustn't come into it. Even if it costs you every penny you have, you must get rid of her. Because you don't love her.

MARQUIS. Her or someone else. What's the difference? Apart from you, they're all the same to me. Blonde, big, small, dark. It's you I wanted. It's you I can't have. It's only you I've ever loved.

COUNTESS. You'll have to get things worked out for yourself. Surely you can't be telling me that I have to marry you, just to get you out of the appalling situation in which you find yourself? That's not particularly subtle!

MARQUIS. I didn't say you had to do anything. You make me seem even more ridiculous than I am. I'm fully aware of the fact that you owe me nothing. It's not your fault that I happen to be in love with you. And I'm not pretending in any way that you're in love with me. In fact I'm being particularly discreet about the whole business.

COUNTESS (*impatient and serious*). Which is much to your honour. Your discretion is nothing but intelligent. I didn't expect any less from you, and you're wrong in thinking that I believe you to be more ridiculous than you are.

MARQUIS. The problem, in a nutshell, is the following. I am entering into marriage with this young woman with a heart a little more heavy than it would have been, had I never met you, Countess. That is the only thing I hold against you. Adieu.

COUNTESS. So you're off?! Just like that! Without even stopping to consider any other possible alternative!

MARQUIS. What alternative? There isn't an alternative. There was an alternative. And it failed. Flopped. So there's nothing else to be done. Please excuse me I . . .

COUNTESS. Good evening, Marquis. Please. Don't waste precious seconds bowing. Chop chop. Time is running out.

[*Lightning.*]

Scene 20

COUNTESS [*alone. Steams, grits teeth. Kicks a flowerpot*]. Would someone be so kind as to point out to me what I've said or what I've done that has implanted in this man's brain the idea that I am not in love with him? I am, I must admit, more and more sorely tempted, prompted by no more than impatience, to tell him outright that, yes, I do love him. There. If only to show him . . . what a stupid idiot he is. [*Thunderclap. Calm descends.*] I must. I will.

Scene 21

LÉPINE. Could I take the liberty of requesting a brief word with madame?

COUNTESS. What is it?

LÉPINE. I just wondered if the Countess might be able to do something to patch things up between me and the Marquis?

COUNTESS. I do sympathise. You serve him loyally and well and what does he do in return? He punishes you. He is twisted.

LÉPINE. I was gratified to note that madame did seem to approve of my refusal to leave for Paris. If my memory serves me right 'bijou' was the word used.

COUNTESS. And I've no reason to retract my compliment.

LÉPINE. It is, however, this very excellence which is jeopardising my present employment. However worthy the Countess finds me, the Marquis is going to give me the boot.

COUNTESS. I won't hear of it. I'll speak in your favour.

LÉPINE. Perhaps madame might explain to the Marquis why I did what I did. I got a bit over-excited. The solicitor business worried me. So first I made him sick. Then I made him dead. Given half a chance, I'd have buried him. And all this out of nothing but affection for the Marquis. And what thanks do I get? (*He approaches the* COUNTESS. *Confidential.*) I do happen, incidentally, in passing to be aware of the fact that the Marquis is in love with you. Lisette knows it too. The Marquis and I even had a little word with her to see if she wouldn't soften you up in his favour, so to speak. But she wouldn't. She was frightened it might compromise her . . . tips.

COUNTESS. Come again?

LÉPINE. The story is the following. She's got it worked out that if you remain a widow, you're more advantageous to her than if you got married. In terms of her profit margins, you're more lucrative unattached. That's what Lisette says.

COUNTESS. Lucrative! Me?! (*Pause.*) How wonderfully loyal! What a charming servant!

LÉPINE. Not particularly flattering, is it? And that kind of mentality you doubtless find repugnant. Your sensitivity is sorely offended. That's what makes you a Countess. But, everyone is not a Countess, are they? What I've just told you, that's how a servant's mind works. And servants . . . you just have to accept them for what they are. I mean, do we get angry with an ant for crawling? You get my point. Lowly status, lowly

ideas. Lisette hasn't got any money. She thinks she can get
some by being mean.

COUNTESS. The nerve! Here she comes in person. Leave
us alone. I'll fix things with the Marquis. Tell him to come
and see me.

Scene 22

LÉPINE (*low to* LISETTE). The immediate forecast is none too
promising. But don't worry. It's all just part of my plan to win
your heart. (*Exits.*)

Scene 23

[*The light is white and cold.*]

LISETTE (*as she moves towards the* COUNTESS). And what the
hell does that mean?

COUNTESS. Ah, Lisette. It's you.

LISETTE. It is, madame. The post hadn't left. Well? What did the
Marquis have to say for himself?

COUNTESS. I think I ought to marry him. If only to teach you
a lesson.

LISETTE. I don't know about lessons. But I can tell you that I was
just coming to see you, to tell you to do exactly that. (*Under her
breath.*) Swim with the tide.

COUNTESS. Oh, really? I find that a little surprising. Wouldn't
you run the risk of ending up out of pocket?

LISETTE. Who's talking about money?

COUNTESS. You told Lépine that it wouldn't be to your financial advantage if I re-married. So I was just thinking that I might indeed have to, in order to elude the clutches of my venal servants.

LISETTE. He told you that, did he? So he kept his word. There's something that perhaps you don't know, madame. He's in love with me. Therefore it is very much in his interest that you marry the Marquis. When I refused to help, he felt slighted. He told me I'd regret it. This is him punishing me. But, to be honest, does all this ring true? Do you really think I'd have said that? I mean, would your opinion of me change if you were married? Would you be in any way less generous, any less warm-hearted?

COUNTESS. I don't think I would, no.

LISETTE. I mean, especially if you married the Marquis who happens to be one of the nicest men in the world. It's crazy. What have I got to lose? In fact I could only gain – if I'm so interested in money. My potential source of income would double.

COUNTESS. You're right.

LISETTE. But finally, if you want real proof that I'm the opposite of the person Lépine has just described, how do you account for the fact that I was on my way to see you to press you into this marriage – which I now consider to be urgent?

COUNTESS. I do believe you, Lisette. And I feel most relieved. I had no idea that Lépine was in love with you. That explains everything.

LISETTE. The only cloud, of course, is that it seemingly doesn't take much to make you suspect me. You don't seem to appreciate the extent of my loyalty.

COUNTESS. Wrong. I have a very high opinion of you. And I didn't suspect you half as much as you think. Now. Let's forget the whole matter. What did you want to tell me?

LISETTE. What I told you. That the Marquis is a very nice man.

COUNTESS. I've never thought any different.

LISETTE. A true friend, a companion, and in no way a tyrant.

COUNTESS. You've never said a truer word.

LISETTE. And then, all your paperwork is getting on top of you.

COUNTESS. Worse. I can't even understand most of it. Added to which, I'm lazy.

LISETTE. And all this sparks off bouts of bad temper, which are not good for you.

COUNTESS. I've only had migraines since I was a widow.

LISETTE. Lawyers, tenants, debtors, the Marquis would deal with all that.

COUNTESS. Heavens. You seem to have considered all this far more constructively than I have. And I must say your arguments are very convincing.

LISETTE. I'd even go as far as to say that there's only one man in the world at this very moment to whom you're really suited. Him.

COUNTESS. In that case I ought to give the matter serious thought.

LISETTE. You don't find him unattractive.

COUNTESS. Absolutely not. I wouldn't go as far as to say that my feelings could be characterised as passion. But on the other hand I have nothing with which to reproach him.

LISETTE. What more could you ask for? I mean to say! Passion?! If you had to hang around waiting for passion to come flaming down out of the skies, you'd be a widow until the cows come home. And, anyway, it's not the man that's important. It's his temperament.

COUNTESS. Which is, it must be said, in his case, quite exceptional.

LISETTE. And think of the good deed you'll be doing getting him to break off this awful marriage, which he's contracted more out of despair than love.

COUNTESS. You're right. It would be a humane gesture. And we are all called upon to do our little bit.

LISETTE. In the present instance, a little bit which is not going to involve any great sacrifice on your part.

COUNTESS. You plead his case with pleasing conviction, Lisette. Suddenly I feel warmly disposed in his favour. Only, I'm afraid, it's going to be very difficult to get him round to our way of thinking.

LISETTE. What do you mean? He told you he loved you, didn't he?

COUNTESS. Yes, he did. He told me he loved me. And my first reaction was to act surprised. I mean, it's the least one can do. But do you know what happened? He mistook the surprise for anger, deduced I couldn't stand him, and concluded that I was furious with him for being in love. That's where things stand at the moment. And I'm finding it very difficult to persuade him of the opposite. I can hardly turn on him and say, 'Stop talking such utter rubbish', can I? That would be throwing myself at his feet. So I don't do anything.

LISETTE. I see what you mean. Tricky. You're quite right. You can't do that. But if you can't do that, you can't do anything. Perhaps the best solution is to forget the whole business.

COUNTESS. What?! Make up your mind! First you want me to marry him. Then you want me to forget him. You go from one extreme to the other. But, perhaps it's not all entirely his fault. I am sometimes a little on the rough side.

LISETTE. Just what I was going to say. Would you like me to have a word with Lépine? He could encourage the Marquis to press on regardless.

COUNTESS. Certainly not. Unless of course I have nothing to do with the request.

LISETTE. It wasn't your idea. It was mine.

COUNTESS. In that case I don't want to know anything about it. If, however, he does manage to marry me, it will of course be entirely of your doing, and I'll make sure that he is aware of the fact.

LISETTE. You're too kind, madame.

COUNTESS. Talking of which. That brown dress I don't like. Take it. A present.

LISETTE. And who said marriage was going to make you less generous? I'll go and find Lépine. No point. I'll leave you alone with the Marquis.

Scene 24

MARQUIS (*aside, without seeing the* COUNTESS). Here's the . . . letter for the solicitor. Just written it . . . But . . . I don't know whether to send it or not. In a bit of a tizzy. (*To the* COUNTESS.) You . . . wished to see me?

COUNTESS. I wanted to speak in favour of Lépine. He only acted from the best of intentions. And now he's afraid you want to get rid of him. I'd be most grateful if you'd think again. I'm sure you won't refuse me this little favour – that is, as you've said you love me.

MARQUIS. Oh, yes, I do. And will. For a long time yet. Ever, even.

COUNTESS. I'll do nothing to prevent you.

MARQUIS. But you can't. Couldn't. If I can't and couldn't, how could you? Anyway. I wouldn't let you.

COUNTESS (*laughs*). Oh, these tough manly tones.

MARQUIS. Go on. Laugh. Enjoying yourself, are you?

COUNTESS. More than you could imagine.

MARQUIS. My God. If only I had never set eyes on you.

COUNTESS. You do wield the most exquisite turns of phrase.

MARQUIS. What's the point of being exquisite? Doesn't get me very far, does it? Given that you hate me.

COUNTESS. This hate business is beginning to get slightly on my nerves. What proof have you? The only quality of mine you can be sure of is my patience – my patience in listening to your hare-brained ramblings. Have I ever once used any of the offensive adjectives you so willingly attribute to me? Nothing

I've ever said could be possibly thought to communicate anger, hate or scorn. All these ideas are cooked up in that odd brain of yours. They are your own concoctions. And every time you reply, you make things worse. You are without any stretch of the imagination the most clumsy man I've ever met. And I'm even wrong to say you reply, because I don't ever get a chance to talk to you. And still you complain!

MARQUIS. Perhaps . . . Yes . . . I am . . . a shade fantastical . . .

COUNTESS. No, you're not. You are the most unbearable man I have ever met. That's what you are. Believe me. Your so-called conversations are unique. Incredible.

MARQUIS. Hurt me. Go on. I love it.

COUNTESS. Wait. You say you love me. I believe you. But, then, what? What do you want from me in way of reply?

MARQUIS. What do I want?! Hardly the most difficult question in the world. You know just as well as I do, what I want!

COUNTESS. Well, then! Think! Haven't I already said it. What a way to reply! Look, let's call it a day. I shall never ever love you, monsieur. [*At last . . . she take the fan from the table, flicks it open to calm herself with a mannered breeze. But the moths fly out. The fan is bare bones. They've eaten it all. The sight brings her back to her senses.*]

MARQUIS. Too bad. Hard luck on me. All I ask is that you appreciate why I am so miserable.

COUNTESS. Get this into your head. Once and for all. When you tell someone that you love them, the least you can do is to ask them what their reaction is.

MARQUIS. You're getting angry with me again.

COUNTESS. I can't bear it. Adieu.

MARQUIS. All right, madame, I love you. What do you think? And, once more with feeling. What do you think?

COUNTESS. What do I think? I'm delighted. That's what I think. Understand? I'll say it again. I'm delighted. Got it? Good grief. If I hadn't got you by the scruff of the neck we'd have been in this greenhouse for years.

MARQUIS. She's delighted! I love her! And she's delighted! Heavens! I do feel better. May I . . . kiss your hand?

Final Scene

HORTENSE. Is your letter ready, Marquis? But . . . do my eyes deceive me? You appear to be kissing the Countess's hand!

MARQUIS. Precisely. It is my way of thanking her for making the loss of the 200,000 francs I am about to give you unimaginably painless.

HORTENSE. How wonderful that, at last, you've decided to be a good sport.

CHEVALIER. Then everyone's happy. Allow me to embrace you, Marquis. This, Countess, is the happy end we have all been waiting for.

COUNTESS. Then there's no point in waiting any longer, is there? [*She takes the* MARQUIS *by the hand.*]

LISETTE. [*alone on stage with* LÉPINE.] Well. It looks as though I'm going to have to marry you after all.

LÉPINE. I had it all worked out from the beginning. [*A long and very French kiss. They look at each other. Exit.*]

[*For the first time and very rapidly the empty greenhouse is bathed in warm sunlight.*
    Loud birdsong.
    By magic a dead geranium bursts into bloom.]

A Matter of Dispute

Translated by John Walters

from LA DISPUTE
First performed by the Comédie-Française (1744)

CHARACTERS

HERMIONE

THE PRINCE

MEZURU

CARISA

EGLEA

AZORO

ADINIA

MEZIRION

MEZILIUS

DEENA

The PRINCE's retinue

The scene is set in the country.

Scene 1

HERMIONE. Where are we going, my lord? This is the wildest and loneliest place in the world, and there is no sign here of the entertainment you promised me.

PRINCE (*laughing*). Everything's ready for it.

HERMIONE. I don't understand a thing. What's this house you're taking me into? What a strange building it is! And the tremendous height of the different walls surrounding it. Where are you taking me?

PRINCE. To a very strange spectacle. You know the matter we were discussing yesterday evening? You were arguing against the whole of my Court that it wasn't your sex, but ours, who had first been fickle and faithless in love.

HERMIONE. Yes, my lord, and I still maintain it. The first betrayal, the first infidelity, can only have started with someone bold enough to blush at nothing. Women were shy and modest by nature then, and have been so long as the world and its corruption have lasted – so how can anyone suppose that they were the first to fall into vices of the heart requiring such boldness, such dissolute feelings, such effrontery, as those we are discussing? It just isn't credible.

PRINCE. Oh, certainly, Hermione, I don't find it any more plausible than you do. You don't have to fight *me* over this. I am of the same opinion as you against everyone else, you know that.

HERMIONE. Yes, but purely out of gallantry, I have noticed.

PRINCE. If it is out of gallantry, I'm not aware of it. It's true I love you, and my extreme desire to please you may well persuade me you are right. But what is certain is that it persuades me so subtly that I don't even notice it. I have no respect for a man's heart, and you may keep it as far as I'm concerned – I believe it to be incomparably more prone to fickleness and infidelity than a woman's. I make an exception only of my own, and even then I wouldn't do it that honour if I loved anyone else but you.

HERMIONE. I detect a great deal of irony in your remarks.

PRINCE. I shall soon be punished for it then, because I'm going to give you something to confound me with if I don't think as you do.

HERMIONE. What do you mean?

PRINCE. Yes, we are going to ask Nature herself about it. Only she can decide the matter irrefutably, and she will surely pronounce in your favour.

HERMIONE. Explain yourself. I don't understand.

PRINCE. If we wanted to know for certain whether it was a man who was first fickle and faithless, as you claim, and me too, we would have had to be present at the beginning of the world and of society.

HERMIONE. Of course. But we weren't.

PRINCE. We are going to be. Yes, the men and the women of that time, the world and its first love-affairs are going to reappear before our eyes just as they were, or at least just as they must have been. Perhaps they won't be the same affairs, but the character will be the same. You're going to see hearts in the same state, souls as brand-new as the first ones – even newer, if that is possible. (*To* CARISA *and* MEZURU.) Carisa, and you, Mezuru, go now, and when it's time for us to withdraw, give the signal we agreed. (*To the retinue.*) And all of you, leave us.

Scene 2

HERMIONE. You arouse my curiosity, I must admit.

PRINCE. Here's how it is. About eighteen or nineteen years ago, the same matter came up for discussion at my father's Court. It was a matter of dispute for a long time, and very heated. My father was not of your opinion, but being drawn by nature to rational enquiry, he resolved to find out the truth of the matter by means of an experiment which would leave nothing to chance. Four babies, two of your sex and two of ours, were taken from their cradles into the forest where he had had this house built specially for them. Each one of them was accommodated separately, and each one even now occupies a plot of land beyond which they have never strayed. So they have never seen one another. They still know only Mezuru and his sister, who have brought them up and always had charge of them, and who were chosen for the colour of their skin,[1] so that their charges would be surprised when they saw other human beings. So for the first time we're going to let them loose, allow them to leave their enclosures and get to know one another. They have been taught the language we speak, and we may think of the dealings they will have together as the first days of the world. The world's first love-affairs are about to start all over again, and we shall see what will happen with them. (*Here, a sound of trumpets is heard.*) But hurry, let's withdraw, I hear the signal which warns us our young people are about to appear. Here's a gallery which runs all the way round the building. We can see and hear them from it, no matter which way they come out. Shall we go?

They exit. Enter CARISA *and* EGLEA.

Scene 3

CARISA. Come on. Eglea, follow me. Here are new lands you have never seen, where you can wander in safety.

---

[1] Carisa and Mezuru are black.

EGLEA. What's this I see? So many new worlds!

CARISA. It's still the same one, but you haven't seen it all.

EGLEA. So much land, so many dwellings! In such a great space I feel as if I am nothing at all. It pleases me and frightens me. (*She stops at a stream and looks at herself.*) What is this water I can see running across the ground? I have seen nothing like that in the world I come from.

CARISA. You are right. It's what they call a stream.

EGLEA (*looking*). Oh! Carisa, come here, come and look! There's something living in the stream! It's made like a person. She seems as surprised by me as I am by her.

CARISA (*laughing*). No, no, it's yourself you can see. All streams have that effect.

EGLEA. What! Is that me, is that my face?

CARISA. It certainly is.

EGLEA. But do you realise it's beautiful, it's delightful to look at? What a shame I didn't know earlier.

CARISA. You are beautiful, it's true.

EGLEA. What do you mean, 'beautiful'? Wonderful! This is a delightful discovery. (*She looks at herself again.*) The stream copies all my expressions, and I like all of them. You and Mezuru must really enjoy looking at me. I could spend my entire life looking at myself like this. How I am going to love myself now!

CARISA. Walk around as much as you wish. I must just leave you, and go back into our home. I have something to do there.

EGLEA. Go on, that's all right, I shan't be bored with the stream.

Scene 4

EGLEA *is alone for a moment.* AZORO *appears, opposite her.*

EGLEA (*continuing, and feeling her face with her fingertips*). I am

not getting tired of myself. (*Then fearfully, seeing* AZORO.)
What's that? A person like me? Don't come any closer! (AZORO
stretches out his arms in admiration, and smiles.) The person is
laughing. She seems to be admiring me. (AZORO *takes a step*.)
Wait . . . She's looking at me very gently, though . . . Can you
speak?

AZORO. The pleasure of seeing you robbed me of speech at
first.

EGLEA. The person can hear me, and answers me. And so
pleasantly!

AZORO. I find you quite bewitching.

EGLEA. That's good.

AZORO. And enchanting.

EGLEA. I like you too.

AZORO. So why do you stop me from coming forward?

EGLEA. I'm not so keen on stopping you now.

AZORO. I'm going to come towards you, then.

EGLEA. I wish you would. (*He comes forward*.) Stop a little . . . I'm
quite overcome!

AZORO. I obey you, because I am yours.

EGLEA. She obeys me. Come right up to me then, so you can
be mine from near at hand. (*He comes*.) Oh! Here she is!
It's you! How well she is fashioned! Really, you are as beautiful as me.

AZORO. I'm dying with joy at being so close to you. I give myself to
you. I don't know what it is I'm feeling, I can't begin to say.

EGLEA. Oh, it's just the same with me!

AZORO. I'm happy and nervous at the same time.

EGLEA. I'm sighing.

AZORO. No matter how close I am to you, I still can't see you
enough.

EGLEA. That's what I'm thinking too. But we can't see more of
one another, because we're already here.

AZORO. My heart desires your hands.

EGLEA. Here, mine gives them to you. Are you happier now?

AZORO. Yes, but no calmer.

EGLEA. That's how it is with me too. We are alike in everything.

AZORO. Oh, but what a difference! Everything I am is nothing compared with your eyes. They are so gentle!

EGLEA. And yours are so lively!

AZORO. You're so dainty and delicate!

EGLEA. Yes, but I assure you it suits you very well not to be as much so as I am. I wouldn't want you to be other than you are. It's a different kind of perfection. I don't deny mine, please keep yours for me.

AZORO. I shan't change it, I shall always have it.

EGLEA. Oh! Tell me, where were you when I didn't know you?

AZORO. In my own world, where I shall never return, since you are not part of it, and I want to have your hands for ever. My mouth and I cannot do without them.

EGLEA. Nor can my hands do without your mouth. But I can hear noises. It's somebody from my world. Hide behind the trees in case you frighten them. I'll call you back.

AZORO. Oh, but I'll lose sight of you.

EGLEA. No, all you have to do is look in this flowing water. My face is there, you'll see it.

Exit AZORO. *Enter* MEZURU *and* CARISA.

Scene 5

EGLEA (*sighing*). Oh, I'm missing her already.

CARISA. Eglea, you seem to be worried. What's the matter?

MEZURU (*aside*). Her eyes are even more expressive than usual.

EGLEA. It's because I have great news. You think there are only three of us. Well, I can tell you there are four. I have just taken

possession of something which was holding my hand just
now.

CARISA. Holding your hand, Eglea! Why didn't you call for
help?

EGLEA. Help against what? Against the pleasure it gave me? I am
very happy for it to hold my hand. It held it with my
permission, and it kissed it as much as it could. And it will kiss it
again for my pleasure and its own as soon as I call it back.

MEZURU. I know who it is. In fact, I think I caught a glimpse of
him going away. This 'something' is called a man, it's Azoro.
We know him.

EGLEA. It's Azoro? What a pretty name! Dear Azoro! Dear Man!
He's going to come back.

CARISA. I'm not surprised that he loves you and you love him.
You have been made for one another.

EGLEA. That's exactly what we realised for ourselves. (*She calls
him.*) Azoro! My man, my Azoro! Come here, quickly!

Scene 6

AZORO. Oh, it's Carisa and Mezuru, they're my friends.

EGLEA (*gaily*). They've told me. You have been made specially
for me, and me specially for you. They've just told me that.
That's why we love each other so much. I am your Eglea,
you my Azoro.

MEZURU. One is the man, and the other the woman.

AZORO. My Eglea, my joy, my delight, and my woman.

EGLEA. Here, take my hand. Console yourself for having had to
hide. (*To* MEZURU *and* CARISA.) Look, this is what he was
doing just now. Did I need to call for help?

CARISA. My dear children, I've already told you, you are pre-
ordained by nature to be delighted by each other.

EGLEA (*holding him by the hand*). Nothing could be clearer.

CARISA. But there's one thing to watch if you want to love each other for ever.

EGLEA. Yes, I understand. We must always be together.

CARISA. On the contrary. From time to time you must deprive yourself of the pleasure of seeing each other.

EGLEA (*astonished*). Pardon?

AZORO (*astonished*). What?

CARISA. Yes, I tell you. Otherwise, your pleasure will diminish and you will become indifferent to it.

EGLEA (*laughing*). Indifferent? Indifferent, my Azoro! Ha, ha, ha ... What a funny idea!

AZORO (*laughing*). She doesn't know what she's talking about!

MEZURU. Don't laugh, it's good advice she's giving you. The only way Carisa and I go on loving each other is by practising what she just said and separating from time to time.

EGLEA. Well, yes, I can believe it. That might be useful for you two – you're both so black, and you must have run away from one another in terror the first time you saw each other.

AZORO. The very most you were able to do was to put up with each other.

EGLEA. And you would soon be sick of the sight of each other if you never separated, because you have nothing beautiful to show each other. For instance, I love you, but when I don't see you I can do without you. I don't need to have you there. And why? Because you don't delight me, whereas we do delight each other, Azoro and me. He is so handsome, and I am so wonderfully attractive that we are in raptures when we look at one another.

AZORO (*taking* EGLEA's *hand*). Just Eglea's hand, see, just her hand, I'm suffering when I'm not holding it. And when I am holding it, I'm dying if I'm not kissing it. And when I've kissed it, I'm still dying.

EGLEA. The man is right. Everything he's just said, I feel too. That's where we are. You speak of our pleasure, but you don't know what it is. Even we don't understand it, and we're the ones who feel it. It's infinite.

MEZURU. We're only suggesting that you separate for two or three hours a day.

EGLEA. Not for a minute.

MEZURU. That's too bad.

EGLEA. You're annoying me, Mezuru. Are we going to become ugly by seeing each other? Shall we stop being delightful?

MEZURU. No, but you will stop feeling that you are.

EGLEA. And what's going to stop us feeling it since we are?

AZORO. Eglea will always be Eglea.

EGLEA. And Azoro always Azoro.

MEZURU. I agree, but who knows what might happen? For instance, suppose that I became as handsome as Azoro, and Carisa as beautiful as Eglea?

EGLEA. What difference would that make to us?

CARISA. You might be glutted with seeing each other, and you might be tempted to abandon one another and fall in love with us.

EGLEA. Why would we be tempted? Do you abandon someone you love? What kind of reasoning is that? Azoro and I love each other, and that's all there is to it. Become as handsome and beautiful as you like, what does it matter to us? It will be your business. Ours is already fixed.

AZORO. They'll never understand. You need to be us to know what it's all about.

MEZURU. As you wish.

AZORO. My love is my life.

EGLEA. Do you hear what he says? His life. How could he leave me? He must live, and me too.

AZORO. Yes. My life. How is it possible for anyone to be so beautiful, to have such beautiful looks, such a beautiful mouth, and everything so beautiful?

EGLEA. I do so like him admiring me.

MEZURU. He certainly does adore you.

AZORO. Ah, that's well said – I adore her. Mezuru understands me, I adore you.

EGLEA (*sighing*). Well, adore me then, but give me time to breathe. Ah!

CARISA. What tenderness! I'm quite bewitched by it myself. But there's only one way of keeping it, and that's to believe us. And if you are wise enough to make up your mind to do so, here, Eglea, give this to Azoro. It will help him to bear your absence.

EGLEA (*taking a portrait which* CARISA *gives her*). What's this? I recognise myself. It's me again, and much better than in the water of the stream. It's got all my beauty, and it's me exactly. How delightful to find yourself everywhere! Look, Azoro, look at me and all my beauty.

AZORO. Oh, it's Eglea, it's my own dear woman. There she is, except that the real one is even more beautiful. (*He kisses the portrait.*)

MEZURU. Well, at least it's an image of her.

AZORO. Yes, it makes you long for her. (*He kisses it again.*)

EGLEA. There's only one thing wrong. When he kisses it, my likeness gets it all.

AZORO (*taking her hand and kissing it*). Let's remedy that.

EGLEA. Oh, I say, I want one too, so I can enjoy myself.

MEZURU. Choose between his portrait and yours.

EGLEA. I'm going to keep both of them.

MEZURU. Oh, you must choose, please. I'd rather like to keep one of them.

EGLEA. Well, in that case, I don't need your help to have Azoro, because I already have his portrait in my mind. So give me mine, and then I shall have both.

CARISA. Here it is in a different form. It's called a mirror. You just have to press it here to open it. Goodbye. We'll come back and look for you in a little while. But I beg you to think about short periods of separation.

Scene 7

EGLEA (*trying to open the case*). Let's see. Oh, I've no idea how to open it. Azoro, you have a try. She said to press there.

AZORO (*opens it and looks at himself*). Right! It's only me, I think. It's my face, the one the stream near here showed me.

EGLEA. Oh, let me see, let me see! No, dearest man, it's not you at all. It's more than ever me. It's really and truly Eglea. Here, come here.

AZORO. Oh yes, it is you! No, wait – it's both of us, it's half one and half the other. I would prefer it to be just you, because I'm preventing myself from seeing you fully and completely.

EGLEA. Ah, but I'm quite happy to be able to see a bit of you as well. You don't spoil it at all. Come forward a little. Hold it there!

AZORO. Our faces are going to touch. Now they're touching! How lucky for mine, how delightful!

EGLEA. I can smell you, and it feels good.

AZORO. What if our mouths got closer?

He steals a kiss from her.

EGLEA (*turning*). Oh, now you've disturbed us – I can only see me. What a wonderful thing is a mirror!

AZORO (*taking the portrait from* EGLEA). Oh, a portrait is an equally wonderful thing! (*He kisses it.*)

EGLEA. Carisa and Mezuru are good kind people, though.

AZORO. They only want the best for us. I was going to talk to you about them, and the advice they gave us.

EGLEA. About these little separations, you mean? I was thinking about it too.

AZORO. Yes, my Eglea, I am a little bit frightened by their warnings. I'm not afraid of anything on my own account, but please don't get bored with me, I should be absolutely desperate.

EGLEA. Watch out for yourself. Don't grow tired of adoring me. To tell the truth, beautiful as I am, your fear makes me afraid too.

AZORO. Well that's amazing! You've no need to be afraid. What are you thinking of?

EGLEA. All right, come on then. All things considered, I've made up my mind. Let's give ourselves some pain, let's separate for two hours. I love your heart and your adoration more than your presence, and yet that's very dear to me.

AZORO. What! Go away from one another!

EGLEA. Oh, I shan't want to in a minute if you don't do it now!

AZORO. Alas, my courage fails me!

EGLEA. That's too bad, I must tell you that mine is nearly at an end.

AZORO (weeping). Goodbye, Eglea, since we must.

EGLEA. Are you crying? Well, stay then, so long as there is no danger.

AZORO. But what if there were!

EGLEA. Well, go then!

AZORO. I'm going.

Scene 8

EGLEA (alone). Oh, he's gone! I'm alone, I can't hear his voice any more, there's only the mirror left. (*She looks at herself in it.*) I was wrong to send my man away. Carisa and Mezuru don't know what they're saying. (*Looking at herself.*) If I had had a better look at myself, Azoro would not have gone. To love for ever what I am looking at, he had no need of absence. I'm going to sit by the stream – it's an extra mirror. But what's this I see? Yet another person!

Scene 9

ADINIA. Oh, what's this new creature? (*She comes forward.*)

EGLEA. She's looking at me carefully, but not admiring me. It isn't another Azoro. (*She looks at herself in the mirror.*) Still less is it another Eglea . . . But I think she's comparing herself with me.

ADINIA. I don't know what to think about the way this creature looks. I don't know what's missing from it. There's something insipid about it.

EGLEA. I don't like the look of her sort.

ADINIA. Does she have any language? Let's see . . . Are you a person?

EGLEA. Yes, certainly, and very much a person.

ADINIA. Well, have you nothing to say to me?

EGLEA. No. People usually forestall me by speaking to me first.

ADINIA. But don't you find me enchanting?

EGLEA. You? I'm the one who enchants people.

ADINIA. What! You aren't really delighted to see me?

EGLEA. Sorry, I'm neither delighted nor upset. What does it matter to me?

ADINIA. Well, that's very peculiar! You look at me, I show myself, and you don't feel anything! You must be looking somewhere else. Have a good look at me. Now, what do you think of me?

EGLEA. But what's all this about you? Is it you that matters? I tell you, it's me that people see first, me they tell what they're thinking. That's the way things are done. And you want me to admire you when I'm around!

ADINIA. Of course I do. The most beautiful woman must expect to be noticed and admired.

EGLEA. Well, admire then!

ADINIA. Don't you know what I'm saying? It's the most beautiful woman who must expect it.

EGLEA. And I tell you she is expecting it.

ADINIA. But where is she, if it isn't me? I am the object of admiration for three persons living in the world.

EGLEA. I don't know your persons, but I know there are three that I enchant, and they regard me with wonder.

ADINIA. And I know that I am so beautiful, so beautiful, that I bewitch myself every time I look at myself. You see how it is.

EGLEA. What are you saying? I who am talking to you cannot look at myself without swooning with delight.

ADINIA. Swooning with delight! It's true you're not bad, and even quite nice. I do you justice, I'm not like you.

EGLEA (*aside*). I could cheerfully beat her with her justice.

ADINIA. But to believe you can compete with me, it's a joke! You only have to look.

EGLEA. But it's precisely by looking that I find you rather ugly.

ADINIA. All right! So you feel envious of me, and prevent yourself from finding me beautiful.

EGLEA. It's only your face that prevents me.

ADINIA. My face! Oh, that doesn't worry me, I've seen it. Go and ask the flowing waters of the stream, go and ask Mezirion who adores me.

EGLEA. The waters of the stream care nothing for you – they will tell me there is nothing as beautiful as me, and they have already told me so. I don't know what kind of thing a Mezirion is, but he wouldn't look at you if he saw me. I have an Azoro who is worth more than him, an Azoro I love. He is nearly as wonderful as me, and says I am his life. You aren't anybody's life. I also have a mirror, and it finally confirms all that Azoro and the stream have told me. What stronger proof could anyone want?

ADINIA (*laughing*). A mirror! You have a mirror too! But what use is it to you? For looking at yourself? Ha, ha, ha!

EGLEA. Ha, ha, ha! Didn't I just know that I wouldn't like her?

ADINIA (*laughing*). Look, here's a better one. Come and get to know yourself in it. That'll shut you up.

CARISA appears in the distance.

EGLEA (*ironically*). Cast your eyes on this if you want to know your own mediocrity, and the modesty which is fitting when you're with me.

ADINIA. Please go away. Since you refuse to take any pleasure in looking at me, you're no use to me, and I'm not going to speak to you any more.

They stop looking at each other.

EGLEA. Well, I don't know you're there.

They move away from one another.

ADINIA (*aside*). She's crazy!

EGLEA (*aside*). She's out of her mind! Whatever planet is she from?

Enter CARISA.

Scene 10

CARISA. What are you doing, the two of you, so far apart and not speaking to one another?

ADINIA (*laughing*). It's a new person I've met, and she's in despair because I'm so beautiful.

EGLEA. What do you think of this vapid creature, this rather ridiculous person who thinks I should find her amazing? She asks me what I feel when I see her, she expects me to be overcome with pleasure when I look at her. She says, 'I say, have a good look at me!' I say, 'What do you think of me?' and she claims to be as beautiful as me.

ADINIA. I don't say that, I say more beautiful, as may be seen by looking in the mirror.

EGLEA (*showing hers*). But let her see herself in this one then, if she dares!

ADINIA. I only ask her to have a quick glance in mine, because that's the real one.

CARISA. Take it easy, both of you, don't lose your temper. Instead, take advantage of this chance meeting, and let's all get together. You could become friends, and combine the pleasure of seeing one another with the delight of being adored, Eglea by the charming Azoro whom she treasures dearly, and Adinia by the charming Mezirion whom she loves. Come on, kiss and make up.

EGLEA. Well, let her get rid of her notion of beauty that I find so boring.

ADINIA. Look, I know how to make her see reason. All I have to do is take her precious Azoro off her. I don't care about him, but at least it would be a way of getting some peace.

EGLEA (*angry and upset*). Where is her idiotic Mezirion? Woe to her if I meet him! Goodbye, I'm going away, I can't stand her.

ADINIA. Ha, ha, ha! . . . Her loathing is a measure of my true worth.

EGLEA (*turning round*). Ha, ha, ha! What an ugly mug!

She exits.

Scene 11

CARISA. Never mind, just let her say what she likes.

ADINIA. Very well, all right. I feel sorry for her.

CARISA. Let's leave. It's time for your music lesson, and I shan't be able to give it to you if you don't hurry.

ADINIA. I'm coming, but I can see Mezirion. I just want to say
    something to him.
CARISA. You've only just left him.
ADINIA. I shan't be a moment.

Scene 12

ADINIA (*calling*). Mezirion!
MEZIRION (*running up*). What! It's you, my Adinia, you've come
    back! I'm so happy! I was missing you so much!
ADINIA. No, no, hold back your joy – I haven't come back, I'm just
    leaving. It's pure chance I'm still here.
MEZIRION. You should have been with me by pure chance,
    then.
ADINIA. Listen, listen to what's just happened to me.
CARISA. Get to the point, I've got other things to do.
ADINIA. I am doing. (*To* MEZIRION.) I am beautiful, aren't I?
MEZIRION. Beautiful? Are you beautiful?
ADINIA. *He* doesn't hesitate. He says what he sees.
MEZIRION. Are you divine? The very essence of beauty!
ADINIA. Yes, yes, I have no doubt about it. And yet we are
    mistaken, you, Carisa, and me. I am ugly.
MEZIRION. My Adinia!
ADINIA. Her very self. When I left you, I met a new person from
    another world. Now, instead of being amazed and sent into
    raptures by me, as you are and as she should have been, she on
    the contrary wanted me to be enchanted with her! And when I
    refused, she accused me of being ugly –
ADINIA. You're making me so angry!
ADINIA. – and maintained that you would leave me when you had
    seen her.
CARISA. She was upset.

MEZIRION. But . . . is she really a person?

ADINIA. She says so, and she seems to be one, more or less.

CARISA. She is one.

ADINIA. She'll be coming back, I expect, and I insist that you despise her. When you find her, I hope she frightens you.

ADINIA. She must be really horrible, then?

MEZIRION. She's called . . . wait a moment, she's called . . .

CARISA. Eglea.

ADINIA. Yes, she's an Eglea. Now this is what she's like. The face is cross and crabby. It isn't black like Carisa's face, or white like mine. It's difficult to put a name to the colour.

MEZIRION. But it's not very nice?

ADINIA. Oh, not at all, it's an indifferent sort of colour. Her eyes . . . how shall I say? Her eyes give no pleasure, they just look at you, that's all. Her mouth is for speaking, her figure is straight up and down, but it would be more or less like ours if it were well made. She's got hands that come and go, and long, skinny fingers, I think. Her voice is rough and strident. Oh, you'll easily recognise her.

MEZIRION. I feel as though I can see her. Leave it to me. She needs to be sent back to another world after I've well and truly humiliated her.

ADINIA. Well and truly crushed and mortified her.

MEZIRION. And well and truly mocked her. Oh, don't you worry about it! Give me your hand.

ADINIA. Oh, take it. It's for you that I have it.

MEZIRION *kisses her hand.*

CARISA (*taking the hand from him*). Come on, you've said it all. Let's go.

ADINIA. When he's finished kissing my hand.

CARISA. Come on, Mezirion leave go of it. I'm in a hurry.

ADINIA. Goodbye to all I love. I shall not be long. Remember my revenge.

MEZIRION. Goodbye, all my delight. I am in a fury!

Scene 13

MEZIRION (*alone for the first few words, repeating the description*).
A colour that's neither black nor white, a figure that's straight
up and down, a mouth for speaking . . . Where might I find her?
(*He sees* AZORO.) But I can see someone. It's a person like me.
Could it be Eglea? No, it isn't deformed.

AZORO (*looking at him*). You seem to be the same as me?

MEZIRION. That's what I was thinking.

AZORO. So are you a man?

MEZIRION. So I am told.

AZORO. I've been told that I am too.

MEZIRION. You've been told? Do you know some persons?

AZORO. Oh yes, I know all of them, two black ones and one
white.

MEZIRION. It's the same with me. Where do you come from?

AZORO. From the world.

MEZIRION. From the same one as me?

AZORO. Oh, I've no idea. There are so many.

MEZIRION. What does it matter? I like the look of you. Put your
hand in mine, we must love one another.

AZORO. Oh yes, you make me very happy. I like looking at you,
even though you aren't attractive.

MEZIRION. And neither are you. I don't care about you except
that you're nice and friendly.

AZORO. That's how it is. I find you the same, a good friend. Me,
another good friend. I don't care about your face.

MEZIRION. Oh, absolutely! It's your good nature that attracts
me. By the way, do you take your meals?

AZORO. Every day.

MEZIRION. Well, I take them too. Let's take them together to
entertain ourselves. That'll keep us lively! All right, that'll be
quite soon. We'll laugh and jump about, won't we? I'm already
jumping!

He jumps. AZORO *jumps too.*

AZORO. Me too, and there'll be two, maybe four of us, because I'll tell my little white one – she has a face, you've got to see it, oh, she's the one who has a face worth more than our two put together.

MEZIRION. Oh, I believe you, friend, because you're nothing at all to look at, and neither am I, alongside another creature I know that we'll put with us, one that sends me into raptures and has such soft white hands that she lets me kiss so much!

AZORO. Hands, friend? Well, hasn't my little white one got hands too? They're heavenly, and I stroke them as much as I want. I'm waiting for them.

MEZIRION. Lucky you! I've just left mine, and I have to leave you as well – I have a small matter to attend to. Stay here until I come back with my Adinia and let's jump about again to celebrate our happy meeting! (*They both jump and laugh.*) Ha, ha, ha!

Scene 14

EGLEA (*as she approaches*). What are you so pleased about?

MEZIRION (*seeing her*). Oh, what a beautiful creature listening to us!

AZORO. It's my little white one, it's Eglea.

MEZIRION (*aside*). Eglea – is that the crabby face?

AZORO. Oh, how happy I am!

EGLEA (*coming closer*). Is this a new friend who's just suddenly turned up?

AZORO. Yes, it's a friend I've made. He's called Man, and he comes from a nearby world.

MEZIRION. Oh, what pleasure there is in this one!

EGLEA. More than in yours?

MEZIRION. Oh, I should say so!

EGLEA. Well then, Man, all you have to do is stay here.

AZORO. That's what we were saying, because he's really kind and cheerful. I love him, not in the way I love my enchanting Eglea, whom I adore. With him I don't think about it – it's just his company I seek, to talk about you, about your mouth, your eyes, your hands that I've been longing for.

He kisses her hand.

MEZIRION (*taking her other hand*). I'm going to take the other one, then.

He kisses this hand. EGLEA *laughs and says nothing.*

AZORO (*takes this hand from him*). Oh, steady now! This isn't your little white one, it's mine. These two hands are mine, there is nothing for you here.

EGLEA. Oh, there's no harm in it. But by the way, you must go away, Azoro – you know very well that separation is necessary, and ours hasn't lasted long enough.

AZORO. What! It's hours and hours since I saw you!

EGLEA. You're mistaken. It isn't long enough, I tell you. I can count, and if I've made a resolution, I want to keep it.

AZORO. But you'll be left all alone.

EGLEA. Well, I shall make do with it.

MEZIRION. Don't upset her, friend.

AZORO. I think you're cross with me.

EGLEA. Why are you arguing with me? It only makes me more determined. Weren't you told that there was nothing so dangerous for us as seeing one another?

AZORO. It may not be the truth.

EGLEA. And I suspect it isn't a lie.

CARISA *appears in the distance and listens.*

AZORO. Then I shall leave to please you, but I shall soon be back. Come on, friend – you said you have a small matter to attend to.

Come with me, and help me to pass the time.

MEZIRION. Yes, but . . .

EGLEA (*smiling*). What?

MEZIRION. I've been walking a long time.

EGLEA. He must rest.

MEZIRION. And I would have prevented the beautiful woman from being bored.

EGLEA. Yes, he would prevent it.

AZORO. Didn't she say she wanted to be alone? Otherwise, I would relieve her boredom even better than you. Let's go!

MEZIRION (*aside, with great vexation*). Let's go!

Exit MEZIRION *and* AZORO.

Scene 15

CARISA (*comes up and looks at* EGLEA, *who is lost in thought*). What are you thinking about?

EGLEA. I'm thinking I'm not in a very good mood.

CARISA. Are you upset about something?

EGLEA. No, it's not that. It's more a sort of mental confusion.

CARISA. Where does it come from?

EGLEA. You were saying to us just now that you can never tell what might happen so far as love is concerned.

CARISA. It's true.

EGLEA. Well, I don't know what's happening to me.

CARISA. But what's the matter?

EGLEA. I feel as though I'm angry with myself, and angry with Azoro. I don't know who I've got it in for.

CARISA. Why angry with yourself?

EGLEA. Because I intend to love Azoro for ever, and I'm afraid of failing.

CARISA. Do you think you might?

EGLEA. Yes, I'm angry with Azoro, because his behaviour is at the root of it.

CARISA. I suspect you're trying to pick a quarrel with him.

EGLEA. Just carry on answering me like that, and I shall soon be angry with you as well.

CARISA. You really are in a bad mood. But what has Azoro done to you?

EGLEA. What has he done to me? We agree to separate, he goes away, he comes back at once, he wants to be there all the time. It'll end up with what you predicted happening to him.

CARISA. What? You'll stop loving him?

EGLEA. Probably. Is it my fault if the pleasure of seeing one another goes away when you enjoy it too often?

CARISA. You maintained that it couldn't happen.

EGLEA. Don't quibble with me – how was I to know? I maintained it out of ignorance.

CARISA. Eglea, it can't be his over-eagerness to see you that's harming him in your eyes. You haven't known him long enough for that.

EGLEA. Oh, quite a long time. We've already had three conversations together, and long discussions are apparently bad for us.

CARISA. You're still not saying what his real fault is.

EGLEA. Oh, he has another. Even two! I don't know how many he has. In the first place, he annoyed me. Because my hands are mine, I think they belong to me, and he forbids that anyone should kiss them!

CARISA. And who wanted to kiss them?

EGLEA. A friend he'd just discovered, called Man.

CARISA. And he is attractive, yes?

EGLEA. Oh, quite charming! Gentler than Azoro. He suggested staying with me to keep my company, but that crazy Azoro took it into his head to refuse him both my hand and my company. He gave him a good telling off, and dragged him away without stopping to ask me what my feelings were on the matter. So I'm not the mistress, eh? So he doesn't trust me, he's afraid of people loving me, is he?

CARISA. No, but he's afraid you might find his friend attractive.

EGLEA. Well, all he has to do is make himself more attractive to me. Because I'm quite happy to be loved, if that's what it's about, I can tell you, and if he had a hundred friends instead of one, I would like them all to love me. That's what gives me pleasure. He wants my beauty to be for him alone, and I say it should be for everybody.

CARISA. Listen, your aversion towards Azoro doesn't come from what you've just said. It comes from the fact that right now you love his friend more than him.

EGLEA. Do you think so? You could well be right.

CARISA. Tell me, don't you feel a little ashamed of being so fickle?

EGLEA. I think I do. What's happened to me makes me blush. I'm still ignorant in that way.

CARISA. It isn't ignorance. You had made so many promises to go on loving him!

EGLEA. But wait – when I made that promise, there was only him. He should have remained alone. The friend didn't enter into my calculations.

CARISA. Those are not very good reasons, you must admit. You had already refuted them in advance just a little while ago.

EGLEA. I don't think much of them either, to tell the truth. But there is one reason which is excellent – the friend is better than Azoro.

CARISA. You're still mistaken – it isn't that he's better, just that he has the advantage of being a newcomer.

EGLEA. But that's a considerable advantage. Isn't being different worth something? At any rate, it's very nice – he has attractions that Azoro doesn't have.

CARISA. Perhaps you're also thinking that this newcomer is going to love you.

EGLEA. Exactly. He will love me, I hope. He still has that quality.

CARISA. Whereas Azoro is not about to love you.

EGLEA. Well, no – he loves me already.

CARISA. What strange reasons for change! I'd like to bet you are not very happy with them.

EGLEA. I'm not at all happy. This change gives me pain on the one hand, and pleasure on the other. I can't prevent one any more than the other. Both are important, but to which do I owe the greater obligation? Must I give myself pain, or must I give myself pleasure? I challenge you to say.

CARISA. Listen to the goodness of your heart. You'll find it will condemn you for being fickle.

EGLEA. Are you not listening to what I'm saying? My heart condemns in its goodness and approves in its goodness. It says 'yes' and it says 'no'. It's in two minds, so all I can do is choose the most convenient.

CARISA. Do you know what you must do? You must run away from Azoro's friend. Come on, let's go. Then you won't have the trouble of fighting.

EGLEA (*seeing* MEZIRION *coming*). Yes, but we're running away rather late. Here comes the fight! The friend is here.

CARISA. Never mind, force yourself! Be brave, don't look at him!

Scene 16

MEZURU (*from the distance, trying to hold back* MEZIRION, *who breaks away*). He's escaping me, he wants to be unfaithful. Don't let him near.

CARISA (*to* MEZIRION). Don't come any closer.

MEZIRION. Why?

CARISA. Because I forbid it. We must have some authority over you, Mezuru and me; we are your masters.

MEZIRION (*rebelling*). My masters? What's a master?

CARISA. Well, I don't order you, then, I beg you. And the lovely Eglea begs you too.

EGLEA. Me? No, I don't. I'm not doing any begging.

CARISA (*aside to* EGLEA). Let's go in. You still aren't sure he loves you.

EGLEA. Oh, I'm not expecting the opposite. All we have to do is ask him about it. What do you want, pretty friend?

MEZIRION. To see you, to look at you, to admire you, and to call you 'my soul'!

EGLEA. You see, he's talking about his soul. Do you love me?

MEZIRION. Like a madman.

EGLEA. Didn't I say so?

MEZIRION. Do you love me too?

EGLEA. I would like to be able to do without if I could, because of Azoro who is counting on me.

MEZURU. Mezirion, follow Eglea's example – don't be unfaithful.

EGLEA. Mezirion! The man is called Mezirion!

MEZIRION. Yes!

EGLEA. The lover of Adinia?

MEZIRION. I used to be, but I don't need her portrait any more.

EGLEA (*takes it*). Her portrait, and the lover of Adinia! He has that quality as well! Oh, Carisa, here are too many attractions, there's no way of resisting. Mezirion, come here and let me love you.

MEZIRION. Oh, delicious hand that I possess!

EGLEA. Incomparable lover that I've won!

MEZURU. But why abandon Adinia? Have you cause for complaint with her?

MEZIRION. No, it's this beautiful face that wants me to leave her.

EGLEA. He has eyes in his head, that's all.

MEZIRION. Oh, I know I'm being unfaithful, but I don't know what to do about it.

EGLEA. Yes, I'm forcing him. We're both forcing one another.

CARISA. She and Azoro are going to be in despair.

MEZIRION. Too bad.

EGLEA. What solution is there?

CARISA. If you like, I know how to end their grief and their love at the same time.

MEZIRION. Well, do it then.

EGLEA. No, I should be quite happy for Azoro to miss me. My beauty deserves it. There's no harm either if Adinia has to sigh a little. I'll teach her to have too high an opinion of herself!

Scene 17

MEZURU. Here comes Azoro.

MEZIRION. I'm embarrassed by my friend. He's going to be very surprised.

CARISA. Judging by his face, I would say he's already guessed the wrong you've done him.

EGLEA. Yes, he's sad. He has plenty to be sad about. (AZORO *comes forward, ashamed. She continues.*) Are you very upset, Azoro?

AZORO. Yes, Eglea.

EGLEA. A lot?

AZORO. Yes, I really am.

EGLEA. It's obvious. Well, how do you know I love Mezirion?

AZORO (*surprised*). What?

MEZIRION. Yes, friend.

AZORO. Eglea loves you? She doesn't care about me any more?

EGLEA. That's right.

AZORO (*cheerfully*). Oh, that's good! Carry on. I don't care about you any more, either. Wait there, I'll be back.

EGLEA. Wait a minute, what are you trying to say? You don't love me any more? What does that mean?

AZORO (*as he goes off*). You'll find out the rest shortly.

Scene 18

MEZIRION. Hey, I say! You're calling him back! What for? What have you to do with him, since you love me?

EGLEA. Oh, leave me be! I shall love you all the more if I can have him back. It's just that I don't want to lose anything.

CARISA }
MEZURU } (*laughing*). Ha, ha, ha!

EGLEA. I can't see anything to laugh at.

Enter AZORO *and* ADINIA.

Scene 19   .

ADINIA (*laughing*). Well hello, it's the lovely Eglea! You must apply to me if you want to see yourself. I've got your portrait. It's been handed over to me.

EGLEA (*throwing hers at her*). Here, you can have yours back. It isn't worth keeping.

ADINIA. What, Mezirion? My portrait! And how does she come to have it?

MEZIRION. I gave it to her.

EGLEA. Come here, Azoro, and let me speak to you.

MEZIRION. Speak to him? What about me?

ADINIA. Mezirion, come over here. What are you doing there? You must be raving!

Final Scene

HERMIONE (*comes bursting in*). No, Prince, leave me alone, I don't want to see any more. I find this Adinia and this Eglea quite unbearable. Fate must have chosen the most hateful members ever of our sex.

EGLEA. Who are all these creatures who've just arrived? They look very angry. I'm off.

They try to leave.

CARISA. Stay, all of you, don't be afraid. Here come some new friends. Don't frighten them, and let's see what they think.

MEZILIUS (*stopping in the middle of the stage*). Oh, dearest Deena, what a lot of people!

DEENA. Yes, but we have nothing to do with them.

MEZILIUS. You're probably right – there isn't a single one like you. Oh, it's you, Carisa, and Mezuru. Are all these men or women?

CARISA. There are as many women as there are men. These are the women, and these are the men. But, Mezilius, have a look at the women, and see if there isn't one you might like even better than Deena. We'll give her to you.

EGLEA. I would like his love.

MEZILIUS. Don't like it, because you won't get it.

CARISA. Choose another.

MEZILIUS. Thank you very much, I don't dislike them, but I don't care about them, there's only one Deena in the world.

DEENA (*putting her arm over his*). Oh, that's well said!

CARISA. And you, Deena, you have a look at them.

DEENA (*taking him under the arm*). I've seen them all. Let's go.

HERMIONE. What a delightful child! I will take care of her.

PRINCE. And I will take care of Mezilius.

DEENA. We have enough with the two of us.

PRINCE. We shall not separate you. Now, Carisa, see that they are kept to one side, and that the others are placed according to my orders. (*To* HERMIONE.) The two sexes have nothing to reproach one another with, madame. Vices and virtues are equally shared between them.

HERMIONE. Oh, please see some difference! Your sex is horribly treacherous – it changes for no reason at all, and without even looking for an excuse.

PRINCE. I must admit, yours at least goes about things in a more hypocritical way, and therefore more respectably. It makes more of a fuss with its conscience than ours does.

HERMIONE. We have no grounds for joking, believe me. Shall we go?

The Constant Players

Translated by Donald Watson

from LES ACTEURS DE BONNE FOI
Published in 1757

CHARACTERS

MADAME ARGANTE, *Angélique's mother*

MADAME AMELIN, *Eraste's aunt*

ARAMINTE, *a friend of both ladies*

ERASTE, *Mme Amelin's nephew in love with Angélique*

ANGÉLIQUE, *Mme Argante's daughter*

MERLIN, *Eraste's valet de chambre*

LISETTE, *lady's maid to Angélique*

BLAISE, *the son of Mme Argante's farmer, in love with Colette*

COLETTE, *the gardener's daughter*

A VILLAGE NOTARY

The scene is set in a country house belonging to Madame Argante.

Scene 1

MERLIN. Yes, monsieur. All will be ready. You have but to set the hall in good order. After noon today, at three o'clock, I promise to stage a comedy for you.

ERASTE. You will greatly please Madame Amelin, who awaits it with impatience. And for my part I rejoice to procure her this little diversion. I truly owe her a courtesy or two. You know what she does for me. I am merely her nephew, yet she makes her entire fortune over to me, in order to marry me to Angélique, the girl I love. Were I her son, could she treat me with more consideration?

MERLIN. It must indeed be said, sir, that she is the kindest aunt in the world. You are right. You could hardly derive greater benefit, had she been your own mother.

ERASTE. But tell me, will this comedy which you present for our enjoyment keep us amused? You are no dullard, but have you wit enough to produce a piece that passes muster?

MERLIN. Passes muster? No, monsieur. That is not within my range. Men of my genius ignore the mediocre. Whatever they do is either delightful or detestable. Either I excel or I fail. Never the unhappy medium.

ERASTE. I tremble for your genius.

MERLIN. Are you afraid I may fail? Take heart. Did you ever buy the *Songbook of the Pont-Neuf*? All the songs you find pleasing there will be mine. Half-a-dozen in particular, anacreontic in style, are in such good taste . . .

ERASTE. Anacreontic! Oh, since you are familiar with that word, you are skilful enough and I shall doubt you no more. But take care lest Madame Argante comes to hear of our plan. Madame Amelin wishes to surprise her.

MERLIN. Lisette, who is one of us, is sure to have kept our secret. Mademoiselle Angélique, your intended, is bound to have held her peace. You in turn have said nothing. And I have been discreet. My players have been paid to keep quiet. So we shall be a surprise, monsieur. We shall surprise her.

ERASTE. And who are your actors?

MERLIN. To start with, myself. I name myself first, to inspire you with confidence. Then there is Lisette, lady's maid to Mademoiselle Angélique, an exceptional soubrette. Colette, the gardener's daughter, and her lover, Blaise, the son of Madame Argante's farmer.

ERASTE. That shows promise of merriment.

MERLIN. And 'tis a promise will be kept. I have studied everything. If you knew what a stroke of artistry is contained in my piece!

ERASTE. What's that, then, tell me?

MERLIN. We shall play it impromptu, sir, impromptu.

ERASTE. How mean you, impromptu?

MERLIN. Ay! All I have furnished is a summary of the action. What we *beaux esprits* term a 'scenario'. Nature alone will provide the dialogue. And nature in this case will be in humorous vein.

ERASTE. A singular sort of comedy! Methinks it should divert us.

MERLIN. You shall see, you shall see! But there is one subtlety in my piece I have forgotten to speak of. 'Tis Colette who shall be in love with me and I am to play her lover. We are both agreed to observe the manner in which Blaise and Lisette respond to all the naive expressions of love we shall affect for one another. And all this to discover if it alarms them and makes them jealous. For, as you know, Blaise is betrothed to Colette, whereas Lisette and I have promised love to each other. But Lisette, Blaise and Colette are about to come and try out their scenes. They are my leading actors. And I wish to know how they will comport themselves. Leave me to hear them out and instruct them on my own. Here they come now.

ERASTE. I withdraw, then. Adieu. Give us cause to laugh. We ask no more of you.

Scene 2

MERLIN. Come, children, I've been waiting for you. Give me a taste of your talents. And let us try to earn our payment as best we can. Let us start the rehearsal.

LISETTE. What pleases me in your comedy is that we pretend to one another. For I believe we shall hold the prettiest discourse.

MERLIN. Very pretty, I'm sure. For in the way my piece is planned, you none of you play false to your own nature. You, Lisette, are an artful soubrette always hard to deceive, and that fits you like a glove. Blaise looks like a nincompoop caught napping, and that's his role. A country coquette and Colette, they're no different. A handsome brute and myself, they're one and the same. All fine-looking men are inconstant. There's no such thing as a faithful coquette. Colette always betrays Blaise and I care little for your passion. Blaise is a tearful buffoon and you are a furious scold. And there lies the matter of my play. Oh, I'd challenge anyone to order things more choicely.

BLAISE. Ay! But what if what we plays should turn out true? Be on your guard, at least! We mustn't 'ave nothing for real. 'Cos, Lord knows, I truly love Colette.

MERLIN. Perfect, Blaise! You sound like a blockhead. Exactly what I want from you in this play.

LISETTE. Now listen to me, Master Handsome Brute! He is right. This had best go no further than a jest. 'Tis not in me to be long-suffering, I warn you!

MERLIN. Splendid, Lisette! Keep it up! That's the bitter-sweet note you have to strike.

COLETTE. Come, come, Miss Lisette! You 'ave nothing to fear. You're more prettier than me, like Mr Merlin knows.

MERLIN. Bravo, saucebox! There you have it! 'Tis the very manner you must play your role. Come, let's improvise our parts.

LISETTE. You and I are to begin, I think.

MERLIN. Yes, the first scene is ours. Sit over there, you others, and we'll start. You know what happens, Lisette. (COLETTE *and* BLAISE *sit down as spectators to watch a scene in which they play no part.*) You come on stage and I am discovered there. Pensive, abstracted. Draw back a little and allow me to compose myself.

Scene 3

LISETTE (*feigning her entry on stage*). What's the matter, Mr Merlin? You look thoughtful.

MERLIN. I am out for a walk.

LISETTE. And when you are walking, is it your custom to turn aside from those who approach you?

MERLIN. When I walk, I am inattentive.

LISETTE. What sort of reply is that? I call it impertinent.

MERLIN (*interrupting the scene*). Gently, Lisette. If at the start of the scene you abuse me, how will you end it?

LISETTE. Oh, expect no consistency from me! I speak as it comes. Let's proceed.

MERLIN. Where were we?

LISETTE. I said you were impertinent.

MERLIN. Well, you *are* out of humour. Let us go our separate ways and speak no more.

LISETTE. Mr Merlin, do you wait here for Colette?

MERLIN. There's a question that portends a quarrel.

LISETTE. You think you know where you stand, but you are not there yet.

MERLIN. It's enough for me to know where I'm standing right now.

LISETTE. I know you've been avoiding me. These last few days I bore you.

MERLIN. You know so much, there is nothing one can teach you.

LISETTE. What's this, you rascal? You don't even trouble to defend yourself? To refute what I've just said?

MERLIN. I never contradict a woman.

LISETTE. Come hither! Speak! Confess that Colette pleases you.

MERLIN. Why should she displease me?

LISETTE. Confess you love her.

MERLIN. I never confide in a woman.

LISETTE. Faugh! I need no confession from you.

MERLIN. So don't ask for one!

LISETTE. To leave me for a minx from the village!

MERLIN. I'm not leaving you! I'm standing stock still.

COLETTE (*interrupting from her seat*). Nay, but this bain't fair play, abusin' me be'ind me back!

MERLIN. Indeed, 'tis not! But can't you see this is a jealous girl who scorns you?

COLETTE. Ay, that I can! So when I says my piece, I'll turn the tables on s'er.

LISETTE. And now I don't know where I am.

MERLIN. Taking me to task.

LISETTE. Oh yes! But tell me: in this scene is it allowed I slap you?

MERLIN. As you're no better than a lady's maid, a blow should not come amiss.

LISETTE. Let us go on, then, so I deliver it.

MERLIN. No, no! Till the performance, let us withhold the blow. We'll make as though it were done already. A gratuitous slap would serve no purpose now.

LISETTE. I am so chagrined, methinks I could shed tears too.

MERLIN. No doubt you could. Don't contain yourself. My merit and your vanity require it.

LISETTE (*breaking into laughter*). I laugh to think how your merit merits it. (*Pretending to cry.*) What a wretch I am, to have fallen

for this rogue's blandishments! Farewell! Here's little Miss
Impudence approaching. You leave her to me. (*She interrupts
herself.*) Couldn't I give her a slap or two?

COLETTE (*who has jumped to her feet*). No, please, not that! I
don't want no beatings in it. I won't be slapped on account of no
farce! Though, if 'twere for real, I'd know 'ow to endure it.

LISETTE. Hark to the sly hussy!

MERLIN. Let us stop wasting time, interrupting one another. Go
off, Lisette. Here comes Colette, who enters while you're
leaving, so you have no place here now. Come, let's proceed.
Move back a few steps, Colette, so I can come to meet you.

Scene 4

MERLIN. Good morning, my beauty. I vow 'tis not I you are
seeking.

COLETTE. No, Mr Merlin. But that's no matter. I'm fair pleased
to find you 'ere.

MERLIN. And I am charmed to meet you, Colette.

COLETTE. Most obliging, I'm sure.

MERLIN. Have you never remarked how pleased I always am to
see you?

COLETTE. Ay, but I daren't 'ardly dare remark it. 'Cos it'd make
me feel likewise.

MERLIN (*interrupting*). Careful, Colette. 'Tis not decent you
should declare yourself so soon.

COLETTE. Faith, in this affair, since I'm meant to feel fondly for
you, I thought there weren't time to waste.

MERLIN. Wait till *I* make a firm declaration first.

BLAISE (*interrupting from his seat*). Now you see 'ow 'asty she be!
Anybody 'ould say she's in earnest. I think it do' bode no good
for me!

LISETTE (*seated and interrupting*). That sally doesn't please me much, either.

MERLIN. 'Tis because she knows no better.

COLETTE. Well now I'm all at sixes and sevens. With them beratin' me, I'm too shy to go on no more. 'Less they go away.

MERLIN. Move further off, then. To encourage her.

BLAISE (*rising from his seat*). No, by the Lawd, I don' wan' 'er 'avin' no more courage! I wan' to 'ear all they says.

LISETTE (*seated and interrupting*). 'Tis true, dear girl, it's most strange of you to expect us to go away.

COLETTE. Why are you pickin' on me too?

BLAISE (*interrupting, but seated*). And why are you itchin' so to be fancyin' Mr Merlin? Is it love you're feelin'?

COLETTE. 'Pon my word! Bain't I obliged to feel it truly, since I'm obliged to play it in the play? 'Ow do you think I can do it contrariwise?

LISETTE (*seated, interrupting*). What's this? You are truly in love with Mr Merlin!

COLETTE. 'Tis my duty! Me labour of love!

MERLIN (*to* LISETTE). You and Blaise are a fine pair of innocents. Can't you see how her words confound her? 'Tis not that she loves me truly. All she signifies is that she must show that she does. Is that not right, Colette?

COLETTE. As you please, Mr Merlin.

MERLIN. Let's continue then. So wait till I make my declaration before you show how you respond to my love.

COLETTE. I'll wait, Mr Merlin. But be quick about it.

MERLIN (*taking up the scene again*). How lovable you are, Colette! And how I envy Blaise, whose good fortune it will be to wed you!

COLETTE. Oh, Lord-a-mercy! Can it be you love me, Mr Merlin?

MERLIN. These seven days or more I've been seeking the moment to tell you.

COLETTE. The pity of it! 'Cos we would suit very well together.

MERLIN. Why is that, Colette?

COLETTE. 'Cos, if you do love me . . . nay . . . shall I say it?

MERLIN. You must!

COLETTE. 'Cos if you do love me, that's good. There bain't no 'arm in it.

MERLIN. Why, dear Colette, does your heart whisper words in my favour?

COLETTE. Oh, it don't just whisper, it speaks out plain.

MERLIN. You lovely child, how you enchant me! Grant me that dainty hand of yours, that I may thank you.

LISETTE (*interrupting*). I'll not have hands!

COLETTE. But *I* can't 'elp 'aving 'em!

LISETTE. That is as may be. But there is no cause to kiss them.

MERLIN. Between lovers, the hands of one's mistress are ever part of the discourse.

BLAISE. Don' you permit it, Miss Lisette!

MERLIN. Don't alarm yourselves. We'll simply cut that part out.

COLETTE. They're only 'ands, for all that.

MERLIN. I shall be content to hold her hand in mine.

BLAISE. No 'and-'olding neither. Eh, Miss Lisette?

LISETTE. That would be for the best.

MERLIN. Then too little will happen to bring this scene alive.

COLETTE. I agrees with you, Mr Merlin. I bain't got nothing 'gainst 'ands.

MERLIN. Since they're not welcome, it seems, we shall leave them out. Let's resume. (*He picks the scene up again.*) So you do love me, Colette? Yet you will marry with Blaise?

COLETTE. That don' please me much neither. 'Cos it's not me that's takin' 'im. It's me father and mother what's chose 'im.

BLAISE (*interrupting, in tears*). That don' spell no good for me!

MERLIN. Peace! Be still! It's all part of the scene, as you know.

BLAISE. I'm willin' to wager 'tis true.

MERLIN. 'Tis not true, I tell you. Either we abandon our project or we hold to it. Madame Amelin has promised a reward. 'Tis

well worth our pains to earn it. I regret this particular plan
I thought up, but I've no time to imagine another. So let us
pursue it.

COLETTE. 'Tis a fine idea, methinks.

LISETTE. I shall not *say* what I think, but I'll think it all the more.
However, we had best proceed. No need to put our earnings
at risk!

MERLIN (*taking the scene up again*). So, Colette, you care naught
for Blaise, as 'tis your parents who wish you to wed him.

COLETTE. Nay, I can't abide 'im. And if I could contrive some
way not to 'ave 'im for my man, I'd as soon be rid of 'im. 'Cos 'e's
a foolish fellow.

BLAISE (*interrupting, seated*). S'Death! What a scurvy comedy
is this!

MERLIN (*to* BLAISE). Hold your peace! (*To* COLETTE:) You have
but to tell your parents that you don't love him.

COLETTE. Right! But ain't I tole 'im myself to 'is face? And still
that don' change nothing.

BLAISE (*standing to interrupt*). And that's the truth, it is! She did
tell me!

COLETTE (*continuing*). But, Mr Merlin, if you asked me for me
'and in marriage, it may be you could 'ave me? Would it worry
you to 'ave me for wife?

MERLIN. I should be enchanted. But we'll have to handle the
matter with guile. On account of Lisette, who in her jealous
spite might injure us and spoil our enterprise.

COLETTE. If she weren't present 'ere, I'd find out a way to do it.
But we shouldn't 'ave left 'er 'ere to eavesdrop on us.

LISETTE (*rising to interrupt*). What in Heaven's name does that
signify? That's a speech, to be sure, which has no place in the
performance of your scene. For when you're playing it, I shall
not be here.

MERLIN. 'Tis true you will not be here. But now, seeing you in
front of her, and misunderstanding, she takes her cue from
that. Have you never heard the dictum according to which a

sighted object always attracts attention? 'Tis for that reason
she is in error. Had you studied a little, you would be less
surprised by it. Now it's your turn, Blaise. You make your
entrance here, coming to interrupt us. Take four paces back, to
pretend you have just arrived. I have seen you coming, so I say
to Colette: 'Here is Blaise coming, my dear Colette. We'll
resume our conversation later.' (*To* COLETTE.) And you leave
the stage.

BLAISE (*approaching, to come on stage*). I be all confused. I knows
not what to say.

MERLIN. You fall in with Colette on your way, and you ask her
what company she's been keeping.

BLAISE (*starting his scene*). Where you coming from then,
Colette?

COLETTE. Why, from where I were, o' course.

BLAISE. That's too pert an answer!

COLETTE. To be sure it is! Make the best of it! Take it or leave it!
Adieu!

Scene 5

MERLIN (*interrupting the scene*). Now you have to confront me.

BLAISE. Now 'ark 'ee, Mr Merlin! I could'n never suffer you to
filch my mistress.

MERLIN (*interrupting the scene*). '*Hark 'ee, Mr Merlin!*' What
manner is that to open a scene? Did I not tell you, in the notes
I gave you, to question me concerning my encounter with
Colette?

BLAISE. S'Blood! But I know all 'bout that, don' I? 'Cos I
were 'ere!

MERLIN. Can't you remember you weren't supposed to be here?

BLAISE (*starting again*). Well, then! So it were you Colette went
with, Mr Merlin!

MERLIN. Yes, we just happened to meet by chance.

BLAISE. But they says you're in love with 'er, Mr Merlin, and that, d'you see, perturbs me? 'Cos she's to be my betrothed a week from Tuesday.

COLETTE (*rising and interrupting*). Oh! Not to interrupt, but it's been put off till *two* week from Tuesday. Twixt now and then, I'll wait and see.

MERLIN. Never mind that! 'Tis a fault of no consequence here. (*Continuing the scene.*) And who was it informed you, Blaise, that I love Colette?

BLAISE. You said it yourself jus' now.

MERLIN (*interrupting the scene*). Take care, now! Try and fix it in your mind that you weren't there!

BLAISE. Then 'tis Miss Lisette, she tol' me. And for all this she puts blame on you too. And she be over there to bear me out.

LISETTE (*interrupting in a threatening tone of voice*). Nay, proceed! I'll give tongue to my sentiments after the play.

MERLIN. We shall make nothing of this magpie. Anything within sight is a magnet to him.

LISETTE. Proceed, go on with it. During the performance, he will not see a thing. And that will set him right. When a man loses his mistress, Mr Merlin, one may allow him a moment's distraction.

BLAISE (*interrupting*). There bain't but one reason for this comedy, Miss Lisette. To see us both cast off!

COLETTE. Well, cast away, Mutton 'ead! Cast me off too!

BLAISE (*weeping*). S'death! That bain't no way to treat a lad who's to be betrothed to you next week!

COLETTE. And I says I'll not be! Not next week nor any week!

MERLIN. Farewell, my comedy! Ten pounds I'd been promised to mount it, and this renegade runs off with them as sure as if he'd picked my pocket.

COLETTE. Oh, Lord-a-mercy, Mr Merlin, 'ere's a fine 'ow-d'ye-do! And all 'cos you're agreeable to me and I feels kindly to you.

Ay! I do please 'im. We please each other. 'E's a boy and me's a girl. 'E's illegible. Me too. Once he wanted Miss Lisette, and now 'e don't. 'E leaves 'er. I leaves you. 'E takes me. I takes 'im. As for you two, you'll just 'ave to suffer in silence.

BLAISE. A fine betrothal I'll 'ave.

LISETTE (*to* MERLIN, *tearing up a paper*). And you daren't say a word, you rascal! Here's what I think of this plan for your comedy! And you merit the same done to you!

MERLIN. But, children, let's earn our money first! We can finish our arguments later.

COLETTE. That's well said. We can squabble later. It don't make no difference.

LISETTE. Hold your tongue, little Miss Pert!

COLETTE. Jealous cats don't 'ave no manners!

MERLIN. Peace, I say! Peace!

COLETTE. Is't my fault, to be a better catch than 'er?

LISETTE. Can no one stop our little country cousin shrieking in my ear?

COLETTE. Look at 'er, the proud beauty! With a face like a scullery maid!

MERLIN. This caterwauling is enough to bring the whole household down on us. And that's Madame Argante, I think, hastening here already.

LISETTE (*leaving*). Farewell, scoundrel.

MERLIN. I can match your scoundrel, if you please, and call you madcap.

BLAISE. I be on my way too. I'll go protest to 'er fam'ly about the wanton jade.

COLETTE. I'll be seein' you, Mr Merlin, won' I?

MERLIN. Yes, Colette. 'Tis all working to perfection. Those two love us truly. But we'll keep up our pretence.

COLETTE. As long as you will. We're not in no danger, since they love us so.

Scene 6

MME ARGANTE. What is this hullabaloo? Who was that you were brawling with just now.

MERLIN. 'Tis naught, madame. Blaise and Colette were leaving with Lisette.

MME ARGANTE. Why, then? Were they in disputation? I require to know the matter.

MERLIN. It concerned a little project which we ... a little idea that had come to us, and we find it hard to unite in a harmonious ensemble. (*Indicating* ERASTE.) Monsieur Eraste will explain what it is.

ERASTE. 'Tis a trifling affair, madame. All will soon be made clear to you.

MME ARGANTE. Then why all this mystery now?

ERASTE. Since you oblige me to reveal it, what is in question is a little piece ...

MME ARGANTE. A piece of what?

MERLIN. 'Tis a play, madame. A comedy. A contrivance to divert you. A surprise.

ANGÉLIQUE. And I, mother, did promise Eraste and Madame Amelin, not to breathe a word of it to you.

MME ARGANTE. A comedy!

MERLIN. Yes, a comedy of my own devising. Which must promise well.

MME ARGANTE. So why this cat and dog fight?

MERLIN. None of that is in the play, madame. The conflict you heard was but an interlude. My actors fell into disagreement during a break in the action. Discord in the ranks. 'Tis no uncommon occurrence. They were itching to jump out of their comic socks and climb on buskins, and I shall try to induce in them a less tragical disposition.

MME ARGANTE. No, let's forget all about your less tragical disposition and abandon this divertissement. You never

considered, Eraste, how absurd it would be for a woman of my
age to patronise a home-grown comedy.

ERASTE. 'Tis the most innocent thing in the world, madame.
Besides, Madame Amelin has been eagerly awaiting this
performance.

MERLIN. She it is who rewards us for putting it together. And
I have already received monies from her in person. My
merchandise has been sold and I must make delivery. Once a
bargain has been struck, madame, I dare swear you are not one
to break it. I would have to make restitution, and the
commitments I have taken no longer permit me to do so.

MME ARGANTE. Do not trouble yourself. I shall see you are all
reimbursed.

MERLIN. Not to speak of the twelve pence it has cost me to hire
the services of a candle-snuffer, the three bottles of wine I have
passed on to some village fiddlers who will make up my
orchestra, plus another four I have promised to drink with
them as soon as the performance is over. And half a quire
of paper I covered with my scribble as I tried to establish the
right scenario . . .

MME ARGANTE. You will not be out of pocket, I tell you. Here
comes Madame Amelin. You will see that she shares my
sentiments.

Scene 7

MME ARGANTE (*to* MME AMELIN). You will never divine,
madame, what these young people were concocting for us? A
comedy fashioned by Monsieur Merlin. They tell me you know
of it, but I am persuaded that cannot be.

MME AMELIN. 'Twas I first conceived the idea.

MME ARGANTE. You, madame?

MME AMELIN. Yes, i' faith. You must know how much I enjoy laughing. And you shall see how well this will divert us. But I had expressly forbidden that you should be informed.

MME ARGANTE. I was apprised of it by the clamour they created in this hall. But I have a favour to ask of you, madame. That you would have the goodness to abandon the project. For my sake. Given my years and my disposition . . .

MME AMELIN. Nay, but then all is decided, madame. Do not alarm yourself. The affair is at an end. There shall be no further question of it.

MME ARGANTE. A thousand thanks, madame. I own that I was fearful at the thought it might be carried to fruition.

MME AMELIN. I am pained at the agitation it has caused you.

MME ARGANTE. I'll go rejoin the company with my daughter. Will you not come too?

MME AMELIN. In a while.

ANGÉLIQUE (*aside to* MME ARGANTE). Mother, Madame Amelin is displeased.

MME ARGANTE (*aside to* ANGÉLIQUE). Peace, girl. (*To* MME AMELIN.) Adieu, Madame. Remember to follow us.

MME AMELIN. Yes, I shall. (*To* ERASTE.) Nephew, when you have attended on Madame Argante, come and speak with me.

ERASTE. At once, madame.

MERLIN. So I'll be left with nothing but the printed page. 'Tis shameful.

Scene 8

MME AMELIN (*alone for a moment*). Madame Argante, you may say what you will. I wanted to laugh and I shall.

ARAMINTE. Well, my dear? What progress for our comedy? Will it be played?

MME AMELIN. No. Madame Argante wishes the money to be returned at the door.

ARAMINTE. How's this? She is against it being performed?

MME AMELIN. So it appears. However it *will* be played. Either this one. Or another. All this shall have but one consequence. Instead of my putting on a comedy for her, she must perform one for me, and what she'll find even worse, play a part in it herself. And I pray you to assist me in this ploy.

ARAMINTE. It will be curious indeed to see her mount upon a stage! But I am good for nothing, except to watch it from my box.

MME AMELIN. Now listen to me. I shall feign such great offence at her failure to indulge my caprice that I'll appear to renounce my nephew's marriage to Angélique.

ARAMINTE. Your nephew is indeed so great a match for her —

MME AMELIN. — that her mother never dared hope I would consent to it. Imagine then the fright she shall have and the stratagems she'll devise? Think you she'll play her part well?

ARAMINTE. Oh, to the life!

MME AMELIN (*laughing*). And my nephew and his mistress? Will they prove, do you think, good actors too? For they shall not know, any more than the others, that this is for my own amusement.

ARAMINTE. 'Twill be most diverting. But I am puzzled by my part in this. How can I be of use to you?

MME AMELIN. Your fortune is three times greater than Angélique's. You are a widow and still young. You have confided in me your own inclination for my nephew. That says it all. You have but to fall in and follow where I lead. Here comes my nephew now, so this is our opening scene. Are you ready for it?

ARAMINTE. I am.

Scene 9

ERASTE. I have returned, madame, at your command. What do you wish from me? The company awaits you.

MME AMELIN. Let them wait, nephew. I am not yet prepared to rejoin them.

ERASTE. You have a most serious, air, madame. What can be the matter?

MME AMELIN (*indicating* ARAMINTE). Eraste, what think you of madame?

ERASTE. I? What everyone believes. That madame is the most amiable of ladies.

ARAMINTE. A flattering response.

ERASTE. A simple, honest one.

MME AMELIN. Do not her heart and hand, nephew, together with an income of £3000, make her a desirable match?

ERASTE. Could there by anyone would need persuading of so evident a truth?

MME AMELIN. I rejoice that you yourself are thus persuaded.

ERASTE. For what reason, madame, does this cause you to rejoice?

MME AMELIN. The reason, nephew, is that 'tis my purpose you should marry with her.

ERASTE. That I should, aunt? You jest. I vow that madame could never share that sentiment.

MME AMELIN. Yet 'tis she who made me the proposal.

ERASTE (*surprised*). To marry me? You, madame?

ARAMINTE. Why not, Eraste? It would seem fitting enough to me. What say you?

MME AMELIN. What says he? Are you tongue-tied for an answer?

ARAMINTE. Still he says nothing.

MME AMELIN. Joy or amazement silence him. Is't not so, nephew?

ERASTE. Madame ...

MME AMELIN. Well?

ERASTE. No man can wed two wives.

MME AMELIN. Where do two spring from? Madame is the only one in question.

ARAMINTE. And, I warrant, you'll have the goodness to wed no one else but me.

ERASTE. Whole-hearted devotion, madame, is what you justly deserve. And, as you know, I worship Angélique. To give my heart to another is impossible.

ARAMINTE. Impossible, Eraste! Impossible! Oh! Since you adopt that tone, you shall love me, please you or no.

ERASTE. Of that, madame, I have no expectation.

ARAMINTE. You shall love me, I say. Your heart has been promised to me and I lay claim to it. To give 200,000 pounds for it is, I believe, to put it at its true worth. Few hearts could exact such a price.

ERASTE. Angélique would value it more highly.

MME AMELIN. Value it as she may, I have given my word that 'tis madame should have it. Have it she must and you shall redeem my promise.

ERASTE. Ah, madame! Will you drive me to despair?

ARAMINTE. What's this *despair*?

MME AMELIN. Pay no heed to him. Have courage, nephew, be brave!

ERASTE. Heavens above!

Scene 10

MME ARGANTE. As you fail to attend us, madame, I come in search of you. But what do I see? Eraste sighing and in tears! He seems distraught. What can have happened to him?

MME AMELIN. Naught but a stroke of good fortune, were he sensible of it. I was, however, about to apprise you, madame, of our imminent departure – Araminte, my nephew and I. Have you no commission for us in Paris on your behalf?

MME ARGANTE. In Paris? How come, madame? Are you going there?

MME AMELIN. On the hour.

MME ARGANTE. Madame, you jest! And this marriage . . .?

MME AMELIN. I think it best to let it ride. The marked distaste with which you viewed the trifling divertissement on which my heart was set has given me cause to reflect. Your cast of mind is too serious for me. I am all for innocent enjoyment, which displeases you. We had designed to stay together. But we might end at loggerheads. Let us pursue things no further.

MME ARGANTE. What's this? Break a marriage, madame, for want of a play? So let us have it, madame. 'Tis of small consequence. And if that suffice not, let us have opera as well, a puppet-show or what you will, a fun-fair or even a circus.

MME AMELIN. No. The decision I have taken will spare you that ordeal. We shall, if you please, be no worse friends for all this. But I have just pledged my word to Araminte and resolved that my nephew shall wed her.

MME ARGANTE. Araminte and your nephew, madame! Your nephew to wed Araminte! What! This young man . . .!

ARAMINTE. And why not, pray? If Angélique can marry, why not I?

ANGÉLIQUE (*sadly*). And Eraste gives his consent?

ERASTE. You witness my confusion. I no longer know where I stand.

ANGÉLIQUE. Is that all you can answer? Take me away, mother. Let's withdraw. On every side we are betrayed.

ERASTE. I betray you, Angélique! I who live for you alone!

MME AMELIN. How can you speak of loving another, nephew, in the presence of madame, to whom I have destined you.

MME ARGANTE (*strongly*). Nay, truly, all this can be but a dream.

MME AMELIN. We are all, I imagine, wide awake.

MME ARGANTE. Indeed, madame. Regrettably. A dream and naught but a dream can excuse the inexcusable. And only the performance of your wretched comedy can dissipate this folly. Let us at once prepare ourselves. This piece, they say, is an impromptu. I wish to take part in it myself. Let them try and contrive a role for me. Let us all play in it. You too, my child.

ANGÉLIQUE. Let us leave them, mother. There's nothing else we can do.

MME ARGANTE. I shall never make a great actress, so I shall amuse you all the more.

MME AMELIN. You will play your part to perfection, madame. Your vivacity gives proof of that. But it fills me with misgivings that, with your sober principles, I should bring you to such a pass.

MME ARGANTE. Have no fear on that score. Merlin is the author of the play, and I see him now in the offing. I shall tell him myself that I assent to it. Merlin! Merlin! Come here!

MME AMELIN. Why no, madame, I beg you.

ERASTE (to MME AMELIN). Let it be played, madame. Do you wish my fate to hang upon a comedy? My life to depend upon two or three lines of dialogue?

MME ARGANTE. No, no, it shall never depend on that.

Scene 11

MME ARGANTE (continuing). This comedy you intend for us, is it soon ready?

MERLIN. I have all our actors assembled. They are all here, and if so desired we can complete our rehearsal.

MME ARGANTE. Let them come in.

MME AMELIN. Truly, there is no point in this.

MME ARGANTE. On the contrary, madame.

ARAMINTE. I could never imagine, whatever we do, that madame would fail to honour the promise she has made me. Play the comedy whenever you wish. But Eraste will still, if it please you, marry me.

MME ARGANTE. You, madame? Together with your forty odd years? If it please you, madame, that will never be. I tell you frankly, madame, that your procedures are in uncommon bad taste. You, a friend of ours, are invited to my daughter's marriage, and you aspire to make it your own and steal her husband away from her, in spite of the repugnance he himself has made manifest. For he rejects you, and you well know this exchange would disadvantage him. In truth, your conduct is beyond belief. That forty years could compete with twenty! You live in a dream world, madame. Come, Merlin, let us conclude.

Scene 12

MME ARGANTE (*continuing*). I'll add ten pounds to what has been promised you already, to incite you to do your best. Let us be seated, madame, and listen.

MME AMELIN. Since that is your wish, let us hear it then.

MERLIN. Step forward, Blaise. We'll take up where we left off. You were complaining about my love for Colette. And 'tis Lisette, you say, who informed you of it?

BLAISE. Ay! So what more d'you wan' me to say?

MME ARGANTE. Would you please continue, Blaise?

BLAISE. Nay, I will not. Our mother has forbid me to mount upon a stage.

MME ARGANTE. And I forbid her to prevent you doing so. Am I not *in loco parentis*? Here *I* am your mother.

BLAISE. What's more to the point, our lady mistress, is that they make mock of me in this plaguey play of theirs. Colette, she pretends 'er 'eart's tender for Mrs Merlin and Mr Merlin's lost 'is for 'er. And spite of it's a comedy, mistress, it's all true. 'Cos they only pretends to pretend, to pull wool over our eyes, and they're both mean enough to be in love for real, spite of Lisette, who won't relish it much, and spite of me who me father-in-law's chose to be 'is own son-in-law. (*The ladies laugh.*)

MME ARGANTE. Oh, you great oaf! Your nonsense is no concern of ours. And you, Merlin, what are you thinking of, passing this tomfoolery off as truth? You leave Colette to him and set his mind at rest.

COLETTE. Yes, but I don' wish 'im to leave me. I wan' 'im to keep me.

MME ARGANTE. What does that signify, child? Step aside. You have no place in this scene. When the time comes, you'll make yourself known. Play on, the rest of you.

MERLIN. Come now, Blaise. Can you blame me for loving Colette?

BLAISE. Well, Lord love us, it be really true, bain't it?

MERLIN. What do you expect, my lad? She's such a dainty morsel, I couldn't help myself.

BLAISE (*to* MME ARGANTE). There, you see, Madame Argante? 'E jes confess it 'isself.

MME ARGANTE. What's that to you, since this is but a play?

BLAISE. S'blood! What do I care 'bout some 'ole farce? It can go to the divil, with all the rest of you!

MERLIN. Again!

MME ARGANTE. Faith! Is there no way to persuade you to proceed?

MME AMELIN. Ah, madame! Leave the poor boy alone. You can see dialogue is not his strong point.

MME ARGANTE. Strong or weak, that's as maybe, but I wish him to say what he knows and answer as best he can.

COLETTE. 'E'll go bellowin' on as long as you like. But that's as much as you'll get out of 'im.

BLAISE. Ay, what's left but to bellow, when you've got good reason!

LISETTE. What use is all this you're doing, madame? If we were to finish this scene, there would be no other to follow. For it is I who must play it and I shall do no such thing.

MME ARGANTE. Oh, you'll play it, I assure you!

LISETTE. We'll see if I can be made to play my part against my will.

Final Scene

NOTARY (*addressing* MME AMELIN). Madame, here is the contract you required me to draw up. Your instructions have been followed to the letter.

MME AMELIN (*aside, to* ARAMINTE). Make it appear to be yours. (*To* MME ARGANTE.) Will you not honour this contract with your signature, madame?

MME ARGANTE. And whom does it concern, madame?

ARAMINTE. Eraste and myself.

MME ARGANTE. Sign your marriage contract? *I*, madame? No, that honour shall not be mine. And you will, if you please, have the kindness to go and sign it yourself, elsewhere. (*To the* NOTARY.) Remove it, monsieur, take that thing away! (*To* MME AMELIN.) You are not thinking straight, madame. Such conduct is indefensible. One has never seen the like.

MME AMELIN. It appeared to me, madame, I could hardly marry my nephew off in your house, without offering you this courtesy. And, to speak plainly, I will not desist till you have signed it. And sign it you shall.

MME ARGANTE. I'll do nothing of the sort. Oh, no! For I am leaving now.

MME AMELIN (*preventing her*). You will remain here, if you please. Without you, this contract would be invalid. (*To* ARAMINTE.) Assist me, madame. We must prevent Madame Argante from walking off.

ARAMINTE. Hold firm! And I shall not give way, either.

MME ARGANTE. To what condition are we thus reduced, ladies? Am I not in my own home?

ERASTE. Gad, what are you thinking of, madame? I myself would rather die than sign that contract.

MME AMELIN. In a moment you will sign it. And we shall all sign.

MME ARGANTE. For want of the comedy she so sorely regrets, madame, it seems, is bent on staging her own.

MME AMELIN (*laughing*). Ha-ha-ha! How right you are. I dislike to be deprived of anything.

NOTARY. Decide amongst you, then, ladies. For I am sent for on other business. To all appearances, moreover, this contract is valueless now and no longer furthers your intentions, since it was drawn up yesterday in the names of Monsieur Eraste and Mademoiselle Angélique.

MME AMELIN. Is that right? Oh, in that case, it is not worth altering. We had best sign it as it stands.

ERASTE. What's this I hear?

MME ARGANTE. Ha! Ha! So now I see it all. You were taking part in your own play and you have made a fool of me. So let us sign the contract. You are both very wicked ladies.

ERASTE. Ah! I breathe again!

ANGÉLIQUE. Who could have thought it! What can one do but laugh?

ARAMINTE (*to* MME ARGANTE). Never will you love me as much as you hated me just now. But my 'forty odd years' still rankle, since I have known but thirty-nine and a half.

MME ARGANTE. I was in such a passion, I could have saddled you with a hundred. You have every right to complain, when I've just made such a scene to you.

MME AMELIN. And you have no further objection to Merlin's play?

MME ARGANTE. Oh no! I'll dispute with you no more. I'm amused by the whole affair. And if any of the actors provoke me again, I'll be ready to prompt them myself.

LISETTE. Now you are all reconciled. As for us, we –

MERLIN. Well, shall I tell you, then? We regaled ourselves in my impromptu with the chance to tease you in your affections.

COLETTE. And you, Blaise, 'ave an 'eart of oak. Enough to please me.

BLAISE (*jumping*). Truly? Pledge me a kiss then to make up for all me fuss and bother.

LISETTE. As for me, I love you still. But I'll make you pay for all this. You must wait six months before I'll wed you.

MME ARGANTE. Fiddlesticks! Shorten that sentence! Reduce the time to two hours! Meanwhile, we'll bring the play to a close.